Max Planck Institute for
Innovation and Competition

More information about this series at
http://www.springer.com/series/7760

MAX-PLANCK-GESELLSCHAFT

MPI Studies on Intellectual Property and Competition Law

Volume 29

Edited by

Josef Drexl
Reto M. Hilty
Joseph Straus

Michèle Finck • Matthias Lamping •
Valentina Moscon • Heiko Richter
Editors

Smart Urban Mobility

Law, Regulation, and Policy

Springer

Editors
Michèle Finck
MPI for Innovation and Competition
Munich, Germany

Matthias Lamping
MPI for Innovation and Competition
Munich, Germany

Valentina Moscon
MPI for Innovation and Competition
Munich, Germany

Heiko Richter
MPI for Innovation and Competition
Munich, Germany

ISSN 2191-5822 ISSN 2191-5830 (electronic)
MPI Studies on Intellectual Property and Competition Law
ISBN 978-3-662-61919-3 ISBN 978-3-662-61920-9 (eBook)
https://doi.org/10.1007/978-3-662-61920-9

This Springer imprint is published by the registered company Springer-Verlag GmbH, DE, part of Springer Nature.
The registered company address is: Heidelberger Platz 3, 14197 Berlin, Germany

Contents

Smart Urban Mobility as a Regulatory Challenge

Michèle Finck, Matthias Lamping, Valentina Moscon, and Heiko Richter

Contents

Abstract The 'smart city' has become shorthand for developments in technology that influence how cities are organised and how citizens coexist in them. 'Smart mobility', one of its most visible sub-domains, has been considerably affected by ecological, demographic and economic pressures. Emerging methods of transportation and innovative business models can overcome old problems, but they also pose new societal, economic and legal challenges. This introduction aims to shed light on the law, regulation and policy of 'smart urban mobility' by critically examining its substantial transformation from a regulatory perspective. It outlines the notion of the 'smart city', highlights trends in 'smart' urban mobility, points to related legal challenges and explains the conception and chapters of this book.

We would like to thank Carolina Banda, Anja Geller and Charles Heard for their excellent support in editing this volume. The editors are Senior Research Fellows at the Max Planck Institute for Innovation and Competition, Munich, Germany.

M. Finck · M. Lamping · V. Moscon · H. Richter (✉)
Max Planck Institute for Innovation and Competition, Munich, Germany
e-mail: michele.finck@ip.mpg.de; matthias.lamping@ip.mpg.de; valentina.moscon@ip.mpg.de; heiko.richter@ip.mpg.de

M. Finck et al. (eds.), *Smart Urban Mobility*, MPI Studies on Intellectual Property and Competition Law 29, https://doi.org/10.1007/978-3-662-61920-9_1

1 Towards the 'Smart' City

American philosopher and architectural critic Lewis Mumford described the city as "a geographic plexus, an economic organisation, an institutional process, a theatre of social action, and an aesthetic symbol of collective unity".[1] He wrote this on the verge of the Second World War. The globalised and digitally integrated 'smart city' of the twenty-first century still resembles his notion, but it has come a long way. Prior to the Industrial Revolution, most cities were self-contained, fairly static organisms with an overall similar appearance: a market, a town hall and a church in the centre; a baker, a butcher and a locksmith in their vicinity; residences of the better situated *citoyen* in between; and a wall enclosing all of it. Beyond that wall one would typically find a river or some other water source, farms and a gallows symbolising the power of high justice. This stereotype began to change with the advent of industrialisation and free trade.[2] Following the disruption of traditional feudal structures and patterns in Europe, cities became more dynamic, open and inclusive.[3] For better or worse, the 'modern' city is a chaotic melting pot with its own momentum—unpredictable and in many respects uncontrollable.

Nowadays, cities are anything but isolated entities. Globalisation and digitalisation have turned them into interdependent hubs, inextricably embedded in the worldwide urban network.[4] This greatly impacts urban planning. It has become much more difficult to predict the dynamics of urban life and to react to them, let alone to control them. Traditional views on the 'form' and 'function'[5] of a city have been altered by digital media and the way in which digital natives live, move and interact. What used to be a bilateral relationship between the citizen and the city is augmented by the internet as an additional, almost parallel dimension in which the citizen—i.e. its digital identity—acts, exists, interacts and coexists.

In the city itself, technology is redefining space. The European Commission considers the smart city "a place where traditional networks and services are made more efficient with the use of digital and telecommunication technologies for the benefit of its inhabitants and business".[6] The use of sensors and other IoT ('Internet of Things') technologies makes it possible to monitor all kinds of events and changes in the environment, such as human and vehicle movement, congestion on the roads, occupation levels of public transport, availability of public parking spaces, soil

---

[1]Lewis Mumford, 'What is a City?' (1937) 82 Architectural Record 59.

[2]On the transition of space and the development towards modern cities, see Michael Batty, *Inventing Future Cities* (MIT Press 2018) 19ff and 77ff on standard models of cities.

[3]See JP O'Malley, 'Inventing Future Cities' (*Scenario Magazine*, 30 April 2019) <www.scenariomagazine.com/inventing-future-cities/> accessed 8 April 2020.

[4]See also Batty (n 2) 14, on the ongoing transition from 'nonurban' to 'urban'.

[5]On the relation between 'form' and 'function', see Michael Batty and Paul Longley, *Fractal Cities – A Geometry of Form and Function* (Academic Press 1994).

[6]European Commission, *Digital Agenda for Europe - Rebooting Europe's Economy* (Publications Office of the European Union 2014) 6.

moisture in public parks or fill levels of litter bins. The citywide coverage of such sensors has amplified points of connection and data collection. It increasingly blurs the line between the analogue and the digital world. Sensors based in homes, paired with machine learning, may even provide insights into the cognitive and physical state of their inhabitants.[7] Such developments promise to provide a number of benefits, including gains in efficiency, transparency and sustainability. But they also entail considerable security risks[8] and threats to data protection and privacy.[9] One can also question whether the net ecological effect is positive in light of the heavy environmental footprint of pervasive computing.[10] Furthermore, the public-private partnerships underlying many smart city projects face major challenges regarding data usage, power dynamics and the privatisation of public space.[11]

The technological penetration of private and social life has already left clear marks on our cities. Institutions which were the cornerstones of urban life in the twentieth century are facing extinction. The disappearance of shopping malls[12] and retail businesses as well as the displacement of private ownership and transport solutions by the sharing economy's business models merely foreshadows the radical change that urban life will undergo in the twenty-first century.[13] For the longest time, it was taken for granted that a city is built around the town hall and the central market, but city life no longer revolves around the *agorá*. Paradigms change in a world where personal communication and commercial exchange increasingly take place in virtual environments. Urban planners need to understand the dynamics of the information society and translate them into urban design measures that reflect modern lifestyles.

---

[7]See Poppy Crum, 'When the Walls Can Talk – Space is the Next Frontier in Personalisation' (*Wired*, 3 February 2020) <www.wired.co.uk/article/smart-home-technology-tracking> accessed 8 April 2020.

[8]See Lily H Newman, 'The Sensors That Power Smart Cities Are a Hacker's Dream' (*Wired*, 8 September 2018) <www.wired.com/story/sensor-hubs-smart-cities-vulnerabilities-hacks/> accessed 8 April 2020.

[9]See Antoine Picon, 'Smart Cities, Privacy and the Pulverisation/Reconstruction of Individuals' (2019) 5 European Data Protection Law Review 154; Esther Keymolen, 'When Cities Become Smart, Is There Still Place for Trust?' (2019) 5 European Data Protection Law Review 156.

[10]See Lorenz M Hilty, Claudia Som and Andreas Köhler, 'Assessing the Human, Social, and Environmental Risks of Pervasive Computing' (2004) 10 Human and Ecological Risk Assessment: An International Journal 853.

[11]Jonathan K Law, Rit Aggarwala and Ester Fuchs, 'How Can the Private and Public Sectors Work Together to Create Smart Cities?' (*McKinsey*, 2 January 2019) <www.mckinsey.com/industries/capital-projects-and-infrastructure/our-insights/how-can-the-private-and-public-sectors-work-together-to-create-smart-cities> accessed 8 April 2020.

[12]See, for example, Matevž Straus, '3 Potential Futures for Dying Shopping Malls' (*Scenario Magazine*, 27 April 2017) <www.scenariomagazine.com/3-potential-futures-for-dying-shopping-malls/> accessed 8 April 2020.

[13]On the 'sharing economy' in detail, see Nestor Davidson, Michèle Finck and John J Infranca (eds), *The Cambridge Handbook of the Law of the Sharing Economy* (Cambridge University Press 2018).

In socio-economic terms, ‘smart’ is more than an allusion to technology. Technological innovation does indeed facilitate the provision of public services such as transportation, security, power and water, but it takes more than a pinch of technology to tackle ubiquitous societal challenges like inequality, social exclusion, urban poverty and deprivation, gentrification,[14] demographic transition, social and political polarisation and pollution. Even if some of these issues could be addressed by technological solutions, not all cities are equally well equipped to implement them. In many parts of the world, governments are struggling to provide their citizens with even the most basic needs, which makes climate neutrality a luxury they may not be able to afford without jeopardising social, economic and political stability.

Population growth and urbanisation add fuel to the fire. According to the United Nations' median prognosis, the world's population will reach 8.6 billion by 2030, 9.8 billion by 2050, and 11.2 billion by 2100.[15] Today, 55% of the world's population resides in urban areas, a proportion that is expected to increase to 68% by 2050.[16] For Europe and Northern America alone, the median level is projected to rise to 83% by the middle of the century.[17] Even beyond these dates, the urbanisation trend will most likely remain uninterrupted due to the ‘urban advantage’: economic opportunities, education, healthcare and public services are more accessible in urban centres than in rural areas.[18] From a macroeconomic perspective, urbanisation goes hand in hand with economic growth.[19] Cities provide the economies of scale that serve to justify and redeem investments in urban infrastructure and services. They are key drivers of the economy, contributing up to 85% of the EU’s GDP.[20] Even though we will certainly witness recurring revivals of rural areas at various points in time, it therefore seems reasonable to believe that the vast majority of us will be living in an urban area by the end of this century.[21]

All of this increases the complexity of urban planning. New technologies and the business models that emerge around them must be implemented in an inclusive manner in order to create cities that live up to the demands of all their residents and

---

[14]See, for example, Camilla Warmedinger, ‘Gentrification and the Search for Authenticity’ (*Scenario Magazine*, 9 March 2016) <www.scenariomagazine.com/gentrification-and-the-search-for-authenticity/> accessed 8 April 2020.

[15]United Nations, ‘World Population Prospects: The 2017 Revision – Key Findings and Advance Tables’ (2017) Working Paper No. ESA/P/WP/248, 1ff <https://population.un.org/wpp/Publications/Files/WPP2017_KeyFindings.pdf> accessed 27 August 2020.

[16]United Nations, *World Urbanization Prospects: The 2018 Revision* (United Nations 2019) 1, 9ff.

[17]ibid 38.

[18]United Nations Human Settlements Programme (UN-HABITAT), *State of the World’s Cities 2010-2011: Bridging the Urban Divide – Overview and Key Findings* (UN-HABITAT 2010) 13, 15ff.

[19]ibid 6ff.

[20]European Commission, *Innovation in Urban Mobility: Policy Making and Planning* (Office for Official Publications of the European Union 2013) 2.

[21]Michael Batty, quoted by O’Malley (n 3).

visitors, irrespective of age, income, origin, (dis)abilities or social status. In that regard, transport and mobility can be seen as key drivers. They are the gateway to the city. The future city's appearance will thus heavily depend on how it absorbs technological advancements in these areas.[22] This in turn will largely depend on how regulators deal with new technologies and the 'raw material' needed to implement and effectuate them (e.g. personal data generated by the citizens' movements, choices, etc.).

In order to respond to these developments and challenges, cities need to expand their urban infrastructure and adapt their transport networks. At the same time, they need to ensure social cohesion and sustainable growth while prioritising the respective solutions. In any case, one has to bear in mind that cities are very much like living organisms.[23] They may be thoroughly planned and their development may be strictly controlled, but there is no certainty that they will behave as anticipated. At the end of the day, without its infrastructure, a city amounts to a conglomeration of people—idiosyncratic, unpredictable and in many respects uncontrollable.

2 Trends in Urban Mobility

The advancement of transport technologies changes the role of distance. It is therefore a major factor in allowing cities to grow.[24] At the same time, progress does not come without problems, in this case for the daily mobility needs of commuters, residents and visitors.

Undeniably, most cities are suffering from heavy congestion, which translates into a plethora of socio-economic concerns. Demand for passenger and freight transport is on the rise, but so are their negative externalities. When we think of urban mobility, what instantly comes to mind are rush hours, traffic jams, accidents, noise and pollution. It is said that "commuters can spend 90 hours a year stuck on the road, and drivers can spend 106 days of their lives looking for parking spots".[25] The environmental perspective does not look much better. Urban centres "consume 78% of global energy and produce more than 60% of carbon and greenhouse gas emissions despite holding less than 2% of global surface".[26] After housing and food, transport is the third largest contributor to these figures, accounting for almost

[22]Lasse Jonasson, quoted by O'Malley (n 3).

[23]See Batty (n 2) 5.

[24]ibid 168ff.

[25]Monica Porteanu, 'Sustainable Urban Mobility Networks' (*Scenario Magazine*, 9 April 2015) <www.scenariomagazine.com/sustainable-urban-mobility-networks/> accessed 8 April 2020.

[26]Liyana Othman, 'Shaping Urban Landscapes in the Age of Sustainability 1'(*Scenario Magazine*, 23 December 2015) <www.scenariomagazine.com/shaping-urban-landscapes-in-the-age-of-sustainability-1/> accessed 8 April 2020; source of percentages undisclosed.

one quarter of a city's greenhouse emissions.[27] Urban mobility accounts for 40% of carbon dioxide (CO_2) emissions and up to 70% of other pollutants produced by road transport.[28]

Considering that climate and consumer protection are powerful policy arguments, many developments in urban mobility are underpinned by environmental, comfort and safety concerns. Technology serves as a catalyst for solutions to these problems. It is therefore an integrated component of most urban mobility strategies. Reducing congestion lies at the heart of such strategies, but social inclusion and cohesion are also on the policy agenda. This is reflected in the goal to promote "smart, green, and integrated"[29] transport solutions.

Back in the 1960s, Jane Jacobs criticised the fact that urban centres were increasingly built for automobiles rather than humans.[30] Numerous cities are now attempting to reverse that phenomenon through the creation of car-free zones, particularly in city centres. This has happened in Copenhagen, Madrid, Barcelona and Oslo, to name just a few.[31] One of the main goals of these efforts is the improvement of public health through the reduction of emissions in densely populated areas. In fact, research has confirmed that such measures can reduce up to 40% of nitrogen dioxide (NO_2) levels.[32] On a related note, London started charging a congestion fee to enter the city centre in 2003.[33] Many European cities have followed suit, although some of them are beginning to reverse their policies. More recently, a number of German cities (e.g. Stuttgart, Frankfurt and Cologne) started banning diesel vehicles from their centres.

---

[27]See Peter-Paul Pichler and others, 'Reducing Urban Greenhouse Gas Footprints' (2017) 7 Scientific Reports 14659; Commission, 'Roadmap to a Single European Transport Area – Towards a Competitive and Resource Efficient Transport System (White Paper)' COM (2011) 144 final, para 30; for all transport emissions, see European Environment Agency, 'Greenhouse Gas Emissions from Transport in Europe' (*EEA*, 17 December 2019) <www.eea.europa.eu/data-and-maps/indicators/transport-emissions-of-greenhouse-gases/transport-emissions-of-greenhouse-gases-12> accessed 8 April 2020.

[28]Commission, 'Towards a New Culture for Urban Mobility (Green Paper)' SEC (2007) 1209 final 2.

[29]See European Commission, *Innovation in Urban Mobility* (n 20) 5.

[30]Jane Jacobs, *The Death and Life of Great American Cities* (Vintage Books 1961), 338ff.

[31]See Porteanu (n 25); Terry Nguyen, 'Car-Free Zones Could Be the Future of Cities' (*Vox*, 28 October 2019) <www.vox.com/the-goods/2019/10/28/20932554/new-york-san-francisco-car-free-zones> accessed 8 April 2020; Stephen Moss, 'End of the Car Age: How Cities Are Outgrowing the Automobile' *The Guardian* (28 April 2015) <www.theguardian.com/cities/2015/apr/28/end-of-the-car-age-how-cities-outgrew-the-automobile> accessed 8 April 2020; all with further references.

[32]See Mark J Nieuwenhuijsen and Haneen Khreis, 'Car Free Cities: Pathway to Healthy Urban Living' (2016) 94 Environmental International 251.

[33]Raphael Minder, 'As Cities Limit Traffic Pollution, Madrid Reverses a Driving Ban' *The New York Times* (Madrid, 1 July 2019) <www.nytimes.com/2019/07/01/world/europe/madrid-low-emission-zone.html> accessed 8 April 2020.

Temporary measures are also gaining popularity. In 2015, for example, Paris reacted to an air pollution spike by reducing speed limits and allowing only cars with odd-numbered license plates or more than three passengers on board to enter the city. In return, parking for cars with even-numbered plates, public transport as well as car and bike sharing services were offered free of charge.[34] Similar measures have been implemented in the years to follow.[35] Notwithstanding all the horrors of the corona pandemic, the lockdown strategies imposed by many cities show that even such short-term measures can have a big impact.[36]

Reducing the number of cars and roads creates more space for other means of transport. All over the globe, cities are expanding their walking and cycling infrastructures.[37] Copenhagen, Utrecht and Amsterdam are usually the poster children.[38] In Helsinki, for example, even suburban neighbourhoods have been turned into car-free communities,[39] which are linked to the city centre by buses and trains. Shared bikes and scooters bridge the last part of the journey from the bus or train station to the citizen's final destination. Such policies can provide further benefits, such as a healthier population due to increased physical exercise.[40] However, it remains to be seen to what extent this effect will be mitigated by the increasing availability of electrified transport solutions. Effectively, e-bikes and e-scooters

---

[34]See Nick Van Mead, 'Paris is Banning Traffic from Half the City – Why Can't London Have a Car-Free Day? *The Guardian* (22 September 2016) <www.theguardian.com/cities/2016/sep/22/paris-ban-traffic-london-world-car-free-day> accessed 8 April 2020; Kim Willsher, 'Paris Bans Cars for Second Day Running as Pollution Chokes City' *The Guardian* (Paris, 7 December 2016) <www.theguardian.com/world/2016/dec/07/paris-bans-cars-for-second-day-running-as-pollution-strikes> accessed 8 April 2020.

[35]See Forrest Crellin, 'Paris Bans up to 60% of Its Cars as Heatwave Worsens Pollution' (*Reuters*, 27 June 2019) <www.reuters.com/article/us-france-pollution/paris-bans-up-to-60-of-its-cars-as-heatwave-worsens-pollution-idUSKCN1TS2Z0> accessed 8 April 2020; Hellen Coffey, 'Paris to Ban Cars in City Centre One Sunday a Month' *The Independent* (3 October 2018) <www.independent.co.uk/travel/news-and-advice/paris-car-free-sundays-city-centre-france-pedestrian-a8566991.html> accessed 8 April 2020.

[36]See, for instance, the lockdown's positive effect on congestion and pollution in the lagoon and the canals of Venice, which are usually heavily frequented by shipping traffic, see Jack Guy and Valentina Di Donato, 'Venice's Canal Water Looks Clearer as Coronavirus Keeps Visitors Away' (*CNN*, 16 March 2020) <https://edition.cnn.com/travel/article/venice-canals-clear-water-scli-intl/index.html> accessed 8 April 2020.

[37]See Porteanu (n 25); Mikael Colville-Andersen, 'The 20 Most Bike-Friendly Cities in the World, From Malmö to Montreal' (*Wired*, 14 June 2017) <www.wired.com/story/world-best-cycling-cities-copenhagenize/> accessed 8 April 2020; Athlyn Cathcart-Keays, 'Where Is the Most Cycle-Friendly City in the World?' *The Guardian* (5 January 2016) <www.theguardian.com/cities/2016/jan/05/where-world-most-cycle-friendly-city-amsterdam-copenhagen> accessed 8 April 2020.

[38]See Colville-Andersen (n 37).

[39]See Porteanu (n 25).

[40]See Adele Peters, '7 Cities That Are Starting To Go Car-Free' (*Fastcompany*, 13 January 2015) <www.fastcompany.com/3040634/7-cities-that-are-starting-to-go-car-free> accessed 8 April 2020.

imply less rather than more exercise, and one may seriously question how the abundance of such transport products—most of which just stand around and take up public space—will affect the environment and consumers at the end of the day.

In any case, an accessible, reliable and affordable public transport system is a prerequisite for such initiatives to work without frustrating those who need to move into, out of and around the city. In the urban context, the methods of public transport available to the general public are abundant. Most cities are served by buses, trams, metros, ferries or any combination of these. Special lanes for buses, cabs and first responders are a common sight. But there are also more exotic transit services, such as the ropeway that extends over the Bolivian city of La Paz, New York's Roosevelt Island Tramway or London's 'Emirates Air Line'. Dubai's flying drone taxi, 'vactrains' such as the 'Hyperloop' envisaged by Tesla and SpaceX and the moving underground sidewalk proposed by a London architecture firm[41] are just hints as to what else the future might hold for public transport. Ideally, all methods of conveyance form an integrated intermodal urban transport network that allows passengers to seamlessly transfer from one mode to another.

Technology is a key driver for progress across the board: electrification, smart grids, solar power, electromagnetic induction, digital bus shelters, smart ticketing systems, public transit apps, automation, etc. Sustainability also drives progress. Some companies put much effort into reducing the environmental footprint of urban transport by developing smaller and lighter vehicles that are made out of recycled and recyclable materials and powered by new and sustainable fuels and alternative propulsion systems. In this regard, public transport can be seen as a "test bed for new technologies" and an "opportunity for early market deployment".[42]

Whether by road, rail or water, public transport needs to meet the expectations of a motley collection of users and user groups. Accessibility is one of the main concerns. The urban transport network must be accessible not only to those who use it out of conviction or convenience but also—and in particular—to those who have no other choice because they are physically, socially or economically dependent. The objective of an inclusive urban mobility strategy is to provide all commuters, residents and visitors with access to urban transport. Considering that this is a monetary issue, some cities offer public transport free of charge, such as Estonia's capital, Tallinn. As of 2020, Luxembourg is the first country to provide all modes of public transport—trams, trains and buses—nationwide for free.[43] In light of all this,

---

[41] Jason Sayer, 'Walk This Way: Architecture Firm NBBJ Proposes a Moving Sidewalk to Replace London Underground Circle Line' *The Architect's Newspaper* (11 September 2015) <https://archpaper.com/2015/09/walk-way-architecture-firm-proposes-travelator-replace-london-underground-line/> accessed 8 April 2020.

[42] COM (2011) 144 final para 32.

[43] Daniel Boffey, 'Luxembourg to Become First Country to Make All Public Transport Free' *The Guardian* (Luxembourg, 5 December 2018) <www.theguardian.com/world/2018/dec/05/luxembourg-to-become-first-country-to-make-all-public-transport-free> accessed 8 April 2020; Marc Auxenfants, 'The Cost of Luxembourg's Free Public Transport Plan' (*BBC*, 29 January 2019) <www.bbc.com/worklife/article/20190128-the-cost-of-luxembourgs-free-public-transport-plan> accessed 8 April 2020.

the bicycle—once considered "a means of transportation for children and the poor"[44]—may witness an unexpected revival, whereas the future of the car—*the* status symbol of the twentieth century—does not appear bright. Some even predict its extinction, or at least its disappearance from the urban landscape: "In the future, we will look at the car the way we look at the horse today. Something for hobbyists. Not as a means of transportation."[45]

In the spirit of making cities greener and cleaner, most trends in urban mobility are accompanied by a transition to alternative propulsion systems and fuels, such as electric, hydrogen and hybrid technologies. According to a report commissioned by Greenpeace, by the end of 2013 almost 93% of all transport energy needs came from oil products, whereas only 1% came from electricity.[46] The message behind the report is unmistakable: fossil fuels are bad, electric power is good. The automotive industry has been quite successful in transporting that notion into consumers' minds; it is not a coincidence that car manufacturers have chosen green and blue for their range of electric and hybrid, allegedly environmental-friendly models. Whether the overall environmental footprint of electric energy is really as small as the industry would like to make us believe lies beyond the scope of this introduction. In any case, urban mobility strategies devote considerable attention to replacing conventional fuels and driving systems with alternative technologies that have a lesser—or at least less visible—impact on the environment.[47]

3 Digitalisation, Data and 'Smartification'

Many current advances in urban mobility are based on embedding information and communication technologies in the very fabric of cities.[48] With the 'third wave' of digitalisation,[49] cities—and along with them, urban mobility—are becoming 'smart' in an unprecedented way.

In the urban mobility context, one of the main fields of application of digital technologies is the automation of products, services and processes. Back in the

[44]See Klaus Æ Mogensen, 'The Bicycle – The Future Means of Transportation' (*Scenario Magazine*, 27 February 2013) <www.scenariomagazine.com/the-bicycle-the-future-means-of-transportation/> accessed 8 April 2020, arguing that the bicycle is the means of transportation for the 21st century.

[45]Peter Schwartz, quoted by Adam Cowart, 'Future of Autonomous Spaces' (*Scenario Magazine*, 3 September 2015) <www.scenariomagazine.com/future-of-autonomous-spaces/> accessed 8 April 2020.

[46]Greenpeace and others, *Energy [R]evolution: A Sustainable World Energy Outlook 2015* (2015), 12, 287ff.

[47]See, for example, European Commission (n 27) 9; European Commission (n 20) 8ff.

[48]See Batty (n 2) 176.

[49]See Martin Kruse, 'Digitalisation' (*Scenario Magazine*, 25 December 2010) <www.scenariomagazine.com/digitalisation/> accessed 8 April 2020.

1980s, the French city of Lille was one of the first worldwide—preceded only by Kobe, Japan—to serve its city centre with a fully automated, driverless train. Today, driverless trains are a common sight throughout Europe, and other modes of transport are catching up. In 2016, for instance, driverless public buses started to operate in the Swiss city of Sion. It was the first time that an automated vehicle operated on public roads in Switzerland. However, it will still take some time until driverless buses and cars become a common sight on public roads in Europe. There are too many legal and regulatory variables that remain unsolved. But the technology is almost there.

Beyond the individual vehicle, information and communication technologies serve as a basis for smart urban traffic management systems, which operate on the basis of real-time information about traffic flows, weather, road conditions, vehicle occupancy, etc. The technical infrastructure behind such systems consists of a multi-layered network that connects traffic participants—pedestrians, cars, bicycles, cabs, buses, trains, metros, trams, ferries, first responders, etc.—with each other as well as with the city's infrastructure. An integrated traffic management system helps to manage traffic flows and public transport services; reduce congestion, emissions and accidents; facilitate intermodal transport; and balance the use of public roads by private cars, public transport and freight vehicles.[50] Copenhagen, for instance, has implemented an 'intelligent transport system' that adjusts traffic signals depending on real-time weather and traffic conditions.[51] For bicycles and buses, in particular those that are full and behind schedule, green lights can be kept on just a little longer than for others. Similar systems—while obviously less sophisticated than today's—were put in place back in the 1990s in order to speed up public road transport.[52] In a fully interconnected world, the possibilities are endless. For instance, based on the information provided by smart watches, mobile phones or fitness trackers, buses or trams carrying passengers with increased stress hormone levels could be given priority over others. Similarly, traffic in neighbourhoods with high rates of congestion, accidents, noise or air pollution could be regulated on the basis of algorithms that optimise traffic flows in real time and make sure that the available public transport services run at full capacity.

A prerequisite for the functioning of smart traffic management is the interoperability of information and communication technologies. Consequently, technical standardisation and all the problems associated with it are ubiquitous.[53] The information collected and processed must be accessible and processable by infrastructure managers, service operators, product developers and other stakeholders in order to

---

50 See European Commission (n 20) 8ff.

51 See City of Copenhagen, 'Better Mobility in Copenhagen – ITS Action Plan 2015-2016' (2014).

52 See, for example, Eric Taub, 'System Lets Traffic Lights Wave Buses Through' *The New York Times* (14 September 2000) <www.nytimes.com/2000/09/14/technology/system-lets-traffic-lights-wave-buses-through.html> accessed 8 April 2020.

53 In the IoT context, see Beatriz Conde Gallego and Josef Drexl 'IoT Connectivity Standards: How Adaptive is the Current SEP Regulatory Framework' (2019) 50 IIC 135.

help customers make traveling choices. For the same reason, interoperability is a *conditio sine qua non* for any driverless vehicle to operate on public roads. Even the transition to new fuels and propulsion systems cannot work without standardisation, which ensures that recharging stations are compatible across different manufacturers and types of vehicles, such as trucks, buses, cars or even bicycles.

All these developments would hardly be possible without data—and to a considerable extent *personal* data, e.g. about our location, movement patterns, choices, preferences, etc. Most citizens carry sensors capable of registering all kinds of data about their physical and mental condition, movements and choices. 'Smart dust' might be employed to register additional data on the citizen's environment, such as sound, light, pressure, acceleration, humidity and more. Datification is becoming an intrinsic part of our being and activity. Data fuels technical solutions that make our everyday life not only easier but more transparent. An illustrative example is 'smart velomobility', which refers to the emergence of networked practices, systems and technologies of cycling.[54] Reporting platforms allow cyclists to easily report road conditions and unexpected incidents to local authorities.[55] Maps track the movement of cyclists through location data collected on mobile phones, smart watches or fitness trackers. In fact, it has become standard for bike-sharing schemes to track their users.[56] Whoever processes that data may get to know almost everything about the cyclist's driving patterns and style.

The resulting data collection and data mining[57] obviously raise data protection concerns. Movement data can reveal intimate details about citizens' lives, and it is also difficult to anonymise. If a mobile device is involved, a plethora of additional personal information about the cyclist's physical condition and social life is at stake. For a long time, most of us have lived unaware of, or at least indifferent to, the collection, processing and monitoring of information on our identity and behaviour by private and public actors. This has changed in recent years. With the digital penetration of everyday lives, the economic value of personal data has grown, as has public awareness about the risks and costs of digital transparency. This does not necessarily imply that people are being more careful or prudent with regard to the exposure of their digital identity. But at least data protection has become a top priority for most legislators.

[54]See Frauke Behrendt, 'Why Cycling Matters for Smart Cities. Internet of Bicycles for Intelligent Transport' (2016) 56 Journal of Transport Geography 157.

[55]See Karen R Greiderer, 'Die kluge Stadt von morgen – Köln ruft zur "Smart Bicycle Traffic Challenge"' (*Bikecitizens*, 24 September 2018) <www.bikecitizens.net/cologne-smart-bicycle-traffic-challenge/> accessed 8 April 2020; on the significant role of platforms for integration and coordination in the city context, see Batty (n 2) 179.

[56]See Rosamond Hutt, 'Mapping of Bike-Sharing Data Will Change the Way You See These Cities' (*World Economic Forum*, 10 August 2016) <www.weforum.org/agenda/2016/08/what-bike-share-data-can-tell-us-about-our-cities/> accessed 8 April 2020.

[57]For details, see Dmitry Namiota and Manfred Sneps-Sneppe, 'On Bikes in Smart Cities' (2019) 53 Automatic Control and Computer Sciences 63.

Whatever technological innovations the future may bring, urban mobility strategies will have to embrace them. But they must equally consider that beyond being 'smart', transport needs to be accessible, sustainable and inclusive in order to keep pace with the societal and environmental challenges of urban life, which will only become bigger in the course of further urbanisation.

4 Legal Challenges and Affected Areas

How does smart urban mobility challenge the law? To answer this question, one has to bear in mind that much of smart urban mobility refers to policies and principles which are not necessarily reflected in—or have not yet been transposed into—legal rules.[58] At the same time, there can also be private arrangements which do not involve the state as lawmaker, an illustrative example being modes of self-regulation through review and rating systems.[59] It is therefore important to envision the broader picture of how smart urban mobility challenges policy, law and regulation alike and how it affects their interaction.

In any case, smart urban mobility raises issues in various legal fields that pinpoint the interaction between technology, law and public policy. Law is a seminal, yet ambiguous factor in this context. Here, it is understood in a dynamic way as it both *shapes* and *is shaped by* techno-economic and societal change. This dynamic perception of the law is key for inquiring into the challenges of technology-driven fields like smart urban mobility.

How does the law *shape* techno-economic and societal change? It can set out conditions for technological and economic development and provide incentives for adapting behaviour. This concerns the prerequisites for a functioning market as well as market intervention, e.g. industrial policies which are transposed into binding rules, such as provisions according to which emissions must be reduced or the development of clean technologies must be fostered. How is the law *shaped by* techno-economic and societal change? Techno-economic and societal change can put existing rules under pressure and demand their revision. An illustrative example is the evolvement of the 'platform economy', which plays a critical role for new urban mobility services. At the same time, it calls the applicability of existing rules into question and triggers a policy discussion as to whether the law must be changed in order to adequately respond to such developments. The responsibility for this rests on courts,[60] policymakers and the legislature alike. The chapters of this book cover

[58]For the distinction, see Josephine van Zeben, 'Environmental Implications of the EU's Urban Mobility Agenda', in this volume.

[59]See, for example, Rossana Ducato, 'Private Ordering of Online Platforms in Smart Urban Mobility: The Case of Uber's Rating System', in this volume.

[60]See Case C-434/15 *Asociación Profesional Élite Taxi v. Uber Systems Spain SL* [2017] EU:C:2017:981.

both the proactive and the reactive role of policies and the law. Often, these roles are intertwined.

This cursory description of trends in urban mobility and the smart city underlines that smart urban mobility is a dynamic phenomenon which is neither clearly defined nor easily referable to a legal category. For a legal analysis, it is therefore important to determine the relevance of distinct legal areas and focuses. Smart urban mobility cuts through many legal and policy areas which—either on the basis of their regulatory purpose or as a mere reflex—are becoming increasingly relevant. As this book focuses on EU policies, laws and regulations, a basic assumption is the existence of a market economy, which sets the framework conditions for economic and technological development, including innovation and competition. The development, provision and exchange of smart mobility products and services therefore largely depend on competition as a 'discovery procedure' and the competitive market as an allocation and price-setting mechanism. In this light, smart urban mobility pressures regulators to reconsider those legal areas which facilitate the functioning of the market, namely property, competition and contract law.

To identify relevant fields of law beyond those mentioned, it appears helpful to break the term 'smart urban mobility' down into its parts and see which legal issues revolve around each component. 'Smart' stands for digitisation and datification. Accordingly, data regulation (e.g. data protection, data ownership, data contract law) plays a seminal role. 'Urban' indicates the local and therefore public dimension; it ties together public interest, legal competences and state intervention as well as laws which address the interaction between public and private actors. 'Mobility' refers to different transport means and movement. It shifts the focus to liability and safety law as well as to transport innovations (data and devices).

5 Goal and Perspectives for Analysis: Public, Businesses and Citizens

5.1 Goal and Three Perspectives

This book aims to analyse current developments of smart urban mobility in order to provide a basis for further research, policy debate and ultimately regulation. To this end, a diverse group of scholars from different legal disciplines and from across the EU has examined ongoing transformations from the perspective of various areas of the law. This includes competition law, intellectual property law, contract law, data protection law, consumer law, legal philosophy, environmental law, public procurement law and fundamental rights.

To structure and conceptualise this analysis, one could imagine different ways of exploring the interaction between technology, law and public policy. An evident approach would be to discuss it according to specific areas and sub-domains of law. Yet this book deliberately follows a different approach by analysing the phenomenon of smart urban mobility from three different angles: the public perspective, the business perspective and the citizens' perspective. Each of these interrelated perspectives highlights issues related to each other, but with a different focus depending on the subject under consideration. Considering the diverging purposes and functional contexts of different areas of law, it is a natural consequence that these different perspectives also emphasise different legal areas. Needless to say, this delineation is of an ideal-typical nature and many overlaps can be identified in the details.

5.2 Public Perspective

The public perspective regards smart urban mobility as a phenomenon which systematically affects public interests and impacts the society at large. This appears obvious, as mobility takes place in public space and therefore has a public dimension by definition. The respective rules are designed to balance different public interests and to address externalities. A key aspect of the public perspective is the relationship between smart urban mobility and sustainability, including environmental policies, public safety and social inclusion. Moreover, the public perspective regards the state itself as an actor—be it as a regulator who designs rules affecting mobility or as a public buyer who himself provides mobility infrastructure and mobility solutions. The significance of smart urban mobility from a public perspective and the interplay between policies and laws become clearer when looking at the chapters in detail:

Caroline Mullen (chapter "Governing a Risky Relationship Between Sustainability and Smart Mobility") leads off by exploring an eminent public policy goal: the use of new mobility concepts for improving the social and economic sustainability of urban mobility, especially decarbonisation. However, new mobility services involve major complexities and uncertainties, and their effects therefore appear ambiguous. Mullen highlights the importance of collaboration between multiple affected stakeholders and argues that collaborative and reflexive governance is key for steering the nature of mobility services towards sustainability.

Josephine van Zeben (chapter "Environmental Implications of the EU's Urban Mobility Agenda") then focuses on concrete policies and laws. While there is no such thing as 'EU urban mobility law', she explores the interaction of the developing EU smart urban mobility policy on the one hand and EU environmental law and policy on the other. She makes suggestions for how to better align and integrate environmental and mobility goals in the future.

Sofia Ranchordás (chapter "Smart Mobility, Transport Poverty and the Legal Framework of Inclusive Mobility") turns to another major challenge for the sustainable development of urban mobility: social exclusion. She explores the important, yet often overlooked phenomenon of 'transport poverty' and asks what is necessary to design forms of mobility that are inclusive, equitable and non-discriminatory. By stressing the notion of public interest and considering the fundamental rights dimension, she argues that inclusive mobility should be acknowledged as part of the right to equal treatment.

Andrés Boix Palop (chapter "Local Leadership and Its Limits in the Deployment of Sustainable Mobility Policies") focuses on the role of local authorities and their legal instruments to implement new urban mobility policies. He outlines the regulatory context and identifies traditional intervention titles and taxation as important instruments. He discusses limitations that local authorities face in their attempts to pursue and implement more ambitious policies.

Albert Sanchez-Graells (chapter "Some Public Procurement Challenges in Supporting and Delivering Smart Urban Mobility: Procurement Data, Discretion and Expertise") focuses on the state as an actor and explores the challenges that public buyers face regarding the design of public tenders to support smart urban mobility. This concerns the re-use of and access to transport data, relevant areas of procurement practice where contracting authorities can exercise their discretion to foster sustainability, as well as the professionalisation and networking of procurement officials.

Jannice Käll (chapter "Governing Smart Spaces Through Autonomous Vehicles") completes the public perspective on smart mobility by inquiring into how autonomous vehicles govern the spaces around them. Based on the theory of special property, she argues that the interaction between autonomous vehicles and their surrounding environment in itself can be considered a new form of control.

5.3 *Business Perspective*

The business perspective focuses on private undertakings, which are the central actors in a market economy. As key determinants for fostering social welfare, the freedoms of property, competition and contract enable undertakings to make use of their autonomy to satisfy demand and innovate products and services. As has already been pointed out, the seminal enabler for smart urban mobility is data. In this regard, mobility solutions are often forms of data-driven innovation. Therefore, the question arises to what extent concepts and laws in the fields of property, competition and contract apply and how they should be further developed.

Giulia Priora and Caterina Sganga (chapter "Smart Urban Mobility: A Positive or Negative IP Space? A Case Study to Test the Role of IP in Fostering Digital Data-Driven Innovation") inquire into the incentives for innovation in the smart urban mobility context. For this purpose, they observe the interface between smart urban mobility and intellectual property. By conducting interviews, they explore the motivations to innovate. They argue that the significance of big data and software infrastructure for innovation in the smart urban mobility sector calls for more openness and inclusion rather than a paradigm of propertisation.

Giancarlo Frosio (chapter "Sharing or Platform Urban Mobility? Propertization from Mass to MaaS") adds the perspective of the sharing economy, which he applies to smart urban mobility. He contextualises the idea of Mobility as a Service (MaaS) and criticises the neo-liberal perspective, which has transformed the sharing economy into a platform economy. Considering the fundamental role of data ownership and protection, he emphasises the negative externalities of data propertisation and pleads for the development of smart urban mobility according to a ‘3C model’: commons, collaboration and crowdsourcing.

Björn Lundqvist and Erion Murati (chapter “Collaborative Platforms and Data Pools for Smart Urban Societies and Mobility as a Service (MaaS) from a Competition Law Perspective”) also elaborate on MaaS, yet from the angle of competition policies and laws. They point out that data can be pooled on MaaS data ecosystems and analyse the issue of MaaS collaborations and platform building with regard to their conformity with EU competition law, specifically Arts. 101 and 102 TFEU. They plead for more guidance from the European Commission.

Mariateresa Maggiolino and Laura Zoboli (chapter “Smart Mobility and Technological Compatibility from an Antitrust Perspective”) take a competition-related view as well in exploring the significance of technological compatibility for smart mobility. They refer to antitrust experience as a benchmark to identify guidelines which can inform public authorities when intervening in the market. For this purpose, they examine how competition law addresses technological incompatibility and examine the role of standard-setting organisations in this context.

Martin Fries (chapter “Efficient Mobility: Lessons on Dynamic Pricing and Sustainable Passenger Service”) then turns the focus to the core parameters of the market: prices and contracts. He argues that the use of mobility services can be optimised (e.g. congestion-free driving, search-free parking and switching transport means) by introducing auction structures. Data allows one to put a price tag on the smallest traffic areas, which can then be auctioned off to the highest bidder. Such transactions could be largely automated. The legislator should unlock the potential of such structures while also safeguarding the public from the associated risks.

5.4 Citizens’ Perspective

Finally, the citizens’ perspective focuses on how smart urban mobility affects the individual rights of subjects. Such individuals include users of mobility products and services as well as those who are indirectly affected. The concept of the citizen points to the importance of fundamental rights, but citizens are also consumers and therefore market participants. This is especially true in the sphere of mobility services, which are not only offered by private providers.[61] From a legal perspective, consumer contract law and data protection law as well as the fundamental right of privacy are at the centre of attention. They are conceptually distinct from one

[61] For differences, see Sofia Ranchordás, ‘Citizens as Consumers in the Data Economy: The Case of Smart Cities’ (2018) 8 Journal of European Consumer and Market Law 154.

another, but there are also overlaps, and one can discuss their relationship and future development in this light.

Zohar Efroni (chapter "Location Data as Contractual Counter-Performance: A Consumer Perspective on Recent EU Legislation") takes the perspective of consumers by enquiring into the current regulation of digital consumer law in the EU, in particular as it pertains to the 'data as a counter-performance' dilemma. He applies it to location data, which is seminal for the provision and functioning of smart urban mobility. He touches on the intersection with data protection law and pleas for a more coherent approach that would balance personal autonomy, state intervention and the market economy.

Catalina Goanta (chapter "Yes Means No(thing): Bridging Consent in Contract Law and Data Protection in the Context of Smart Mobility") further elaborates on the intersection of contract and data protection law. She identifies consent as seminal for the functioning of many business models (e.g. through tracking and profiling users) and points to the differences between contractual consent and 'informed consent'. Goanta reflects upon whether these concepts must converge or diverge in the future if they are to serve the pursuit of sustainable smart mobility policies.

Rossana Ducato (chapter "Private Ordering of Online Platforms in Smart Urban Mobility: The Case of Uber's Rating System") focuses on the significance of rating and review systems for smart urban mobility. Such systems enable private ordering and can therefore be seen as self-regulatory mechanisms. The focus lies on Uber, which is currently the world's largest shared mobility platform. Ducato discusses its conformity with European data protection rules and elaborates on the aspect of automated decision-making.

Jonathan Andrew (chapter "Challenges to Locational Privacy: The Transformation of Urban Mobility") completes the citizens' perspective by discussing challenges to locational privacy. He describes the transformation of urban mobility towards a system which monitors individual and group movements and points to the risk that smart infrastructure will open the door to an era of omnipresent surveillance. Andrew highlights the relevance of locational privacy for safeguarding the fundamental right to privacy in urban settings.

Part I
Public Perspective

Governing a Risky Relationship Between Sustainability and Smart Mobility

Caroline Mullen

Contents

Abstract New mobility services, enabled by developments in digital technology, could be the making of sustainability in urban mobility. Alternatively, they could act to increase car dependence and so worsen what are already severe sustainability problems. Governance of new mobility services needs to steer implementation towards sustainability, and this chapter explores what that governance might look like. The stakes are high because of the extent of sustainability impacts of transport, especially the increasingly urgent need to decarbonise the sector. There is evidence that reductions in car dependence are required to address many of the pressing social, environmental and economic transport problems, including carbon dioxide emissions. Uncertainties about the sustainability implications of new mobility services present challenges for governance. Those governance challenges are heightened by the complex landscape of actors, with new developers and service providers joining an already complicated multi-level system. I argue that collaborative and reflexive governance provides a basis for meeting these challenges of uncertainty and complexity. However, its implementation should involve reframing the relationships

---

Caroline Mullen is a Senior Research Fellow at the Institute for Transport Studies, University of Leeds, UK.
This work is supported by U-PASS Urban Public Administration and Services innovation for Innovative Urban Mobility Management and Policy ESRC Grant ref: ES/T000074/1, Co-funder: JPI-Europe.

C. Mullen (✉)
Institute for Transport Studies, University of Leeds, Leeds, UK
e-mail: c.a.mullen@leeds.ac.uk

M. Finck et al. (eds.), *Smart Urban Mobility*, MPI Studies on Intellectual Property and Competition Law 29, https://doi.org/10.1007/978-3-662-61920-9_2

between transport authorities and developers of mobility services such that innovation is rewarded, but priority is given to responding to evidence on sustainability impacts as they emerge.

1 Introduction

It is becoming commonplace to draw attention to, and to question, the optimism placed in what is called smart mobility, that is the use of digital technologies to provide and coordinate new mobility services including (where legal) ride sharing, car sharing, shared cycles and scooters, and possibly combinations of these. The optimism is amplified by progress in electrification of transport, and anticipation of increasing automation. The promise is that these new mobility services will reduce reliance on private motor vehicles and so will tackle major problems associated with our current mobility systems.[1] Conversely, the concern is that if we do not get the governance of new mobility services right, then we will be faced with increasing reliance on motor vehicles. Such caution is far from overstated as traffic increases bring problems for social, economic and environmental sustainability, and there is an increasingly acute need for reductions in traffic in order to meet the requirements for decarbonisation. The basis for concern that traffic may increase is the modelling evidence that new mobility services could encourage—and then embed—greater use of vehicles. Researchers, and some governments, have made the case for the importance of good governance of these mobility services, and there have been efforts at outlining the sorts of governance measures which might be required to steer the new mobility services.[2]

---

[1]For instance: Iain Docherty, Greg Marsden and Jillian Anable, 'The Governance of Smart Mobility' (2018) 115 Transportation Research Part A: Policy and Practice 114; Achille Fonzone, Wafaa Saleh and Tom Rye, 'Smart Urban Mobility – Escaping the Technological Sirens' (2018) 115 Transportation Research Part A: Policy and Practice 1; Mahtot Gebresselassie and Thomas W Sanchez, '"Smart" Tools for Socially Sustainable Transport: A Review of Mobility Apps' (2018) 2 Urban Science 45; Enrica Papa and António Ferreira, 'Sustainable Accessibility and the Implementation of Automated Vehicles: Identifying Critical Decisions' (2018) 2 Urban Science 5; Department for Transport, 'Future of Mobility: Urban Strategy: Moving Britain Ahead' (Department for Transport 2019) <https://assets.publishing.service.gov.uk/government/uploads/system/uploads/attachment_data/file/846593/future-of-mobility-strategy.pdf> accessed 10 March 2020; Miloš N Mladenović, 'How Should We Drive Self-driving Vehicles? Anticipation and Collective Imagination in Planning Mobility Futures' in Matthias Finger and Maxime Audouin (eds), *The Governance of Smart Transportation Systems* (Springer 2019); Fariya Sharmeen and Henk Meurs, 'The Governance of Demand-Responsive Transit Systems—A Multi-level Perspective' in Matthias Finger and Maxime Audouin (eds), *The Governance of Smart Transportation Systems* (Springer 2019).

[2]Zia Wadud, Don MacKenzie and Paul Leiby, 'Help or Hindrance? The Travel, Energy and Carbon Impacts of Highly Automated Vehicles' (2016) 86 Transportation Research Part A: Policy and

Alongside this consideration of substantive measures, there has been research focusing on how governance can effectively involve the multiple actors engaged in the development of smart mobility.[3] New mobility services are not unique in bringing public, private and non-governmental actors together in the provision of mobility,[4] however it is noticeable that new actors—many of whom had not previously been involved in the mobility sector—are now participating. This may bring into focus the significance of collaboration between actors to enable governance which takes account of, and is informed by, the interests and knowledge of the multiple stakeholders whose actions will shape the use and impact of new mobility services.

What has not yet been given significant attention is the processes of governance as they occur over time, and which are needed to improve the prospects that smart mobility will contribute to, rather than further damage, sustainability. As I argue in this chapter, these processes will be central to the prospects for effective governance for two major and related reasons. The first of these is common to many sectors, and arises from a recognition that the future is uncertain, and that any governance or regulation which ignores this, and attempts to plan for every eventuality, will run into problems. This recognition underpins a large body of work on collaborative and reflexive governance.[5] However, as the following sections explore, uncertainty and

Practice 1; Docherty, Marsden and Anable (n 1); Fonzone, Saleh and Rye (n 1); David A Hensher, 'Tackling Road Congestion – What Might it Look Like in the Future Under a Collaborative and Connected Mobility Model?' (2018) 66 Transport Policy A1; Jennifer Kent, 'Three Signs Autonomous Vehicles Will Not Lead to Less Car Ownership and Less Car Use in Car Dependent Cities – A Case Study of Sydney, Australia' (2018) 19 Planning Theory & Practice 767; Glenn Lyons, 'Getting Smart About Urban Mobility – Aligning the Paradigms of Smart and Sustainable' (2018) 115 Transportation Research Part A: Policy and Practice 4; Greg Marsden, 'Planning for Autonomous Vehicles? Questions of Purpose, Place and Pace' (2018) 19 Planning Theory & Practice 771; Department for Transport (n 1); Eva Fraedrich and others, 'Autonomous Driving, the Built Environment and Policy Implications' (2019) 122 Transportation Research Part A: Policy and Practice 162; Anthony D May and others, 'The Potential Impacts of Automated Cars on Urban Transport: an Exploratory Analysis' (World Conference on Transport Research, Mumbai, May 2019); Sharmeen and Meurs (n 1).

[3]Docherty, Marsden and Anable (n 1); Louise Reardon, 'Ensuring Good Governance: The Role of Planners in the Development of Autonomous Vehicles' (2018) 19 Planning Theory & Practice 773; Jingrui An and others, 'Collaborative Governance in the Sharing Economy. A Case of Free-Floating Bicycle Sharing with Visualized Analyzation' (2019) 22(supp 1) The Design Journal 777.

[4]For instance, David A Hensher and John Stanley, 'Contracting Regimes for Bus Services. What Have We Learnt after 20 years?' (2010) 29 Research in Transportation Economics 140; Ian Bache and others, *Multilevel Governance and Climate Change: Insights from Transport Policy* (Roman and Littlefield 2015); Robert Hrelja, Tom Rye and Caroline Mullen, 'Partnerships Between Operators and Public Transport Authorities. Working Practices in Relational Contracting and Collaborative Partnerships' (2018) 116 Transportation Research Part A: Policy and Practice 327.

[5]David M Van Slyke, 'Collaboration and Relational Contracting' in Rosemary O'Leary and Lisa Blomgren Bingham (eds), *The Collaborative Public Manager: New Ideas for the Twenty-First Century* (Georgetown University Press 2009); Jacques Lenoble and Marc Maesschalck, *Democracy, Law and Governance* (Ashgate 2010); Peter Vincent-Jones and Caroline Mullen, 'From Collaborative to Genetic Governance: The Example of Healthcare Services in England' in Olivier

the beliefs which uncertainty allows take on a particular importance in governing the mobility system. The second reason stems from a combination of the path-dependency which is characteristic of the mobility system, and the acute sustainability problems which are exacerbated by our current mobility system. I will argue that this means that not only is there a risk that smart mobility could increase the difficulty of achieving sustainable mobility, but also that the severity of this risk is heightened by the need to act rapidly to address sustainability concerns. In other words, we cannot afford to go backwards with sustainability of transport. The argument of the chapter indicates that the processes needed to govern new mobility services involve an acceptance that planning and decision-making are reflexive processes which take account of new evidence. An acceptance that we need to rethink the role of both public and private sector service providers, and the way in which service providers can expect to participate in, and benefit from, their engagement in the mobility system is also crucial. Since the argument is concerned with how smart mobility can contribute to sustainability, it concerns what needs to happen, rather than what is easy or perhaps even likely. The justification for this approach is that unless we consider what is required we will not know what to aim for, or how to assess our existing state of affairs.

The chapter is organised into six sections. After this introduction, the next section outlines how and why mobility matters for sustainability. This is a vast area, and space allows us only to focus on the most pressing concerns particularly relevant to new mobility services. So, this section will outline the need for transport to decarbonise, the problems of poor local air quality associated with transport, and the relationship between social exclusion and transport. This section will also briefly review existing literature on the potential sustainability implications of new mobility services. Section 3 will outline historical and current efforts to improve governance for the sustainability of transport and will discuss some of the major challenges for those efforts. This will include an outline of literature and discussions to date on governance of smart mobility. This section briefly describes previous and ongoing hopes for technological solutions and some of the criticisms of what is sometimes held to be a reliance on seeking technological fixes. It will then discuss the evidence that for effective change we need to intervene at the level of the mobility system: that is, in order to change the way in which travel is used we need to change the infrastructure, the provision of services, and the economic and social pressures which encourage particular travel practices. It will also indicate the counterpart to this point, which is that the structure and nature of the mobility system influences the way in which people travel. So, if the mobility system develops in a way which privileges motorised mobility then it becomes harder for people to move away from reliance on that mobility. I argue that two points follow from this section. The first of these is that it would be unrealistic to expect the tendency to look to technology to

---

De Schutter and Jacques Lenoble (eds), *Reflexive Governance* (Hart Publishing 2010); Peter Vincent-Jones, 'Contractual Governance: A Social Learning Perspective' in Pekka Valkama, Stephen J Bailey and Ari-Veikko Anttiroiko (eds), *Organizational Innovation in Public Services* (Palgrave Macmillan 2013).

solve complex mobility problems to suddenly disappear. The more so as we are currently witnessing optimism about the potential of new mobility services. Consequently, we might expect this optimism to influence planning decisions. The second point is the case for ongoing monitoring of the way in which the mobility system is developing, particularly since that development in turn tends to affect prospects for subsequent changes to the mobility system. Section 4 outlines the powers of, and constraints on regional, city, and national governments or transport authorities, when seeking to steer the mobility system. This looks at the legal powers of planners at different levels of government, and at the capacities that those planners have (since the two are not the same). This section informs the subsequent discussion of how new mobility services might be governed to support sustainability. Understanding the constraints and limitations on government actors is, as we would expect, important if we are to understand their powers and possibilities in relation to steering the development of new mobility services and the actions of non-governmental mobility providers. Then it is in Sect. 5 (informed by the argument of the previous sections) that the argument for a collaborative and reflexive approach to governance of new mobility services is presented. By investigating the circumstances and implications of mobility, the section makes the case that governance of new mobility services requires significant reassessment of the relationship between public and private actors. The argument also contributes to wider debate about the role of planning authorities at local and national level in shaping the mobility system if we are to support sustainability. Section 6 concludes the chapter.

2 Sustainability and Mobility

Understanding mobility as a matter of sustainability is something that has been mainstream for over two decades, since increasing political and public concern that the previously dominant approach of predict and provide—that is predict traffic increases and build road capacity to accommodate that—was not only failing to bring social and economic benefits, but was also having serious detrimental impacts on the environment and quality of life.[6] The relationship between mobility and sustainability is complex and vast, and we cannot do more here than to outline some of the major components which will be particularly relevant in thinking about new mobility services. As I have argued elsewhere, in thinking about sustainability and transport, it is helpful to begin by reflecting on the importance that mobility, including all forms of movement from walking to driving to cycling to passenger transport, has in our lives. Mobility enables social, political, personal and economic activities, and is vital for sustaining our lives, particularly given our complex social

[6]For instance, Caroline Mullen and Greg Marsden, 'Mobility Justice in Low Carbon Energy Transitions' (2016) 18 Energy Research & Social Science 109; Stefan Gössling, 'Urban Transport Justice' (2016) 54 Journal of Transport Geography 1.

and economic organisation. So individually and collectively we all benefit from a functioning mobility system, although those benefits are often uneven.[7] A lack of available, affordable, or accessible transport hampers opportunities, and social and economic welfare.[8] This lack of access to mobility can be a consequence of poor public transport services, or not owning a car; but it can also be something brought about by high levels of traffic which mean non-vehicular mobility is difficult or even dangerous.[9] There is significant work on the ways in which planning predicated on car use tends to encourage urban sprawl, which means everyday life involves travel over long distances or complex journeys.[10] There is also evidence that fear of traffic is one of the greatest barriers to cycling.[11] Further, there is long standing evidence—since the famous study by Appleyard—that high levels of motor traffic impedes and prevents local mobility on foot.[12] All of this can mean social exclusion for those who cannot drive or cannot own a private vehicle, it can also mean that people take on vehicle ownership even when doing so causes economic hardship.[13] Alongside all of this is the prominent notion that congestion on the roads is a barrier to economic activity and development.[14] Our use of transport is also responsible for deaths and serious injury through collision, with something under 2000 people killed each year in Britain on the roads, and between 1.2 and 1.3 million people killed worldwide.[15] As with other aspects of transport the burden of risks on the roads are unevenly distributed. As an indication of this, consider that car occupants are more than

[7]Mullen and Marsden, 'Mobility Justice' (n 6).

[8]John Preston and Fiona Rajé, 'Accessibility, Mobility and Transport-Related Social Exclusion' (2007) 15 Journal of Transport Geography 151; Karen Lucas and others, 'Transport Poverty and its Adverse Social Consequences' (2016) 169 Proceedings of the Institution of Civil Engineers - Transport 353; Giulio Mattioli, '"Forced Car Ownership" in the UK and Germany: Socio-Spatial Patterns and Potential Economic Stress Impacts' (2017) 5 Social Inclusion 147; Caroline Mullen, Greg Marsden and Ian Philips, 'Seeking Protection from Precarity? Relationships Between Transport Needs and Insecurity in Housing and Employment' (2020) 109 Geoforum 4.

[9]Colin Pooley and others, 'Policies for Promoting Walking and Cycling in England: a View from the Street' (2013) 27 Transport Policy 66; Caroline Mullen and others, 'Knowing their Place on the Roads: What Would Equality Mean for Walking and Cycling?' (2014) 61 Transportation Research Part A: Policy and Practice 238.

[10]Mattioli (n 8); Mullen, Marsden and Philips, 'Precarity' (n 8).

[11]Pooley and others (n 9).

[12]Donald Appleyard, *Liveable Streets* (University of California Press 1981).

[13]Mattioli (n 8); Mullen, Marsden and Philips 'Precarity' (n 8).

[14]See Caroline Mullen and Greg Marsden, 'Transport, Economic Competitiveness and Competition: A City Perspective' (2015) 49 Journal of Transport Geography 1. This understanding of the relationship between economic activity and congestion is not without controversy, especially where the understanding relies on views about the economic cost associated with travel time, see for instance David Banister, 'The Sustainable Mobility Paradigm' (2008) 15 Transport Policy 73.

[15]World Health Organization, *Global Status Report on Road Safety 2018* (World Health Organization 2018).

10 times less likely to be killed per given distance travelled than cyclists or pedestrians.[16] Reflecting on these issues brings to the fore ways in which mobility matters for social and economic sustainability.

Major environmental concerns associated with transport include greenhouse gas emissions (for which carbon dioxide emissions is often used as a shorthand), local air pollution, pollution of land and water from transport run-off, and land taken by transport which can damage biodiversity.[17] In thinking about the environmental impacts of transport it is important to keep in mind that it is people, and other living beings, who are affected by environmental damage.[18] As such it can be misleading to think of environmental sustainability as something distinct from social sustainability or from economic sustainability, if we consider the economic impacts of environmental harm and of ill health. We have already noted how urban sprawl can be associated with high levels of car use, and that infrastructure and patterns of motor vehicle use have implications for the possibilities of movement on foot or by bicycle and so for the activities associated with that mobility. Beyond this, surface transport is responsible for over one quarter of carbon dioxide emissions in Britain, a proportion which is increasing as other sectors have some success in decarbonisation,[19] and worldwide road transport accounts for between one fifth and one quarter of carbon dioxide emissions.[20] Concern about climate change is at the top of the policy agenda at the moment, although—or perhaps because—efforts at decarbonisation are falling well short of levels which appear required if we are to avoid more dangerous climate change.[21] Transport is faring badly even against this backdrop of inadequate action. The Committee on Climate Change holds that transport needs to decarbonise completely, and it suggests that to successfully achieve this in the time required involves not only the most rapid progress viable on the development and roll out of cleaner vehicles (that is electric vehicles and

[16] Mullen and others, 'Knowing their Place on the Roads' (n 9).

[17] An assessment of how land use taken for transport can impact fauna is given in Mårten Karlson and Ulla Mörtberg, 'A Spatial Ecological Assessment of Fragmentation and Disturbance Effects of the Swedish Road Network' (2015) 134 Landscape and Urban Planning 53.

[18] Will Steffen and others, 'Planetary Boundaries: Guiding Human Development on a Changing Planet' (2015) 347 Science 6223.

[19] Committee on Climate Change (CCC), 'Reducing UK Emissions: 2018 Progress Report to Parliament' (CCC 2018) <www.theccc.org.uk/publication/reducing-uk-emissions-2018-progress-report-to-parliament/> accessed 10 March 2020.

[20] International Energy Agency, 'CO2 Emissions from Fuel Combustion: Highlights' (IEA Publications 2018) <www.indiaenvironmentportal.org.in/files/file/CO2_Emissions_from_Fuel_Combustion_2018_Highlights.pdf> accessed 10 March 2020.

[21] Intergovernmental Panel on Climate Change, 'Summary for Policymakers of IPCC Special Report on Global Warming of 1.5 °C Approved by Governments' (*IPCC*, 2018) <www.ipcc.ch/2018/10/08/summary-for-policymakers-of-ipcc-special-report-on-global-warming-of-1-5c-approved-by-governments/> accessed 10 March 2020.

improvements in the efficiency of conventional vehicles), but also a reduction in motor traffic demand.[22,23] As we shall see in the following sections this need to decarbonise is particularly important when thinking about sustainability of new mobility services. Local air pollution from transport, such as nitrogen dioxide and particulate matter, is associated with thousands of early deaths in Britain and millions of early deaths worldwide. The majority of health problems associated with this pollution appear to be cardiovascular, however there is also evidence that pollution from diesel vehicles causes lung cancer, and as time goes on further evidence emerges of links to other forms of ill health.[24]

Recognition of major sustainability concerns associated with transport is not something fixed but rather something which develops over time as our scientific and social understanding develops (consider for instance our developing understanding of the health impacts of transport pollution such as nitrogen dioxides and particulates). Further, the sustainability impacts of transport change over time.[25] Keeping this developing picture in mind is important, as it reminds us that further, as yet unknown or weakly understood sustainability concerns may occur in the future and our governance should be capable of responding to this.

3 Governance and Politics of Mobility

At a high level there is little dispute about the types of measures which will support sustainable mobility or specific components of sustainable mobility. Those include a move to cleaner vehicles, and a reduced reliance on motor traffic enabled by a shift towards more walking and cycling and shared or public transport. However, there can be a worry that there is not enough substance beneath this high-level agreement to tackle the challenges of sustainable mobility. In other words, there is a policy ambition to improve sustainability, but this is not supported by planning or measures to realise the ambition. An example of this is the recent criticism by the Committee

[22]The CCC is an independent body which advises the British government on decarbonisation and which produces assessments of the sufficiency of government action on climate.

[23]Annex to letter from CCC Lord Deben, Chair of Committee on Climate Change, to Secretaries of State for Transport and Business, Energy and Industrial Strategy (11 October 2018).

[24]International Agency for Research on Cancer, *Outdoor Air Pollution: IARC Monographs on the Evaluation of Carcinogenic Risks to Humans* (vol 109, International Agency for Research on Cancer 2015); World Health Organization, *Ambient Air Pollution: A Global Assessment of Exposure and Burden of Disease* (World Health Organization 2016).

[25]Consider the increasingly acute impacts of failure to decarbonise transport. See also John Bowers, *Sustainability and Environmental Economics: An Alternative Text* (Longman 1997).

on Climate Change of the British government's strategy to decarbonise transport in compliance with the Climate Change Act 2008.[26]

Related to this is a well-recognised and widely critiqued tendency for planners and politicians to place a high level of hope on technology. This includes the sort of technology which will improve energy efficiency and reduce pollution from vehicles, and increasingly digital technology to coordinate mobility services and reduce reliance on private vehicles (whether automated or driven by humans). While there may be little dispute that technology has a major role to play in sustainable mobility, the concern is that the level of faith placed on technology is unwarranted and may act as a distraction to the sorts of actions required to improve sustainability. We can see this in efforts to decarbonise transport which tend to emphasise technological development.[27] However, even where technology brings some progress in relation to pollution, problems for sustainability remain. We have seen a reduction in carbon emissions per kilometre travelled on average for cars in Europe (although the level of this reduction is widely disputed given the increasing gap between reported and real-world efficiency).[28] Yet this improvement in efficiency has not led to a corresponding reduction in carbon dioxide emissions from vehicles because traffic volume and vehicle sizes have increased.[29] Further, even if technological change were to bring about a substantial reduction in tail pipe emissions, this would still not be sufficient to address sustainability concerns. There would still be problems of emissions, other pollution and resource use (for example carbon dioxide embodied in vehicles and particulate pollution from tyre wear), and complex concerns around the resources required for vehicles, and especially for the batteries in electric vehicles. Beyond this, any approach which does not tackle traffic and car dependence, will at best sustain and at worst exacerbate the social and economic injustices associated with our mobility system which were discussed in the previous section.[30]

This recent history of a failure of efficiency improvements to turn into a reduction in carbon dioxide emissions serves as a warning in thinking about smart mobility.

---

[26]CCC Lord Deben (n 23). Note that this letter pre-dates the amendment committing the country to net-zero emissions by 2050: Climate Change Act 2008 (2050 Target Amendment) Order 2019, SI 2019/1056.

[27]See for instance Transport and Environment, 'Draft National Energy and Climate Plans Transport Ranking' (Transport & Environment 2019) <www.transportenvironment.org/sites/te/files/publications/2019_06_Draft_NECP_transport_analysis_final.pdf> accessed 10 March 2020; HM Government, 'Carbon Plan' (Department of Energy & Climate Change 2011) <https://assets.publishing.service.gov.uk/government/uploads/system/uploads/attachment_data/file/47621/1358-the-carbon-plan.pdf> accessed 26 August 2020; Department for Transport, *Road to Zero Strategy* (Department of Transport 2018).

[28]See Georgios Fontaras, Nikiforos-Georgios Zacharof and Biagio Ciuffo, 'Fuel Consumption and CO2 Emissions from Passenger Cars in Europe – Laboratory Versus Real-World Emissions' (2017) 60 Progress in Energy and Combustion Science 97.

[29]CCC, 'Progress Report' (n 19); Jillian Anable, Christian Brand and Caroline Mullen, 'Transport: Taming of the SUV?' in UK Energy Research Centre (ed), 'Review of Energy Policy 2019: December 2019' (*UKERC*, 2019) 10 <https://ukerc.rl.ac.uk/UCAT/PUBLICATIONS/UKERC_Review_Energy_Policy_2019.pdf> accessed 10 March 2020.

[30]Mullen and Marsden, 'Mobility Justice' (n 6).

One of the anticipated benefits of automated transport is improvements in efficiency from the prospect that automated cars will use the roads more efficiently than human drivers, and will not engage in the sorts of inefficient driving practices (those practices being the opposite of what is called eco-driving) which characterise driving by humans.[31] The questions about whether these efficiencies would really lead to energy and emissions reductions were raised early in research on automation. Those investigating the question have presented modelling evidence which indicates that much depends on how automated vehicles are used and that there is a risk that automation could not only fail to bring hoped for improvements but could actually induce greater use of motor vehicles and hence greater energy consumption and emissions. We return to this question below when looking at how smart technology might influence the way in which transport is used.

Despite uncertainty about the extent to which technology can solve problems of sustainability and transport, it is perhaps understandable at some level that politicians seek to rely on technological solutions. Changing travel demand, and in particular reducing reliance on private vehicles, has proved difficult both politically and practically. The discussion of the last section outlined how a mobility system based to a large extent on motor traffic use becomes one in which it is difficult to travel by other means. The problem is one of path dependency in that once we start to use and accommodate particular ways of travelling and moving goods we then increasingly plan our infrastructure, built environment, and even economic and social activities in a way which comes to depend on those ways of travelling and moving goods. It is not difficult to see the problems that planners face in encouraging or insisting that people change the way in which they travel. We can see this when economic measures, such as fuel tax or road user charging, are used to reduce car use. There are numerous examples of efforts to introduce such measures, and they are generally accompanied by political dispute or protest—sometimes to the extent that the measures cannot be implemented.

Of course, the ideal is to intervene in the mobility system to make life easier to manage without owning a private car, and as the discussion above indicates, the elements which may achieve this would include improving public and shared transport, as well as improving conditions for walking and cycling. The challenge here is to provide the investment and planning which creates an accessible and affordable mobility system, with coverage (that is provision across areas and at times) which enables people to make what are often complex everyday journeys without relying on cars. Such measures, if successful, can improve environmental and social sustainability. Given this, the potential of new mobility services to support sustainability appear very promising. Digital technologies can provide the sorts of information which enables services to be coordinated, and which allows users to navigate their way through multi-modal forms of mobility. For users, the lack of information has been a barrier to reducing car dependence. This has been recognised for well over a decade, and during that period there have been efforts to provide

[31] Wadud, MacKenzie and Leiby, 'Help or Hindrance' (n 2).

travel planning tools.[32] The limitations previously have been a lack of real time information, and sometimes a lack of information about how to use public transport (since this is not always obvious to unfamiliar users).[33] In this way information technology can provide a relatively simple but perhaps very important solution to non-private car travel. It can also be used by service providers to monitor and coordinate public transport and shared transport and to coordinate different modes. However, it is recognised that much of this depends on different providers being willing to share information, and using compatible systems to do so.[34] Information technology can also be used to provide pedestrians with information about a route, and this can be particularly helpful for people with mobility difficulties who may need to know about flights of steps or the condition of a footway. For providers, digital technologies underpin the prospects for effectiveness of shared mobility services, including shared bikes and electric scooters, ride sharing (where people pay to travel in a car owned by another person), or car sharing where people collectively own a car. Providers need to be able to track vehicles and to provide users with information about where vehicles located and to coordinate their use.

Yet as noted above there is some discussion about whether automation could increase or decrease transport energy and emissions, and this is tied up with the issue of car sharing or ride sharing. On one hand if people do give up private cars then there is the potential for reductions in emissions and energy use, however this still depends on the way in which ride sharing and car sharing is used. One concern is empty cars driving around waiting for passengers. A further concern is that ride sharing will simply make it easier to travel by car, so even though individual journeys become more efficient, the number of them increases. Added to this is the question of whether, or the extent to which, ride sharing attracts people away from private cars, or instead lures passengers from public transport or discourages walking and cycling.[35] There is early empirical evidence emerging that ride sharing, even prior to any automation, is indeed leading to increased traffic. This is happening with ride sharing services such as Uber, for example.[36] If new mobility services act

---

[32]Sendy Farag and Glenn Lyons, 'To Use or Not to Use? An Empirical Study of Pre-trip Public Transport Information for Business and Leisure Trips and Comparison with Car Travel' (2012) 20 Transport Policy 82; Jan-Willem Grotenhuis, Bart W Wiegmans and Piet Rietveld, 'The Desired Quality of Integrated Multimodal Travel Information in Public Transport: Customer Needs for Time and Effort Savings' (2007) 14 Transport Policy 27; Susan Kenyon and Glenn Lyons, 'The Value of Integrated Multimodal Traveller Information and its Potential Contribution to Modal Change' (2003) 6 Transportation Research Part F: Traffic Psychology and Behaviour 1.

[33]See Tim Chatterton and others, 'Flexi-Mobility: Helping Local Authorities Unlock Low Carbon Travel?' (University Transport Studies Group (UTSG) 47th Annual Conference, London, January 2015).

[34]This also raises questions about data protection which are largely outside the scope of this chapter.

[35]See, for instance Christina Pakusch and others, 'Unintended Effects of Autonomous Driving: A Study on Mobility Preferences in the Future' (2018) 10 Sustainability 2404.

[36]John M Barrios, Yael V Hochberg and Hanyi L Yi, 'The Cost of Convenience: Ridesharing and Traffic Fatalities' (2018) Becker Friedman Institute Working Paper No. 2018-80 <https://bfi.uchicago.edu/wp-content/uploads/BFI-WP-2018-80.pdf> accessed 10 March 2020; Bruce

to increase traffic, this in turn could further exacerbate car dependence, albeit a form of dependence less predicated on private car ownership than we have at present. So, the risk is that if we begin to use new mobility services in ways which increase rather than reduce traffic, then we may be locking in practices and a mobility system which becomes even more difficult to change than is currently the case. This risk is further increased when we consider how much and how fast our mobility system needs to change if we are to tackle sustainability concerns, particularly those presented by climate change and the need to rapidly reduce carbon emissions.

Questions around bike sharing are slightly different. There are considerations about the attractiveness of shared bicycles for people who do not currently cycle. These are the very people who need to be attracted to bicycle use if we are to see increases in levels of cycling.[37] Factors such as the quality of the bicycles, ease of hire, and conditions of use will be relevant. We might also anticipate that the barriers to cycling at present, of which the largest is fear of traffic,[38] are going to remain unless that problem is tackled, and a bicycle sharing scheme itself cannot achieve this. There are also questions around the possible implications of shared bicycle and shared scooter schemes (in countries where this is legal) if they are used on footways, and for footway clutter. Both can create safety problems and obstacles for pedestrians, and particularly so for those with any form of mobility difficulty.[39] If the pedestrian environment is degraded, this may be a further barrier to sustainable mobility.

4 Transport Planning: Powers and Capacity

In thinking about the power and capacities of local and national governments to steer smart mobility towards sustainability we can begin by reminding ourselves of the existing conditions of a mobility system that is very far from sustainable. Transport authorities are aware that they have legal obligations regarding sustainable mobility and some of those are being pressed by non-governmental organisations and the public.[40] Yet transport authorities find difficulty in bringing about change. In this context bringing in new actors, and the new mobility services discussed in the last section, may present a solution to a very difficult problem.

Schaller, 'The New Automobility: Lyft, Uber and the Future of American Cities' (*Schaller Consulting*, 2018) <www.schallerconsult.com/rideservices/automobility.pdf> accessed 9 January 2020.

[37]Pooley and others (n 9).

[38]ibid.

[39]See for instance, Sustrans, 'Our Position on Micromobility' (*sustrans*, 1 January 2019) <www.sustrans.org.uk/our-blog/policy-positions/all/all/our-position-on-micromobility> accessed 10 January 2020.

[40]Alan Andrews, *The Clean Air Handbook: A Practical Guide to EU Air Quality Law* (Client Earth 2014).

One set of questions regarding new mobility services is how transport authorities can commission or find new providers. Transport authorities may have reasons to draw on the expertise of a range of actors to steer mobility, and this could extend to wanting to commission providers who can offer the sorts of information technology discussed in the previous section. The question is whether, or how well, the authority is able to specify what is needed. Further there are substantial ethical concerns around data protection and consent to use of data. Even if the public fully understand that their data will be used by private companies or the public sector, it is very difficult to say that they have a genuine choice about providing their data if that is a requirement for accessing the mobility that they need for everyday life.[41]

Further sets of questions surround the mobility parts of the new services and the extent to which there can be alignment between the needs of a functioning sustainable mobility system, and the interests of private providers. On one hand—as has been discussed earlier in this chapter—there are hopes that new mobility services could contribute to developing a sustainable mobility system, something which transport authorities will be aiming to achieve. Moreover, transport authorities in some places may be somewhat reliant on non-governmental and private sector providers of mobility services, if they lack the capacity or resource to run public services themselves. As Docherty et al. have argued, public (transport) authorities in many countries have faced the same sort of hollowing out of the state to which other sectors have been subject over recent decades.[42] Therefore, new service providers and transport authorities may begin from a position where each has interests in working with the other. Yet it is far from obvious that the interests of different actors can be easily aligned. One consideration is that the interests of private providers are not likely to tend towards providing services in less densely populated areas or providing services at different times of day or night outside peak times. In relation to this we might look at recent history of deregulation of buses in Britain (by the Thatcher government in the 1980s) with the concern over many years that this has meant private providers 'cherry-pick' profitable routes, leaving routes to less populated areas to be paid for by public sector providers. Scarcity of resources for public sector providers as meant those services are often cut.[43] The result has been a fragmented bus network, to the extent that politicians from left and right have passed legislation intended to enable transport authorities to take bus networks back under public control through franchising. The first such legislation was brought in as part of the Transport Act 2000 and amended in Local Transport Act 2008 by the Blair (Labour government). There have been subsequent efforts by transport authorities to use this legislation to introduce franchising, so while the private sector may actually

[41]See Jonathan Andrew, 'Challenges to Locational Privacy: The Transformation of Urban Mobility', in this volume.

[42]Docherty, Marsden and Anable (n 1).

[43]Campaign for Better Transport, 'Buses in Crisis: a Report on Funding Across England and Wales 2010-2018' (*Campaign for Better Transport*, June 2018) <https://bettertransport.org.uk/sites/default/files/research-files/19.04.12.bic-2018.pdf> accessed 10 January 2020.

provide the services, it will be done to a specification set by the transport authority. However, this was not successful partly due to opposition from private bus providers, and perhaps also partly because the legislation was not sufficiently robust to enable transport authorities to push their case. The Bus Services Act 2017, brought in by the May (Conservative) government, was intended to improve the legislation to enable franchising and at the time of writing Greater Manchester is consulting on the introduction of bus franchising. Another factor which might stand in the way of aligned interests is where new mobility services take up either footway or carriageway space, the providers of those services would not have an automatic interest in taking responsibility for the space used, and if there are no restrictions then that may be to their advantage. The problem is that space is scarce, and vehicles left by the side of the carriageway reduce space for other road users. In addition, as noted in the last section, anything left on pavements—such as shared bicycles—can create obstacles to pedestrians, especially those with mobility difficulties.[44] A further area where misaligned interests present a substantial risk concerns safety. This includes the safety of vehicles, other road users related to the new mobility services, and drivers of ride sharing services (at least unless all until full automation becomes commonplace). There is some emerging empirical evidence of safety concerns associated with ride sharing, if those working as drivers on the new services have low rates of pay and so need to work long hours, become tired, and are therefore less able to drive safely. In other words, drivers are working for long periods which presents a risk to themselves (in relation to their health and their safety) and to others.[45]

Where interests are not aligned, transport authorities may consider how to shape, or in some cases restrict or constrain new mobility services in their jurisdiction. We can note that some services in some places will be illegal unless laws are changed—this is the case in Britain with electric scooters which are neither allowed on the public carriageway nor the footway.[46] Beyond this, transport authorities do have legal powers to prevent or restrict the way in which mobility services run. As Marsden has argued, transport authorities have significant powers over the way in which carriageways and kerbsides are used, and the exercise of these powers could be influential in determining how or whether new mobility services function in a given area.[47] Authorities may also have powers over licensing, such as licensing of taxis and shared ride services, and again these could be used to steer a functioning of services. A challenge for transport authorities may come from the service providers however, if they decide to test the legality of any restrictions. This type of challenge presents difficulties for transport authorities. First is that there may be uncertainty about the outcome until something is tested by the courts, and this can lead to caution on both sides. However, transport authorities face a further challenge from scarcity,

---

[44] Marsden, 'Planning for Autonomous Vehicles?' (n 2); Pooley and others (n 9).

[45] Barrios, Hochberg and Yi, 'The Cost of Convenience' (n 36).

[46] Road Traffic Act 1988.

[47] Marsden, 'Planning for Autonomous Vehicles?' (n 2).

something which has arguably increased over the past decade in many countries, and this could add to a view that they do not have the resources to risk taking on legal cases.[48] For similar reasons of scarce resources, transport authorities may also have limited capacity to enforce restrictions of powers. However, these powers may at least provide a negotiating tool to help bring different actors together to find common ground.

5 Reflexive and Collaborative Processes of Smart Mobility Governance

Our central question is how can governance develop to support sustainability of smart mobility? As has been recognised in other literature the introduction of new actors increases the case for collaborative approaches to governance.[49] As we noted in the introduction the mobility system has always been a system of multiple actors rather than one governing actor, but it has not always been conceptualised as such. The work on collaborative governance recognises that different actors have different interests and that they have different expertise and knowledge. Collaborative and reflexive governance also brings recognition of uncertainty centre stage. This matters because it is always the case that we do not know how exactly transport measures will play out, and that uncertainty may be increased with the introduction of new mobility services. In assessing the likely implications of changes to the mobility system, we can be guided by evidence from modelling and previous cases. Yet transport policy is littered with examples of poor forecasting, which is all too frequently used in the development of transport decisions. Arguably, one of the problems with forecasting is the assumptions used to explain existing transport behaviour. A further and related problem in assessments of future mobility is a tendency to adopt what is frequently shown to be an erroneous assumption that things will carry on as before, rather than considering the implications of the range of factors which can influence mobility including wider systemic economic and social changes.[50] So there is a case for governance which expects uncertainty and which seeks to take account of that in the processes of decision-making.

There has been attention to collaborative and reflexive governance in many sectors over decades. Although this came late to transport, it has been considered for several years. It is worth briefly mentioning some of the characteristics underlining this form of governance. To begin, and as was touched on in the last section of this chapter, collaborative and reflexive governance recognises that

---

[48]Docherty, Marsden and Anable (n 1).

[49]An and others (n 3).

[50]Chatterton and others (n 33); Mullen and Marsden 'Mobility Justice' (n 6); Greg Marsden and others, *All Change? The Future of Travel Demand and the Implications for Policy and Planning: the First Report of the Commission on Travel Demand* (Commission on Travel Demand 2018).

different actors have different expertise and different interests.[51] It is intended to enable each party to learn from others. It also identifies the need to seek a sufficient commonality between actors, so that they can understand they are engaged in a common project. This does not mean that they will be able to realise all their interests, but the intention is that they will better meet their individual interests in this way than if they see themselves solely in competition. We can see from this that reflexivity is central, so this is more than a negotiation. Instead it is intended to be a process of learning which enables the development of decisions which are informed by the knowledge of all the different actors and which can best meet the interests of those actors.[52] The common interests are set as high level principles designed to take account of uncertainty. Rather than trying to plan for every eventuality (something which is unlikely to succeed) the principles can guide decision-making over time as events unfold.[53] What is crucial is a process of decision making that the actors are content with, and this requires a level of trust among actors. This trust is not something that would be expected to be placed without justification.[54] Much of the work on reflexive governance emphasises the importance of continuing relationships through which trust is built. So, there has to be trust that, in the process of decision-making, actors will not seek to undermine each other at every turn but will instead accept the spirit of the principles on which they have agreed. Alongside this, those working on collaborative and reflexive governance recognise the importance of monitoring and benchmarking as means of assessing how well decisions are being made given the principles which are intended to guide them.[55] In transport we might see benchmarking against cases in other cities and countries.

So, on one level we might say that there is a case for collaborative and reflexive governance because of the multiple actors and because of the uncertainty of new mobility services. However, there are characteristics of smart mobility which have some quite specific implications for the way in which reflexive governance would need to work. These raise challenges for reflexive governance, and also arguably strengthen the case for such an approach. To recap, the questions around the way in which new mobility services actually work are particularly important given the acute sustainability concerns, especially on decarbonisation. We cannot afford to be taking decisions which increase carbon emissions. The risks here are exacerbated by path

[51]For instance, James Bohman, 'The Coming of Age of Deliberative Democracy' (1998) 6 The Journal of Political Philosophy 400; Hrelja, Rye and Mullen, 'Partnerships Between Operators' (n 4).

[52]Charles F Sabel, 'Learning by Monitoring: The Institutions of Economic Development', in Neil J Smelser and Richard Swedberg (eds), *The Handbook of Economic Sociology* (Russell Sage Foundation 1994). Van Slyke (n 5); Lenoble and Maesschalck, *Democracy, Law and Governance* (n 5); Vincent-Jones and Mullen, 'Collaborative to Genetic Governance' (n 5); Hrelja, Rye and Mullen, 'Partnerships Between Operators' (n 4).

[53]Sabel (n 52); Van Slyke (n 5); Hrelja, Rye and Mullen, 'Partnerships Between Operators' (n 4).

[54]Onora O'Neill, *Question of Trust: The BBC Reith Lectures 2002* (Cambridge University Press 2002).

[55]Sabel (n 52); Van Slyke (n 5); Hrelja, Rye and Mullen, 'Partnerships Between Operators' (n 4).

dependency, so that the more we lock ourselves into increased energy use and carbon emissions the harder it is to get ourselves out of it. This makes managing uncertainty particularly important. Given this, we need to take seriously the tendency towards optimism which is particularly prominent in relation to (hoped-for) technological solutions. What we have seen is that strategies attempting to tackle serious sustainability concerns in mobility can amount to little more than a high-level ambition without a robust plan to support it. Since these historical and contemporary examples are quite well recognised, we might hope that it will guard against a similar tendency in future. Yet this itself may be overly optimistic, and a more risk averse approach would be to try and take account of this tendency within processes of governance. A governance process which recognises uncertainty, and which recognises we need to adapt to unfolding events may offer some protection against previous over-optimism, since it at least offers the possibility of changing approach if that optimism is recognised to be unfounded. The effectiveness of this will depend on the quality and sensitivity of monitoring, and the ability to set up assessment processes which pick up early signs if mobility services are not supporting sustainability. This might include measures such as assessing the comprehensiveness and affordability and accessibility of services, and congestion levels. This approach also keeps open the possibility of benefiting from new mobility services, and in that sense it guards against greater risk aversion towards new mobility services. In other words, it could act as a sort of insurance about the new mobility services which might otherwise face opposition from the public and from transport authorities.

However, there is a potentially serious barrier to reflexive governance in this case. Reflexive governance requires careful monitoring of the implications of new mobility services, and responding if those new services are acting to the detriment of sustainability rather than supporting it. The question is what form this response takes. It may be that services simply need to be altered and that this can be done without greatly affecting the interests of the service providers. Yet this might not be the case, and it could be that the service needs radically changing, restricting, or even removing all together. To a private provider this presents a significant risk, and we might question whether it is one that they would be willing to sign up to. One issue is whether the benefits to service providers are substantial enough to take the chance that their services may be cut. However, the risk for the transport authority and planners (and so for the wider public) is that this acts as an obstacle to service providers developing services which may bring sustainability benefits. So, if mobility systems could benefit from new services brought by private or non-governmental providers, then this form of reflexive government may need to be coupled with a system of rewards which is not predicated primarily, or solely, on the service provision. Instead it may need to give significant attention to rewarding engagement with public sector transport planners on problem solving and rewarding experimentation which might (but which also might not) lead to successful new services. This would require public sector investment for the experimentation, something which may appear unappealing when compared with the prospect of bringing in private sector providers who are rewarded by users rather than the state. However, governments and the public sector already invests in mobility through infrastructure and maintenance, and often through service provision. They also pay indirectly through the health services needed to respond to road traffic collisions and poor health from transport related pollution. Governments and the public sector, along with private sector organisations, will also face financial costs associated with climate change.[56] There are of course wider risks associated with this idea, including risks of exploitation by private actors, and there remains a burden on decision makers to consider who to engage with. Nevertheless, the risks of this approach do allow us to avoid some of the more substantial risks of becoming locked into services which are detrimental and the corresponding risk of ignoring the possibility of services which may bring improvements.

It may be quite apparent from this that the reflexive governance we are considering is not a meeting of two equal parties, and as such is unlike the sort of engagement we might get between two companies. Instead it fixes the role of transport authorities in steering, planning and assessing public transport. Given this, there is a wider case for a collaborative or participatory approach to transport governance which involves robust public participation, in part to draw on the public's knowledge about what mobility services they require in order to enable them to go about daily activities without relying on private motor transport.

6 Conclusion

The risks of technological optimism have not been overlooked in relation to smart mobility and in fact there has been a good awareness of these risks both in research literature and policy. However, within the debate around smart mobility there is a more limited awareness of the scale of the challenge facing us. This is particularly so in relation to the need for decarbonisation and to reduce traffic in order to decarbonise at the rates required to avoid more dangerous climate change. Much of the attention has been focused on the risks of increasing congestion, and while this is important it may be distracting from the problem that simply keeping traffic at existing levels is not enough to tackle decarbonisation. The scale of sustainability challenges coupled with path dependency creates a strong case for governance capable of taking account of uncertainty. This should be done in a way that avoids continued use of services when evidence emerges that they are detrimental to sustainability, whilst leaving open the prospect of new services which can support major sustainability aims.

There has been attention elsewhere on the need for collaboration and for adaptation in relation to mobility, particularly to new mobility services. However, this chapter has shown it is only when we work through the processes of governance and consider what this means in the case of mobility, that we can see there are some quite

[56] A point made over a decade ago by Nicholas Stern, *Economics of Climate Change: The Stern Review*. (Cambridge University Press 2007).

specific implications. There is a case for changing the relationship between service providers and transport authorities, and also a case for changing expectations of the potential rewards for private service providers. The prospect that services may need to be discontinued reframes arguments about the rewards which service providers may expect. The need to monitor services, and to assess whether or how they are supporting sustainability, clarifies the role and responsibility of public sector transport providers in steering the nature of mobility services.

Environmental Implications of the EU's Urban Mobility Agenda

Josephine van Zeben

Contents

Abstract This volume discusses the impact of technology on urban mobility and its regulation within the EU. In turn, this chapter explores the interaction of the developing smart urban mobility agenda with EU environmental law and policy. At the moment, EU action on urban mobility mostly takes the form of policy, not law. Conversely, there is a rich body of EU environmental law, much of which sets goals and obligations that directly affect urban mobility. This chapter provides an overview of the most important existing initiatives regarding urban mobility. It then considers how technology may affect these initiatives, both positively and negatively. It identifies areas of overlap with EU environmental law and offers suggestions for the future alignment and integration of environmental and mobility goals.

I would like to thank Joshua Pike for his excellent editorial support. Josephine van Zeben is Professor and Chair of the Law Group at Wageningen University and Research, the Netherlands.

J. van Zeben (✉)
Law Group, Wageningen University and Research, Wageningen, The Netherlands
e-mail: josephine.vanzeben@wur.nl

M. Finck et al. (eds.), *Smart Urban Mobility*, MPI Studies on Intellectual Property and Competition Law 29, https://doi.org/10.1007/978-3-662-61920-9_3

1 Introduction

The centrality of cities within our economic, social and political life is widely accepted among policymakers and academics. At the moment, more than half of the world's population resides in an urban environment, a number which is only expected to increase over the coming decades.[1] Although most of this urbanization will not take place in the European Union,[2] which is already largely urbanized,[3] environmental, social and economic pressures on European urban centers will nonetheless continue to increase.

Urban governance touches on virtually every aspect of daily life. Some of these aspects speak to issues that remain within the Member States' exclusive competence, such as land use and the internal organization of the state.[4] More specifically, in the national context, the management of some of these policy questions can lie within the exclusive competence of regional and local authorities within the Member States. While this internal division of competence is formally unaffected by European decision-making, it is in fact often and meaningfully influenced by it.[5] Equally, urban governance touches on numerous topics that are governed through the exercise of shared competences between the EU and its Member States, such as environment and the internal market,[6] as well as on policies within the exclusive competence of the EU, such as competition law.[7] In lieu of a clear and comprehensive legislative mandate on urban development, the EU has developed an Urban Agenda that creates possibilities for information exchange, best practices, coordination and policy integration on issues related to urban governance. Urban mobility

[1]Today, 55% of the world's population lives in urban areas, a proportion that is expected to increase to 68% by 2050. See Population Division of the UN Department of Economic and Social Affairs (UN DESA), *2018 Revision of World Urbanization Prospects* (United Nations 2019) <www.population.un.org/wup/Publications/Files/WUP2018-Report.pdf> accessed 4 January 2020.

[2]Close to 90% of the increase is expected to take place in Asia and Africa: ibid.

[3]In 2018, the rate of urbanization in the EU was 74%: ibid. For the purposes of the UN report, 'Europe' comprised all EU Member States as well as Iceland, Kosovo, the former Yugoslav Republic of Macedonia (Republic of North Macedonia as of February 2019), the Russian Federation and the Ukraine. EU policy documents largely refer to UN reporting on this matter, supplementing it with its own data, including Mariana Kotzeva and others (eds), *Urban Europe: Statistics on Cities, Towns and Suburbs* (European Union 2016) <www.ec.europa.eu/eurostat/documents/3217494/7596823/KS-01-16-691-EN-N.pdf> accessed 4 January 2020.

[4]See Consolidated Version of the Treaty on the Functioning of the European Union [2012] OJ C326/47 (TFEU), art 4(2).

[5]See in detail Michèle Finck, *Subnational Authorities in EU Law* (Oxford University Press 2017).

[6]TFEU, art 4(2)(e) and (a) respectively.

[7]TFEU, art 2.

(UM) has been a central theme within this Agenda since 2007,[8] 20 years after the first Commission Urban Agenda Communication.[9]

The importance of mobility within an urban agenda is self-evident: transport and traffic affect the ability of people to get to and from urban areas, and to move around within them; environmental and human health are directly, and often adversely, affected by concentrated traffic flows through emissions and noise; mismanagement of traffic flows can create unsafe situations leading to bodily harm and even death.[10] Moreover, high concentrations of traffic can lead to congestion, which in turns creates economic loss due to delays and loss of work time.[11] Mobility also has a wide range of implications for the livability of urban areas, the social inclusion or exclusion of various groups[12] and the relationship between an urban area and its (rural) surroundings.

Issues related to mobility are also almost invariably issues related to the environment: air quality, noise, land use decisions and health are all affected by mobility. This means that most policies adopted under the EU's mobility agenda exist in a legislative space that is already occupied by environmental standards. Moreover, while urban planning is outside the EU's competence, transport and mobility—including urban mobility—are firmly within the shared competences of the EU,[13] governed by DG MOVE.[14] Even before considering the impact of technology on urban mobility, urban mobility brings together at least three policy areas[15]—urban

[8]The main EU policy documents related to mobility are: Commission, 'Towards a New Culture for Urban Mobility' (Green Paper) COM (2007) 55 final; Commission, 'Action Plan on Urban Mobility' COM (2009) 490 final; Commission, 'Roadmap to a Single European Transport Area – Towards a Competitive and Resource Efficient Transport System' (White Paper) COM (2011) 144 final; Commission, 'Together Towards Competitive and Resource-efficient Urban Mobility' (Communication) COM (2013) 913 final.

[9]Commission, 'Towards an Urban Agenda in the European Union' (Communication) COM (97) 197 final.

[10]In 2017, there were 26 000 traffic-related deaths in the EU, 38% of which took place in urban areas (as compared to 67% of all road traffic accidents). Moreover, traffic accidents in urban areas tend to cause more serious injury than those outside of urban areas: European Commission, *European Urban Mobility: Policy Context* (European Union 2017) 9 <www.civitas.eu/sites/default/files/booklet_1_-_en.pdf> accessed 4 January 2020.

[11]In 2011, the cost of congestion was estimated at EUR 130 billion/year: COM (2011) 144 final.

[12]The elderly are particularly dependent on mobility policies that provide for public transport: European Commission, *Sustainable Urban Mobility: European Policy, Practice and Solutions* (European Union 2017); see also Sofia Ranchordás, 'Smart Mobility, Transport Poverty and the Right to Inclusive Mobility?', in this volume.

[13]TFEU, art 4(2)(g).

[14]European Commission, 'Mobility and Transport Mission Statement' (European Commission) <www.ec.europa.eu/transport/sites/transport/files/move-mission-statement.pdf> accessed 4 January 2020.

[15]Additional policy areas can easily be identified, for example, the internal market implications of the production and sale of transport modalities or the competition and state aid law implications of public transport contracts.

policy, transport policy and environmental policy—all of which speak to different areas and levels of competence of the EU and the Member States (supplemented by local and regional governments).

The question asked in this volume concerns not only the effect of technology on mobility and the role law plays in shaping this effect, but also how law itself is shaped by these technological changes. This chapter explores this question from the perspective of EU environmental law.

There is a longstanding link between technological change and environmental regulation. Much of EU environmental law concerns environmental impacts caused by technologically advanced activities.[16] The development of new technologies with new environmental impacts continues to shape environmental law, as does our changing understanding of these impacts in step with scientific and technological progress. The precautionary principle is an important driver in the EU's legislative and regulatory responses to these developments.[17] At the same time, technological progress has changed the way environmental law is applied, monitored and enforced.[18] Technology is also often presented as one of the main mechanisms through which environmental impacts may be managed and alleviated.[19] Similarly, there is a sense of optimism regarding technology's ability to help address certain mobility problems.[20] In developing a smart urban mobility strategy, inspiration can—and arguably should—be taken from the existing legal framework of environmental law, especially as many of the technological changes in urban mobility directly affect environmental conditions.

Bringing these policy areas together and asking what influence environmental law might have on smart urban mobility (and vice versa) is therefore a multifaceted task. The EU's urban mobility agenda is mostly a coordinating device for Member States and subnational actors that links to legislation in several policy areas, including environment. One of the many challenges facing the agenda is the combination of policy goals that it needs to speak to and the lack of hierarchy between them. While there is ample scope for interaction and overlap between these policy areas, it is not yet clear what principles govern the relationship between mobility and environmental policy. One overarching principle relevant to these policy areas—and more generally to *all* Union policies—is the integration principle of Art. 11 TFEU. The integration principle stipulates that environmental protection

[16]In this context, 'technologically advanced' refers to human activities that have developed since the Industrial Revolution. Naturally, technology can also have a mitigating effect on environmental impacts, but on the whole the most severe impacts are caused by relatively advanced technological activities.

[17]TFEU, art 191(2).

[18]See eg Cathy C Conrad and Krista G Hilchey, 'A Review of Citizen Science and Community-based Environmental Monitoring: Issues and Opportunities' [2011] Environmental Monitoring and Assessment 273.

[19]See also Caroline Mullen, 'Governing a Risky Relationship Between Sustainability and Smart Mobility', in this volume.

[20]ibid.

requirements are to be integrated into the definition and implementation of all Union policies and activities with a view to stimulating sustainable development.[21] However, it does not tell us how potential clashes between goals within and between policies should be resolved,[22] especially as there are several 'horizontal' principles in EU law that may apply.[23]

This chapter will provide an overview of the most important initiatives regarding urban mobility and how they speak to EU environmental law and policy. It will then consider how the integration of technology into mobility and the mobility agenda may affect this status quo. It concludes by identifying areas where legislation is particularly needed and what principles of environmental law and EU law more generally could provide guidance.

2 Urban Mobility and the Environment

2.1 History of EU Urban Mobility Policy

EU policy on Urban Mobility (UM) gained momentum between 2007 and 2013. The agenda-setting 2007 Green Paper 'Towards a New Culture for Urban Mobility' defined five main challenges: free-flowing towns and cities, greener towns and cities, smarter urban transport, accessible urban transport and safe and secure urban transport.[24] These challenges were accompanied by several proposed solutions and options for change, as well as several follow-up questions regarding feasibility and next steps. Within these next steps, it was made explicit that the role of the EU was open-ended and to be determined.[25] The EU's ability and willingness to contribute to urban mobility projects financially has been a marked exception to this; the Green Paper refers to a number of existing and potential financial instruments available to Member States and local authorities, including Structural Funds, the Cohesion Fund and loans from the European Investment Bank.[26] Already before the publication of the Green Paper, the European Regional Development Fund had contributed more than EUR 2 billion to urban transport projects, a number which increased to EUR 8 billion in the 2007–2013 period.[27]

[21]TFEU, art 11.

[22]Unless we accept that the principle is autonomously normative, see in-depth André Nollkaemper, 'Three Conceptions of the Integration Principle in International Environmental Law' in Andrea Lenschow (ed), *Environmental Policy Integration: Greening Sectoral Policies in Europe* (Earthscan 2002).

[23]See eg TFEU, arts 8, 9, 10 and 12.

[24]COM (2007) 55 final 6ff.

[25]See eg ibid 8.

[26]ibid 9.

[27]ibid.

After the Green Paper, several rounds of consultation and debate followed, which culminated in the 2009 Action Plan on Urban Mobility.[28] In this Action Plan, the role of the European Union in UM is explicated, referencing the Common Transport Policy,[29] as well as the central role of urban mobility and transport in other EU policies such as cohesion policy, environment policy and healthy policy.[30] Reference is also made to technological and environmental research and innovation agendas, as well as to the coordinating role the EU can play through the internal market.[31] However, it is made equally clear that the EU's role (for now) continues to be one of information exchange and coordination through policy development rather than through the creation of a legal agenda.[32]

These policy documents developed in parallel to the EU's general transport policy, the European Transport Policy (ETP), which has been undergoing redevelopment since 2001.[33] Notably, the 2009 Action Plan was published at the same time as the ETP Communication 'A Sustainable Future for Transport: Towards an Integrated, Technology-led and User-friendly System'.[34] In these documents, sustainability becomes a shared policy direction for urban mobility and more general transport policy, with the Action Plan explicitly referring to the 'sustainable future for transport'.[35] In 2011, the White Paper 'Roadmap to a Single European Transport Area – Towards a competitive and resource efficient transport system' (the Roadmap)[36] brought these two policy areas together, repositioning urban mobility as part of a broader transport strategy.

The focus on environmental sustainability with respect to UM can be seen most clearly when we consider the financing instruments set out in the 2007 Green Paper, particularly through the European Regional Development Fund and the Cohesion Fund.[37] The 2009 Action Plan developed this focus further, setting out possibilities for 'greening urban transport', relying on clean(er) technologies, internalizing transport externalities, facilitating information exchange and creating urban pricing plans.[38] In the 2011 Roadmap, these policy suggestions are incorporated under the heading 'clean urban transport and commuting'.[39] In the eyes of the Commission,

---

28 COM (2009) 490 final 3.

29 Consolidated Version of the Treaty on European Union [2002] OJ C325/33, arts 70 and 80.

30 COM (2009) 490 final 3.

31 ibid.

32 ibid 9-10 (Action 18).

33 See eg Commission, 'European Transport Policy for 2010: Time to Decide' (White Paper) COM (2001) 370 final and a mid-term review of the agenda: Commission, 'Keep Europe Moving – Sustainable Mobility for Our Continent' COM (2006) 314 final.

34 Commission, 'A Sustainable Future for Transport: Towards an Integrated, Technology-led and User Friendly System' (Communication) COM (2009) 279 final.

35 COM (2009) 490 final 2.

36 COM (2011) 144 final.

37 COM (2007) 55 final 20.

38 COM (2009) 490 final 7-8.

39 COM (2011) 144 final 9ff.

the sustainability of transport systems has a dual meaning: on the one hand, the need for a 'clean' (urban) transport system is emphasized through measures such as halving the use of conventionally-fueled cars and achieving CO_2-free logistics in major urban centers by 2030;[40] on the other hand, the importance of reducing reliance on imported oil is stressed.[41] Another important area where sustainability gains are envisaged is the creation of more efficient infrastructures, moving towards rail- and water-based transport and away from cars and other road transport.[42]

The latest restatement of EU Urban Mobility policy is the 2013 Urban Mobility Package (UMP).[43] The UMP is structured around the Commission Communication 'Together Towards Competitive and Resource-efficient Urban Mobility'.[44] The accompanying staff working papers detail policy ambitions regarding urban logistics (movement of goods, equipment and waste into, out of, within or through urban areas),[45] urban access regulations (focusing on congestion issues),[46] urban road safety[47] and the use of 'Intelligent Transport System' solutions.[48] The latter is particularly relevant in the move to smart urban mobility and is discussed in more detail in Sect. 3.

The Communication reflects on the successes of the 2009 Action Plan[49] and proposes Sustainable Urban Mobility Plans (SUMPs) as a framework for further local level initiatives regarding mobility.[50] While these SUMPs are meant to consider a range of policy areas, including environment, their aim is to foster 'a balanced development and a better integration of the different urban mobility modes'.[51] Moreover, the Commission emphasizes that urban mobility is 'primarily about people'.[52] Within the UMP, the Commission takes a coordinating role, creating

[40]COM (97) 197 final 15.

[41]ibid.

[42]COM (2011) 144 final 10.

[43]Available in full at: European Commission, 'Urban Mobility Package' (*European Commission*, 27 August 2020) <www.ec.europa.eu/transport/themes/clean-transport-urban-transport/urban-mobility/urban-mobility-package_en> accessed 27 August 2020.

[44]COM (2013) 913 final.

[45]Commission, 'A Call to Action on Urban Logistics' (Commission Staff Working Document) SWD (2013) 524 final.

[46]Commission, 'A Call for Smarter Urban Vehicle Access Regulations' (Commission Staff Working Document) SWD (2013) 526 final.

[47]Commission, 'Targeted Action on Urban Road Safety' (Commission Staff Working Document) SWD (2013) 525 final.

[48]Commission, 'Mobilising Intelligent Transport Systems for EU Cities' (Commission Staff Working Document) SWD (2013) 527 final.

[49]Ricardo JM Poppeliers and Andrea Ricci, 'Review of the Action Plan on Urban Mobility' (European Commission Report 2013) <www.ec.europa.eu/transport/sites/transport/files/themes/urban/studies/doc/2013-07-review-of-the-action-plan-on-urban-mobility.pdf> accessed 4 January 2020.

[50]COM (2009) 279 final 3ff.

[51]ibid 3.

[52]ibid.

the European Platform on Sustainable Urban Mobility Plans and (financially) supporting the local, national and regional development of SUMPs.[53]

2.2 *Interactions with Environmental Policy*

The most obvious link between (urban) mobility and environmental policy lies in the pollutive effects of transportation. The EU's environmental acquis contains a rich body of pollution control measures, many of which relate directly to transportation, for instance the regulation of vehicle emissions.[54] The greenhouse gas emissions and particulate matter caused by traditional combustion engines create severe adverse effects for human, plant and animal life.[55] The 2009 UMP recognizes the existing legal requirements stipulated in EU legislation regarding air quality, referring specifically to the high share of transport emissions from urban areas (23%) and the failure of cities across all Member States to comply with legal requirements.[56] Within the UMP, much attention is paid to the possibilities for technology to help achieve these aims through cleaner forms of transportation.[57]

The Commission has demonstrated its commitment to (financially) supporting the shift to cleaner transport through exemptions in its Guidelines on State aid for

[53]ibid 4.

[54]See among others Parliament and Council Directive 2009/28/EC of 23 April 2009 on the promotion of the use of energy from renewable sources and amending and subsequently repealing Directives 2001/77/EC and 2003/30/EC [2009] OJ L140/16, art 3(4); Parliament and Council Directive 2009/30/EC of 23 April 2009 amending Directive 98/70/EC as regards the specification of petrol, diesel and gas-oil and introducing a mechanism to monitor and reduce greenhouse gas emissions and amending Council Directive 1999/32/EC as regards the specification of fuel used by inland waterway vessels and repealing Directive 93/12/EEC [2009] OJ L140/88; Parliament and Council Directive 2008/50/EC of 21 May 2008 on ambient air quality and cleaner air for Europe [2008] OJ L152/1; Parliament and Council Regulation (EC) 715/2007 of 20 June 2007 on type approval of motor vehicles with respect to emissions from light passenger and commercial vehicles (Euro 5 and Euro 6) and on access to vehicle repair and maintenance information [2007] OJ L171/1; Parliament and Council Regulation (EC) 443/2009 of 23 April 2009 setting emission performance standards for new passenger cars as part of the Community's integrated approach to reduce CO2 emissions from light-duty vehicles [2009] OJ L140/1.

[55]For example, car exhaust emissions contain, among other things, considerable levels of dioxins and furans, both of which are highly toxic: Qing Qing Li and others, 'Persistent Organic Pollutants and Adverse Health Effects in Humans' (2006) 69 Journal of Toxicology and Environmental Health, Part A 1987, 1992. Pollutants such as these are slow to biodegrade and thus accumulate in soil and water. As a result, they enter the food chains of various plants and animals: ibid.

[56]COM (2009) 279 final 2.

[57]ibid 5.

environmental protection and energy[58] and the 2014 Block Exemption Regulation.[59] These exemptions cover all forms of transport, including rail transport. In order to achieve the emission and particulate matter reductions needed, reductions in the use of conventionally fueled cars will not be sufficient; the uptake of other forms of transportation, especially public transportation and bicycles, will also have to increase. The dual benefit of this is that greater shares of public transportation contribute to reductions in congestion, another key aim of the UMP.[60]

Naturally, the environmental implications of continuing urbanization go well beyond transportation emissions. Energy efficient design and the construction of new housing stock as well as the retrofitting of existing buildings is another significant set of challenges faced by national and local authorities.[61] Relatedly, the expansion of existing urban areas in order to accommodate growth puts pressure on existing green spaces and the habitats and migration patterns of wildlife. Similarly, the need to accommodate increasing numbers of vehicles on land, water and air affects land use decisions and cuts into habitats and animal populations.[62] This chapter highlights the most well-known and relevant interactions between urban mobility and environmental concerns. However, we should be mindful of the fact that the full range of urbanization's environmental impacts is open-ended and continues to develop alongside our understanding of the environmental and public health effects of mobility.

2.3 *Jurisdictional Questions*

Another challenge in considering the interplay between urban mobility and EU environmental law and policy is the relationship (or lack thereof) between the relevant governmental and non-governmental actors. Member States have strongly

[58]Commission Communication on guidelines on state aid for environmental protection and energy [2014] OJ C200/1.

[59]Commission Regulation (EU) 651/2014 of 17 June 2014 declaring certain categories of aid compatible with the internal market in application of Articles 107 and 108 of the Treaty [2014] OJ L187/1, section 7.

[60]COM (2009) 279 final 9.

[61]See among others the Parliament and Council Directive (EU) 2018/844 of 30 May 2018 amending Directive 2010/31/EU on the energy performance of buildings and Directive 2012/27/EU on energy efficiency [2018] OJ L156/75.

[62]For example, one study found that the construction of roads led to a habitat loss of around 8 % for grizzly bears, often around areas with important food sources; it was also found that the bear population became more vulnerable to hunting: Bruce N McLellan and David M Shackleton, 'Grizzly Bears and Resource-extraction Industries: Effects of Roads on Behaviour, Habitat Use and Demography' (1988) 25 Journal of Applied Ecology 451.

diverging needs, ambitions and abilities related to urban mobility, including important differences between urban (and rural) areas within Member States.[63] In some Member States, urban centers have started to collaborate with one another on specific issues and/or generally in order to achieve economies of scale and scope.[64] At the same time, most urban regions, especially those resulting from the gradual merging of several cities or urban centers, tend to lack formal status within Member States' legal frameworks. An example of this is the Randstad area in the Netherlands. The exact contours of the Randstad vary depending on how broadly one seeks to define this region; at the very least, it encompasses the urban areas of Amsterdam, Rotterdam, The Hague and Utrecht.[65] Depending on one's definition, the Randstad represents up to half of the country's population and economy. Administratively, the region is managed partly by the respective provinces in which the cities are located, partly by the cities themselves and partly by the *metropoolregios* Amsterdam and Rotterdam-The Hague.

The political, economic and social importance of these regions remains unaffected by the uncertainty surrounding their delimitations and status and their political representation at the national level is often strong, at times to the (perceived) disadvantage of other regions.[66] At the same time, these urban centers and the EU only have an 'indirect' formal relationship through the conduit of the Member State and/or a body such as the Committee of the Regions,[67] and their ability to legally act with respect to questions of mobility (and the environment) primarily depends on national arrangements. For example, the *metropools* Amsterdam and Rotterdam-The Hague are also 'Transport Authorities', which assigns them formal responsibilities with respect to mobility and makes them the recipient of national funds for transportation as well as the sole contracting entity for regional and city transportation services within the region.[68] In the case of the *metropool* Rotterdam-The Hague, this regulatory power over mobility overlaps with that of the *metropoolregio*

[63]Tim Richardson and Ole B Jensen, 'Discourses of Mobility and Polycentric Development: A Contested View of European Spatial Planning' (2000) 8 European Planning Studies 503.

[64]For example, the Scotland's Towns Partnership and the Scottish Cities Alliance, representing different sizes of local governments in Scotland: see for further details (*STP*) <www.scotlandstowns.org> accessed 4 January 2020 and (*scottishcitiesalliance*) <www.scottishcities.org.uk/about-us/policies> accessed 4 January 2020. Some initiatives are regional or global, such as the Covenant of Mayors for Climate and Energy: (*Covenant of Mayors for Climate & Energy*) <www.covenantofmayors.eu/en/> accessed 4 January 2020.

[65]An impression of the difficulties in definition is provided by the Randstad monitor: Walter Manshanden and Olaf Koops, 'Randstad Monitor 2016: De Top-20 van Europese grootstedelijke regio's 1995-2016' (10th edn, 2017) 17-19 <www.neo-observatory.nl/site/wp-content/uploads/2017/10/PDF-121.pdf> accessed 4 January 2020.

[66]See for example Jan G Lambooy, 'Polynucleation and Economic Development: The Randstad' (1998) 6 European Planning Studies 457.

[67]Finck (n 5).

[68]See in detail the 'Wet personenvervoer 2000' [People transport Act], wet van 6 juli 2000, Stb 2000, 314 <www.wetten.overheid.nl/BWBR0011470/2019-06-16> accessed 4 January 2020.

Rotterdam-The Hague, a formal administrative entity composed of 23 local authorities;[69] conversely, the *metropoolregio* Amsterdam is an informal collaboration which overlaps only partially with the membership of the Transport Authority Amsterdam.[70]

At the European level, questions of competence continue to be relevant. As urban mobility increasingly becomes subsumed under EU transport policy—as suggested by the integration of the two areas in the 2011 White Paper—the EU may be expanding its competence regarding urban mobility towards a shared, rather than solely supporting, competence. At the same time, this heterogeneity in formal arrangements both nationally and at the EU level suggests that supporting coordination is at least as valuable at the moment—possibly more so. Although the clear emission standards set for transport are helpful in assessing the environmental implications of urban mobility, they still present an incomplete picture due to the many indirect environmental impacts and the fragmented implementation of these goals. An outstanding question therefore is how the EU's environmental competence will continue to affect its decisions on urban mobility.

3 Towards Smart Urban Mobility

3.1 Technology for Mobility

Technology has played a role within the urban mobility agenda from an early stage, primarily as a promising source of solutions. Technological developments and innovations are referenced frequently and presented as methods that can be used or developed in order to accommodate or speed up the transition towards greater energy efficiency and/or cleaner mobility.[71] The use of technology to speed up and facilitate the move towards more sustainable (in terms of environmental impacts) and inclusive (in terms of access and affordability) transport is often presented by policymakers as the most viable policy option.[72] Specific examples of smart mobility

[69]See also 'Over MRDH' (*Metropoolregio Rotterdam Den Haag*) <www.mrdh.nl/over-mrdh> accessed 4 January 2020.

[70]More information available via (*metropool regioamsterdam*) <www.metropoolregioamsterdam.nl/about-mra> accessed 5 January 2020.

[71]San Murugesan, 'Harnessing Green IT: Principles and Practice' (2008) 10 IT Professional 24; Sunil Mithas, Jiban Khuntia and Prasanto K Roy, 'Green Information Technology, Energy Efficiency, and Profits: Evidence from an Emerging Economy' (Proceedings of the International Conference on Information Systems, ICIS 2010, Saint Louis, Missouri, USA, 12-15 December 2010) <www.pdfs.semanticscholar.org/0698/05bbc124e3ba6f16ff4d41be99531493322b.pdf> accessed 4 January 2020.

[72]Indeed, there is some evidence that experts in general prefer technology-based solutions, whereas the layperson prioritizes behavioral changes and public transport: Dimitrios Xenias and Lorraine Whitmarsh, 'Dimensions and Determinants of Expert and Public Attitudes to Sustainable Transport Policies and Technologies' (2013) 48 Transportation Research Part A: Policy and Practice 75.

include the use of apps for ridesharing,[73] better information regarding public transport routes and times, digital ticketing for public transport,[74] the automation of cars and the facilitation of other types of vehicle sharing, such as bicycles and scooters.[75]

It is no longer controversial to highlight some of the potential environmental pitfalls of these technological advances.[76] There are still many puzzles to be solved for a successful transition to smarter and greener mobility through technology, many of which revolve more around the use of such technologies than their technical viability. The human factor in transport use and mobility needs is crucial and increased attention is being paid to incentivizing behavioral changes.[77] In the interim, however, this means that the theoretical potential for these technologies and their practical resolution of mobility issues tend to diverge. Five particularly relevant puzzles are listed here, but many more exist and are coming to light as an increasing number of smart mobility initiatives are piloted.

First, studies have shown that a reduction of emissions per vehicle can be negated by an increased aggregate use of vehicles, which is a trend that is caused in part by the increased use of vehicles through mobility sharing services;[78] moreover, a reduction of greenhouse gas emissions does not automatically solve other public health problems related to vehicle emissions. Secondly, it is unclear how successful these technological changes have been in shifting people's use of cars or other semi-private vehicles to public transport; while private car ownership may be declining thanks to these services, the overall reliance on cars continues, as do problems of congestion.[79] Only in the case of actual car sharing, for example through carpooling, are substantial reductions in CO_2 achieved.[80] Thus far, the most effective changes for improving public transport uptake tend to be information based, but personal

[73]Eg Uber and Lyft.

[74]Eg Cicero in Italy.

[75]Eg Santander cycles, London; emmy scooters, Munich; Lime, Copenhagen; Voi, Copenhagen; Vélib, Paris.

[76]See also in this volume Mullen (n 19).

[77]Linda Steg and Gerard Tertoolen, 'Sustainable Transport Policy: The Contribution from Behavioural Scientists' (1999) 19 Public Money and Management 63; Raman Kazhamiakin and others, 'Using Gamification to Incentivize Sustainable Urban Mobility' (IEEE First International Smart Cities Conference, Guadalajara, 25-28 October 2015) <www.core.ac.uk/download/pdf/226064365.pdf> accessed 4 January 2020.

[78]See eg Greenwheels in the Netherlands or Enjoy in Italy: (*greenwheels*) <www.greenwheels.com/nl/nl-en/private> accessed 4 January 2020 and (*enjoy*) <www.enjoy.eni.com/en> accessed 4 January 2020. There are numerous other car sharing platforms in most other European countries.

[79]Scarlett T Jin and others, 'Ridesourcing, the Sharing Economy, and the Future of Cities' (2018) 76 Cities 96.

[80]T Donna Chen and Kara M Kockelman, 'Carsharing's Life-cycle Impacts on Energy Use and Greenhouse Gas Emissions' (2015) 47 Transport Research Part D: Transport and Environment 276; Hans Nijland and Jordy van Meerkerk 'Mobility and Environmental Impacts of Carsharing in the Netherlands' (2017) 23 Environmental Innovation and Societal Transitions 1.

preferences continue to be an important determinant of outcomes.[81] Thirdly, increasing the share of non-motorized transport presents different questions and appears to be driven by factors beyond technology; that is, even where bicycle sharing is technologically possible, demographic factors such as the female population and the unemployment rate can prove more decisive in demand and uptake.[82] Fourth, incentivizing greater uptake of pedestrian activity—by far the most effective in terms of improving sustainable, clean and affordable transport—proves to depend largely on characteristics of the built environment, which means that technology can only play a very limited role.[83] Finally, and relatedly, some forms of smart urban mobility have negatively affected road safety; for example, the rise of electric scooter sharing in many European cities has resulted in a sharp increase of injuries, mostly to pedestrians.[84]

3.2 EU Policy Responses to Smart Urban Mobility

Keeping in mind these (at times negative) interactions between technology and mobility, the EU's urban mobility framework has given rise to programs that have explicitly embraced an approach that combines smart mobility with green mobility. There are two main ways in which policy has sought to use technological changes for greening mobility: by creating cleaner and more efficient modes of transport and by making transport more efficient through improvements to infrastructure and 'transport chains'.

---

[81]See eg Florian Drevs and others, 'Crowding-in or Crowding out: An Empirical Analysis on the Effect of Subsidies on Individual Willingness-to-pay for Public Transportation' (2014) 59 Transportation Research Part A: Policy and Practice 250.

[82]See eg Robert C Hampshire, 'An Analysis of Bike Sharing Usage: Explaining Trip Generation and Attraction from Observed Demand' (2011) <www.nacto.org/wp-content/uploads/2012/02/An-Analysis-of-Bike-Sharing-Usage-Explaining-Trip-Generation-and-Attraction-from-Observed-Demand-Hampshire-et-al-12-2099.pdf> accessed 4 January 2020 and Stephen D Parkes and others, 'Understanding the Diffusion of Public Bikesharing Systems: Evidence from Europe and North America' (2014) 31 Journal of Transport Geography 94.

[83]Paulus Teguh Aditjandra, Xinyu (Jason) Cao and Corinne Mulley, 'Exploring Changes in Public Transport Use and Walking Following Residential Relocation: A British Case Study' (2016) 9 (3) Journal of Transport and Land Use 77.

[84]See eg Ben Hamilton, 'Electric Scooter Injuries in Copenhagen: Over a Hundred and Counting!' *The Copenhagen Post Online* (Copenhagen, 5 August 2019) <www.cphpost.dk/news/electric-scooters-injuries-in-copenhagen-over-a-hundred-and-counting.html> accessed 4 January 2020; James Tapper, 'Invasion of the Electric Scooter: Can Our Cities Cope?' *The Guardian* (Copenhagen, 15 July 2019) <www.theguardian.com/cities/2019/jul/15/invasion-electric-scooter-backlash> accessed 4 January 2020.

With respect to the former, CIVITAS is the most established program under the Urban Mobility Agenda,[85] set up by the Commission with the aim to assist local governments in piloting integrated policy and technological measures to achieve 'more sustainable, clean and energy-efficient urban transport systems'.[86] In parallel, the Smart Cities and Communities European Innovation Partnership was launched in 2012. This program was set up to contribute to the '20/20/20' climate action goals,[87] taking into consideration the use of technology for both human and environmental health as well as energy concerns.[88] The goals of this program are set broadly, referring to the EU's climate action goals that relate to improving energy efficiency, increasing the use of renewable energy and reducing energy consumption, greenhouse-gas emissions, bad air quality and congestion. Similarly, the Intelligent Energy Europe (IEE) Programme, financed under the Competitiveness and Innovation Programme (CIP), which ran from 2007 to 2013,[89] supported initiatives relating, for example, to new and renewable energy sources, the promotion of alternative fuels and the promotion of energy efficiency in transport.[90]

When considering the optimization of 'transport chains', Intelligent Transport Systems (ITS) play a key role. A key source of inefficiency in mobility, both environmentally and economically, is the set of challenges posed by intermodal transport—situations where people have to use at least two modes of transport for one door-to-door journey. Improving intermodality through the use of smart technology is central to several EU initiatives, including NODES (New Tools for Design and Operation of Urban Transport Interchanges), CLOSER (Connecting Long and Short-distance Networks for Efficient Transport) and Superhub, which provides real-time information for personalized travel advice.[91] Intelligent Transport Systems

[85]See European Commission, 'Clean Transport, Urban Transport: Programmes and Projects' (*European Commission*, 26 August 2020) <www.ec.europa.eu/transport/themes/urban/programmes_projects_en> accessed 4 January 2020.

[86]See European Commission, *Sustainable Urban Mobility: European Policy, Practice and Solutions* (n 12).

[87]See in detail European Commission, '2020 Climate and Energy Package' (*European Commission*) <www.ec.europa.eu/clima/policies/strategies/2020_en> accessed 4 January 2020.

[88]See European Commission, 'Smart Cities' (*European Commission*) <https://ec.europa.eu/info/eu-regional-and-urban-development/topics/cities-and-urban-development/city-initiatives/smart-cities_en> accessed 4 January 2020.

[89]Parliament and Council Decision 1639/2006/EC of 24 October 2006 establishing a Competitiveness and Innovation Framework Programme (2007 to 2013) [2006] OJ L310/15. Results available at European Commission, 'Competitiveness and Innovation Framework Programme (CIP)' (*European Commission*, 3 September 2015) <www.ec.europa.eu/cip/> accessed 4 January 2020.

[90]This program has since been replaced by COSME (Competitiveness of Enterprises and Small and Medium-sized Enterprises), running from 2014-2020 with a EUR 2.3 billion budget: Parliament and Council Regulation (EU) 1287/2013 of 11 December 2013 establishing a Programme for the Competitiveness of Enterprises and small and medium-sized enterprises (COSME) (2014 - 2020) and repealing Decision No 1639/2006/EC [2013] OJ L347/33.

[91]European Commission, 'NODES' (*European Commission*) <www.trimis.ec.europa.eu/project/new-tools-design-and-operation-urban-transport-interchanges> accessed 4 January 2020;

speak to all these issues by managing specific traffic operations through improving traffic signals, creating journey planners and providing for smart ticketing, among other things. The Expert Group on Urban ITS has developed a set of guidelines and best practices in order to streamline the use of ITS solutions within the EU.[92] Moreover, a framework Directive was adopted to accelerate the take-up of some of the smart solutions suggested.[93] The 2008 Action Plan that was adopted as a result was a collaborative effort of five DGs: DG Mobility and Transport (lead), DG Communications Networks, Content & Technology, DG Research & Innovation, DG Enterprise & Industry and DG Climate Action.[94] The measures proposed under the Action Plan can in part be financed by the Regional Development Fund, especially when the measures more broadly relate to environmentally sustainable urban transport projects or provide access to normal public transport services for certain target groups of the population (elderly, handicapped).[95]

The integration of smart technology into urban mobility policy through these programs suggests that technology is mainly seen as a means to achieve mobility and/or environmental policy aims as opposed to a change in our practical reality that necessitates its own policy response.[96] The latter will become increasingly true and pose an additional challenge for these policy areas. The concluding section will consider the interplay between policy areas and the demands posed on regulation in more detail.

European Commission, 'CLOSER' (European Commission) <www.trimis.ec.europa.eu/project/connecting-long-and-short-distance-networks-efficient-transport> accessed 4 January 2020; European Commission, 'Superhub' (*European Commission*) <www.ec.europa.eu/digital-single-market/en/content/superhub-tailor-made-mobility> accessed 4 January 2020.

[92]Available here: European Commission, 'Register of Commission Expert Groups and Other Similar Entities' (*European Commission*, 27 November 2015) <www.ec.europa.eu/transparency/regexpert/index.cfm?do=groupDetail.groupDetail&groupID=2520> accessed 4 January 2020.

[93]Parliament and Council Directive 2010/40/EU of 7 July 2010 on the framework for the deployment of Intelligent Transport Systems in the field of road transport and for interfaces with other modes of transport [2010] OJ L207/1.

[94]Commission, 'Action Plan for the Deployment of Intelligent Transport Systems in Europe' (Communication) COM (2008) 886 final.

[95]COM (2007) 55 final 20.

[96]On the kinds of legal and social challenges posed by this technology that might require such a policy response, see eg Brishen Rogers, 'The Social Costs of Uber' (2015) 82 University of Chicago Law Review Dialogue 85; on the legal challenges posed by the gig economy more generally, see Jeremias Prassl, *Humans as a Service: The Promise and Perils of Work in the Gig Economy* (Oxford University Press 2018).

4 Moving Forward

EU urban mobility policy is undeniably moving towards smart urban mobility policy. Unlike the technological changes that necessitate this move, the regulatory changes appear to be fairly slow. This last section will consider two elements which will be important as this policy area moves forward: the way (environmental) regulation deals with smart technologies and the ways in which environmental goals are integrated into smart urban mobility policy.

4.1 Smart Technology Versus Smart Regulation

The uncertainty that goes hand in hand with continuous and non-linear technological progress is not easily accommodated within existing regulatory frameworks. In relation to smart urban mobility, two challenges deserve specific attention: the need to balance technological innovation with public safety and the possibility of updating regulation in the event of technological change and/or knowledge.

With respect to the former, there is a longstanding tension between innovation and public safety (broadly defined). The EU has traditionally relied on regulatory expertise and scientific information, coupled with the precautionary principle, to steer decision-making.[97] The precautionary principle has allowed for regulatory intervention even when supporting evidence for the regulation in question is incomplete or speculative and its economic cost is high.[98] Some have argued that the resulting regulatory framework is excessively rigid and stifling,[99] whereas others believe that even more caution should be exercised in order to safeguard human and environmental health.[100] Depending on the interpretation of the principle, these

[97]European Communication, 'Better Regulation Principles' (*European Commission*, 15 April 2019) <www.ec.europa.eu/commission/news/better-regulation-principles-2019-apr-15_en> accessed 4 January 2020; European Commission, *Science for Environment Policy Future Brief: The Precautionary Principle: Decision-making Under Uncertainty* (European Union 2017); for the precautionary principle itself, see TFEU, art 191.

[98]European Commission, *Science for Environment Policy Future Brief: The Precautionary Principle: Decision-making Under Uncertainty* (n 97) 4.

[99]See eg 'Statement by the Group of Chief Scientific Advisors: A Scientific Perspective on the Regulatory Status of Products Derived from Gene Editing and the Implications for the GMO Directive' (European Commission 2018) 6 <www.op.europa.eu/en/publication-detail/-/publication/a9100d3c-4930-11e9-a8ed-01aa75ed71a1/language-en/format-PDF/source-94584603> accessed 4 January 2020: 'There is danger that unless the EU improves the regulatory environment for products of gene-editing, it will be left behind in this field, which could also diminish EU influence on ongoing debates at the international level with respect to specific applications and regulatory processes.'

[100]See eg the recent CJEU's Mutagenesis ruling on neonicotinoids: Kathleen Garnett, 'Hold Your Pipettes: The European Court of Justice's Findings in Confédération Paysanne & Others Stirs

critiques can be justified to different extents.[101] Some have argued for the development of a principle to counter-balance the precautionary principle: the so-called innovation principle.[102] With respect to smart urban mobility, however, these principles have limited utility: the precautionary principle can be found within the environmental title of the TFEU and little smart urban mobility policymaking takes place under this title. More generally, the programs adopted thus far suggest that the EU has adopted an experimental approach to regulation where local authorities can use smart mobility as they see fit; the precautionary principle only applies to policies adopted by EU institutions, not to local governments. This approach is partly born of necessity, considering limited EU regulatory competence, but it also makes sense given the many technological unknowns. Regardless of the policy area or regulatory level, however, the tension between innovation and public safety will need to be addressed.

In instances where the balancing act between technological innovation and public safety has resulted in regulatory action, continuous (and often rapid) technological change will require regulatory measures and programs to be frequently updated. This may be due to a change in the technological possibilities or in our knowledge about their impacts. In both cases, reflexive or adaptive legislation that takes account of new evidence is desirable.[103] Research on path dependency shows that regulations are 'sticky' and costly to change; as a result, successful changes tend to be incremental.[104] The stickiness of legislation in fast-moving policy areas has led to the creation of private standards and regulations.[105] While there is much to be said for this development in terms of effectiveness and efficiency, the potential lack of public

---

GMOtions' (2019) 28 Review of European, Comparative and International Environmental Law 349.

[101]Andy Stirling, 'Precaution in the Governance of Technology' (2016) University of Sussex Science Policy Research Unit Working Paper Series SWPS 2016-14 <https://papers.ssrn.com/sol3/papers.cfm?abstract_id=2815579> accessed 4 January 2020.

[102]See eg European Risk Forum, 'The Innovation Principle – Letter to the Presidents of the European Commission, the Europe Council, and the European Parliament' (2013) <www.riskforum.eu/uploads/2/5/7/1/25710097/erf_communication_12.pdf_innovation_principle.pdf> accessed 4 January 2020; René von Schomberg and Jonathan Hankings (eds), *International Handbook on Responsible Innovation* (Edward Elgar 2019).

[103]See Mullen (n 19), on reflexive legislation. On adaptive legislation, see Lori S Bennear and Jonathan B Wiener, 'Adaptive Regulation: Instrument Choice for Policy Learning Over Time' (2019) Draft Working Paper <www.hks.harvard.edu/sites/default/files/centers/mrcbg/files/Regulation%20-%20adaptive%20reg%20-%20Bennear%20Wiener%20on%20Adaptive%20Reg%20Instrum%20Choice%202019%2002%2012%20clean.pdf> accessed 4 January 2020.

[104]Daniel H Cole, 'Explaining the Persistence of 'Command-and-control' in US Environmental Law' in Kenneth R Richards and Josephine van Zeben (eds), *Policy Instruments in Environmental Law* (Edward Elgar 2020) (forthcoming).

[105]See generally Veerle Heyvaert, *Transnational Environmental Regulation and Governance: Purpose, Strategies and Principles* (Cambridge University Press 2018).

and/or democratic oversight combined with transparency and accountability concerns can undermine these alternatives.[106]

These questions are neither unique to smart urban mobility nor exclusive to its environmental impacts; scholarship on smart cities studies the role of technology in urban development more generally. It considers smart urban systems from three vantage points: as cities using smart technology, as cities with smart collaboration and governance, as cities with smart people or as cities that bring together these three ideal types.[107] As discussed in this volume, smart urban mobility mostly refers to the city as a smart technology user. However, in our analysis of smart urban mobility, it soon becomes clear that smart collaboration and governance are likely to precede—indeed, to be a necessary precondition of—smart urban mobility usage. The interrelatedness of mobility with other elements of urban life makes it nearly impossible to regulate in isolation.

4.2 *Policy Integration and Hierarchies*

An important aim of this chapter has been to identify areas of overlap between EU (smart) urban mobility policy and environmental law and policy, with a view to considering the alignment and integration of environmental goals with smart urban mobility policy.[108]

Many of the EU's environmental goals, specifically those related to energy, climate and air quality, are explicitly referenced by urban mobility policy.[109] Moreover, sustainability is a leading principle in the latest iteration of EU urban mobility policy and technology is viewed as a crucial tool in achieving sustainability and environmental goals.[110] Unsurprisingly, the nexus between environment, urban mobility and technology underpins numerous EU programs, policy documents and regulations, as discussed in this chapter. The goal of this reflection is not to problematize the existing—though arguably under-explored—interactions between EU mobility and environmental policy: generally speaking, the aims of these policy areas are complementary and even mutually reinforcing. The problem is therefore one of missed opportunity rather than of overt policy conflict.

---

[106] See eg Richard Sclove, *Democracy and Technology* (Guilford Press 1995).

[107] Albert Meijer and Manuel P Rodriguez Bolivar, 'Governing the Smart City: A Review of the Literature on Smart Urban Governance' (2016) 82 International Review of Administrative Sciences 392, 396.

[108] While very important in many respects, the distinction between smart UM policy and 'general' UM policy has proven to have limited relevance with respect to the interaction with environmental policy.

[109] Meijer and Rodriguez Bolivar (n 107).

[110] See eg European Commission, *European Urban Mobility: Policy Context* (n 10) 16-19 and section 3.

That said, as EU UM policy becomes increasingly formalized, conflict may become more likely through its integration with transportation policy (a shared competence), especially as urban mobility policy has thus far been anthropocentric rather than ecocentric. This is true despite the existence of the integration principle of Art. 11 TFEU, which requires all EU policies and activities to take into consideration environmental protection with a view to achieving sustainable development. Unlike the precautionary principle which can be found in the environmental title, the integration principle has general application and (is meant to) provide legal support for the intuitive synergies that should arise between areas like environmental policy and smart urban mobility policy.

However, the CJEU has interpreted the obligation to integrate environmental protection in such a way that there are no procedural requirements and very limited substantial review.[111] The AG has gone so far as to say that 'it is only where ecological interests manifestly have not been taken into account or where they have been completely disregarded that Art. [11 TFEU] may serve as the standard for reviewing the validity of Community legislation'.[112] The EU and its Member States thus have considerable discretion in how to balance environmental protection with other policy aims.[113] Perhaps even more importantly, there is ample evidence that policy integration rarely takes place in practice.[114] This would also undermine the potential of smart urban mobility to contribute to the EU's environmental goals in the most efficient way, a worrying situation given the need to grow and maintain our urban centers in the most sustainable way possible.

---

[111] See Julian Nowag, 'Article 11 TFEU and Environmental Rights' in Sanja Bogojević and Rosemary Rayfuse (eds), *Environmental Rights in Europe and Beyond* (Hart Publishing 2018) 13. See also Case C189/01 *H Jippes v Minister van Landbrouw, Natuurbeheer en Visserij* [2001] ECR I-5689.

[112] Case C161/04 *Republic of Austria v European Parliament and Council* [2006] ECR I-7209, Opinion of AG Geelhoed, para 59.

[113] This is easily justified with reference to the democratic process, according to which elected representatives are to decide between conflicting policy aims rather than courts. At the same time, we see courts playing an increasingly important role in environmental protection, for example in HR 20 December 2019, NL:HR:2019:2006 (*Nederlanden/Urgenda*).

[114] Andrew Jordan and Andrea Lenschow, 'Environmental Policy Integration: a State of the Art Review' (2010) 20 Environmental Policy and Governance 147; Kati Kulovesi, Elisa Morgera and Miquel Muñoz, 'Environmental Integration and Multi-Faceted International Dimensions of EU Law: Unpacking the EU's 2009 Climate and Energy Package' (2011) 48 CML Rev 829; Jeroen JL Candel and Robbert Biesbroek, 'Toward a Processual Understanding of Policy Integration' (2016) 49 Policy Sciences 211.

Smart Mobility, Transport Poverty and the Legal Framework of Inclusive Mobility

Sofia Ranchordás

Contents

Abstract Smart mobility aims to provide efficient, sustainable and connected mobility solutions to congested urban centers. It is often assumed that smart mobility will benefit cities' residents and improve overall accessibility. Nevertheless, smart mobility strategies presuppose that transport users are digitally literate, autonomous and capable of affording either public or private transportation. For the millions of citizens throughout the world who are affected by transport poverty, this is not the case. Transport poverty is a multidimensional phenomenon which is often overlooked in the legal literature. Yet this specific type of poverty can limit individuals' upward mobility and impede their ability to exercise social and economic rights. This paper explores the phenomenon of transport poverty and delves into the possibility of designing smart mobility policies that address this type of poverty. It discusses existing or proposed policies of free public transit and explains why

I would like to thank the participants of the Smart Mobility Workshop at the Max Planck Institute for Innovation and Competition for their insightful comments. Sofia Ranchordás is Professor of European and Comparative Public Law, University of Groningen, Faculty of Law, The Netherlands.

S. Ranchordás (✉)
University of Groningen, Faculty of Law, Groningen, The Netherlands
e-mail: s.h.ranchordas@rug.nl

M. Finck et al. (eds.), *Smart Urban Mobility*, MPI Studies on Intellectual Property and Competition Law 29, https://doi.org/10.1007/978-3-662-61920-9_4

inclusive mobility should be regarded as a concretization of the right to equal treatment. This paper contributes to the existing scholarship on smart cities, smart mobility and fundamental rights with a novel interdisciplinary analysis of urban mobility. Furthermore, it draws attention to the need to design connected transport systems that are inclusive.

1 Introduction

Transport poverty is not the first thing that comes to mind in the context of smart mobility.[1] Smart mobility refers to the use of digital technology, connected transportation and accessibility systems which contribute to the creation of a sustainable and efficient traffic system.[2] However, current smart mobility projects are not always inclusive. They assume that individuals have access to the internet, own a smartphone or a tablet, are digitally literate and can afford public or private transportation,[3] which is not the case for millions of individuals in the North and the Global South.[4] In cities where urban sprawl increasingly separates affordable housing from well-paid jobs, transport poverty is a daily struggle.[5]

---

[1]Despite the limited scholarship on the topic of transport poverty and smart mobility, there are some exceptions: Sören Groth, 'Multimodal Divide: Reproduction of Transport Poverty in Smart Mobility Trends' (2019) 125 Transportation Research Part A: Policy and Practice 56; Aaron Golub and others, 'Assessing the Barriers to Equity in Smart Mobility Systems: A Case Study of Portland, Oregon' (2019) 7(4) Case Studies on Transport Policy 689. See also Ke Fang, '"Smart Mobility:" Is It Time to Re-think Urban Mobility?' (*Transport for Development/World Bank Blogs*, 29 April 2015) <http://blogs.worldbank.org/transport/smart-mobility-it-time-re-think-urban-mobility> accessed 7 January 2020 (drawing attention to the need to 'enable all people, regardless income or other social status, to better access the urban services they need, while also reducing motorized traffic').

[2]Tan Yigitcanlar and Md Kamruzzaman, 'Smart Cities and Mobility: Does the Smartness of Australian Cities Lead to Sustainable Commuting Patterns?' (2019) 26(2) Journal of Urban Technology 21.

[3]Diana Andone, Carmen Holotescu and Gabriela Grosseck, 'Learning Communities in Smart Cities. Case Studies' (International Conference on Web and Open Access to Learning (ICWOAL), Dubai, 25-27 November 2014) <https://ieeexplore.ieee.org/document/7009244> accessed 7 January 2020.

[4]Alan Wiig, 'The Empty Rhetoric of the Smart City: From Digital Inclusion to Economic Promotion in Philadelphia' (2016) 37(4) Urban Geography 535. According to the European Commission, 80 million Europeans never use the internet because 'they don't have a computer or it is too expensive [...] or they find it too difficult'; see European Commission, 'Digital Inclusion for a Better Society' (European Commission - Digital Single Market, 19 June 2019) <https://ec.europa.eu/digital-single-market/en/digital-inclusion-better-eu-society> accessed 1 December 2019.

[5]The burden of transport prices on household budgets is difficult to determine, but the World Bank has conducted several studies showing that this burden varied between 8 and 16% of household

Transport poverty refers to the social exclusion of marginalized individuals (e.g. those with low income, low education, limited digital literacy or precarious employment) who do not have access to public or private transportation.[6] Transport poverty has been detected in large European cities and metropolitan areas such as London, Greater Manchester, Leeds, Helsinki, Lyon and Nantes.[7] The literature has demonstrated that unequal access to transportation and accessibility systems limits individuals' social and economic mobility, particularly regarding access to education and economic opportunities.[8] Yet legal scholars have thus far overlooked this phenomenon and underexplored the link between poverty and public interest in regard to technological design.[9] Since the events of October 2019, however, when a $0.04 metro fare increase ignited violent protests in Chile, the social relevance of transport poverty has become difficult to deny.[10] It is also worth noting that one year earlier, the *gilets jaunes* (yellow vests) demonstrations were initially motivated by rising fuel prices.

While transport poverty and the need for higher connectivity have been discussed in the rural context, the debate on smart mobility is still failing to address urban inequalities.[11] Furthermore, smart mobility might insufficiently address or even

---

expenditures in developing countries in Africa and was 15% in certain developed countries (including France); see http://siteresources.worldbank.org/INTURBANTRANSPORT/Resources/Chapter3.pdf. In many Latin American cities, such as Lima and Rio de Janeiro, the poor are also being driven to inexpensive dwelling areas up to 40 kilometers away from potential employment areas, increasing the commuting time as much as three hours per day; see Julie Babinard, 'Is Public Transport Affordable?'(*World Bank Blogs*, 1 May 2014) <https://blogs.worldbank.org/transport/public-transport-affordable> accessed 18 March 2020.

[6] Groth (n 1) 57.

[7] Richard Crisp, Edward Ferrari and others, 'Tackling Transport-related Barriers to Employment in Low-income Neighbourhoods' (Project Report, Joseph Rowntree Foundation, York 2018) <http://shura.shu.ac.uk/24128/1/tackling_transport-related_barriers_low-income_neighbourhoods.pdf> accessed 18 March 2020.

[8] Diego Hernandez, 'Uneven Mobilities, Uneven Opportunities: Social Distribution of Public Transport Accessibility to Jobs and Education in Montevideo' (2018) 67 Journal of Transport Geography 119.

[9] See in this context the report of the Pathways for Prosperity Commission, 'The Digital Roadmap: How Developing Countries Can Get Ahead' (Oxford University 2019) <https://pathwayscommission.bsg.ox.ac.uk/digital-roadmap> accessed 18 March 2020. Energy poverty and fuel poverty have received more attention from other disciplines; see, for example, Kristian Fabri (ed), *Urban Fuel Poverty* (Academic Press 2019). On social exclusion and mobility, see Noel Cass, Elizabeth Shove and John Urry, 'Social Exclusion, Mobility and Access' (2005) 53(3) Sociological Review 539.

[10] John Bartlett, 'Chile Students' Mass Fare-Dodging Expands into City-Wide Protest' *The Guardian* (Santiago, 18 October 2019) <www.theguardian.com/world/2019/oct/18/chile-students-mass-fare-dodging-expands-into-city-wide-protest> accessed 18 March 2020; Dominique Mignot and others 'Mobilité et grande pauvreté' (HAL Archives Ouvertes 2001) <https://halshs.archives-ouvertes.fr/halshs-00110400/document> accessed 8 January 2020.

[11] Nagendra R Velaga and others, 'Transport Poverty Meets the Digital Divide: Accessibility and Connectivity in Rural Communities' (2012) 21 Journal of Transport Geography 102.

aggravate transport poverty depending on how the technology is designed.[12] This paper offers a legal analysis of transport poverty and explores the legal framework of inclusive mobility in the urban context.[13] Inclusive mobility would entail that cities embrace wide-ranging smart mobility strategies and public interest technology (within the limits of their budgets) to ensure that citizens have access to affordable, efficient, equitable and sustainable transportation.[14] This paper also explores whether there should be a separate 'right to mobility' without delving into the legal issues of international mobility (migration or other types of international travel).[15]

This paper does not aim to add another fundamental right to the longstanding proliferation of fundamental rights.[16] I argue instead that inclusive mobility is grounded in the right to equal treatment, particularly in the case of physical or psychological disabilities.[17] Moreover, I draw attention to the fact that transport poverty sets limits on the exercise of multiple socio-economic rights.[18] Although mobility might not always be necessary to have access to knowledge, health and labor in the digital age, adequate and inclusive mobility allows individuals to lead a life of dignity—a life 'without shame', as Amartya Sen puts it.[19]

This paper analyzes recent proposals and experiments on assisted mobility, the adoption of 'universal basic mobility policies' and discounted public transit as ways

---

[12]See Rodolfo Benevenuto and Brian Caulfield, 'Poverty and Transport in the Global South: An Overview' (2019) 79 Transport Policy 115. Guilio Mattioli, Karen Lucas, and Greg Marsden, 'Transport Poverty and Fuel Poverty in the UK: From Analogy to Comparison' (2017) 59 Transport Policy 93.

[13]See also Thomas W Sanchez and others, *The Right to Transportation: Moving to Equity* (Routledge 2008).

[14]The leading proponent of Public Interest Technology is Bruce Schneier; see Bruce Schneier, 'Cybersecurity for the Public Interest' (2019) 17(1) IEEE Security & Privacy 84. On governing smart mobility from a public value perspective, see Iain Docherty, Greg Marsden, Jillian Anable, 'The Governance of Smart Mobility' (2018) 115 Transportation Research Part A 114. See also (though as a rather implicit position) Agusti Cerrillo-i-Martinez, 'Fundamental Interests and Open Data for Re-use' (2012) 20(3) International Journal of Law and Information Technology 203.

[15]On this subject, see Andrew Geddes and Christina Boswell, *Migration and Mobility in the European Union* (Palgrave Macmillan 2011).

[16]See Janneke Gerards, 'Fundamental Rights and Other Interests: Should it Really Make a Difference?' in Eva Brems (ed), *Conflicts between Fundamental Rights* (Intersentia 2008) 655.

[17]Aart Hendriks, 'Disabled Persons and their Right to Equal Treatment: Allowing Differentiation while Ending Discrimination' (1995) 1(2) Health and Human Rights 152.

[18]On socio-economic rights, see Ingrid Leijten, *Core Socio-Economic Rights and the European Court of Human Rights* (Cambridge University Press 2017).

[19]David Bilchitz, *Poverty and Fundamental Rights: The Justification and Enforcement of Socio-economic Rights* (Oxford University Press 2008) 192. Amartya Sen, 'The Standard of Living: Concepts and Critiques: Lecture I', in Geoffrey Hawthorn (ed), *The Standard of Living* (Cambridge University Press 1987) 1, 18.

to address mobility inequality.[20] Smart technology consisting of ride-sharing, platform transportation systems and micromobility (electric bikes and scooters) has been suggested here as the supporting pillar for these universal basic mobility policies.[21]

This paper is organized as follows. Section 2 provides an overview of the potential and challenges of smart mobility. In Sect. 3 I delve into the concept of transport poverty as discussed in existing interdisciplinary scholarship (e.g. urban studies, transport policy and economics). Section 4 discusses the legal nature of mobility and existing proposals to implement (smart) inclusive mobility in cities. Section 5 reflects on the loose legal ends of smart inclusive mobility.[22]

2 Smart Mobility

2.1 Smart Cities and Mobility

Cities are inherently defined by a number of key elements, such as densely populated areas, cross-border trade through connectivity, innovation and influence over systems of exchange, diverse and entrepreneurial populations and growing urban sprawl.[23] Transportation systems ensure that city residents and visitors can commute between their homes and workplaces, have access to different city services and interact with each other for both economic and social purposes.[24] Mobility cannot be reduced to the physical movement of people, capital or ideas or their access to opportunity.[25] Mobility is a cornerstone of modern society which translates into personal control, freedom and access to new opportunities and risks.[26]

[20]Matt Caywood and Alex Roy, 'Universal Basic Mobility Is Coming: And It's Long Overdue' (*CityLab*, 3 October 2018) <www.citylab.com/perspective/2018/10/universal-basic-mobility-is-coming-and-its-long-overdue/572017/> accessed 18 March 2020.

[21]Daniel Comeaux, 'Movement Matters: Why We Should Commit to Universal Basic Mobility' (Kennedy School Review, 30 July 2019) <https://ksr.hkspublications.org/2019/07/30/movement-matters-why-we-should-commit-to-universal-basic-mobility/> accessed 18 March 2020.

[22]Lynn Scholl and others, 'Urban Transport and Poverty: Mobility and Accessibility effects of IDB-Supported BRT Systems in Cali and Lima' (Inter-American Development Bank 2016) <https://publications.iadb.org/en/urban-transport-and-poverty-mobility-and-accessibility-effects-idb-supported-brt-systems-cali-and> accessed 18 March 2020.

[23]Greg Clark, *Global Cities: A Short History* (Brookings Institution Press 2016) 3.

[24]On the notion of mobility, see Timothy Cresswell, *On the Move: Mobility in the Modern Western World* (Routledge 2006) 3-5.

[25]Mary Gilmartin, Patricia Burke Wood, and Cian O'Callaghan, *Borders, Mobility and Belonging in the Era of Brexit and Trump* (University of Bristol Policy Press 2018) 37.

[26]Randi Hjorthol, 'Transport Resources, Mobility and Unmet Transport Needs in Old Age' (2013) 33 Ageing & Society 1190; John Urry, *Sociology beyond Societies: Mobilities for the Twenty-first Century* (Routledge 2000).

Cities depend nowadays on their ability to design efficient, connected and smart mobility.[27] While urban mobility is essential to the economic growth and competitiveness of cities, there are growing concerns regarding the side effects of transport, particularly congestion, accidents and pollution.[28] This is one of the key issues that smart cities seek to address. In a smart city, technology and traditional infrastructures are merged in order to improve the quality of life of its citizens and commuters and to stimulate the development of social, economic and ecological areas of the urban environment.[29] The elusive term 'smart cities' refers to urban geographical areas in which public officials implement data-driven technologies to create benefits for citizens in terms of inclusion and participation, environmental quality and well-being.[30] Although there is no consensus on the definition of smart cities, scholars agree that these cities aim to address severe urban challenges such as traffic jams, pollution and social exclusion.[31] Smart mobility has become one of the most important pillars of smart cities: traffic management systems in their different applications are a clear example of data-driven solutions that can contribute to the realization of smart city goals.[32] Smart mobility also promises to reduce CO_2 emissions, which are largely caused by road transport.[33]

[27]Fumihiko Nakamura, 'Role of Connected Mobility for Twenty-first-century Cities—Trial Approach for Conceptualization of Connected Mobility through Case Studies' (2014) 38(1) International Association of Traffic and Safety Sciences IATSS Research 52.

[28]European Commission, 'European Urban Mobility, Policy Context' (European Commission 2017) <https://ec.europa.eu/transport/sites/transport/files/2017-sustainable-urban-mobility-policy-context.pdf> accessed 18 March 2020.

[29]Clara Benevolo, Renata P Dameri and Beatrice d'Auria, 'Smart Mobility in Smart City' in Teresina Torre, Alessio Braccini, Ricardo Spinelli (eds), *Empowering Institutions. Lecture Notes in Information Systems and Organisation*, vol 11 (Springer 2016) 13; Neus Baucells Aletà, Concepción Moreno Alonso and Rosa M Arce Ruiz, 'Smart Mobility and Smart Environment in the Spanish Cities' (2017) 24 Transportation Research Procedia 163.

[30]For a literature review on the definition of smart cities, see, for instance, Margarita Angelidou, 'The Role of Smart City Characteristics in the Plans of Fifteen Cities' (2017) 24(4) Journal of Urban Technology 3; Andrea Caragliu, Chiara del Bo and Peter Nijkamp, 'Smart Cities in Europe' (2011) 18(2) Journal of Urban Technology 6.

[31]Eduardo M Costa and Alvaro D Oliveira, 'Humane Smart Cities' in Robert Frodeman (eds), *The Oxford Handbook of Interdisciplinarity* (Oxford University Press 2017).

[32]Sandra Melo, Joaquim Macedo, Patrícia Baptista, 'Guiding Cities to Pursue a Smart Mobility Paradigm: An Example from Vehicle Routing Guidance and its Traffic and Operational Effects' (2017) 65 Research in Transportation Economics 24.

[33]According to the European Commission, urban mobility accounts for 40% of all CO^2 emissions from road transport and up to 70% of other pollutants from transport; see European Commission, 'Urban Mobility' (European Commission-Mobility and Transport 2019) <https://ec.europa.eu/transport/themes/urban/urban_mobility_en> accessed 17 March 2020.

2.2 *Smart Mobility*

Smart mobility is a novel and complex concept which refers to transportation and more broadly to mobility solutions based on IT. The concept of smart mobility has been defined in the literature by reference to four central elements: first, it includes vehicle technology (e.g. alternative fuels, electric mobility, autonomous driving and vehicle dynamics); second, it is supported by Intelligent Transport Systems such as connected vehicles or intelligent traffic management; third, it requires large amounts of data on transportation, weather and traffic conditions that corresponds to the real-time demand of passengers; fourth, it includes the development of new mobility services such as ride-sharing, new biking systems and multimodal transportation.[34]

The term ‘smart mobility’ also refers to the transition from traditional transportation systems to multimodal transportation, which relies heavily upon new technologies to facilitate both individual and collective mobility.[35] Multimodal transportation refers to the combination of different modes of transportation such that at least two modes are integrated in terms of schedule and route. Multimodal transport enables sustainable and efficient travel within cities and includes rapid bus transit, metro and light rail, and shared mobility services such as bike or car-sharing. It is a system which allows passengers to be connected to public transportation from the first to the last mile and typically includes an online mobility platform that provides real-time information to passengers regarding ongoing disruptions. The interconnection of different modes of transportation often also relies on the Internet of Things and the integration of different transportation platforms.

The advancement of smart mobility strategies in cities and the idea of ‘mobility as a service’ (MaaS) translate not only into integrated modes of transport but also into the creation of additional incentives to not own a private vehicle. Examples of these initiatives include the widespread use of ride-sharing services (e.g. Uber) and micromobility services such as shared electric scooters (e-scooters) and bicycles. These platforms have disrupted the market of personal transportation by offering alternatives to licensed taxicabs. Smart mobility platforms (e.g. Uber) match demand and supply more efficiently and allow individuals in areas with limited public transportation to hail and share a ride at more affordable prices.[36] Ride-sharing could thus in theory promote social inclusion. In the last decade, urban mobility has indeed been transformed by the introduction of platforms. New technologies have shown the potential to improve mobility and to efficiently match demand and supply without building additional transport infrastructure.[37]

---

[34]Hans Jeekel, ‘Social Sustainability and Smart Mobility: Exploring the Relationship’ (2017) 25 Transport Research Procedia 4296, 4305.

[35]Docherty, Marsden and Anable (n 14).

[36]Daniel E Rauch and David Schleicher, ‘Like Uber, but for Local Government: The Future of Local Regulation of the Sharing Economy’ (2015) 76(4) Ohio State Law Journal 901.

[37]Margaret Grieco, ‘Poverty Mapping and Sustainable Transport: A Neglected Dimension’(2015) 51 Research in Transportation Economics 3, 8.

To sum up, smart mobility promises to deliver more sustainable and efficient mobility and accessibility options. This promise is ideally framed as a multimodal system of connected, on-demand vehicles with flexible and personalized services that are supported by real-time information.[38]

2.3 *Criticism*

Despite the expansion of smart mobility strategies in smart cities, the acceptance of smart mobility is far from universal. On the one hand, smart mobility has been defined by the enhanced movement of people and goods in terms of efficiency, sustainability, interconnection and speed.[39] On the other, studies have shown that the social sustainability of smart mobility is highly dependent on the type of systems used and the ability of citizens to actively participate in sustainability policies.[40] Songdo, one of the most celebrated smart cities, has been criticized for its top-down character, which allows limited citizen participation.[41] This top-down approach relies heavily upon partnerships with technology companies whose goals are not always aligned with the public interest.[42] Socio-spatial issues and inclusive and sustainable growth in the mobility sector are thought to be at risk when citizens are not adequately involved in the design of smart mobility policies.[43]

The potential of smart mobility to improve accessibility in urban centers can also be criticized from an economic perspective. In several Western cities (e.g. in the United States), owning a private vehicle remains more convenient for low-income commuters than using public transit because of the latter's limited network and schedules.[44] For low-income households that are not adequately served by public transit, expenditures on private vehicles, insurance and fuel can be disproportionately high relative to their means.[45] Moreover, although ride-sharing platforms have

---

38 Docherty, Marsden and Anable (n 14) 115.

39 Glenn Lyons, 'Getting Smart about Urban Mobility—Aligning the Paradigms of Smart and Sustainable' (2018) 115 Transportation Research Part A 4, 6.

40 ibid.

41 Jung I Kim, 'Making Cities Global: The New City Development of Songdo, Yjiapu and Lingang' (2014) 29(3) Planning Perspectives 329, 351-2; Islam Bouzguenda, Chaham Alalouch, Nadia Fava, 'Towards Smart Sustainable Cities: A Review of the Role Digital Citizen Participation Can Play in Advancing Social Sustainability' (2019) 50 Sustainable Cities and Society 101627.

42 Lyons (n 39).

43 Tan Yigitcanlar and others, 'Can Cities Become Smart without Being Sustainable? A Systematic View of the Literature' (2019) 45 Sustainable Cities and Society 348, 360.

44 Institute for Transportation and Development Policy ITDP, 'The High Cost of Transportation in the United States' (*ITDP Blog*, 23 May 2019) <www.itdp.org/2019/05/23/high-cost-transportation-united-states/> accessed 9 January 2020.

45 Nicolas Valenzuela-Levi, 'Why Do More Unequal Countries Spend More on Private Vehicles? Evidence and Implications for the Future of Cities' (2018) 43 Sustainable Cities and Society 384.

ostensibly offered a new transport service to underserved communities, low-income commuters tend to find ride-sharing too expensive to use regularly, particularly when compared to traditional public transit options.[46]

Infrastructure is an additional issue when it comes to smart mobility. Several cities around the world are not yet well equipped for the safe circulation of bicycles and electric scooters. Moreover, the rapid expansion of electric scooters among young middle-income earners and tourists in cities has been criticized due to the rising number of accidents and nuisances (e.g. scooters that are abandoned on sidewalks or narrow streets).[47] Bike-sharing systems have been frowned upon due to poor management and vandalism (e.g. in Paris, where vehicles were often not returned to stations or properly taken care of). These criticisms have called into question the sustainability of a mobility model based on access rather than ownership.[48]

Finally, smart mobility can also give rise to a wide array of legal problems, ranging from liability for accidents caused by automated vehicles and insurance for ride-sharing vehicles to law enforcement, privacy and security.[49] Moreover, in challenging the longstanding regulation of taxicabs, the regulation of many of these connected vehicle technologies (including private ride-sharing operated by online platforms) is famous for having sparked a great deal of controversy throughout the world.[50] As the regulation of ride-sharing becomes clearer, many other legal, economic and social problems continue to accompany the academic and policy debates on smart mobility. One of them is its social inclusiveness and in particular its ability to address transport poverty.

---

[46]McKinsey and Company, 'Smart Cities: Digital Solutions for a More Livable Future' (McKinsey Global Institute, June 2018) 105 <www.mckinsey.com/~/media/mckinsey/industries/capital%20projects%20and%20infrastructure/our%20insights/smart%20cities%20digital%20solutions%20for%20a%20more%20livable%20future/mgi-smart-cities-full-report.ashx> accessed 17 March 2020.

[47]For a thorough discussion of some of these problems and how mobility platforms are reshaping the public values of cities, see Sofia Ranchordas and Catalina Goanta, 'The New City Regulators: Platform and Public Values for Smart and Sharing Cities' (2020) 36 Computer Law & Security Review (in press, corrected proof available) <https://doi.org/10.1016/j.clsr.2019.105375> accessed 17 March 2020.

[48]On the definition of access and the disruption of property as a model of stability, see Shelly Kreiczer-Levy, *Destabilized Property: Property Law in the Sharing Economy* (Cambridge University Press 2019) 78-80.

[49]Nynke Veilinga, 'From the Testing to the Deployment of Self-driving Cars: Legal Challenges to Policymakers on the Road Ahead' (2017) 33(6) Computer Law & Security 847; Nynke Veilinga, 'Automated Driving and its Challenges to International Traffic: Which Way to Go?' (2019) 11 (2) Law, Innovation, and Technology 257.

[50]See, for example, Brishen Rogers, 'The Social Costs of Uber' (2017) 82 University of Chicago Law Review Online 82.

3 Transport Poverty and Smart Mobility

Existing scholarship has devoted great attention to the need to improve the connectivity of rural communities and to help rural communities overcome transport poverty and social exclusion.[51] However, city dwellers also face important challenges concerning the affordability of public transportation and its accessibility. As cities grow and the price of housing in neighborhoods near employment centers increases, it becomes increasingly important to discuss the problem of transport poverty in urban centers and to explore whether technology can be a solution for the exclusion of individuals who are too poor to travel.[52]

Transport poverty has been defined as 'the systemic lack of (usually motorized) transport that generates difficulties in moving, often (but not always) connected to a lack of services or infrastructures'.[53] Transport poverty can be divided into different categories: mobility poverty, transport affordability, accessibility poverty and exposure to transport externalities. While for some individuals transport poverty means spending three hours commuting between their homes and jobs in crowded public transit systems, for others it means not being able to attend medical appointments outside their residential area due to the prohibitive prices of public transit or the lack of physical mobility.[54] Existing scholarship in both developed and developing countries has shown that there is a correlation between the lack of access to suitable transport and better employment opportunities and healthcare.[55]

In multiple Western countries, at least 20% of households are affected by or at risk of transport poverty: they are unable to afford public transportation or a private

[51]Nagendra R Velaga and others, 'Transport Poverty Meets the Digital Divide: Accessibility and Connectivity in Rural Communities' (2012) 21 Journal of Transport Poverty 102. Philip Alston, United Nations Special Rapporteur on extreme poverty and human rights, drew attention to the problem of rural poverty and the geographical isolation experienced by rural dwellers; see Philip Alston, 'Statement on Visit to the United Kingdom' (United Nations Human Rights Office of the Higher Commissioner, 16 November 2018) <www.ohchr.org/EN/NewsEvents/Pages/DisplayNews.aspx?NewsID=23881&LangID=E> accessed 9 January 2020.

[52]On the relationship between technology and social inequality, see Susan Halford and Mike Savage, 'Reconceptualizing Digital Social Inequality' (2010) 13(7) Information, Communication & Society 937.

[53]Karen Lucas and others, 'Transport poverty and its adverse social consequences' (2016) 169 (6) Proceedings of the Institution of Civil Engineers - Transport, 353 <https://doi.org/10.1680/jtran.15.00073> accessed 9 January 2020.

[54]Samina Syed and others, 'Traveling Towards Disease: Transportation Barriers to Health Care Access' (2013) 38(5) Journal of Community Health 976.

[55]Margaret Grieco, 'Transportation in African Cities: An Institutional Perspective' in Nancy Brooks, Kieran Donaghy, and Gerrit-Jan Knaap (eds), *The Oxford Handbook of Urban Economics and Planning* (Oxford University Press 2011) 834, 835. Social Exclusion Unit, 'Making the Connections: Final Report on Transport and Social Exclusion' (Office of the Deputy Prime Minister, February 2003) <www.ilo.org/wcmsp5/groups/public/%2D%2D-ed_emp/%2D%2D-emp_policy/%2D%2D-invest/documents/publication/wcms_asist_8210.pdf> accessed 7 January 2020. See also Giuseppina Pellegrino (ed), The Politics of Proximity: Mobility and Immobility in Practice (Routledge 2011).

vehicle. This number tends to be higher among underrepresented groups (e.g. 33–35% of African-American and Hispanic households in the United States).[56] In the United Kingdom, research has shown that there are important inequalities in the provision of transport services and the impact of their costs on household budgets.[57] In Finland, a growing number of citizens are falling below the poverty line because of the high costs of public transportation.[58] This problem also affects the Netherlands despite the popularity of micromobility, namely bicycles, in the country. The Dutch Central Bureau for Statistics developed an indicator to determine the risk of individuals falling into transport poverty.[59] This indicator's variables are income, vehicle ownership, distance to public transport, distance to public services, physical or mental disability and age. According to this indicator, the risk of being affected by transport poverty in the Netherlands was the highest in Heerlen (18.2%) and the lowest in Utrecht (1.9%). This indicator draws on the literature that recognizes transport poverty as a multi-dimension phenomenon caused by the intersection of different social, economic and personal factors.[60]

According to a report authored by the Verne Transport Research Centre in Finland, the causes of transport poverty tend to fall into two main categories: personal features such as needs, resources and personal capabilities; and housing location and choices related to the distance between residence and employment.[61] Transport poverty can result from the lack of affordable options as well as from internal or psychological elements such as the feeling that available modes of transport are unsafe or unreliable.[62] The most vulnerable groups are typically low-income groups, aging individuals, migrants, minority households, individuals

[56]Kevin DeGood and Andrew Schwartz, 'Can New Transportatin Technologies Improve Equity and Access to Equity and Opportunity' (*Center for American Progress*, 27 April 2016) <www.americanprogress.org/issues/economy/reports/2016/04/27/135425/can-new-transportation-technologies-improve-equity-and-access-to-opportunity/> accessed 17 July 2020.

[57]Sustrans, 'Locked Out: Transport Poverty in England' (Sustrans, 2012) <www.sustrans.org.uk/media/3706/transport-poverty-england-2012.pdf> accessed 21 October 2019; Karen Lucas and others, 'Inequalities in Mobility and Access in the UK Transport System' (Foresight, Government Office for Science 2019) <https://assets.publishing.service.gov.uk/government/uploads/system/uploads/attachment_data/file/784685/future_of_mobility_access.pdf> accessed 21 October 2019.

[58]Verne Transport Research Centre, 'Report: What is Transport Poverty? Is there Transport Poverty in Finland? Who are the Victims of it?' (Verne Transport Research Centre, 12 February 2018) <www.tut.fi/verne/transport-poverty-preliminary/#more-7252> accessed 21 October 2019.

[59]Centraal Bureau van Statistiek CBS, 'Risico op vervoersarmoede. Een eerste aanzet tot een indicator' (CBS 2018) <www.cbs.nl/nl-nl/achtergrond/2019/42/indicator-risico-op-vervoersarmoede> accessed 21 October 2019.

[60]A Church, M Frost, and K Sullivan, 'Transport and Social Exclusion in London' (2000) 7 (3) Transport Policy 195.

[61]Verne Transport Research Centre (n 58).

[62]This was concluded in two case studies on transport poverty in Rotterdam and The Hague; Rob van der Bijl, 'Vervoersarmoede in de grote stad ontrafeld' (*Verkeerskunde*, 25 April 2019) <www.verkeerskunde.nl/internetartikelen/vakartikelen/vervoersarmoede-in-de-grote-stad-ontrafeld.57552.lynkx?pageStart23314=41> accessed 22 October 2019.

who are either too young or too old to drive and individuals with physical or cognitive limitations.

Transport poverty coexists with other types of urban poverty and tends to aggravate it.[63] Individuals experiencing transport poverty may feel excluded, particularly when there are no local informal networks that can compensate for the lack of transportation and local labor opportunities. Even when individuals do not experience transport poverty in the strict sense, but only have access to slower modes of transportation, they are still put at a disadvantage if they work shifts or live in remote areas. Although transport poverty affects a large number of people, it has remained rather invisible to those engaged in designing smart mobility policies.

A key assumption of the narrative that has thus far accompanied smart cities is that access to more information and additional connectivity are inherently beneficial to a city's residents and visitors.[64] Nevertheless, existing smart mobility narratives are not inclusive enough to account for the needs of those who do not have the financial means or the digital literacy to participate in the smart city and its smart mobility policy.[65] The following section delves into existing or proposed policies that may alleviate transport poverty.

4 Inclusive Mobility

In 2018, Philip Alston, the United Nations Special Rapporteur on extreme poverty and human rights, concluded his visit to the United Kingdom by stating that 'transport, especially in rural areas, should be considered an essential service, equivalent to water and electricity, and the government should regulate the sector to the extent necessary to ensure that people living in rural areas are adequately serviced'.[66] As cities evolve into large urban centers, it is important to highlight that geographical isolation and the need to make transportation universal is no longer limited to rural areas. In megacities with considerable urban sprawl, the lack of

---

[63] Xavier Godard, 'Poverty and Urban Mobility: Diagnosis toward a New Understanding' in Harry T Dimitrou and Ralph Gakenheimer (eds), *Urban Transport in the Developing World: A Handbook of Policy and Practice* (Edward Elgar 2011) 232.

[64] Collin McFarlane, *Learning the City, Knowledge and Translocal Assemblage* (Wiley-Blackwell 2011); Alan Wiig, 'IBM's Smart City as Techno-utopian Policy Mobility' (2015) 19(2) City 258, 260.

[65] Ola Söderström, Till Paasche and Francisco Klauser, 'Smart Cities as Corporate Storytelling' (2014) 18(3) City 307; Skip Descant, 'Digital Literacy is at the Heart of a Thriving Smart City' (Government Technology, 30 March 2018) <www.govtech.com/applications/Digital-Literacy-Is-at-the-Heart-of-a-Thriving-Smart-City.html> accessed 5 January 2020; Melissa Gilbert, 'Theorizing Digital and Urban Inequalities' (2010) 13(7) Information, Communication & Society 1000.

[66] Philip Alston, 'Statement on Visit to the United Kingdom' (United Nations Human Rights, Office of the Higher Commissioner, 16 November 2018), <www.ohchr.org/EN/NewsEvents/Pages/DisplayNews.aspx?NewsID=23881&LangID=E> accessed 5 January 2020.

access to reliable transportation limits the ability of individuals in some areas to escape poverty.

In recent years, the idea that access to transport should assume the same status as other basic utilities has started taking shape. Proposals to provide free transportation to all residents or a 'universal basic mobility' system are becoming increasingly popular in both traditional and social media in the United States and Europe, where many small to medium-sized cities are already experimenting with free or discounted public transit systems.[67] Yet the question of whether transport should be held in the same regard as other utilities remains unanswered. In this section, I discuss the nature of 'a right to mobility', its possible legal framework and existing or proposed policies to further mobility inclusion, including through technological means.

4.1 The Nature of Mobility

If a separate 'right to mobility' were to exist, its first element would be the right to move from one place to another. Indeed, mobility *stricto sensu*, understood as the right to travel within the country and particularly abroad, has been judicially and constitutionally recognized in a number of countries, such as the United States, Germany, Canada and Japan, and it is far from a modern invention.[68] In early common law, subjects were required to ask for the king's license to leave the country, but this soon changed with chapter 42 of the Magna Carta.[69] More recently, the right to travel within one's country has been recognized as a right inherent to citizenship which can only be limited under extraordinary conditions.[70] The right to mobility has also been extensively discussed in the context of civil rights movements. In the United States, the connection between mobility, rights and citizenship has been construed in different decisions of the United States Supreme Court. In *Crandall v State of Nevada* (1867) the Court decided that the right to travel was an essential part of citizenship: the ability to exercise one's citizenship rights as such (e.g. the right to vote) depends on having the right to transport.[71] This debate also includes the question of diversity since each of us exercises mobility in a different way.[72] Citizens with disabilities face numerous obstacles to the exercise of this right.

[67] See, for example, Daniel Comeaux, 'Movement Matters: Why We Should Commit to Universal Basic Mobility' (Kennedy School Review, 30 July 2019) <https://ksr.hkspublications.org/2019/07/30/movement-matters-why-we-should-commit-to-universal-basic-mobility/> accessed 3 January 2020.

[68] Duane W Schroeder, 'The Right to Travel: In Search of a Constitutional Source' (1976) 55 (1) Nebraska Law Review 117.

[69] Leonard B Boudin, 'The Constitutional Right to Travel' (1956) 56(1) Columbia Law Review 47.

[70] See Richard Sobel, 'The Right to Travel and Privacy: Intersecting Fundamental Freedoms' (2014) 30(4) The John Marshall Journal of Information Technology & Privacy Law 639.

[71] Tim Cresswell, 'The Right to Mobility: The Production of Mobility in the Courtroom' (2006) 38 (4) Antipode 735, 743.

[72] ibid 739.

In this context, the right to travel has been discussed in the international context as a right in itself or as part of the right to equal treatment and the prohibition of discrimination.[73]

While the physical element of the 'right to mobility' is well established, the economic dimension of this right has not been widely recognized as a way to address the transport poverty of underprivileged citizens.[74] Citizens may have the right to 'move' and travel from their homes to another destination in order to make a living or for any other legitimate purpose, but it is unclear whether the right to travel should encompass measures to support those who do not have the financial means. Even in countries such as France where legislation includes a right to travel 'on reasonable terms of access, quality and process, as well as of costs to the community', its implementation has remained problematic.[75] While many European countries have subsidized public transport for low income households, senior citizens as well as students, these policies have not fully addressed transport poverty in that they seldom offer coverage for the 'last mile'. Moreover, for a large number of individuals, public transit does not offer an adequate alternative to owning a private vehicle. In this context, the European Energy Poverty Index developed by OpenExp seeks to establish the share of expenditures on transport energy out of the total expenditures for each Member State as well as the percentage of citizens who cannot afford regular public transport.[76] This poverty index seeks to show the trade-off between affordable housing and car dependency. For example, in Hungary in 2016, the share of expenditures on transport energy was as high as 59.2% and the percentage of individuals who could not afford public transportation on a regular basis was 54.9%.

Furthermore, there is a third element of mobility worth considering: digital inclusion/exclusion. In a world where travel information is becoming exclusively digital and smart mobility systems communicate with citizens through platforms, the mobility of citizens with limited digital skills may be impaired.[77] Although this paper does not seek to delve deeper into the broader problem of digital illiteracy, it should not be assumed that users have the required digital literacy to use complex smart mobility applications.[78] In other words, a right to mobility should also be

---

[73]See Lalin Kovudhikulrungsri, 'The Accessibility Standards with respect to Air Travel in the European Union' (2018) 1 Handicap & Recht 20; Lalin Kovudhikulrungsri, 'Human Rights in the Sky: Weighing Human Rights against the Law on International Carriage by Air' (2018) 11(1) European Journal of Legal Studies 39.

[74]Exceptions have been Tallinn, Luxembourg and Cascais (as of 2020), which have adopted a system of free transportation for all registered residents. See Sect. 4.2 for further information.

[75]Loi no 82-1153 du 30 december 1982, art 2. Caroline Gallez, Benjamin Motte-Baumvol, 'Inclusive Mobility or Inclusive Accessibility? A European Perspective' (2017) 56 Deusto Journal of European Studies 79.

[76]OpenExp, 'European Energy Poverty Index EEPI' <www.openexp.eu/european-energy-poverty-index-eepi> accessed 5 January 2020.

[77]Julie Colin, 'Digital Illiteracy: The Challenge of Getting around without a Smartphone' (*InMovement*, 23 November 2018) <www.inmvt.com/en/insight/digital-illiteracy-challenge-getting-around-without-smartphone/> accessed 9 January 2020.

[78]John C Bertot, 'The Multiple Dimensions of the Digital Divide, More than Technology 'Haves' and 'Have-Nots'' (2003) 20(2) Government Information Quarterly 185. On the problem of digital

adapted to the requirements of the digital age. This dimension has nevertheless remained underexplored.

To conclude, while the right to 'move' and travel is well recognized, it is more challenging to argue that the right to mobility should exist on its own and include the right to affordable forms of transportation that meet one's needs. In the remaining part of this section, I will consider inclusive mobility not as a separate socio-economic right but as part of the right to equal treatment.

4.2 *Inclusive Mobility and the Right to Equal Treatment*

A separate right to mobility does not need to be constitutionalized in order to protect inclusive and affordable mobility. Instead, both the physical and economic dimensions of mobility lead us to the same problems: exclusion and poverty. Whenever some citizens are not able to travel because they do not have the financial means or the ability to travel by themselves, they are being treated differently. The same applies to those who are denied access to better healthcare or education because of inefficient transportation.[79] Similar to other forms of poverty, transport poverty is the result of a number of factors (e.g. gender), but it is also the cause of other issues that are central to the study of poverty and inequality, for example, lack of access to education and healthcare.[80] Placing inclusive mobility under the 'umbrella' of the right to equal treatment means that the denial of mobility or accessibility needs to be reasonable and justifiable.[81]

Inclusive mobility entails not only that individuals should be granted reasonable access to public transit but also that other modes of transport should be seen as acceptable, depending on national or local conditions and individual needs. To illustrate, in a case on social security law in Australia, the right to maintain ownership of a private vehicle was considered justified because mobility in several parts of Australia is only possible with a privately owned vehicle.[82]

The abstract meaning of equal and inclusive mobility is hard to determine. Here I draw on Mimmi Sheller's 'mobility bill of rights' and her concept of 'mobility

---

literacy and how it can be addressed with digital literacy courses, see Stichting Lezen en Schrijven, 'Laaggeletterden: achterblijvers in de digitale wereld?' (ECBO, 2015) <www.lezenenschrijven.nl/uploads/editor/ecbo.15-217-Laaggeletterden-achterblijvers-in-de-digitale-wereld-web.pdf> accessed 5 January 2020.

[79] Sandra Fredman, 'The Potential and Limits of an Equal Rights Paradigm in Addressing Poverty' (2011) 22(3) Stellenbosch Law Review 566.

[80] Meghan Campbell, *Women, Poverty, Equality: The Role of CEDAW* (Bloomsbury 2018) 150. Sara Burke, *Tackling Poverty: Tackling Health Inequalities* (Combat Poverty Agency 2009) 26.

[81] Janneke H Gerards, 'Intensity of Judicial Review in Equal Treatment Cases' (2004) 51(2) Netherlands International Law Review 135.

[82] Kieran Tranter and Judith Kelly, 'Private Motor Vehicle Ownership in Australian Social Security Law' (2014) 21(1) Journal of Social Security Law 32, 42.

justice'.[83] This bill of rights not only focuses on an individualistic rights-based approach (the right of citizens to mobility) but also takes into account the impact of transportation on the environment. This bill includes for example 'the right not to harm the environment' as well as the right to 'affordable transportation to meet our basic needs; the right to transportation that does not threaten health, safety, water, air, or the local environment of a community; the right to a fair transport pricing system that does not penalize those that use less; the right to efficient and inviting mobility'. The concept of 'mobility justice' draws attention to the multidimensional complexity of the problems of uneven mobility and accessibility and the need to provide equitable solutions that treat citizens equally, that is, without providing mobility to some citizens at the expense of others or denying access to citizens on the grounds of race, gender and ability.[84]

To conclude, the right to mobility should be interpreted as the right to treat citizens equally in the provision of transportation and the design of (smart) mobility solutions. Complex mobility systems that disproportionately exclude citizens who are not tech-savvy could be regarded as a violation of the right to equal treatment. The same is true for transport pricing systems that do not take into account the varying impact that transport expenditures can have on each household. While it is easy to understand how this generates the obligation to take steps towards the improvement of mobility for disabled persons, this reasoning has not often been applied to poverty. However, poverty is often the result of historical racial and gender discrimination and the lack of equal opportunity.[85]

4.3 Implementation: Free Public Transit?

Universal basic mobility (UBM) proponents argue that mobility should be regarded as an essential utility since it is instrumental to gaining access to other essential resources such as food and education. UBM draws on the well-known principle of universal basic income.[86] This proposal also assumes that UBM could be made

---

[83]Mimmi Sheller, *Mobility Justice: The Politics of Movement in the Age of Extremes* (Verso 2018).

[84]Mimmi Sheller, 'Theorising Mobility Justice' (2018) 30(2) Tempo Social: Revista Sociologica da USP 17, 28-9.

[85]Sandra Fredman, 'The Public Sector Equality Duty' (2011) 40(4) Industrial Law Journal 405, 406-7.

[86]See, for example, Miranda P Fleischer and Daniel J Hemel, 'The Architecture of a Basic Income' (2019) University of San Diego School of Law: Legal Studies Research Paper Series 19-401 <https://ssrn.com/abstract=3346467> accessed 10 January 2020; Erika Schutt, 'A Quasi-Experiment for Universal Basic Income: Evidence from Remittances in Colombia' (2019) University of Miami Business School Research Paper 3430801 <https://ssrn.com/abstract=3430801 or https://doi.org/10.2139/ssrn.3430801> accessed 10 January 2020; Bryant W Sculos, 'Changing Lives and Minds: Progress, Strategy, and Universal Basic Income' (2019) 41(2) New Political Science 234-247.

possible by smart technology and in particular the numerous platforms that connect the demand and supply of mobility, that is, platforms that offer 'mobility as a service'.[87] A consolidated regional MaaS smartphone application could be a potential solution for the provision of accessibility information. This could allow governments to coordinate modes of public transportation and offer subsidized transportation packages. Since the network of public transit is not always sufficient, additional measures (e.g. integration with car-sharing systems) would be necessary to ensure that citizens are also offered transportation for the 'last mile'.

A growing number of mid-sized European cities offer free transportation to their residents. This is the case for 30 French cities, such as Aubagne, Niort and Dunkirk, as well as for Cascais in Portugal, Tallinn in Estonia and Luxembourg. In September 2018, a bill on the promotion of free public transit was introduced for examination in the French Parliament. This bill justified the need for free public transportation on environmental, public health, social and economic grounds.[88] Besides the argument that free transportation would improve the purchasing power of French residents, this piece of legislation also aimed to promote social inclusion. The bill drew upon successful experiments in France as well as on the system in Tallinn. The Estonian capital has been providing free public transportation to the registered residents of Talinn since 2004. Discounted tickets are available to individuals registered as residents of other Estonian cities in the Estonian Population Register.[89] The legality of this measure has nonetheless been questioned in the literature due to the potential risk of residence-based discrimination.[90] Indirect discrimination on the basis of residence can be justified in some cases, particularly when a national measure has a legitimate aim and the discrimination is proportionate.[91]

In Portugal, low-income households were considerably affected by rising transport costs during the financial crisis. The introduction of universal mobility since then has remained limited but holds future potential. In the metropolitan area of Lisbon, recent efforts have been made to reduce the price of public transit and promote the efficiency of multimodal transport. In 2019, a unique discount card for the whole region and a MaaS platform (Moovit) were introduced. The municipality of Cascais, just a few kilometers away from Lisbon, went further and initiated the transition to free public transit in 2019. As of 2020, public transport is free for all residents as well as for individuals studying or working in this municipality. The

---

[87]Vincent Varney, 'Why Universal Basic Mobility Is an Economic Necessity for an Autonomous Future' (*Here360*, 18 January 2019) <https://360.here.com/on-universal-basic-mobility-and-tackling-the-high-cost-of-poor-transport> accessed 5 November 2019.

[88]André Chassaigne and others, 'Proposition de loi visant à encourager la gratuité des transports collectifs urbains et périurbains enregistrée à la Présidence de l'Assemblée nationale' (Assemblée Nationale France, 19 September 2018) <www.assemblee-nationale.fr/15/propositions/pion1242.asp> accessed 10 January 2020.

[89]Carri Ginter, 'Free Public Transport of Tallinn, Estonia: a Case to Justify (Reverse) Discrimination on the Basis of Residence' (2017) 42(6) European Law Review 894.

[90]ibid.

[91]Case C-103/08 *Arthur Gottwald v Bezirkshauptmannschaft Bregenz* [2009] ECR I-09117.

mayor of Cascais has presented this policy as 'a shift to a new paradigm that envisions mobility as a pillar of developed and sustainable democratic societies'. [92]

The policies discussed thus far presuppose that citizens are able to use regular public transit. Nevertheless, these options do not always get them from door to door, which is problematic for individuals with physical impairments. Moreover, only a very small number of individuals with reduced mobility are eligible for paratransit service operators. Technology can nevertheless reduce these impairments. This is the case for a low-cost power wheelchair shared control system recently developed by Imperial College and the National University of Singapore. This system guides users through programmed paths between specific destinations and does not require the user to do more than control speed and avoid obstacles.[93] Research in assistive technologies for the mobility of the elderly seeks to develop specific hardware designs such as smart walkers, mobile devices, personalized travel planning, personal reminders and novel forms of robotic assistance.[94] In the context of smart cities, App & Town Compagnon claims to offer the first smart city solution for assisting people with mobility impairments. This application was developed by a Spanish technology company (Mass Factory Urban Accessibility Mobility) which develops urban applications of social value.[95] This application is an example of a smart mobility application that seeks to advance inclusiveness in smart cities.

From a more theoretical perspective, it should also be mentioned that in the context of Horizon 2020, the European Commission has funded projects to develop new mobility solutions at affordable prices and/or minimum subsidies that aim to eliminate transport poverty.[96] Commercially available smart mobility solutions have thus far not invested enough into developing affordable mobility options for low-income, low-educated individuals or other socially marginalized people.[97] Moreover, smart mobility solutions also require a certain level of digital literacy which, depending on the country and the personal characteristics of each group, might not always be present among those affected by transport poverty.

---

[92] Joao Saramago, 'Transportes gratuitos' (CM, 2 January 2020) <https://www.cmjornal.pt/portugal/cidades/detalhe/transportes-gratuitos-para-todos-em-cascais> accessed 9 January 2020.

[93] Rachel E. Cowan et al., 'Recent Trends in Assistive Technology for mobility' (2012) 9 NeuroEngineering Rehabilation 20 <https://doi.org/10.1186/1743-0003-9-20>.

[94] Christoph Schlieder and others, 'Assisted Technology to Support the Mobility of Senior Citizens' (2013) 27 KI – Künstliche Intelligenz 247.

[95] 'App&Town' (*Mass Factory Urban Accessible Mobility SL*, 2019) <www.appandtown.com/index.html> accessed 10 January 2020.

[96] This is the case for HiReach, coordinated by TRT Trasporti e Territorio (Italy); more information and results available at Community Research and Development Information Services, 'Fact Sheet: High Reach Innovative Mobility Solutions to Cope With Transport Poverty' (*CORDIS*, 22 January 2020) <https://cordis.europa.eu/project/rcn/211649/factsheet/en> accessed 10 January 2020.

[97] Groth (n 1).

5 Conclusion

The advancement of smart cities and smart mobility assumes that citizens have financial, intellectual and physical access to technology and transportation infrastructures. This paper has shown nonetheless that smart mobility policies often neglect groups of citizens that are affected by transport poverty for numerous reasons (e.g. low income, disabilities or reduced digital literacy). The ability of smart mobility to address transport poverty depends on what route smart mobility will take in the future and whether public authorities will start perceiving mobility as an essential utility to which all citizens should have equal access. Designing smart mobility that is inclusive, equitable, non-discriminatory and oriented towards the public interest requires taking a number of considerations into account.

First, this paper has contended that inclusive mobility should be regulated within the framework of the right to equal treatment and prohibition of discrimination. Although mobility is a cornerstone of economic freedom, it is not necessary to constitutionalize a separate right to mobility.[98] As this paper has demonstrated, the different causes of transport poverty can in many cases be boiled down to the unequal treatment of citizens. In other words, citizens should not be excluded from access to (or information on access to) transportation on account of their lack of digital literacy, psychological condition, physical place of residence or low income. Inclusive mobility encompasses not only the right to change locations but also the right to do so under fair and reasonable conditions. As this paper has highlighted, access to public transport is essential to the exercise of fundamental rights (e.g. the right to vote) and to the possibility of escaping the circle of poverty.[99] Equal and inclusive mobility nonetheless requires implementation measures and a new vision of smart mobility.

Second, if smart mobility is to be more inclusive, the design of transport systems technology needs to adopt a clear public interest mission. Thus far, many cities have embraced a vision of smart mobility which serves educated and tech-savvy middle-class residents who live fairly close to centers of employment. This narrative of smart cities and smart mobility is influenced by the power of private technology companies and platforms and private business consultancies.[100] The influence of business consultants on cities has been criticized in the literature and the media as it reflects a selective, tech-savvy and elite-based vision of the city, excluding parts of the population that are not digitally literate, mobile and able to afford public or

[98]Barbara Flügge, 'The Mobility Ecosystem' in Barbara Flügge (ed), *Smart Mobility—Connecting Everyone. Trends, Concepts and Best Practices* (Springer Vieweg 2017) 48.

[99]Thomas Coggin and Marius Pieterse, 'A Right to Transport? Moving Towards a Right-Based Approach to Mobility in the City' (2015) 31(2) South African Journal on Human Rights 294, 296.

[100]Luca Belli, Pedro Francisco and Nicolo Zingales, 'Law of the Land or Law of the Platform? Beware of the Privatisation of Regulation and Police' in Luca Belli and Nicolo Zingales (eds), *Platform Regulations. How Platforms Are Regulated and How They Regulate Us* (FGV Direito Rio 2017) 59.

private transit.[101] Moreover, a multimodal and connected vision of smart mobility with real-time information may optimize transportation systems, but it will not always address the real problems experienced by citizens. To illustrate, citizens who have a private vehicle may still experience transport poverty since they are vulnerable to the rising prices of fuel, tolls or parking fees.[102] Smart mobility that is designed to serve the public interest and local public values should thus consider a thorough understanding of transport poverty, including the appreciation of the needs, lifestyles, constraints and behaviors of a representative and diverse sample of the population.[103] Furthermore, the development of public interest-oriented smart mobility requires more attention to the legal shortcomings of smart mobility, particularly the privacy and security framework of transport systems and connected vehicles.[104]

Third, while digital technology has the potential to alleviate poverty and address the accessibility and inclusion problems it causes both in cities and rural areas, the degree to which technology can mitigate problems is largely dependent on the existence of infrastructure and the available budget.[105] Providing free mobility to all residents is not within the budgetary reach of most developing countries that still struggle with other minimum facilities and essential goods such as water. Yet for many developed countries, particularly in Europe, the provision of discounted transport cards or even free public transportation is already a reality. At a time when smart mobility seeks to promote sustainable transport, reduce car dependency and improve the well-being of citizens, it is important to ensure that reasonable pricing policies and options for users with specific needs are also included.[106]

Digital technology can nowadays reduce transport poverty at a lower cost to governments than some decades ago, as platforms can aggregate supply and demand data, develop better pricing systems and ensure that unused transport capacity is reallocated to those who need it. Nevertheless, smart mobility will only fulfill its potential social value when technology and transport policies are designed according to the view that citizens, regardless of their income, physical ability and digital literacy, are entitled to equal access to mobility.

[101] Ash Armin, 'Telescopic Urbanism and the Poor' (2013) 17(4) City 476.

[102] Jeff Allen and Steven Farber, 'Sizing up Transport Poverty: A National Scale Accounting of Low-income Households Suffering from Inaccessibility in Canada, and What to Do about it' (2019) 74 Transport Policy 214, 215.

[103] Lyons (n 39) 12.

[104] See Shazade Jameson, Christine Richter and Linnet Taylor, 'People's strategies for perceived surveillance in Amsterdam Smart City' (2019) 40(1) Urban Geography 1467.

[105] Velaga and others (n 11) 104-5.

[106] See Sefa A Churchill and Russell Smyth, 'Transport Poverty and Subjective Wellbeing' (2019) 124 (C) Transport Research Part A 40.

Local Leadership and Its Limits in the Deployment of Sustainable Mobility Policies

Andrés Boix Palop

Contents

Abstract The indisputable need for new urban mobility policies, which has already been recognised in numerous international, European and national legal instruments, undoubtedly requires a local role in the redefinition of these policies. This action must be carried out in a regulatory context that does not always provide local authorities with all the legal instruments to do so. In this contribution, the primary measures being used to achieve greater sustainability of urban mobility are outlined, as well as a description of the effective room for manoeuvre local authorities

This work has been developed within the research project PID2019-108745GB-I00 "Digital economy regulation: equality guarantees provided by public powers and algorithmical tools" of the National Plan of R+D+i and the research project PROMETEU/2017/064 'The regulation of the digital transformation and the exchange economy' financed by the Generalitat Valenciana. It is also partly a conclusion of the research part of the SHINE Jean Monnet Network (*Sharing Economy and Inequalities across Europe*) where several European universities, coordinated by the University of Valencia, are studying these issues with the support of the European Commission (611585-EPP-1-2019-1-EN-EPPJMO-NETWORK).

A. Boix Palop (✉)
Universitat de València, València, Spain
e-mail: Andres.Boix@uv.es

M. Finck et al. (eds.), *Smart Urban Mobility*, MPI Studies on Intellectual Property and Competition Law 29, https://doi.org/10.1007/978-3-662-61920-9_5

normally have, analysing the current limitations they face for a more ambitious deployment and possible models of alternative regulation.

1 Introduction

The growing worldwide concern regarding the consequences of global warming associated with human activity in the context of a greater environmental awareness, has led to significant regulatory production at the international, European and national levels. The main objectives of these regulations include the reduction of our carbon footprint and consumption of non-renewable energy, control of polluting emissions, waste generation and many other issues. The United Nations Objectives for Sustainable Development, specified in the Agenda 2030[1] that most European public institutions, as well as other countries, have at least formally and symbolically embraced, are a good example of this change in attitude. On a more concrete level, within the context of the United Nations Framework Convention on Climate Change (UNFCCC), a way to establish specific obligations for signatory countries has finally been achieved.[2] This result is a clear reflection of the priority given by the international community to drastically reduce emissions of gases associated not only with public health problems but also considered to be responsibility for human caused climate change.[3]

With regard to the specific actions to be undertaken to achieve these objectives, many of them relate to areas of traditional local responsibility in many legal orders—for instance, in the European and American traditions—which is the case with all

[1]The Sustainable Development Goals on which Agenda 2030 is based are 17 objectives and 169 targets proposed as a continuation of the Millennium Development Goals previously set up by the United Nations. They were approved by the United Nations General Assembly on 25 September 2015, specified in United Nations General Assembly, 'Transforming Our World: the 2030 Agenda for Sustainable Development' (25 September 2015) A/RES/70/1, which came into force on 1 January 2016.

[2]The United Nations Framework Convention on Climate Change (UNFCCC) was adopted in 1992 and has undergone several revisions that have gradually incorporated stricter obligations for the parties through subsequent agreements. The last of these, the Paris Agreement, establishes concrete measures for the reduction of greenhouse gas emissions and has replaced, since 2020, the well-known Kyoto Protocol, which initiated the path of multinational agreements within the framework of the UNFCCC for the establishment of concrete emission reduction objectives that are obligatory for the signatory parties.

[3]A phenomenon for which there is already an overwhelming scientific consensus, both in terms of its underlying causes and its disastrous environmental consequences, with social and economic effects on human populations and most of our activities. On this issue, see the summary of the state of the art in terms of empirical evidence on the subject by Andreu Escrivà, *Encara no és tard* (Bromera 2017).

aspects related to sustainable urban mobility. Thus, to the extent that traffic in our cities generates a significant percentage of the total emissions that negatively affect health in the condensed spaces of metropolitan environments, it is up to local authorities, metropolitan structures and regional governments to bear a significant responsibility in the coming years in relation to policies to combat pollution and climate change through the implementation of new models of mobility. To achieve this set objectives, these policies will have to undergo a radical and structural transformation, based on a global reconsideration of urban planning as well as many economic, social, developmental and environmental issues related to urban mobility. Without losing sight of the costs, it is currently accepted that these new urban mobility policies will necessarily involve a substantial reduction in the use of private vehicles using fossil fuels and, in general, all forms of mobility with high energy consumption. In this regard, at the Habitat III Conference in Quito, the United Nations approved the so-called New Urban Agenda (NUA)[4] that set down global guidelines from which urban policies have to be developed in many areas, including environmental and mobility issues. Among the most important areas of action that were identified is the emphasis on the value of urban mobility and public transportation as a fundamental characteristic and condition of the quality of urban life. This must be guaranteed by public authorities in order to fulfil their social function in all its dimensions, including the social and ecological spheres.[5]

---

[4]United Nations, *New Urban Agenda* (United Nations 2017). On this document and its effects on the 'right to the city', Juli Ponce Solé, 'El Derecho a la Ciudad, Gobernanza y la Nueva Agenda Urbana', in Juli Ponce Solé, Wellington Migliari and Oscar Capdeferro (eds), *El Derecho, la Ciudad y la Vivienda en la Nueva Concepción del Desarrollo Urbano* (Atelier 2019) 115-151.

[5]The underlying notion of the document, which will be further developed in the specific proclamations of the UN (n 4) paras 113-117 is quite clear: mobility and transportation are as essential today for any human settlement to enable its inhabitants to carry out their activities as they have been historically—and still are—such as the essential resources of guaranteeing universal access to drinking water, the existence of an adequate sanitation network, ensuring food security, providing basic education or monitoring air quality, among others. Therefore, they must be guaranteed by the authorities, at least, with the same standards and degree of legal exigency with which we have historically proclaimed and guaranteed those other rights. It is also important to note that in the document, and immediately following this statement, the importance of transport and mobility is explicitly linked to social inclusion considerations. Thus, s 13.f of the NUA establishes that public authorities must carry out mobility planning that also takes into account considerations of age and gender, thus guaranteeing the availability of transportation systems capable of effectively linking all types of people, places, goods, services and economic opportunities and offering the possibility of carrying out a normal social life, as well as the proper deployment of economic activities to all citizens. Thus, the idea that the promotion of equitable and affordable access to sustainable transport services should ensure the specific needs associated with disadvantaged groups (women, children and youth, older persons and persons with disabilities, migrants, indigenous peoples and local communities, as well as any other group in a situation of vulnerability, ibid. para 34; these vulnerable groups are also taken into account in relation to security in ibid. para 113) is explicitly strengthened and reinforced (e.g. for persons with disabilities, ibid. para 36); for informal and poor settlements (see ibid. para 54). Similarly, the idea of social cohesion and the role that modern and accessible mobility and modern means of transport can play in greater productivity, social,

Given that cities and metropolitan areas are undeniably called upon to play a leading role in these changes,[6] it is interesting to list the traditional instruments of action that we have used in the past to guarantee the deployment of urban policies to improve sustainable mobility; to this end we will look at essentially three issues: (1) how the traditional tools for local action on mobility and urban space have been used until now to achieve improvements in environmental quality; (2) what new regulatory instruments are derived from the new environmental paradigm and how are they being used in different countries; and finally (3), to what extent might local authorities encounter possible legal limitations in the development of some of these policies. It has to be noted that local governments must act within State or regional legal frameworks on many issues, especially when the legality principle is at stake. Therefore, in some cases, further ambitious transformations might sometimes require a prior modification of those legal frameworks or at least some help from other public bodies. In addition, it is also interesting to consider how new technological possibilities offered by new actors within the digital economy are already affecting urban mobility markets. The implications of these possibilities for mobility can hardly be overestimated and are already having an effect that will become even greater in the foreseeable future. Local authorities will have to deal with these new realities when reframing new regulatory approaches.[7]

2 A More Environmental Approach to Urban Mobility Regulation Based on Traditional Intervention Titles

Up to now, municipalities have had a diversity of typically local titles of intervention, all of them with a long tradition in the continental European and American legal systems, that allow cities to organise urban mobility. They can establish regulations

---

economic and territorial cohesion, aligned with security and environmental sustainability (ibid. para 50), is also linked to these equity considerations that bind all public authorities.

[6]Diana Reckien and others, 'How are Cities Planning to Respond to Climate Change? Assessment of Local Climate Plans From 885 Cities in the EU-28' (2018) 191 Journal of Cleaner Production 207.

[7]The phenomenon of the collaborative economy has already been studied in great depth. A selection of recent works that give an idea of the implications of this includes Ming Hu (ed), *Sharing Economy. Making Supply Meet Demand* (Springer 2019) for the study of the economic rationale behind the model and its main effects in terms of efficiency and externalities; Nestor M Davidson, Michèle Finck and John J Infranca (eds), *The Cambridge Handbook of the Sharing Economy* (Cambridge University Press 2018) for the study of the impact of the collaborative economy on various markets and the legal framework of the phenomenon in its various manifestations and repercussions; and Duncan McLaren and Julian Agyeman, *Sharing Cities. A Case for Truly Smart and Sustainable Cities* (MIT Press 2015) for the more concrete effects of the sharing economy on cities, with interesting case studies. Specifically, in relation to the effects of the sharing economy on urban mobility, Andrés Boix Palop, Ana María De la Encarnación and Gabriel Doménech Pascual (eds), *La Regulación del Transporte Colaborativo* (Aranzadi - Thomson Reuters 2017).

concerning traffic, parking and mobility in order to organise the uses of public space and road infrastructure, including in some cases the powers to manage urban transportation services. This makes them protagonists alongside regional governments in providing public mass transportation services. Additionally, cities are also partially responsible for local taxes policies which, within the margins imposed by State and regional regulations, can also be used to achieve environmental objectives. Although all these powers must be exercised within the European and national regulatory framework that may predetermine possible forms of organisation for the provision of local public transportation services to general traffic regulations[8] or the general structure of legal titles that allow certain uses of the public space, it should also be noted that the room for manoeuvre of local authorities in this realm is of real importance. Traditionally, urban mobility policies have resulted from these policies and titles of intervention, which are typically local in nature, thus allowing different approaches depending on the political priorities or specific characteristics of each city.

On the other hand, some legal instruments have traditionally been beyond the reach of local governments. For instance, the establishment of pollution and environmental quality thresholds in cities is effectively unavailable to local authorities. These thresholds currently depend on State regulations within the European Union and on the European standards that frame them. Specifically, the Air Quality Directive (Directive 2008/50/EC of 21 May 2008 on ambient air quality and cleaner air for Europe and its subsequent amendments)[9] currently establishes these thresholds, which in principle must be complied with by the Member States. The Directive also provides for a system of sanctions in the event of non-compliance. This in turn leads to the existence of State legislation—and even incipient regional legislation—that imposes legal limits beyond which it is possible to establish restrictions that may affect freedom of movement with increasing intensity of application.[10] However, interesting developments in recent years have shown how this supranational legislation has enabled local authorities to gain leverage to realign their urban mobility policies in stricter ways, in some cases with the help of judicial powers.

[8]Andrés Boix Palop and Reyes Marzal Raga (eds), *Ciudad y movilidad. La regulación de la movilidad urbana sostenible* (PUV 2014).

[9]Parliament and Council Directive (EC) of 21 May 2008 on ambient air quality and cleaner air for Europe [2008] OJ L 152, 1 (Air Quality Directive).

[10]Antonio J Sánchez Sáez, *Las restricciones de tráfico en las ciudades por motivos ambientales y su afección a la libertad de circulación* (Comares 2019) 37-59.

2.1 A Renewed Judicial Activism That Imposes Action at the Local Level

An initial novelty with regard to the use of these traditional legal titles of intervention for the achievement of environmental objectives and an improvement in the sustainability of urban mobility relates precisely to the recent understanding that, through the direct application of the thresholds laid down in the Air Quality Directive—or of the national rules for transposing it as adopted by different Member States—decisions by local councils establishing restrictions on the circulation of vehicles which go beyond the mere regulation of traffic in cities may be deemed acceptable. Certain additional restrictions were traditionally considered to be problematic, especially if they entail effective limitations on the use of goods—in this case, of certain types of vehicles—which in principle are consumer goods that are bought and sold with total freedom within the margins set by national and international technical standards. As long as free movement of goods, competition or market unity may be affected, the issue can be considered to be beyond local powers. Any intervention or regulation that may affect or distort them is potentially questionable; the more intense the intended restriction, the more problematic from a jurisdiction perspective. However, growing environmental awareness and the existence of the European Directive on air quality, whose thresholds are usually exceeded in many European cities, may have created a new legal environment in which urban powers are considered to be broader than in the past. Increased powers allow cities in some cases to circumvent certain regulations aimed at regulating markets and the tradability of goods.

For instance, in some recent cases, local governments across Europe have been allowed to establish restrictions that may affect certain types of vehicles—logically affecting more intensely those that pollute the most, in order to be aligned with any basic proportionality analysis[11]—as long as these either do not affect the entire metropolitan or regional area or are only temporary measures, or respond to a need sufficiently covered by the already mentioned proportionality criteria. Of great relevance in this matter is the decision of the Court of Justice of the European Union (CJEU) in the case *Ville de Paris & Ville de Bruxelles & Madrid*.[12] Even

---

[11]In particular, the European Commission in Parliament and Council Regulation (EU) 2016/646 of 20 April 2016 amending Regulation (EC) No 692/2008 as regards emissions from light passenger and commercial vehicles (Euro 6) [2016] *OJ L 109/1* defined emission limits for nitrogen oxides not to be exceeded during new tests under real driving conditions, which are allegedly much more demanding than the previous ones. But these limits were in turn less demanding than more advanced environmental standards such as the 2007 Euro 6 vehicle emissions standard. It was therefore questionable whether local authorities should uncritically accept that they could not set limits under the more demanding standard.

[12]The ECJ, in its judgment of 13 December 2018, in joined cases: Case T-339/16 *Commune de Paris v Commission* EU:T:2018:927, Case T-352/16 *Commune de Bruxelles v Commission* EU:T:2018:927 and Case T-391/16 *Commune de Madrid v Commission* EU:T:2018:927 agrees with these municipalities on the understanding that the Commission could not change the emission thresholds already laid down in the Euro 5 and Euro 6 standards with the practical effect of

though it was ultimately decided on the grounds of jurisdiction, the internal logic of the decision allows us to understand how important the proportionality analysis is regarding these issues. As long as the restriction may be considered proportional and necessary to cope with existing and proven pollution issues, European standards can be overcome, even against objections made by the European Commission itself because those cities' regulations were affecting tradability and the use of vehicles that the European technical standards considered within the accepted emission standards. In accepting the possibility that local authorities might have a right to establish regulations that may not precisely fit with the existing rules defined by broader levels of government concerning emissions, the CJEU is clearly enlarging the capacity of local governments to define an autonomous policy on urban mobility, to be decided by local authorities, even in cases of possible contradiction with competition and market provisions. It is then clear from this decision that there is a direct expansion of local regulatory capacity that goes beyond the mere regulation of road traffic in cities. Even though the legal tool being used is the regulation of urban transit, its aim is not only to establish more orderly or fluid traffic conditions, but also to pursue another public interest: the reduction of pollution and emissions, which in a classic understanding would have depended on the title of competence in the field of emissions—as the Commission's approach ultimately intended. In the same vein, the Belgian Constitutional Court has also recently expressly excluded that this type of local regulation aimed at reducing traffic and pollution may collide with the free movement of goods, therefore considering it was perfectly compatible with European and constitutional free market provisions.[13]

This same trend, and the subsequent enlargement of local authorities' capacity to design more ambitious and environmentally conscious urban mobility policies, is already established in a number of European countries. In fact, thanks to a number of concerned citizens and judicial activism, at least in some countries of the European Union, these kinds of policies set up by local authorities can be now considered not only as a legal possibility within the scope of their powers, but even as currently binding legal obligations to act. Some recent decisions taken by different institutions reinforce this idea. For instance, the European Commission has recently initiated infringement proceedings against several Member States for failing to adopt public policies at all levels, including regional and local, to ensure compliance with the provisions of the Air Quality Directive.[14] Of course, it can be argued whether local

increasing the permitted margins and that the municipalities of the cities concerned were therefore not obliged to comply with the new standard set by the Commission in their traffic regulations and the restrictions they had introduced for the circulation of certain types of vehicles. Environmental, competence and legal security considerations are intermingled in an analysis that ends up notably expanding the capacity of municipalities to establish effective restrictions on the use of certain types of vehicles.

[13]Thus the Low-Emission Zone in Brussels was recently endorsed by the Belgian Constitutional Court in its decision of 28 February 2019 (*Arrêt 37/2019 of the Cour constitutionnelle de Belgique*).

[14]The European Commission, on the basis of the aforementioned Air Quality Directive (n 9) and its specific thresholds and limits (which, although they have varied and adapted, have traditionally

governments are among the public bodies directly obliged to take further steps and the necessary regulatory decisions to comply with European standards, but at least in one country the answer to this question has been already given.

A series of judgments have forced several cities in Germany to adopt measures concerning the high level of pollution produced by diesel vehicles, forcing them to establish driving bans for these vehicles in various forms, ranging from a total ban throughout the city centre to partial bans or more limited prohibitions that may only affect older models. On the basis of this disorganised series of judicial decisions,[15] which are the result of complaints by residents' groups and environmental organisations concerned about air quality at the local level, the German Federal Administrative Court ended up validating these jurisdictionally imposed restrictions in its judgment of 27 February 2017.[16] The German Federal Government was thus obliged to design a policy of common action on minimums which has tried to compromise while also validating the possibility—and sometimes the requirement—of establishing this type of restriction at the local level.[17] An absolute *Dieselverbot* within significant parts of cities could therefore also affect vehicles that in theory are still within current international trade agreements, as well as EU and national regulatory thresholds. In practice, their use as an urban transport alternative has been greatly limited, at least in the urban centres affected by the ban, due to the fact

---

been established in Annexes I to XI), has taken action against several Member States in recent years on these issues (Germany, France, Hungary, Italy, the United Kingdom and Romania) on the grounds that their national, regional and local regulations were not achieving a situation in accordance with the established limits. More recently, action has also been taken against Spain following recent changes and amendments made to previous plans to reduce air pollution in cities such as Madrid. See, in this regard, Jaime Doreste 'The European Commission has run out of patience with Spain' *El País* (25 July 2019), <http://agendapublica.elpais.com/a-la-comision-europea-se-le-ha-acabado-la-paciencia-con-espana/> accessed 19 December 2019.

[15] A chronological list of the various local, state and federal court decisions and regulations can be found at Bundesministerium für Umwelt, Naturschutz und nukleare Sicherheit, 'Chronologie zu Diesel und Luftreinhaltung' (*BMU*, 15 March 2018) <www.bmu.de/themen/luft-laerm-verkehr/luftreinhaltung/diesel-und-luftreinhaltung> accessed 15 January 2019.

[16] Following a series of decisions at the local or regional level in *Länder* such as North Rhine-Westphalia or Baden-Württemberg, the possibility of introducing such total bans on the use of such vehicles in certain urban areas has been confirmed by the Federal Administrative Court (*Bundesverwaltungsgericht*, judgment of 27 February 2018, 7 C 26.16 and 7 C 30.17).

[17] German Federal Government, faced with the possibility of diesel bans in more than 50 German cities (Berlin, Köln and Munich among them) as a result of those judicial decisions, proposed an amendment to the German federal emissions law in to limit local government capacity to impose such prohibitions when emissions limits were only slightly exceeded, which was adopted by the German parliament. Under the amended legislation, which was passed by the German parliament this spring, driving bans would only be considered in cities where nitrogen oxide levels were exceeded by 50 µg/m3 or more. But shortly after, the Mannheim Administrative Court reduced this margin to only 25 µg/m3. This particular 'dialogue' between Courts and government is expected to be continued and reinforces the idea that nowadays the rules in the matter established by the European Union or national regulators may not be set down on stone and it is possible to challenge them before the courts.

that their environmental effects, considered on a local scale, outweigh those considerations.[18]

Furthermore, international agreements and empirical considerations regarding climate change and pollution are increasingly analysed in order to extract from them reasons to force public bodies to act, and thereby passing new regulations to strike a fairer balance that may allow stricter management even in contradiction with some previous considerations and granting more power to authorities willing to comply with international treaties and environmental protection. A good example of this trend is the much-commented decision of the Supreme Court of the Netherlands of 20 December 2019, which obliged the government to take all necessary measures to reduce global emissions by an exact percentage—25%—and within a precise period of time—the end of 2020. To this end, the Court mentioned both international treaties and European law, which it considers would be directly binding on the competent public authorities.[19]

It can therefore be said that this line of legal argument is already consolidated. It would not be surprising to see other examples of the practical consequences shortly, thus strengthening not only the capacity of local authorities to act in this direction but even in some cases the obligation for them to do so.[20] Moreover, these precedents are characterised by neighbourhood activism and citizen response to non-compliance, which is also worthy of note. Above all, however, they display a legal understanding that gives local authorities broad powers to establish restrictions to achieve better air quality and more sustainable mobility that should be exploited, stimulating ambitious and innovative policies that, as they are tested and prove to be effective, should be extended.

---

[18]Josef Cyrys, Jianwei Gu and Jens Soentgen, 'Analyse der Wirksamkeit von Umweltzonen in drei deutschen Städten: Berlin, München und Augsburg' (Bundesministeriums für Umwelt 2017) <www.umweltbundesamt.de/sites/default/files/medien/1410/publikationen/2017-06-01_texte_46-2017_umweltzonenwirksamkeit.pdf> accessed 15 January 2020.

[19]Decision NL:HR:2019:2006 of the Dutch Supreme Court (ECLI:NL:HR:2019:2006) is interesting because it not only questions the decision of the Dutch government but also that of the European Union, which had set a reduction target for the Netherlands of 20% for emissions by 2020 (compared to 1990). After a series of appeals by an environmental association Urgenda in The Hague and a first ruling in its favour in 2015, confirmed on appeal, the Supreme Court finally agreed with these previous rulings and established a jurisdictional obligation to further reduce emissions (up to 25% with the same benchmark). It does so directly on the basis of international instruments and the obligations that the court considers to be directly derived for the Dutch State in the area of health protection and the right to a clean environment for citizens from the European Convention for the Protection of Human Rights and Fundamental Freedoms (ECHR). The alleged discretion of the various executives who had determined other thresholds is reviewed and controlled by the court, which bases its decision on various scientific studies on the insufficiency of current efforts to sufficiently reduce emissions.

[20]It should be noted that recently a Bavarian court asked ECJ about the possibility of taking measures against public officials in case of non-compliance with environmental obligations, which is consider to be a legitimate alternative in case there are no alternative possible solutions in national law for administrative authorities to act, see Case C-752/18 *Deutsche Umwelhilfe v Freistaat Bayern* EU:C:2019:1114.

2.2 Environmental Taxation and Urban Charges

A second title of local intervention that allows the development of urban public policies aimed at improving sustainable urban mobility that is currently under steady development involves fiscal incentives for green mobility and the possibility of establishing tax models that integrate environmental considerations into their structure.[21] According to this approach, Pigou's theories come into play concerning the possibility of solving many of the problems caused by certain negative externalities using taxes or equivalent instruments.[22] Due to the importance of negative externalities in environmental matters, this instrument is particularly usefulness in this field. Thus, it is not surprising that its use has become widespread in recent decades.[23] In addition to strictly legal considerations, which have alleviated part of the traditional [illegible] to Pigouvian taxes linked to concerns related to strict compliance with the principle of economic capacity, the reasons for this development are particularly related to the acknowledged effectiveness of Pigouvian taxes. Furthermore, and of particular interest to this analysis, is the fact that these policies are often left to local authorities, allowing them more room for manoeuvre than they would otherwise have in order to design environmentally oriented policies. This is especially true when we refer to public fees that every local council can set for the enjoyment of certain services—for example, with respect to the use of public space, city streets and parking lots.[24] Such fees can be set more easily than taxes related to the economic capacity principle, for which the legality principle—statutory reserve—is usually required in most countries. Therefore, a previous legal provision passed by the State or a regional power establishing the margins and procedures with which the tax ordinances approved by local councils have to comply is needed in these cases. Also, tax exemptions or the implementation of some environmental incentives may also depend on State or regional regulations. However, legal distinctions are not so important from an economic perspective, because taxes or public fees behave in the

[21]Iñaki Bilbao Estrada, 'Transporte Colaborativo, Medioambiente y Beneficios Fiscales: Especial Referencia al Ordenamiento Jurídico Español', in Andrés Boix Palop, Ana De la Encarnación and Gabriel Doménech Pascual (eds), La *Regulación del Transporte Colaborativo* (Thomson Reuters Aranzadi 2017) 297-299.

[22]Christopher R Knittel and Ryan Sandler, 'The Welfare Impact of Indirect Pigouvian Taxation: Evidence from Transportation' (2013) National Bureau of Economic Research Working Paper Series 18849, 20-23; Jonathan S Masur and Eric A Posner, 'Towards a Pigouvian State' (2015) 164 University of Pennsylvania Law Review 93.

[23]Roxana J Javid, Ali Nejat and Katharine Hayhoe, 'Selection of CO2 Mitigation Strategies for Road Transportation in the United States Using Multi-criteria Approach' (2014) 38 Renewable and Sustainable Energy Reviews 960.

[24]Inge Mayeres and Stef Proost, 'Congested Roads and General Equilibrium Pigouvian Tax Solutions', in Jeroen CJM van den Bergh, Peter Nijkamp and Piet Rietveld (eds) *Recent Advances in Spatial Equilibrium Modelling* (Springer 1996) 221-242; see also Danielle Spiegel-Feld, 'Reducing the Cost of Free Parking: How Some American Cities are Decreasing Parking Subsidies to Increase Sustainable Mobility' in Antonio Fortes Martín (ed) *Movilidad Urbana Sostenible y Acción Administrativa* (Thomson Reuters Aranzadi 2019) 293-302.

exact same way, following Pigouvian logic. For local bodies, this is equally relevant to have both at their disposal—but having more discretion to balance the interests in conflict and to decide how to use this tool to achieve policy objectives when using public fees regulatory power instead of local taxation powers if the room for manoeuvre contemplated by the State in the latter case is not wide enough. As a matter of fact, even if coordination among policies is required, this is a field of increasing activity for municipalities which seek to create the conditions for better urban mobility. It is therefore an interesting form of leverage from the local sphere partially at the disposal of municipalities.

One particularly advanced manifestation of this model, already implemented on a large scale in several European cities (London, Milan, Stockholm)—and currently being tested on different scales and a variety of phases of implementation in many other cities around the world[25]—is that of urban charges. The first and most important experience to date, and therefore the most well known, is the London city centre congestion charge,[26] which has been in force for almost two decades. It is interesting to note some of the legal elements that make this model difficult to implement in many countries. In order to respect the legality principle, it was necessary to have a previous law to establish and manage the model in the city of London, as would be the case in many other European countries. This also converges with very interesting lessons regarding its results and possibilities as an example of how ambitious local policies in the area of urban mobility can be game-changing and how important local leadership is in order to achieve effective policies in this field.

We know from the lessons learned from the London experience, in contrast to the initial intentions of the model, which aimed not only to limit traffic in central London but also sought to raise funds to be used for improving public transportation, that the former objective was achieved to a much greater extent than the latter. As a matter of fact, the introduction of the tax has meant that traffic in the city centre has fallen much more than initially expected and is now mainly carried by vehicles authorised to enter the restricted zone without paying the congestion charge. However, and precisely for that reason, the funds collected from the toll have been lower than estimated.[27] In short, it seems that these types of urban charges are particularly useful to reduce traffic in the city centres rather than to achieve a substantial increase

---

[25]Cities such as Stockholm, Milan, Hong Kong and Singapore, as well as New York, San Francisco and especially Beijing, in addition to London, have had experiences in this regard. For more information, see Andrés Boix Palop, 'The Challenges of Urban Mobility Regulation and the New Urban Agenda' in Nestor M. Davidson and Greta Taawari (eds), Law and the New Urban Agenda (Routledge 2020) (forthcoming) previous draft available at <https://papers.ssrn.com/sol3/papers.cfm?abstract_id=3414970> accessed 10 January 2020.

[26]Introduced definitively in 2003, after the approval of the Greater London Authority Act 1999 and the Greater London Congestion Charging Order of 2001, it is the best known and most studied experience. On its effects, see Stephen Glaister and Daniel Graham, *Pricing Our Roads: Vision and Reality* (Institute of Economic Affairs 2005).

[27]Jun Yang, Avralt-Od Purevjav and Shanjun Li, 'The Marginal Cost of Traffic Congestion and Road Pricing: Evidence from a Natural Experiment in Beijing' (2020) 12(1) American Economic Journal: Economic Policy 418 <https://doi.org/10.1257/pol.20170195> accessed 12 January 2020.

in funds for public transportation. At the end, the London congestion charge has been a great success in order to reduce traffic, and the successive extensions of the perimeter in London or the extension of the model to other cities demonstrate it.

This case is an excellent example of a new urban mobility policy experimented in one city, which succeed for a number of reasons, but also due to the fact that London's local government has important regulatory and executive powers as well as granted autonomy. The London model shows which results are to be expected from similar policies and that it could be imitated in some cases, but with some caveats, especially regarding the necessity of having a previous legal framework granting local authorities the powers to act and the fact that is not the best tool to raise money for local public transportation systems. In fact, successful mass transportation systems tend to rely heavily on other sources of income. Essentially there is a combination of fees—although only certain countries such as Luxembourg and some cities are successfully experimenting with tariff elimination to encourage their use and combat climate change[28]—and, increasingly, direct public budget provision—which is more equal in terms of social justice and therefore indirectly encouraged by instruments such as the NUA.

2.3 *Other Traditional Instruments*

Both the provision of public transportation services and the planning and distribution of urban space to prioritise the various modes of mobility have historically been very relevant to the design of urban policies in the field of mobility. In relation to both vectors, the current guidelines for the fight against pollution and climate change must lead us to a more decisive commitment to public transportation—initiatives such as its free provision are very consistent with this idea—and to a distribution of public space that is coherent with this idea. Both guidelines are fully compatible with the principles established by the NUA and its commitment to a more socially inclusive mobility model that promotes public transport, on foot or by human-powered vehicles rather than fuel-driven private vehicles. But this evolution is combined and must necessarily take into account the disruption caused by the emergence of new forms of mobility and modern transport technologies.

---

[28] From 1 March 2020, all public transport in Luxembourg City will be free of charge. See the explanation on the official website of Luxembourg City: Ville de Luxembourg, 'Introduction of free public transport in Luxembourg, from 1 March 2020' (28 February 2019) <https://www.vdl.lu/en/news/introduction-free-public-transport-luxembourg-1-march-2020> accessed 15 January 2020.

3 Local Leadership in the Design of a Global Sustainable Urban Mobility Strategy That Integrates New Forms of Mobility

The so-called 'collaborative economy' and, in particular, the technological advances that have led to the emergence in practically all markets of highly efficient digital platforms and brokerage services—bringing together supply and demand that otherwise would have never met—have also had an impact on mobility markets.[29]

If we take into account that, for a variety of reasons and in more or less restrictive variants, traditional regulation throughout Europe reserved urban transportation to public authorities, preventing or significantly restricting the private provision of this type of service under a free market regime, it is easy to understand the significant legal disruption caused by the appearance of business models such as Uber and the like—initially outside Europe but shortly thereafter arriving to European countries.[30] A forward-looking urban strategy for a city-led regulation of sustainable urban mobility must also enable cities to take decisions in these areas. Without having some capacity to integrate a comprehensive regulation regarding these issues into their global mobility strategy, urban policies would be hardly coherent. To do this, local governments have to act on two different levels: (1) they must act within the legal framework—they have no choice but to comply regarding public service and competition in the local mobility market; and (2) they must integrate their regulation and decisions regarding so-called 'sharing mobility' into a comprehensive design that is consistent with other considerations. As we will explain, with respect of this last element, considerations regarding the use of public space and the impact on public transportation systems are of paramount importance.

3.1 *Public Regulation and Urban Mobility Markets*

Even if the current EU legal framework still allows regulatory restrictions and public money to be spent in transportation public services,[31] the traditionally restricted public regulation of the urban mobility market linked to the idea of public service—no matter how hard we try to maintain it and even tighten it as has been the recent

[29]See note 7.

[30]See the very different experiences and reactions in various European countries in Rozen Noguellou and David Renders, *Uber & Taxis. Comparative Law Studies* (Bruylant 2018).

[31]Stéphane Bracq, 'Droit communautaire materiel et qualification juridique: le financement des obligations de service public au coeur de la tourmente (à propos de la décision: CJCE 24 juill. 2003, Altmark Trans GmbH, aff. C-280/00)' (2004) 40(1) *Révue trimestrielle de Droit Européen* 33.

case of Spain[32]—does not make much sense anymore in urban private transportation services in dense enough cities. None of the justifications derived from the old French *lois du service public*[33] which, in one way or another, were at the root of these limitations in countries that established taxis as a public service or as a highly regulated market with administratively fixed prices and all sorts of entry barriers to the market makes much sense today. The reason lies not only in the fact that European law is clearly evolving in that direction, even though the European Services Directive still accepts an exemption regarding these markets,[34] but also because of the current technological and economic environment, which makes such restrictions difficult to justify, even accepting the traditional legal reasoning of *service public*, where considerations regarding the continuity of the service, its quality and equality issues were accepted as possible reasons for allowing a public regulation limiting competition

The combined forces of the multiplying and powerful logic of the Services Directive and technological drive may end soon with this exception, reducing the room of manoeuvre of EU Member States to avoid competition. There are good reasons to assume that this will happen in the foreseeable future. On the one hand, the continuity of the service and a sufficient supply of it does not seem to be in question in urban mobility markets, at least according to empirical experience, when the sector has been liberalised or new providers have been left to act. On the other hand, digital intermediation, with its effectiveness in matching supply and demand, can be argued to have fulfilled the guarantee function even better on this point than any traditional regulation.[35] The adaptability of the service to new needs, for example, new and stricter environmental provisions, is easily achieved by means of public regulation, either coercive—obliging vehicles providing this service to comply with strict requirements, for example, in terms of emissions—or by using all kinds of incentives, without the further necessity of restricting competition to achieve those goals. Lastly, with regard to the concern for equality and protection of consumers and users, the traditional solution based on establishing regulated public fees for the service in order to prevent abuses seems utterly unnecessary today. At least, under normal conditions and in order to prevent one-off abuses, it would be much less invasive and more consistent with a liberal logic to simply set, where deemed appropriate, a price cap to avoid possible abuses. Additionally, some regulation in order to protect users, or even providers of those services, from new sorts of discrimination, should be enacted.

---

[32]Gabriel Doménech Pascual and Alba Soriano-Arnanz, 'Taxi Regulation in Spain under the Pressure of the Sharing Economy', in Rozen Noguellou and David Renders (eds), *Uber & Taxis: Comparative Law Studies* (Bruylant 2018) 357-376.

[33]Jacques Chevalier, *Le service public* (PUF 1997) 7-15 and 67-69.

[34]Parliament and Council Directive 2006/123/EC of 12 December 2006 on services in the internal market [2006] *OJ L 376/36 (Services Directive), art 2(d) still explicitly excludes transportation from the scope of the Services Directive.*

[35]Katrina M Wyman, 'Taxi regulation in the age of Uber' (2017) 20 Legislation and Public Policy 9.

To sum up, it does not seem that the rules with which certain local or regional governments have initially reacted to the disruptive emergence of new and highly efficient providers by restricting the possibilities of providing these services under a market regime are defensible any longer from a perspective based on the general interest and on parameters consistent with market rules within the European Union. Nor are these rules regulations that can overcome a sufficiently demanding filter if we contrast them with environmental requirements, since they do not generate appreciable benefits in this regard compared to the great advantage of the reduction of emissions that could be achieved with an alternative regulation that takes advantage of their potential instead of establishing restrictions.[36]

In fact, the only purpose envisaged in these rules that makes sense—whether or not this is ultimately a legitimate objective—is the mere protection of the incumbents:[37] something which is clearly not enough to justify them because of the heavy limitations on other freedoms and how costly and burdensome those measures are to the public interest.[38] That is why, little by little, evolution, not only in other continents but also in continental Europe, has been consistently moving towards a liberalisation of those markets or, at least, to alleviate some of the restrictions—even though with some exceptions.[39] This is also why local protagonism in the regulation of those market services is going to be more important, once free from some regulatory limitations that are still of importance in some countries. In doing so, and using this new protagonism to strike a new and fairer balance for consumers and providers of services and public goods, local powers should have to take into account new considerations that perhaps were not so important in the past but that are today essential issues that go well beyond economic efficiency of market regulation of private urban transportation markets. Alongside economic efficiency in service provision, and even beyond the aforementioned potential positive environmental benefits, other social and planning considerations may emerge. These considerations are also closely linked to the local situation, which is why regulatory decisions adopted at a local level are particularly justified in this case.

---

[36]Gabriel Doménech Pascual, 'La regulación de la economía colaborativa. El caso Uber contra el taxi' (2015) 175/176 CEF Legal 89; Katrina M. Wyman, 'The novelty of TNC Regulation', in Nestor M. Davidson, Michèle Finck and John J. Infranca (eds), *The Cambridge Handbook of the Sharing Economy* (Cambridge University Press 2018) 134-137.

[37]Christopher Koopman, Matthew Mitchell and Adam Thierer, 'The Sharing Economy and Consumer Protection Regulation: The case for Policy Change' (2015) 8(2) Journal of Business, Entrepreneurship and the Law 530-545.

[38]Incumbent issues should be compensated only in exceptional cases, but in this cases those issues would be better solved with other types of strategies: transitional measures, public subsidies or cross-subsidies to compensate for the costs of transition to competition, as have been accepted in other markets and which, in general, are the only restrictions which pass the analytical filters, see Eran Kaplinski, 'Should Licence Plate Owners Be Compensated when Uber Comes to Town?' in Derek McKee, Finn Makela and Teresa Scassa, *Law and the 'Sharing Economy': Regulating Online Market Platforms* (University of Ottawa Press 2018) 311-317.

[39]Dirk Uwer and Alla Drössler, 'Germany' in Rozen Noguellou and David Renders (eds), *Uber & Taxis, Comparative Law Studies* (Bruylant 2018) 231-250.

3.2 *Congestion, Public Transportation, Digital Platforms and the Design of New Urban Mobility Policies*

As mentioned above, it is not only the economic efficiency of the local transportation market, as well as its intersection with environmental policies aimed at reducing emissions, that must be taken into account. At least two other considerations closely linked to the local situation must also be integrated into the design of any sustainable urban mobility policy which properly integrates and takes advantage of these new technological possibilities: (1) the effects that some possible regulations may have on the congestion of certain urban spaces—which is a dimension that, although closely linked to pollution, goes beyond it and which has more to do with the fair distribution of urban space and the uses to which we believe it should be [illegible] and rather than with questions of pollution in the strict sense, and (2) the possible effect on public transportation systems, which are at risk of being cannibalised if they lose enough users who may turn to other alternatives, which are now cheaper and more efficient than in the past, until reaching the point where they risk falling below the critical mass required for full or partial viability of the system.

Thus, while it is difficult at present to understand the justification for restrictions on the provision of certain types of local transportation based on market regulation considerations—for example, those that may be offered by digital intermediary platforms—congestion or public transportation protection considerations might provide a sufficient legal basis for some limitations. The higher efficiency of digital intermediary platforms can lead to a drop in prices that makes the offer of transportation services made by private vehicles increasingly attractive. This can lead to their use being increased at such a pace that it will provoke an undesirable saturation of the public space in cities. It is worth remembering here that the public space is scarce, and the fact that its occupation with private vehicles may displace or threaten other mobility models—e.g. cyclists, pedestrians or even public transportation—which are normally considered to be a priority for any urban mobility model.[40] In such a case, quantitative restrictions by local public authorities are completely justified, as those already established on an experimental basis in cities such as New York.[41] The same considerations may also be valid for business models based on the supply of mobility services that, even if they are not as objectionable from an

---

[40]On congestion problems in San Francisco or New York, respectively, and their effects on urban mobility policies and regulatory options for digitally mediated transport, Gregory D Erhardt and others, 'Do transportation network companies decrease or increase congestion' (2019) 5(5) Science Advances <https://advances.sciencemag.org/content/5/5/eaau2670.full> accessed 21 December 2019; and Natasha Bhatia, 'The Second Avenue Subway's Effect on Ride-Hail, Rideshare, and Taxi Usage in New York City' (2019) <https://ssrn.com/abstract=3258592 or https://doi.org/10.2139/ssrn.3258592> accessed 21 December 2019.

[41]In June 2019, New York City announced the extension of the quantitative limitation and the decision to make these quotas permanent. See the city's own statement on this subject: Official Website of the City of New York, 'Mayor de Blasio Announces Extending FHV Caps to Protect Hardworking Drivers, Increase Their Pay & Reduce Cruising by Empty Cars in Manhattan'

environmental perspective as fossil fuel-driven vehicles,[42] renting electric cars, electric motorcycles, e-scooters or bicycles may still create similar saturation problems. In practice, local authorities will have to address those issues to the benefit, for instance, of pedestrians or mobility alternatives which are not dependant on electricity.[43] Obviously, this hypothetical saturation could be fought with various strategies—from bans to the regulation of public spaces and also using taxes or public fees—and each city should assess the most appropriate path, if possible, for its own situation and particular needs and experiment with its consequences. These range from setting limits on the number of authorisations to establishing tax measures or public fees or prices for the occupation of the public space that will make the provision of these service more expensive and, therefore, less competitive by making them compensate for the externality derived from the congestion that could occur in the absence of these measures. This is a very interesting example of how local experimentalism and a non-negligible amount of administrative and political discretion have a large role to play in the future of the regulation and the establishment of different models of urban mobility policies. It also explains why local leadership is so important in this field.[44]

In a very similar sense, we already have some empirical studies showing that the high efficiency of the provision of some digitally brokered mobility services can drain users of public transportation systems, with the risk of them becoming less competitive than those other forms of private mobility[45]—a problem that is bound to increase as they become even cheaper as technology evolves. If this loss of users calls into question the viability of public transportation in certain areas, since public

(12 June 2019) <www1.nyc.gov/office-of-the-mayor/news/301-19/mayor-de-blasio-extending-fhv-caps-protect-hardworking-drivers-increase-their-pay-#/0> accessed 9 January 2020.

[42]Troy R Hawkins and others, 'Comparative Environmental life cycle assessment of conventional and electric vehicles' (2012) 17(1) Journal of Industrial Ecology 53.

[43]Rafael Leal-Arcas, 'Electric Vehicles, Sustainability and Decarbonization', in Antonio Fortes Martín (ed) *Movilidad urbana sostenible y acción administrativa* (Thomson Reuters Aranzadi 2019) 257-279.

[44]For instance, regarding how sharing and urban mobility policies may merge resulting in an alternative and innovative model after proactive local leadership, the case of Copenhagen may be a perfect case study: Duncan McLaren and Julian Agyeman, *Sharing Cities: a Case for Truly Smart and Sustainable Cities* (Massachusetts Institute of Technology 2015) 137-143.

[45]It should be noted, moreover, and as is obvious, that for public transportation most of the network economic effects also apply, where the effective density of the network is key to enabling the platform to be competitive. Conversely, the risk of losing some 'transactions', users and connections should not be underestimated: once a certain threshold is reached, the mere existence of the entire network as a viable alternative may be at risk if users are lost due to the emergence of very competitive private services, which in turn may generate potential problems of congestion or social equity. See Orly Lobel, 'Coase and the Platform Economy', in Nestor M Davidson, Michèle Finck and John J Infranca (eds), *The Cambridge Handbook of the Sharing Economy* (Cambridge University Press 2018) 71-74; Yemi Adediji, Liam Donaldson and Murtaza Haider, 'Regulating Vehicles-for-Hire in Toronto: a Review of the Regulatory Frameworks' (Ryerson Urban Analytics Institute 2019) <https://urbananalyticsinstitute.com/wp-content/uploads/2019/06/UAI_VFH_Report_June-2019.pdf> accessed 9 January 2020.

mass transportation systems require a minimum critical mass to function properly, it would also be completely justifiable to establish measures to protect them. This conclusion is supported by the importance of public transportation not only as one of the least polluting alternatives in some of its modalities, but also by the importance of public supply being underpinned by social considerations. Indeed, as the NUA emphasises,[46] public transportation is the only urban mobility alternative effectively available to particularly vulnerable groups and communities, so its conservation and improvement must be a priority of sustainable urban mobility policies.[47]

4 Conclusion

In conclusion, from all of these variables which must be taken into account, many options are available for the establishment of very diverse regulatory models with necessarily different points of balance. The conditions of each city and of each urban environment are different, and for this reason it is very reasonable that these decisions are made at the local level. The relevant decisions for establishing an urban policy of sustainable mobility have to do with traditional local powers, e.g. on how to regulate the use of public space, on a sustainable strategy for urban public transportation, and what is the better solution for traffic regulation. Such solutions are also sometimes limited by excessively rigid State legal frameworks, which prevent full development. Alternative and innovative models associated with the needs of each specific city with all the required ambition can only be designed and fully implemented if the required leadership of local governments to address those issues is completely acknowledged by State and regional powers, thus granting them a suitable legal framework. In absence of enough space for local authorities to decide their urban mobility policies, in addition to depriving us of better regulatory solutions for today, we would be also limiting the possibilities of promoting policies of experimentation and innovation at a local level[48] that can offer clues about what would be the best practices and policies for the regulation of sustainable urban mobility for each urban typology.

[46] UN (n 4) para 50.

[47] Also, the European Union and United Nations Human Settlements Programme (UN-Habitat), *The State of European Cities: Cities Leading the Way to a Better Future* (Publications Office of the European Union 2016) 122-135.

[48] Sofia Ranchordás, 'Innovation Experimentalism in the Age of the Sharing Economy' (2015) 19 (4) Lewis & Clark Law Review 871.

Some Public Procurement Challenges in Supporting and Delivering Smart Urban Mobility: Procurement Data, Discretion and Expertise

Albert Sanchez-Graells

Contents

Abstract This chapter explores three of the challenges that public buyers face when designing public tenders to support smart urban mobility initiatives and when supervising the execution of the relevant contracts. First, the chapter covers emerging issues around access and re-use of transport data that may be hindering 'outside of the box' thinking and the deployment of artificial intelligence in this area. Second,

---

This chapter was remotely presented at a workshop on smart urban mobility held at the Max Planck Institute for Innovation and Competition, in Munich, on 23 November 2019. I am grateful to the participants and, in particular, to Heiko Richter for useful feedback. I am also grateful to Phinella Henderson and to Karolis Granickas for their comments on earlier drafts. The standard disclaimer applies. Further comments welcome. Albert Sanchez-Graells is Professor of Economic Law and Co-Director of the Centre for Global Law and Innovation, University of Bristol Law School, UK.

A. Sanchez-Graells (✉)
University of Bristol Law School, Bristol, UK
e-mail: a.sanchez-graells@bristol.ac.uk

M. Finck et al. (eds.), *Smart Urban Mobility*, MPI Studies on Intellectual Property and Competition Law 29, https://doi.org/10.1007/978-3-662-61920-9_6

it discusses some well-known 'inside the box' regulatory issues around the exercise of discretion in the choice of sustainable technological solutions, the constraints surrounding certain types of complex and collaborative procurement, and the difficulties in monitoring contract compliance clauses. Third, the chapter arrives at the realisation that the main challenges in delivering and supporting smart urban mobility through procurement relate to the higher-level or cross-cutting challenges of the professionalisation of the procurement workforce and the need to bridge significant (and growing) knowledge gaps. It thus explores existing policy interventions aimed at the professionalisation and networking of procurement officials. The chapter concludes with some overall reflections, and a call for a more active role to be taken by the new Von der Leyen Commission.

1 Introduction

In a Janus-faced fashion, public procurement is simultaneously identified as one of the main levers of, and as one of the main obstacles to, the roll-out of sustainable urban mobility policies in the European Union.[1] With its bright face, the buying power derived from the large volumes of public expenditure through procurement is seen as a catalyst for sustainability and for the creation of an open transport data culture. This is not only in the public sector, but also in the private sector through, for instance, market development and leading by example as a responsible, transparent buyer. With its dark face, however, procurement rules are considered as a tight corset constraining the exercise of the required discretion by the public buyer,[2] thus making the adoption of sustainability policies and their deployment very difficult or even impossible. Procurement rules and the opacity of some procurement systems are also seen as contrary to open data policies.

While these positions hold some truth, they are also both rather distorted. On the one hand the buying power that contracting authorities can exercise is constrained by their ability to identify what they want to buy and by the existence of a competitive market that is capable of offering it, or is capable of engaging in its co-creation

[1]See, eg CIVITAS, 'Procuring Sustainable Mobility Solutions' (CIVITAS 2016) <https://civitas.eu/content/civitas-guide-procuring-sustainable-mobility-solutions> accessed 13 February 2020. See also, Smart procurement for better transport (SPICE), 'D 3 SPICE Analysis and Recommendations' (SPICE 2018) <http://spice-project.eu/wp-content/uploads/sites/14/2019/03/SPICE-D-3-Analysis-and-Recommendations-FINAL.pdf> accessed 13 February 2020; or Frederic Rudolph and Stefan Werland, 'Public Procurement of Sustainable Urban Mobility Measures' (European Platform on Sustainable Urban Mobility Plans 2019) <www.eltis.org/sites/default/files/public_procurement_of_sustainable_urban_mobility_measures.pdf> accessed 13 February 2020.

[2]For extended discussion, see Sanja Bogojevic, Xavier Groussot and Jörgen Hettne (eds), *Discretion in EU Public Procurement Law* (Hart 2019).

through joint innovation projects. On the other hand the constraints on the contracting authorities' discretion to pursue green public procurement goals have been significantly relaxed in the 2014 EU Public Procurement Package[3] and the European Commission is pushing for the exercise of sustainability-oriented discretion as a strategic priority.[4] The Commission is also pushing for more available and higher-quality procurement data.[5] However, the practical effects that can be generated through procurement discretion also hinge on the public buyer's ability to identify what it wants to buy and how to do it, as well as on the broader ability of the public sector to develop an enabling data infrastructure.[6] Ultimately the measure in which public procurement can be a catalyst or will be a neutraliser of efforts to develop sustainable urban mobility solutions will thus hinge on interrelated aspects of procurement data, discretion and expertise and in the public sector's ability to meet these challenges.

This chapter structures the discussion of these issues around three main challenges. First, it discusses the potentially more transformative challenge of 'thinking outside the box' and harnessing the power of big data and artificial intelligence for sustainable urban mobility, which requires an assessment of the current enablers and inhibitors of 'open transport data' as the indispensable input to fuel that transformation (Sect. 2). Second, it focuses on the more immediate challenges in exercising discretion to implement sustainability measures within the existing regulatory framework, which has created significant space for the inclusion of green procurement criteria at all stages of the procurement cycle, but has also increased the complexity of sophisticated procurement activities (Sect. 3). The discussion of both challenges will lead to the realisation of the persistent relevance of the higher-level or cross-cutting third challenge of the professionalisation of the procurement workforce; and the need to bridge the significant (and growing) knowledge gap separating the potential for sustainable procurement from its actualisation in the complex procurement ecosystem of the European Union (Sect. 4). The chapter concludes with some

[3]The 2014 EU Public Procurement Package comprises: Parliament and Council Directive 2014/23/EU of 26 February 2014 on the award of concession contracts Text with EEA relevance [2014] OJ L94/1, Parliament and Council Directive 2014/24/EU of 26 February 2014 on public procurement and repealing Council Directive 2004/18/EC Text with EEA relevance [2014] OJ L94/65 (Public Procurement Directive), and Parliament and Council Directive 2014/25/EU of 26 February 2014 on procurement by entities operating in water, energy, transport and postal services sectors and repealing Directive 2004/17/EC Text with EEA relevance [2014] OJ L 94/243 (Utilities Procurement Directive).

[4]Commission, 'Making Public Procurement Work in and for Europe' (Communication) COM (2017) 572 final.

[5]For discussion, see Albert Sanchez-Graells, 'EU Public Procurement Policy and the Fourth Industrial Revolution: Pushing and Pulling as One?' (2019) <https://ssrn.com/abstract=3440554> accessed 13 February 2020.

[6]For discussion, see Albert Sanchez-Graells, 'Data-Driven and Digital Procurement Governance: Revisiting Two Well-Known Elephant Tales' (2019) 24 Communications Law – Journal of Computer, Media and Telecommunications Law 157.

overall reflections, and a call for a more active role by the new Von der Leyen Commission (Sect. 5).

2 'Outside of the Box' Procurement: Untapped Potential of Big Data for Sustainable Mobility

One of the key challenge areas for a significant transformation of transport and mobility concerns the exploitation of data-based solutions through the deployment of artificial intelligence to, for instance, automate transport and develop smart mobility, based largely on the new approach to 'mobility as a service' (MaaS).[7] Indeed, there are clear examples of how artificial intelligence and big data analysis can streamline urban mobility strategies and deliver sustainability gains,[8] as an aspect of their broader potential to contribute to urban resilience.[9] The importance of open transport data in this context can hardly be overstated. Indeed, the European Commission has placed strong emphasis on the need for shared open transport data as a key enabler of sustainable mobility innovations:

> Companies, governments and public entities should be equally encouraged to provide collected user and urban data on the use of public space and infrastructures wherever it is available (in such a way that protects the privacy of its citizens) so that users, cities, third party apps, operators, developers and innovators can access it to inform their decisions and innovate their applications. Smart mobility and cities will combine publically and privately developed infrastructures; only by making data (such as aggregate dynamic mobile phone and traffic data, the real-time location of buses or the accurate arrival time of trains) 'open' will third parties be able to integrate it into their systems and establish truly 'cross-infrastructure' integrated mobility systems.[10]

[7] As discussed in eg Commission, 'Towards clean, competitive and connected mobility: the contribution of Transport Research and Innovation to the Mobility package' (Staff Working Document) SWD (2017) 223 final.

[8] A recent example concerns the redesign of public school bus routes in Boston by an MIT team, see Kara Baskin, 'Creating Better Bus Routes With Algorithms' (*MIT Sloan blog*, 31 July 2017) <https://mitsloan.mit.edu/ideas-made-to-matter/creating-better-bus-routes-algorithms> accessed 13 February 2020. For examples based on the Singaporean experience, see Mariusz Maciejewski, 'To Do More, Better, Faster and More Cheaply: Using Big Data in Public Administration' (2017) 83(1S) International Review of Administrative Sciences 120, 128-129. More generally, see ARUP, 'Urban Mobility in the Smart City Age' (*ARUP*, 2014) <www.arup.com/perspectives/publications/research/section/urban-mobility-in-the-smart-city-age> accessed 13 February 2020. For a technical account of the possibilities of machine learning use cases to improve transportation and its environmental impact, see David Rolnick and others 'Tackling Climate Change with Machine Learning' (2019) 13ff <https://arxiv.org/abs/1906.05433> accessed 13 February 2020.

[9] See Jean-Noé Landry and others, 'How Can We Improve Urban Resilience With Open Data?' (*OpenData for Development*, 2016) <www.ccmdesign.ca/files/od4d-resilient-cities.pdf> accessed 13 February 2020.

[10] SWD (2017) 223 final 64. Similarly, in relation to transport automation, the document stresses that 'Optimised use of internet of things, big data and innovative data management and governance

In other words, it has been stressed that 'government has an important role to kickstart new services by releasing as much data as possible, both static and real time data',[11] as '[t]he availability of public data provides greater certainty in the value chain, enabling new industry to grow up around the promise of robust and comprehensive data.'[12] This led to the recommendation that '[w]here external service providers and infrastructure operators are procured by government, contracts should outline the need for digital infrastructure and the requirement for operators to supply the output data to government.'[13] Along the same lines, it was pointed out that 'open data policies by national or local governments and respective procurement requirements for data sharing and interoperability of interfaces (APIs) can ... be a useful tool to accelerate the adoption of innovations and new mobility services.'[14]

It is thus pertinent to assess the challenges that exist under current EU rules in relation to the unlocking of open transport data in the context of public procurement, as well as possible paths to develop an open transport data infrastructure.[15] The availability of improved information sources could enable significant changes to the way procurement is used to support the development of sustainable urban mobility under the current rules, in particular if the innovation resulted in superior urban mobility solutions. This is discussed later (Sect. 3). The discussion in this section will follow the logic of a possible progression from the current situation of largely non-existent (transport) procurement data, to an ideal situation of open public and private transport data, concentrating on four levels of data collection and publication: old, new and open public data; and open private data. This section will emphasise the legal issues that arise in the development of such comprehensive open transport data infrastructure. Further reflections are left for the conclusion (Sect. 5).

---

needs to be researched for increasing the performance and efficiency of automated transport technologies, transport systems, mobility and freight delivery services. This includes data mining, access to and innovative uses of data sources, data analytics, innovative business models, and visualisation' (ibid 13).

[11] ARUP (n 8) 36.

[12] ibid 29.

[13] ibid 37.

[14] SPICE (n 1) 5 and 24.

[15] For an in-depth analysis of an ideal open data architecture, though premised on the assumption that there are no data protection issues to address, see Pieter Colpaert, 'Publishing Transport Data for Maximum Reuse' (2017) <https://phd.pietercolpaert.be/> accessed 13 February 2020. For related discussion, see also Laurence Folliot-Lalliot and Peter T McKeen, 'Procurement and Smart Cities: Exploring Examples on Both Sides of the Atlantic' in Gabriella M Racca and Christopher R Yukins (eds), *Joint Public Procurement and Innovation. Lessons across Borders* (Bruylant 2019).

2.1 *Accessing 'Old' Procurement Data: Who Has It and Who Owns It?*

It seems reasonable to start the analysis on the premise that having access to accurate information about the current state of affairs is a precondition for the design of (more) sustainable urban mobility. Improving upon the current situation requires the prior gaining of a sufficient understanding of the way in which mobility solutions operate in a given urban context. However, this seemingly simple task may prove less than straightforward depending on the practical and contractual arrangements in place. Awareness of the importance of consolidated transport data is only now emerging and gradually becoming mainstream. It should thus come as no surprise that legacy procurement contracts are unlikely to have explicitly regulated 'old' data ownership and that cities may not have yet developed comprehensive digitalised systems for the recording, archiving and management of transport data (or procurement data, more generally). It could be that 'old' transport data has simply been lost or recorded in non-digital format in such a way as to make its digitalisation for re-use impractical or too expensive. Even where there are adequate (digital) records, there are a few legal issues that can be relevant in this context, including two which seem particularly relevant.

The first issue concerns cases where some or all of the public transport services of a city have been contracted out to private providers. In such a situation it is likely that any transport data being recorded is under the control of the services provider and that this undertaking has an interest in claiming proprietary protection of the relevant database through the relevant *sui generis* right,[16] or under any other mechanisms, such as the protection of trade secrets.[17] In such a setting, one of the difficulties for the contracting authorities and for any third parties seeking to gain access to the database will be the negotiation of access to and the right to re-use the data.

Where the database has been made public in whatever manner by its maker, contracting authorities could seek an exception from the relevant *sui generis* right and extract and re-utilise the data 'for the purposes of an administrative procedure'.[18] These purposes would include the evaluation of current mobility solutions and the facilitation of the development of new, more sustainable ones, in particular in the context of their tendering or retendering. This possibility to seek access on the basis of an exception to the *sui generis* right would not necessarily be open to third parties. In any case, this approach would not be without the risk of legal challenge by the incumbent operator, as the scope of the exceptions to the *sui generis* right is still

---

[16]Parliament and Council Directive 96/9/EC of 11 March 1996 on the legal protection of databases [1996] OJ L77/20 (Database Directive), art 7.

[17]Parliament and Council Directive 2016/943/EU of 8 June 2016 on the protection of undisclosed know-how and business information (trade secrets) against their unlawful acquisition, use and disclosure [2016] OJ L157/1 (Trade Secrets Directive).

[18]Database Directive, art 9(c).

rather undefined.[19] It is worth stressing that this situation will not be altered by the new Open Data Directive, adopted on 20 June 2019 and due to be implemented by Member States by 16 July 2021.[20] Indeed, the Open Data Directive imposes obligations on public undertakings involved in the provision of public transport services. Crucially, though, the restriction in the exercise of *sui generis* rights on databases[21] only applies to public sector bodies, but not to public undertakings and, much less, to private service providers (as further discussed below).

Moreover, both contracting authorities and third parties would face heightened issues where the relevant database has not been made available to the public, as access would then completely hinge on voluntary disclosure by the provider of the service. While some contract law mechanisms could be explored by the contracting authority to try and force this disclosure—e.g. on the basis of implicit duties of collaboration or good faith in the execution of the relevant contract—this legal avenue also seems less than straightforward, or obviously leading to access to the data, in particular by third parties. It could thus be generally preferable to try to seek contractual access to the database—whether it had been made available to the public or not—but this would probably entail relevant costs. Which leads to the second relevant legal issue.

This concerns the possibility of finding public law solutions to override any contractual or other types of protection that could result in the contracting authority and/or third parties being locked out of the data necessary to develop new more sustainable mobility options. The public law of the relevant jurisdiction will determine this, which could give rise to different treatment across EU jurisdictions. One possibility would be to seek the declaration of the data as (immaterial) public domain or *res communes omnium*, in the sense of an asset that cannot be the subject of private property rights,[22] somewhat along the lines of the 2016 French Digital Republic Law.[23] Another possibility—or an implication of such declaration—would be to seek the expropriation of the database on the basis of the public interest in the data accessibility as an enabler of mobility innovation.[24] Both options are

[19]See eg Commission, 'Evaluation of Directive 96/9/EC on the legal protection of databases' (Staff Working Document) SWD (2018) 146 final.

[20]Parliament and Council Directive 2019/1024/EU of 20 June 2019 on open data and the re-use of public sector information [2019] OJ L172/56 (Open Data Directive).

[21]Open Data Directive, art 1(6).

[22]For an overview of debates on data ownership, see Thomas Hoeren, 'A New Approach to Data Property?' (2018) 2 AMI: Tijdschrift voor Auteurs, Media and Informatierecht 58 <www.itm.nrw/wp-content/uploads/AMI-%e2%80%93-tijdschrift-voor-auteurs-media-en-informatierecht-Nummer-20182-A-New-Approach-to-Data-Property.pdf> accessed 13 February 2020. See also Alberto Alemanno, 'Big Data for Good: Unlocking Privately-Held Data to the Benefit of the Many' (2018) 9 European Journal of Risk Regulation 183.

[23]Loi n° 2016-1321 du 7 octobre 2016 pour une République numérique, in particular arts 17-19. See also Jean-Bernard Auby, 'Public Contracts and Smart Cities' in Racca and Yukins (n 15) 187, 190-191.

[24]For related discussion of four alternative models, see Geoffrey Delcroix, 'Smart Cities and Innovative Uses for Personal Data: Scenarios for Using Data to Restore the Balance between Public

likely to be costly and/or result in legal challenges, which could delay or even prevent completely the access to and re-use of 'old' public transport data linked to legacy procurement arrangements.

It thus seems that access to 'old' procurement data of relevance for the development of new and more sustainable urban mobility could be impossible (where it has not been duly recorded) or problematic from a legal perspective, and that there is a possibility of non-availability of data that could complicate attempts at the development of innovations due to a limited understanding of the status quo. Contracting authorities should thus take every possible step to persuade undertakings in possession of 'old' (or *rectius*, current) transport data to disclose it and, more importantly, contracting authorities must develop adequate data governance in all new public procurement arrangements to avoid perpetuating this situation.

2.2 *Ensuring Access to 'New' Procurement Data: Data Governance in Procurement*

Given the difficulties in accessing 'old' transport/procurement data, contracting authorities willing to facilitate the emergence of more sustainable mobility need to make sure that they create contractual mechanisms that ensure adequate data governance, with a view to the re-use of data where appropriate. Of course, from a transaction cost perspective, it could be desirable to create data governance regimes applicable by default by means of generally-applicable legislative measures—and the transposition of the Open Data Directive could be a good opportunity to develop them. However, in the absence of such regulation, contracting authorities need to include these considerations in their own contractual arrangements, in particular for public transport services, if they want to support more sustainable urban mobility initiatives. Indeed, it has been rightly stressed that

> data ownership is becoming more and more important [. . .] nowadays any development of a mobility service is information and communication driven. Collecting, processing and providing data is crucial and it may come to a point where ownership of information and control of how it is processed and distributed can become more important than owning and operating infrastructure. This poses questions on how cities, procuring mobility services, should consider these trends when planning procurement processes, and questions on how much control of data the cities need in order to ensure effective traffic and mobility management.[25]

As a general starting point, it seems that contracting authorities should at a minimum ensure at least two levels of access to and re-use of mobility data. First, unlimited free access for their own purposes. Second, limited free access by third

and Private Spheres' (2017) Field Actions Science Reports 75 <https://journals.openedition.org/factsreports/4489> accessed 13 February 2020.

[25]SPICE (n 1) 80. Generally, on data issues related to intelligent transportation systems, see ibid 93.

parties in the context of the design of new mobility solutions, which could be restricted by e.g. obligations not to re-use the data for any other purposes and not to further divulge it or publicise it. This minimal approach could be appropriate for cases where the generation and exploitation of the data by the incumbent operator is crucial to the economic viability of the public service and where the value generated by the data cannot be compensated for with other revenue streams by the contracting authority. However, this seems unlikely to be the general case and, ideally, it seems that contracting authorities should ensure unlimited free and open access to mobility data in real time where it relates to the provision of a contracted-out public transportation service.

Under the 2014 EU Public Procurement Package, this could easily be implemented through contractual performance conditions.[26] The contracting authority could then publish such transport data and, where appropriate, aggregate data from different transport operators. Along the same lines, it has also been rightly stressed that

> Open data being a fundamental element in the MaaS developments, *public procurement can also be used to encourage open data by setting data sharing obligations in public tendering.* Open interfaces (APIs) and open platforms encourage the involvement of smaller companies and their access to the mobility service provision. As the first step, publicly funded data registered (containing not-classified information) could be made available for academic and commercial developers and researchers. The public funding may be needed to compensate the expenses related establishment of register (and open interfaces) and maintenance of the data storages if the data has been previously sold, if needed [emphasis added].[27]

Indeed, the current procurement rules allow for these policy innovations, and contracting authorities should take data governance seriously in order to avoid any extensions of lock-out effects as those discussed above (Sect. 2.1). Of course, there will be some difficulties related to the protection of commercially sensitive information,[28] and to compliance with the General Data Protection Regulation (GDPR).[29] Such difficulties will require careful consideration on a case by case basis of the data being generated, its processing, and its publication—which are increasingly important aspects of data governance but of no distinct character in the context of procurement.[30] The issue of funding can be addressed in different ways but, in my

[26]Public Procurement Directive, art 70; Utilities Procurement Directive, art 87.

[27]SPICE (n 1) 18. See also SPICE (n 1) 19ff for discussion of the role of public authorities in a data-driven ecosystem.

[28]For discussion in the context of procurement prior to the execution of the public contracts, see Albert Sanchez-Graells, 'Transparency and Competition in Public Procurement: A Comparative View on a Difficult Balance' in Kirsi-Maria Halonen, Roberto Caranta and Albert Sanchez-Graells (eds), *Transparency in EU Procurements: Disclosure within public procurement and during contract execution* (Edward Elgar 2019) 33-56.

[29]Parliament and Council Regulation (EU) 679/2016 of 27 April 2016 on the protection of natural persons with regard to the processing of personal data and on the free movement of such data, and repealing Directive 95/46/EC (General Data Protection Regulation) [2016] OJ L119/1 (GDPR).

[30]Thus, these issues will not be discussed in any further detail, due to space constraints. See eg Alessandro Mantelero, 'Data Protection, E-Ticketing, and Intelligent Systems for Public Transport'

opinion, the imposition of an obligation to give unlimited open access to mobility data under new (or renegotiated) contracts can be priced into the cost of delivery of the service and the costs associated with the creation of the necessary platforms and APIs could be borne by the contracting authority. This is particularly so where there are economies to be had in the centralisation and aggregation of mobility data generated by the providers of different types of public (transport) services.

2.3 Opening (Public) Transport Procurement Data to Foster Innovation

Once contracting authorities have secured access to new (and to old) transport data in the context of contracted out services, as well as in relation to the data generated by any public transport services they directly manage, they are in a position to publish it in open data formats,[31] ideally following standardised formats that are open, machine-readable, accessible, findable and re-usable, together with their metadata.[32] As mentioned above, the availability of such open data is considered fundamental to the fostering of more sustainable mobility solutions, in particular those based in MaaS.[33] The publication of standardised open data would be of particular interest to avoid legal fragmentation across the board and meet reasonable expectations of companies functioning within the single market. This goal of publication of open transport data is not solely a matter of discretionary choice for the contracting authority, but is about to become an obligation under the Open Data Directive.

Indeed, in order to promote the use of open data and stimulate innovation in mobility services, from 16 July 2021 the Open Data Directive will require public sector bodies holding transport or mobility data[34] and public undertakings involved in the provision of transport services[35] to facilitate access and re-use of mobility data

(2015) 5 International Data Privacy Law 309. The interested reader will find relevant analysis in other contributions to this book.

[31]See European Data Portal, *Analytical Report 11: Re-use of PSI in the Public Sector* (Publications Office of the European Union 2018). For comparative discussion, see Teresa Scassa, 'Public Transit Data through an Intellectual Property Lens: Lessons about Open Data' (2014) 41 Fordham Urban Law Journal 1759.

[32]It is notable that open transport data is amongst the OECD priorities, as stressed in the OECD 'OURdata Index' (*OECD*, 2019) <www.oecd.org/gov/digital-government/open-government-data.htm> accessed 13 February 2020.

[33]SPICE (n 1) 18.

[34]Open Data Directive, art 1(1)(a).

[35]Open Data Directive, art 1(1)(b). That is, transport services procured either under the rules of the Utilities Procurement Directive or Parliament and Council Regulation (EC) 1370/2007 of 23 October 2007 on public passenger transport services by rail and by road [2007] OJ L315/1. There are other rules concerning air and sea transport, although these are less likely to be relevant in the context of urban mobility and will thus not be discussed in detail. The analysis in this and later

generated in the context of the provision of services[36] covered by the relevant procurement rules.[37] The obligation will extend to transport or mobility data generated by private providers of those public services that is in the possession of public sector bodies.[38] The availability of such data for re-use will be mandated by the Directive, except where it is covered by third party intellectual property rights,[39] or its disclosure is excluded on the grounds of protection of sensitive data (including commercial confidentiality i.e. business, professional or company secrets),[40] or the protection of personal data[41] (as discussed above, Sects. 2.1 and 2.2).[42] As mentioned above, in the case of public sector bodies the Open Data Directive imposes restrictions on the exercise of *sui generis* rights on those databases[43] which can be particularly relevant where the contracting authority—or another public sector body—collects and aggregates mobility data for its publication with a view to its re-use.

The obligations resulting from the Open Data Directive are controlled by the general principle that any documents to which it applies shall be re-usable for commercial or non-commercial purposes in the terms of the Directive.[44] The main obligations for public sector bodies include: (1) making their documents available in any pre-existing format or language (and where appropriate by electronic means), in formats that are open, machine-readable, accessible, findable and re-usable, together with their metadata—on the understanding that, where possible, both the format and the metadata shall comply with formal open standards[45]—with emphasis on making the documents 'open by design and by default';[46] and (2) making dynamic data available for re-use immediately after collection via suitable APIs and, where relevant, as a bulk download[47] (although dynamic data can be made available for re-use within a time frame or with temporary technical restrictions that do not unduly impair the exploitation of their economic and social potential, where making dynamic data available immediately after collection would exceed the financial and technical capacities of the public sector body, thereby imposing a

sections, however, applies across all procurement governed by these different sets of EU rules, as their substantive standards are largely coordinated.

[36]Cf Open Data Directive, art 1(2)(a).

[37]Cf Open Data Directive, art 1(2)(b).

[38]Open Data Directive, art 1(1)(a).

[39]Open Data Directive, art 1(2)(c).

[40]Open Data Directive, art 1(2)(d)(iii).

[41]Open Data Directive, art (1)(2)(h).

[42]There are, of course, more exceptions to the obligations under the Open Data Directive, but these seem to be those of more direct relevance in the context of our discussion.

[43]Open Data Directive, art 1(6).

[44]Open Data Directive, art 3(1).

[45]Open Data Directive, art 5(1).

[46]Open Data Directive, art 5(2).

[47]Open Data Directive, art 5(5).

disproportionate effort).[48] In the case of public undertakings, these obligations apply to the documents available for re-use only,[49] which I argue include all data related to mobility, or to the provision of the relevant public transport services.

Moreover, given the explicit inclusion of mobility data under the category of 'high-value datasets' in the Open Data Directive,[50] they shall be available free of charge (subject to the restrictions discussed below); machine readable; provided via APIs; and provided as a bulk download, where that is appropriate.[51] The requirement for these datasets to be made available free of charge will not apply to specific high-value datasets held by public undertakings where that would lead to a distortion of competition in the relevant markets (as specified by the European Commission in the future implementing acts laying down a list of specific high-value datasets held by public sector bodies and public undertakings).[52] Making high-value datasets available free of charge by public sector bodies that are required to generate revenue to cover a substantial part of their costs relating to the performance of their public tasks would lead to a substantial impact on the budget of the bodies involved. To counteract this Member States may exempt those bodies from the requirement to make their high-value datasets available free of charge for a period of no more than 2 years following the entry into force of the relevant implementing act.[53] However, unless and until the European Commission adopts the relevant implementing acts, the re-use of high-value mobility datasets shall not necessarily be free of charge,[54] and the more general rules on charging in the Open Data Directive will be applicable—which, however, also establish the general principle that re-use of documents shall be free of charge.[55] Those rules would also apply to transport data not captured by the definition of mobility data and the relevant implementing acts. In those cases, it will be possible to impose recovery of the marginal costs incurred for the reproduction, provision and dissemination of documents as well as for anonymisation of personal data. Measures taken to protect commercially confidential information may be allowed, and it will also be possible for Member States to allow specific entities to charge above the marginal costs.

The Open Data Directive thus requires a form of revolution in the way in which mobility data is collected, structured and published in the context of the procurement of public transport services and other public services of direct relevance to the development of (more) sustainable urban mobility. Member States would be well-advised to fast-track the preparations for the entry into force of the Open Data Directive and to take this opportunity to turn (procurement) transport data into an

[48]Open Data Directive, art 5(6).
[49]Open Data Directive, art 5(7).
[50]Open Data Directive, Annex I, para 6, in relation to art 13(1).
[51]Open Data Directive, art 14(1).
[52]Open Data Directive, art 14(3).
[53]Open Data Directive, art 14(5).
[54]Open Data Directive, recital (68).
[55]Open Data Directive, art 6(1).

open source input for anyone interested in researching or developing urban mobility solutions.[56] This will require strengthening contract-based data governance and/or the development of a general framework to ensure that the necessary access and publication rights are available to public sector bodies holding mobility data (as discussed in Sect. 2.2) and could be used as a lever to unlock further 'old' mobility data (as discussed in Sect. 2.1). However, given the increasing relevance of privately-generated and privately-held data in urban contexts where there is significant experimentation with MaaS solutions—and, in particular, light urban mobility—there is a clear need to extend the efforts to private transport data.

2.4 *Incentivising Broader Openness of (Private) Transport Data*

Indeed, as just mentioned, not all data required for the development of smart urban mobility will be in the control of the public sector and establishing an open transport data infrastructure as comprehensive as possible will require access to privately-held data.[57] Indeed, current EU legislation does not guarantee free access by public authorities to data generated in the cities if not agreed in advance in specific contractual rules. The difficulty for contracting authorities wishing to promote disclosure of such private data is that this is a controversial issue that is currently under debate at EU level, and which is likely to trigger even more complications than access to privately-held data linked to the contracted-out provision of public services (as discussed above Sect. 2.1).

Indeed, at EU level, the possibility of allowing public authorities to access private sector data of public interest was first mentioned in the January 2017 Communication 'Building a European Data Economy'[58] and, in the May 2017 Digital Single Market Midterm Review,[59] it was identified as an area for further exploration by the Commission.[60] This should lead the Commission to formulate a proposal for an EU regulation on access to and re-use of data by public authorities to data generated and

[56]This should be an opportunity to overcome the barriers to publication of open data that remain despite the improvements introduced by the Open Data Directive. For broad analysis, see Melanie Dulong de Rosnay and Katleen Janssen, 'Legal and Institutional Challenges for Opening Data across Public Sectors: Towards Common Policy Solutions' (2014) 9(3) Journal of Theoretical and Applied Electronic Commerce Research 1.

[57]Along the same lines, ARUP (n 8) 30.

[58]See Commission, 'Building a European data economy' (*European Commission*) <https://ec.europa.eu/digital-single-market/en/policies/building-european-data-economy> accessed 13 February 2020.

[59]Commission, 'Mid-Term Review on the implementation of the Digital Single Market Strategy A Connected Digital Single Market for All' (Communication) COM (2017) 228 final.

[60]See Commission, 'Better Regulation - Action 7: Access and reuse of private sector data of general interest by the public authorities' (*European Commission*) <https://ec.europa.eu/futurium/en/digital-transition/better-regulation-action-7-access-and-reuse-private-sector-data-general-interest> accessed 13 February 2020.

collected in public spaces. However, at the time of writing (November 2019), the progress and timeline for this initiative remain unclear.[61] Similarly, the guidance on private sector data sharing[62] stresses that the European Commission considers that the respect of the principles contained in the Communication 'Towards a Common European Data Space'[63] (i.e. proportionality in the use of private sector data; purpose limitation; 'do no harm' in terms of private commercial interests; mutually-beneficial conditions for data re-use; mitigation of limitations of private sector data; and transparency and societal participation) could support the supply of private sector data to public bodies under preferential conditions for re-use.[64] This led to the creation of an Expert Group on Business-to-Government (B2G) Data Sharing,[65] tasked with an evaluation of the principles, collaboration modes and technical means outlined in the Guidance on private sector data sharing and the endorsement of a framework for B2G data-sharing.[66] Such a framework is unavailable at the time of writing. Given the level of generality of the principles and the extremely difficult balancing act between public interest and private commercial interests, one can but wonder how far this initiative can go in practical terms.

This is thus an area of regulatory experimentation where contracting authorities need to tread carefully. In my view there are two main aspects to consider from a public procurement perspective concern. The first is the extent to which the provision of financial incentives for the disclosure of privately-held data could trigger an

[61] ibid.

[62] See Commission, 'Guidance on private sector data sharing' (*European Commission*) <https://ec.europa.eu/digital-single-market/en/guidance-private-sector-data-sharing> accessed 13 February 2020.

[63] Commission, 'Towards a common European data space' (Communication) COM (2018) 232 final. See also the accompanying Commission, 'Guidance on sharing private sector data in the European data economy, accompanying the document Communication' "Towards a common European data space" (Staff Working Document) SWD (2018) 125 final.

[64] See Begoña Gonzalez Otero, 'Evaluating the EC Private Data Sharing Principles. Setting a Mantra for Artificial Intelligence Nirvana?' (2019) 10 JIPITEC 65 para 1 <www.jipitec.eu/issues/jipitec-10-1-2019> accessed 13 February 2020. See also Emmanuel Letouzé and Nuria Oliver, 'Sharing is Caring. Four Key Requirements for Sustainable Private Data Sharing and Use for Public Good' (*Data-Pop Alliance*, November 2019) <http://datapopalliance.org/wp-content/uploads/2019/11/DPA_VFI-SHARING-IS-CARING.pdf> accessed 13 February 2020; and OECD, *Enhancing Access to and Sharing of Data: Reconciling Risks and Benefits for Data Re-use across Societies* (OECD Publishing, 2019).

[65] See Commission, 'Meetings of the Expert Group on Business-to-Government Data Sharing' (*European Commission*) <https://ec.europa.eu/digital-single-market/en/news/meetings-expert-group-business-government-data-sharing> accessed 13 February 2020.

[66] Relatedly, see European Data Portal, 'Analytical Report 12: Business-to-Government Data Sharing' (European Data Portal 2019) <www.europeandataportal.eu/sites/default/files/analytical_report_12_business_government_data_sharing.pdf> accessed 13 February 2020. See also GovLab, 'Eight phases of B2G data sharing' (*Data Collaboratives*) <http://datacollaboratives.org/canvas> accessed 13 February 2020; and International Data Corporation / Lisbon Council, 'Update of the European Data Market SMART 2016/0063, Story 1 – Opening Up Private Data for Public Interest' (11 November 2017) <http://datalandscape.eu/sites/default/files/report/Story_1_New_format.pdf> accessed 13 February.

obligation to comply with the procurement rules (which is however unlikely to require many formalities beyond specific contract award publications on the basis of the exclusive nature of the data).[67] The second aspect is the extent to which the disclosure of privately-held mobility data could be promoted in the context of market consultations.[68] These are, however, very technical and narrow issues that need not be discussed in detail here.

3 'Inside the Box' Procurement: Promoting Sustainable Mobility Within Existing EU Rules

The previous section discussed the challenge of creating an open transport data infrastructure that could unlock innovation in the development of (more) sustainable urban mobility. An added benefit of the creation of such (big) data architecture would be to allow contracting authorities to gain a much better understanding of urban transport needs, which would then inform the way in which they design their urban mobility strategies and the supporting public procurement arrangements. This could generate significant changes if the emergence of those solutions could be facilitated by the exercise of procurement discretion in specific directions. In this section, the analysis thus focuses on how to foster sustainability in the procurement of urban mobility solutions—however defined—which requires an examination of the space for sustainable or green public procurement within the 2014 EU Public Procurement Package, as well as the challenges in the practical implementation of green procurement. The discussion will be kept general[69] and focus on three main areas of procurement practice where contracting authorities can exercise their discretion to foster sustainability: embedding green considerations in different stages of the procurement process; issues surrounding complex and joint procurement of sustainable mobility solutions; and the monitoring and enforcement of contract performance conditions.

3.1 Embedding Sustainability Through Selection, Technical Requirements and Award Criteria

One of the main goals of the 2014 EU Public Procurement Package and the current 2017 Procurement Strategy of the European Commission concerns the promotion of

---

[67]Public Procurement Directive, art 32(2)(b).

[68]Public Procurement Directive, art 40.

[69]For further discussion and references, see Albert Sanchez-Graells, 'Truly Competitive Public Procurement as a Europe 2020 Lever: What Role for the Principle of Competition in Moderating Horizontal Policies?' (2016) 22 European Public Law Journal 377.

the uptake of green public procurement (GPP). Indeed, current rules allow for the inclusion of GPP considerations in all stages of the procurement process, including requirements related to compliance with environmental management systems or standards;[70] the setting of technical specifications;[71] the use of ecolabels;[72] and the choice of award criteria[73] which includes the option to consider life cycle costing methodologies for the evaluation of tenders.[74] Current rules also allow for the setting of contract performance conditions based on environmental considerations[75] (as discussed in more detail below, Sect. 3.3).

Most of these rules simply generate the possibility of including GPP considerations, which is then left to the discretion of the contracting authority. This is encouraged by the European Commission, in particular through the publication of rather detailed (technical) EU GPP criteria—e.g. for road transport—including criteria applicable to vehicles and to mobility and other services[76] which build on its 'Buying Green Handbook'.[77] There are a number of other available guidance documents, some of which have been funded by the Commission through the Horizon2020 programme.[78] All of this guidance makes it clear that its adoption is voluntary and that contracting authorities still need to make sure that they comply with the constraints derived from the applicable EU procurement rules and the interpretive case law.[79] A similarly voluntary approach concerns safety

---

[70]Public Procurement Directive, art 62.

[71]Public Procurement Directive, art 42.

[72]Public Procurement Directive, art 43.

[73]Public Procurement Directive, art 67(2)(a).

[74]Public Procurement Directive, art 68.

[75]Public Procurement Directive, art 70.

[76]Commission, 'EU Green Public Procurement Criteria for Road Transport' (Staff Working Document) SWD (2019) 2 final. There is further information in the accompanying JRC Science for Policy Report, *Revision of the EU Green Public Procurement Criteria for Transport: Technical Report and Criteria Proposal* (Publications Office of the European Union 2019). There is also a much broader library of green public procurement criteria developed by the European Commission, which is accessible at Commission, 'EU GPP Criteria' (*European Commission*) <https://ec.europa.eu/environment/gpp/eu_gpp_criteria_en.htm> accessed 13 February 2020.

[77]European Commission, *Buying Green! - A Handbook on Green Public Procurement* (3rd edn, Publications Office of the European Union 2016).

[78]Eg BuyZET, 'Procuring Zero Emission Delivery of Goods and Services' (BuyZet Project 2019) <https://civitas.eu/news/guidelines-published-procuring-zero-emission-delivery-goods-and-services-cities> accessed 13 February 2020.

[79]In that regard, some aspects of the guidance are questionable, such as the indication that contracting authorities are free to choose the procedural stage at which to require test reports and the possibility to rely on self-declarations to verify compliance with specific technical specifications. See SWD (2019) 2 final 6 –which it can be argued runs contrary to the principles of the Judgment Case C-14/17 *VAR v ATM* [2018] EU:C:2018:568, where the CJEU required that certificates attesting compliance with established technical specifications must be submitted already with the tender. This can create some legal uncertainty and, in any case, stresses the importance of the independent assessment of legal compliance by the contracting authority, which compounds the issues surrounding knowledge gaps discussed below (Sect. 4).

considerations, which the Commission also expects public procurement to positively influence.[80] There are, however, some mandatory rules concerning aspects of green procurement linked to transport and mobility. For example, in relation to the acquisition of vehicles,[81] where the Clean Vehicles Directive[82] imposes specific obligations on contracting authorities and entities and on operators tasked with the discharge of public service obligations under a public service contract.[83] At the time of writing, the directive is undergoing revision as a part of 2017 Clean Mobility Package, with the aim of drastically increasing the share of the alternatively fuelled vehicles in public or publicly procured fleets.[84]

More generally, though, it is worth stressing that there are mandatory requirements in the EU procurement rules that could generate tensions with specific types of MaaS solutions, and in particular light urban transportation, such as 'design for all' requirements (including accessibility for disabled persons). In particular, the current rules require that '[f]or all procurement which is intended for use by natural persons, whether general public or staff of the contracting authority, the technical specifications shall, except in duly justified cases, be drawn up so as to take into account accessibility criteria for persons with disabilities or design for all users'.[85] This could create some constraints on the public procurement (and funding) of solutions that were not capable of ensuring adequate accessibility to urban mobility systems—although the scope for the exemption based on 'duly justified cases' is likely to be tested by contracting authorities willing to actively purchase light transport MaaS.

Therefore, there seems to be no doubt that the 2014 EU Public Procurement Package creates sufficient policy space for contracting authorities to embed sustainability or GPP considerations in urban mobility procurement. However, with such possibilities also comes complexity and the need for contracting authorities to be able to engage with complex technical issues in a manner that still satisfies the general principles of procurement (and, in particular, the need to respect the principle of proportionality and the prohibition to artificially narrow competition for public

[80]Rudolph and Werland (n 1) 20, by reference to the Commission, 'Europe on the Move: Sustainable Mobility for Europe: Safe, Connected and Clean' (Communication) COM (2017) 293 final, Annex 1.

[81]See eg Clean fleets, 'Guide on Procuring Clean and Efficient Road Vehicles' (*Clean Fleets*, November 2014) <www.clean-fleets.eu/fileadmin/files/documents/Publications/Clean_Fleets_Guide_screen_version.pdf> accessed 13 February 2020.

[82]Parliament and Council Directive 2009/33/EC of 23 April 2009 on the promotion of clean and energy-efficient road transport vehicles [2009] OJ L120/5.

[83]SPICE (n 1) 11.

[84]See Commission, 'Energy Union: Commission takes action to reinforce EU's global leadership in clean vehicles' (*European Commission*, 11 August 2017) <https://ec.europa.eu/transport/modes/road/news/2017-11-08-driving-clean-mobility_en> accessed 13 February 2020.

[85]Public Procurement Directive, art 42(1) para 4.

contracts).[86] So, at this stage, embedding sustainability considerations in procurement rarely faces legal challenges, though it does face some complicated practical issues, as discussed below (Sect. 4).

3.2 *The Relevance of Complex and Joint Procurement, and Their Challenges*

Similarly, another of the goals of the 2014 EU Public Procurement Package is the facilitation of complex and joint procurement as conduits for innovation in procurement sustainability.

The new rules have created significant procedural flexibility for contracting authorities seeking to co-produce innovation in sustainable mobility through the formalisation of the rules on preliminary market consultations and the creation of the innovation partnership,[87] as a new procedure for innovation procurement.[88] Indeed, contracting authorities can consult the market to get a sense of the state of the art and to invite suggestions on how to best satisfy their needs in the fairly unregulated context of preliminary market consultations.[89] The only requirements derived from this possibility of relatively informal, pre-procurement interaction relate to the need to ensure equality of treatment and undistorted competition for public contracts.[90] This is particularly important in terms of neutralising any advantages obtained by those involved in the preliminary consultations[91] and the need to carry out a robust control of any potential conflicts of interest that might arise.[92] On its part, the new innovation partnership is designed as a procedure aimed at the financing[93] and

[86]For discussion and further references, see Albert Sanchez-Graells, 'Some Reflections on the 'Artificial Narrowing of Competition' as a Check on Discretion in Public Procurement' in Bogojevic, Groussot and Hettne (n 2) 79-98. Cf Sanja Bogojevic, 'Mapping Public Procurement and Environmental Law Intersections in Discretionary Space' in Bogojevic, Groussot and Hettne (n 2). See also Jason J Czarnezki, 'EU and US Discretion in Public Procurement Law: The Role of Eco-Labels and Life-Cycle Costing' in Bogojevic, Groussot and Hettne (n 2).

[87]Public Procurement Directive, art 31.

[88]Commission, 'Guidance on Innovation Procurement' (Communication) COM (2018) 3051 final.

[89]Public Procurement Directive, art 40.

[90]Public Procurement Directive, art 40 indeed stresses that 'contracting authorities may for example seek or accept advice from independent experts or authorities or from market participants. That advice may be used in the planning and conduct of the procurement procedure, provided that such advice does not have the effect of distorting competition and does not result in a violation of the principles of non-discrimination and transparency'.

[91]Public Procurement Directive, arts 41, 57(4)(f).

[92]Public Procurement Directive, art 24.

[93]However, the interaction between the innovation partnership and the EU rules on State aid remains somewhat unclear after the adoption by the Commission 'Notice on the notion of State aid as referred to in art 107(1) of the Treaty on the Functioning of the European Union' [2016] OJ C262/1. For discussion, see Grith Skovgaard Ølykke, 'Commission Notice on the Notion of State

co-creation of 'innovative product, service or works that cannot be met by purchasing products, services or works already available on the market'. This requires specific regulation of *inter alia* the ownership and exploitation of the IP derived from the innovation pursued through the partnership.[94]

On the other hand, the new rules have also regulated different possibilities for contracting authorities to seek to 'join forces' and carry out collaborative procurement, including on a cross-border basis.[95] This is particularly relevant in the area of urban mobility, as joint and cross-border procurement have been identified as areas of policy interest in order to support the undertaking of projects that can be too large or complex for a single contracting authority, or as a manner of generating sufficient demand to ensure a minimum scale that makes pilot projects viable (or at least affordable).[96]

In this area, thus, it seems that the 2014 EU Public Procurement Package has also removed most of the legal obstacles to the carrying out of complex or collaborative procurement,[97] but it has also increased the potential complexity of the procurement in a way that also generates complex practical issues, as discussed below (Sect. 4).

3.3 Making Sure Promises Are Kept: Whole-Life Monitoring and Post-Execution Learning

Finally, and as mentioned above, it is worth stressing that the 2014 EU Public Procurement rules allow for the imposition of contractual performance conditions reflecting environmental considerations.[98] This could be used for a variety of purposes and the Commission has developed specific guidance for supplies and services contracts.[99] The main difficulty with the introduction of contractual

Aid as Referred to in Article 107(1) TFEU - Is the Conduct of a Public Procurement Procedure Sufficient to Eliminate the Risk of Granting State Aid?' (2016) 5 Public Procurement Law Review 197-212.

[94]Public Procurement Directive, art 31(6) last sentence.

[95]For discussion and further references, see Albert Sanchez-Graells, 'The Emergence of Trans-EU Collaborative Procurement: A "Living Lab" for European Public Law' (2020) 29 Public Procurement Law Review 16-41.

[96]See eg SPICE, 'Best Practices. New Approaches to Public Procurement of Innovative Transport and Mobility Solutions within the City Environment' (*SPICE*, 2018) <http://spice-project.eu/wp-content/uploads/sites/14/2018/05/Ertico-SPICE-Best-Practice_brochure-20pages-A5-finish_web.pdf> accessed 13 February 2020.

[97]With the exception of cross-border procurement; Sanchez-Graells, 'The Emergence of Trans-EU Collaborative Procurement' (n 95).

[98]Public Procurement Directive, art 70. See also Commission, *Public Procurement Guidance for Practitioners on Avoiding the Most Common Errors in Projects Funded by the European Structural and Investment Funds* (Publications Office of the European Union 2018) 14.

[99]European Commission, *Buying Green!* (n 77) 62-65.

performance conditions is not primarily in their design, but in their monitoring.[100] This is not only a matter of ensuring the effectiveness of the conditions, but also of procurement integrity, as contracting authorities cannot establish tender requirements that they do not intend (or are not capable of) verifying.[101]

Moreover it seems clear that only after the completion of contract execution will it be possible to assess the effectiveness of the contractual conditions in delivering the desired sustainability outcomes in most cases. Other than generating contractual penalties—if foreseen in the contract—any shortcomings in this regard can only result in post-execution learning of value in the re-tendering (or the abandonment) of the relevant service. This is therefore also a possibility for the inclusion of sustainability considerations that increase procurement complexity and generate practical difficulties, which will be discussed immediately below.

4 Knowledge Gaps, Procurement Teamwork and Expertise Networks

The discussion in the earlier sections has a common thread, which is the increasing complexity of carrying out sustainability-orientated procurement, including in a digitalised context and with the aim of deploying artificial intelligence and big data analytics to unlock innovation in the development of (more) sustainable urban mobility. The analysis in Sect. 2 has shown that contracting authorities need to be increasingly savvy in the design of contractualised mechanisms of data governance, in particular with a view to ensuring compliance with the future requirements of the Open Data Directive (which are particularly stringent for high-value mobility datasets). The analysis in Sect. 3 has also shown that the 2014 EU Public Procurement Package has removed most of the obstacles to green and innovation procurement identified in the earlier generation of procurement rules. However, with the increased space for the exercise of discretion also comes the need for public buyers to manage increased complexity, while ensuring compliance with the general principles of public procurement law. All in all, the pursuit of smart procurement in a digitalised environment generates high levels of complexity.

This can only lead to the realisation that the main challenges in delivering and supporting smart urban mobility through procurement relate to the higher-level or cross-cutting challenges of the professionalisation of the procurement workforce and the need to bridge significant (and growing) knowledge gaps. These knowledge gaps mainly concern technical developments in the areas of clean technologies and digital technologies. The detail of each of them is clearly distinct (although there is an overlap to be explored in terms of clean digital technologies) but, from a governance

[100] ibid, 66-67.

[101] For discussion and further references, see Albert Sanchez-Graells, *Public Procurement and the EU Competition Rules* (2nd edn, Hart 2015) 390.

perspective, both knowledge gaps raise the same challenges in terms of professionalisation and procurement expertise.

In that regard, it is worth noting that the European Commission has also identified the professionalisation of the procurement workforce as a top priority in its 2017 Strategy, which led it to adopt a specific recommendation on the professionalisation of public buyers,[102] and a flanking library of good practices and tools.[103] While the recommendation could have a positive impact on the professionalisation of the procurement function in some Member States, it also has significant flaws.[104] One of the main shortcomings of the European Commission's approach to procurement professionalisation is that it seems to be based on the assumption that each and every public buyer is capable of acquiring all skills necessary to carry out complex and smart procurement procedures,[105] and seemingly in all areas of policy and public activity. These can include such diverse and complex issues as digital technologies, environmental technologies, or social and employment requirements.

In simple terms, the entire recommendation on professionalisation is based on the assumption that individuals can carry out complex procurement satisfactorily on their own, provided they are sufficiently skilled and educated. While it is clear that an overall understanding of procurement processes and the business context in which they take place is necessary, it also seems obvious that sophisticated procurement (e.g. projects including elements of innovation or sustainability, or negotiations, or complex goods and services, or infrastructure, or the management of IP rights, and the inclusion of social clauses, etc.) cannot be carried out by individuals, however skilled. More and more, it is necessary to think along the lines of teams with complementary and interdisciplinary expertise. There is no such thing as a 'super-procurer', and the European Commission and the Member States would be foolish to try to find or educate them. In that regard, if there are competency schemes that require development to establish a blueprint for procurement training at EU level,

---

[102] Commission Recommendation 2017/1805/EU of 3 October 2017 on the professionalisation of public procurement — Building an architecture for the professionalisation of public procurement [2017] OJ L259/28.

[103] Available at Commission, *Building an Architecture for the Professionalisation of Public Procurement: Library of Good Practices and Tools Accompanying the European Commission Recommendation* (Publications Office of the European Union 2017).

[104] For discussion, see Pedro Telles, 'The Commission's Recommendation on Professionalisation of Public Procurement' (*Telles.eu*, 10 Oct 2017) <www.telles.eu/blog/2017/10/10/the-commissions-recommendation-on-professionalisation-of-public-procurement> accessed 13 February 2020; and Albert Sanchez-Graells, 'The European Commission's Recommendation on Procurement Professionalisation: Show Me The Money' (*How to Crack a Nut*, 12 Oct 2017) <www.howtocrackanut.com/blog/2017/10/12/the-commissions-recommendation-on-professionalisation-of-public-buyers-show-me-the-money> accessed 13 February 2020.

[105] In particular, as the Recommendation requires that 'Member States ... identify and define the baseline of skills and competences any public procurement practitioner should be trained in and possess, taking into account the multidisciplinary nature of procurement projects, both for dedicated procurement officials and for related functions as well as for judges and auditors', Commission Recommendation (n 102) 3.

they should not be premised on individuality but rather on teamwork and collaborative approaches. This would mean that teams of engineers or technical personnel, data scientists, economists and lawyers would need to be put together so that they can complement each other. Some training to give them an overall understanding of what they are collectively doing would be necessary and helpful, but that is a long way away from expecting them each to master a sufficiently advanced knowledge of law, economics, data sciences and clean technologies. This is highly relevant, and it is necessary to avoid shallow, box-ticking attempts to train the procurement task force in complex issues. For example, it is difficult to see how the entire commercial workforce of a Member State could quickly be trained in any specific aspect or secondary policy (such as the pursuit of sustainability or, more generally, social value through public contracts), or in data management in any meaningful way in a short period of time.[106] In this area, the recognition of the importance of expertise seems paramount if we are to avoid the hype that comes with some technological developments, in particular in the area of big data and artificial intelligence.[107]

Similarly, there are shortcomings in other policy interventions aimed at supporting the uptake of green procurement—such as the EU GPP criteria (above, Sect. 3.1)—or the potential issuance of guidance in the area of procurement data and digitalisation. While capable of making relevant and updated information readily available in their early stages, these initiatives also have very limited potential in terms of making such information *accessible* in terms of enabling public buyers' understanding and supporting their translation into actionable measures. Similarly, initiatives aimed at creating networks of domain-specific experts—including some projects financed under the Horizon2020 programme, such as SPICE,[108] or the more general activities of CIVITAS[109]—are generally constrained by issues of continuity of their activities, language barriers, potentially outdated materials[110] and, more generally, uncertainty about funding continuity. Publishing increasing volumes of material does not necessarily reduce the burden of contracting authorities seeking to facilitate innovation in the development of more sustainable urban mobility.

[106]Cf the claims made by the UK Government in the recent public consultation: Cabinet Office and Department for Digital, Culture, Media and Sport, 'Social Value in Government Procurement' (*GOV.UK*, 11 March 2019) 9 <www.gov.uk/government/consultations/social-value-in-government-procurement> accessed 13 February 2020, where it promised to 'train all 4000 commercial buyers in government in how to design procurement to deliver social value effectively and efficiently'; see public consultation document.

[107]For related discussion, see Albert Sanchez-Graells, '"Screening for Cartels" in Public Procurement: Cheating at Solitaire to Sell Fool's Gold?' (2019) 10 Journal of European Competition Law & Practice 199-211.

[108]CIVITAS (n 1) 18.

[109]CIVITAS (*CIVITAS*) <https://civitas.eu/about> accessed 13 February 2020.

[110]Eg the website of ICLEI, where it is difficult to identify what information is still current; ICLEI, 'Mobility and Transport' (*ICLEI*) <http://iclei-europe.org/topics/mobility-transport/> accessed 13 February 2020.

This is a problem that has no easy fix and the interventions at EU level can only serve to provide some general guidance or a starting point for Member States. At the end of the day, the unavoidable reality is that the deployment of data-driven innovative solutions for (more) sustainable urban mobility—and the conduct of smart procurement more generally—is rather expensive, not only regarding the need to fund the procured solutions themselves, but also in terms of the procurement capability required to identify, design, procure, and manage them while ensuring continuity and interoperability of services. More complex procurement is more expensive. There is no avoiding this. The ultimate challenge in terms of using procurement to foster innovative (more) sustainable urban mobility is thus to generate political buy-in and the commitment of significant volumes of funding in a stable manner. This is not a challenge unique to procurement in this area,[111] but it is probably one of the main determinants of the limited advances we have seen in this area to date, and perhaps particularly acute at local level.

5 Conclusions

The analysis in this chapter has shown how there are significant challenges in supporting and delivering smart urban mobility through procurement. The chapter has concentrated on three challenges of relevance in this area, involving: the creation of an open transport data in the context of contracted-out public services (Sect. 2); the use of procurement to foster sustainability (Sect. 3); and the need to upgrade the skills of the procurement workforce to deal with increased complexity (Sect. 4).

The analysis has shown that there are indeed distinct challenges in unlocking the potential of procurement-related transport and mobility data by making it available on open access. However, this is becoming a policy imperative with the approach of the expiry in July 2021 of the transposition period for the Open Data Directive, when Member States will have to ensure that high-value mobility datasets are freely available for re-use. The clock is thus ticking for contracting authorities to develop more advanced data governance contractual mechanisms. Given the need to take into consideration complex issues of protection of commercial interests and personal data rights, Member States should consider supporting this development by creating generally applicable regulatory frameworks and detailed policies aimed at supporting open access to procurement-related data. This could be an opportunity to also establish a general framework for the development of data exchange in

[111] For an overview of existing capacity constraints at Member State level, see PwC, *Stock-Taking of Administrative Capacity, Systems and Practices across the EU to Ensure the Compliance and Quality of Public Procurement Involving European Structural and Investment (ESI) Funds* (Publications Office of the European Union 2016).

business to government settings, as well as to implement more general mechanisms of open procurement data.[112]

There are also distinct challenges in exercising discretion to embed sustainability considerations throughout the procurement cycle, including in the monitoring of the execution of public contracts, and in the adoption of new procedures for complex and collaborative procurement. However, the analysis in this chapter has shown that the challenges and obstacles are not primarily of a legal nature, but rather relate to practical difficulties. In that regard, the chapter has also stressed how the complexity of the practical implementation of open data and sustainability policies in procurement ultimately compounds the difficulties derived from the higher-level challenge of ensuring professionalisation, sufficient capability and skills in the procurement workforce. The chapter has stressed how, ultimately, this is a matter of resources, which requires political support.

It therefore seems that there is a risk of very unequal development of more sustainable urban mobility across the EU and that, as things stand, it will only be in the better-resourced (and more risk-taking) larger cities that the conditions for the emergence of innovation may lead to practical changes.[113] This would be an undesirable state of affairs, as sustainability needs to be embedded across procurement activities and—with the unavoidable constraint of the imperatives of the minimum scale that can support specific projects—it should reach as many citizens as possible right across the EU.

It therefore seems to me that Member States should take the (anyway unavoidable) opportunity of the transposition of the Open Data Directive to address the largely neglected area of the necessary investments in the digitalisation of procurement. In parallel they should also place significant investment in programmes to upskill the procurement workforce (and not just concerning data sciences). In the context of the climate emergency and growing pressure for political support for meaningful changes, it seems clear that the public sector needs to upskill and significantly invest in the acquisition of expertise in clean technologies and in the measurement of the environmental impacts of different public policies and interventions. The urban mobility setting can serve as a springboard or sandbox to trial pilot programmes that can then be scaled and rolled-out over the rest of the public sector. It would be expensive and difficult to do this. However, continuing to expect more and more from the procurement function in terms of digital adaptation and achievement of sustainability goals without committing significant investments to facilitate it is an unsustainable position to hold.

The new Von der Leyen Commission could perhaps also move past the soft approaches followed by the Juncker Commission and try to find ways to get the

[112]Taking also advantage of the need to adapt to the new rules on eForms by 14 November 2022; see Commission Implementing Regulation (EU) 2019/1780 of 23 September 2019 establishing standard forms for the publication of notices in the field of public procurement and repealing Implementing Regulation (EU) 2015/1986 (eForms) [2019] OJ L272/7.

[113]Along the same lines, Rolnick and others (n 8) 23.

Member States to make these necessary investments, in particular in view of its expressed commitment to digitalisation and tackling climate change.[114] Otherwise, the prospect of more sustainable procurement under the 2014 EU Public Procurement Package—and of more accessible data fuelling a revolution in digital procurement governance under the 2019 Open Data Directive—will remain elusive, marred by the very practical constraints identified in this chapter.

[114]See Commission, 'Press release: The Von der Leyen Commission: for a Union that Strives for More' (IP/19/5542, 10 Sep 2019) <https://ec.europa.eu/commission/presscorner/detail/en/ip_19_5542> accessed 13 February 2020.

Governing Smart Spaces Through Autonomous Vehicles

Jannice Käll

Contents

Abstract Autonomous vehicles may be understood to govern the spaces around them through their technological composites. This understanding of governance, or control, diverges from established perspectives in intellectual property and competition law according to which technological control is assessed in relation to societal, or market, effects. This chapter bypasses such questions by exploring how autonomous vehicles can be understood to interact with their surrounding environment, whether urban or not, and how this in itself can be considered a new form of control.

To arrive at a visualization of this type of governance, a theory of spatial property is here deployed and developed. In short, this theory implies that property can be understood as something that holds up bodies in, and as, space. The aim of pursuing such a perspective is to show that governance occurs through different interfaces between autonomous vehicles and space. In sum, this chapter suggests a threefold understanding of governance in terms of how autonomous vehicles could govern smart spaces: through data commodification, through control over the surrounding space's materialities and through control over the interpretation of space.

Jannice Käll, LL.D. Legal Philosophy, is Postdoctoral Fellow, Department of Sociology of Law, Lund University, Lund, Sweden.

J. Käll (✉)
Department of Sociology of Law, Lund University, Lund, Sweden
e-mail: jannice.kall@soclaw.lu.se

M. Finck et al. (eds.), *Smart Urban Mobility*, MPI Studies on Intellectual Property and Competition Law 29, https://doi.org/10.1007/978-3-662-61920-9_7

1 Introduction

As this volume makes apparent, we are currently experiencing a new shift in the digitalization of society. The so-called '4th revolution'[1] includes an increased focus on various digital innovations such as artificial intelligence and smart objects. As is increasingly well known, this is a development that started with technological objects such as mobile phones but has spread to such a degree that we now see advanced attempts to make entire cities smart.[2] The various digital phenomena integrated into smart cities, such as autonomous vehicles, have also been researched in their own right. The perspective of smart urban mobility, however, invites a further consideration of these two different perspectives—on the city as a smart space and on the smart objects that improve mobility, such as autonomous vehicles—together.

Studies of objects and spaces and their interconnectivity come from different theoretical streams as well as areas of empirical focus. One perspective that is specifically relevant to the interaction and interdependency of autonomous vehicles and spaces is the work carried out on the entanglements between code and space. An early and significant contribution was made by Rob Kitchin and Martin Dodge in their work 'Code/Space' from 2011. In this book, they explain how code and space need to be read together as code becomes embedded both in objects and spaces to a larger degree than ever before. In short, they argue that '[c]ode/space occurs when software and the spatiality of everyday life becomes mutually constituted, that is, produced through one another. Here, spatiality is the product of code, and the code exists primarily in order to produce a particular spatiality.'[3]

The aim of this chapter is to read the entanglements between coded objects, such as autonomous vehicles, and coded spaces, such as the environments surrounding them, through the lens of property. Through this theorization, the chapter may be understood as a first step towards mapping autonomous vehicles and the way they govern space as a form of spatialized property control. In doing this, the discussion here will mostly focus on providing a theoretical framework for how to consider the connection between autonomous vehicles and space as one that is embedded in, and producing, property in new ways. Examples of related discussions as well as practical cases have been chosen to support this perspective. They should not be understood as empirical proof for the existence of de facto emerging property control. The aim of this chapter is not to substantiate the theory with empirical evidence, but rather to make use of what philosopher Rosi Braidotti, along the lines of Giles Deleuze and Félix Guattari's work, has framed as a cartographical methodology. This implies that boundary cases have been sought out that push current

[1]Luciano Floridi, *The 4th Revolution: How the Infosphere is Reshaping Human Reality* (Oxford University Press 2014).

[2]Jathan Sadowski and Roy Bendor, 'Selling Smartness: Corporate Narratives and the Smart City as a Sociotechnical Imaginary' (2019) 44 Science, Technology, & Human Values 540.

[3]Rob Kitchin and Martin Dodge, *Code/Space, Software and Everyday Life* (MIT Press 2011).

forms of thinking to an extreme.[4] Such a methodology is specifically apt for the study of digital/digitalized innovations since they in themselves tend to uproot many of the binaries—in as well as outside law—that modern understandings of society tend to rely upon.[5] A methodological starting point for this chapter is therefore to situate two things which are usually considered separate—vehicles and space—as interconnected phenomena. From a practical perspective, then, the cases have all been chosen to show where this entanglement becomes especially poignant. The further aim in deploying this methodology is to convey a more complex understanding of what the entanglement between autonomous vehicles and space implies in terms of the boundaries of property rights.

A preliminary conclusion from the present exploration of this entanglement is that its relation to property control is more complex than whether or not there are property rights embedded in the technologies being deployed. The reason for this is that autonomous vehicles' embeddedness in their environments in and of itself challenges traditional boundaries of property control.[6] What is more important in regard to this chapter, however, is to visualize the possibility of using new theories of property to better capture the way in which new forms of governance are embedded in emerging phenomena such as autonomous vehicles. To this end, the present chapter elaborates a theory of spatial property control with the purpose of making visible how autonomous vehicles function as vectors to govern their surrounding space in several ways.

Following the introduction, this chapter is divided into five sections. The first section elaborates on some theoretical and methodological foundations for spatial theory in general and for spatial property theory in particular. The second section discusses how control over spatial property through autonomous vehicles can be seen to unfold similarly to control over digital phenomena in general: through the commodification of data, intellectual property rights, contracts and encryption technologies. The third section delves further into the spatial aspects of property with respect to autonomous vehicles by considering how autonomous vehicles navigate space by making it readable, e.g. through scanning technologies. The fourth section combines the insights from the second and third sections to show that an expanded form of spatial property control in relation to autonomous vehicles may be visualized through the way they interpret their surroundings, e.g. using different forms of artificial intelligence. The fifth section summarizes the preceding sections and demonstrates why spatial property is a fruitful theoretical perspective for understanding the way autonomous vehicles might govern the spaces around them.

---

[4]Rosi Braidotti, *The Posthuman* (Polity Press 2013) 164; Rick Dolphijn and Iris van der Tuin, 'Pushing Dualism to an Extreme: On the Philosophical Impetus of a New Materialism' (2011) 44 Continental Philosophy Review 383, 392f.

[5]For a longer discussion on this perspective, see my doctoral dissertation: Jannice Käll, *Converging Human and Digital Bodies, Posthumanism, Property, Law* (University of Gothenburg 2017) 41-44.

[6]cf Margaret Jane Radin, *Contested Commodities* (Harvard University Press 1996).

2 A Spatial Turn in Law and Property

A theoretical starting point for this chapter is that law needs to be increasingly understood as materially embedded both in and through technologies rather than as an object that can be studied merely by engaging with legislation, legal cases and the other materials that continue to be considered the main sources of law. The move towards a perspective on law that sees beyond the traditional legal sources has to varying degrees been identified as a spatial turn in law. By now, this spatial turn has been developing for a long time and in more or less converging directions,[7] similar to the spatial turn in theory in general.[8] To summarize, the spatial turn in law pays more detailed attention to how law comes to be effectuated through space as well as how law performs and subsequently changes space or holds it up as a specific place.[9] In [illegible] and [illegible] understandings of law under the spatial turn, law is still understood as being ordered by the power of the nation-state (including its legislative or judicial acts of surrendering power to supranational organs). The more full-fledged version of the spatial turn, advocated significantly by Andreas Philippopoulos-Mihalopoulos, understands law as a performative practice that is integrated into space. Philippopoulos-Mihalopoulos exemplifies this by pushing for an understanding of law where law also means '[. . .] the pavement, the traffic light, the hoodie in the shopping mall, the veil in the school, the cell in Guantanamo, the seating arrangement at a meeting, the risotto at the restaurant'.[10]

Such a perspective on law fits well with current developments relating to the perception of law's role in establishing intelligence in objects. The reason for this is that when technology takes on such function it renders capacities for action, including actions that effectuate norms, into objects. Mireille Hildebrandt, e.g., suggests that the operationalization of smart technologies as governance systems can in this way be understood to lead to the end of law as a textual order wherein law is primarily seen as located under the rule of law and effectuated by courts. This implies that understanding law as a facilitator of justice and democracy may be lost if law does not find a way to integrate smart technologies and the current living conditions into its sphere.[11] As a response to this challenge, Hildebrandt suggests that a new position with regard to norms and values such as privacy is imperative. Substance and effectiveness must according to Hildebrandt further be evaluated 'in the light of the relevant new technologies, taking into account that the design of such technologies makes a difference for the values and the legal norms they enable or overrule.'[12] Instead of referring to the development of smart objects as the end of

---

[7]Andreas Philippopoulos-Mihalopoulos, *Spatial Justice, Body, Lawscape, Atmosphere* (Routledge 2015) 15-28.

[8]See eg Doreen Massey, *For Space* (Sage Publications 2006).

[9]Eg Philippopoulos-Mihalopoulos (n 7) 5.

[10]ibid 215.

[11]Mireille Hildebrandt, *Smart technologies and the End(s) of Law* (Routledge 2015).

[12]ibid 216.

law,[13] this section argues that the introduction of intelligence to vehicles, e.g., and the manner in which this intelligence is produced and controlled may function as a way of coming to terms with the fact that law has always been material through and through.[14]

Such a materialistic focus makes it possible to understand that the fundamental technologies that make vehicles autonomous not only create smartness but also new means of control. As outlined in the introduction, this section aims to look beyond productive control over smart urban mobility by reframing it as conceptual control over objects moving around in an environment. This can be summarized as the process of questioning how the pursuit of control manifests in the way that smart vehicles are made to communicate with their environment. The chapter is thus theoretically affiliated with the insight (stemming from the fields of intellectual property and law and technology) that legal control can be exercised through—or even replaced by—code, as will be further explored below. However, the aim here is also to push such perspectives further by applying the recent developments in property theory that build upon the spatial turn in law. This is here referred to as the perspective of spatial property.

This perspective in property theory builds upon work in legal geography that shows how the link between law, space and identity has become connected to such a degree that they are constitutive of each other. As Sarah Keenan describes it, this work attempts to show how law plays a role in the production of particular places, '[...] from nation-states to public parks to eruvs'.[15] This perspective implies that property rights are to be understood not only as a form of control over elements/commodities as fixed matter but as a continuous 'holding up of bodies' through multiple affective as well as material registers.[16] The idea that property is something that holds up bodies as space implies that property can subsequently be understood as '[...] a spatially contingent relation of belonging [...]'.[17] As Keenan further puts it:

> 'Holding up' [...] is a (more) diffuse, heterogeneous, spatial process than state recognition; it invokes a range of social processes, structures and networks that give force to relations of belonging.[18]

Thus, the aim of thinking about property in this register is both to show how material elements are part of what property entails (i.e. 'spatial process') as well as to attend to the notion that other aspects determine which bodies relate to each other or how these bodies are held up in/as space. Keenan develops her theoretical matrix

[13] ibid.

[14] cf Philippopoulos-Mihalopoulos (n 7) 215.

[15] Sarah Keenan, *Subversive Property: Law and the Production of Spaces of Belonging* (Routledge 2015) 17.

[16] ibid.

[17] ibid 6.

[18] ibid 7.

around an intersectional perspective on power.[19] This entails accounting for a matrix of interconnected power regimes, such as those related to race, sexuality and gender. As Kimberlé Crenshaw shows, intersectional understandings of power also takes into account how these different forms of power intersect with each other in the production of society.[20] What connects such intersectional perspectives on power with perspectives on how materialities shape and connect bodies is an understanding of matter, or bodies, as deeply relational and affectively bound together (or kept apart).[21] From the perspective of property, this means that property rights are understood as ongoing forms of control that depend on both matter and social structures for their effectuation. Furthermore, this means that space, as well as one's status as a person, cannot be understood as something that exists apart from property objects but as something entangled with them. To sum up the theoretical argument of spatial property, the aim is to show that property connects the various materialities and forces that arrange space.

3 Controlling Data as a Commodity (as Usual)

The commodification of data is a core aspect of more or less all modern digital technologies. As they continue to be developed, autonomous vehicles are another sphere into which control over data as a business asset will likely extend. This implies that phenomena such as service-based business models as well as the focus on creating intellectual assets that can be controlled under intellectual property rights will likely extend here as well. An example of the migration of such logics to a new area is the conceptualization of Transport as a Service (TaaS). The move to consider transport as well as many hardware-imbued business models as services often comes with the promise of increasing efficiency by sharing resources.[22] As such, if this indeed leads to a more efficient use of resources, it speaks against the view that property is best used when kept exclusively by one owner.[23] The promise of sharing resources may, however, also be complemented by a more troubling prospect in the

[19]Keenan (n 15) 18-20.

[20]Devon W Carbado and others, 'Intersectionality: Mapping the Movements of a Theory' (2013) 10 Du Bois Review: Social Science Research on Race 303.

[21]Käll, *Converging Human and Digital Bodies, Posthumanism, Property, Law* (n 5).

[22]See eg Megan Lampinen, 'Smart Cities and the Vehicle Ownership Shift' (*Automotive World*, 28 February 2018) <www.automotiveworld.com/articles/smart-cities-vehicle-ownership-shift/> accessed 10 January 2020.

[23]Garrett Hardin, 'The Tragedy of the Commons' (1968) 162 Science 1243, see also Giulia Priora and Caterina Sganga, 'Smart Urban Mobility: A Positive or Negative IP Space? A Case Study to Test the Role of IP in Fostering Digital Data-Driven Innovation', in this volume.

event that data becomes a core commodity and the vehicle becomes not only a service but a platform.[24] As Jussi Parikka points out:

> The intensity of imagining practices that relate to autonomous cars is due to their (by necessity) needed capacity to be able to process in-situ loads of incoming data in relation to their environment while simultaneously transmitting this data in real-time with the wider network in which they are connected.[25]

Taking the perspective of the centrality of data to autonomous vehicles, it is also interesting to return to some of the early insights in intellectual property theory that considered bundling up the concepts of intellectual property and contract as a way to produce property control in digital settings. As argued by Margaret Jane Radin, we can note that new forms of the commodification of information have arisen as the conceptual categories of intellectual property commodities (such as computer code) converge with boilerplate contracts (such as standardized service agreements) in ways that go beyond the traditional concept of copyright. As digitalization has moved forward, it has also become increasingly visible that the contract may function as an extended means to control knowledge-based elements as assets. As Radin subsequently points out, one could even argue that the contract as an institution in digital domains has collapsed into the institution of intellectual property.[26] Radin comes to this conclusion by stressing how contracts may be understood to further embody digital technology in the manner of so-called 'boilerplate contracts', which are the main form of contract in digital settings today.[27] These boilerplate contracts are inherently connected to the servitization of digital commodities as the latter are generally offered as streamed services.[28]

Elaborating on Radin's insights into intellectual property rights, contract and technology through the lens of spatial property can function as a first step to making visible the materialization that enables interactions between objects and space. As Radin herself shows, the convergence between intellectual property and contract can be derived from a general development in which digitalization renders information into *tangible objects.* Such information tangibility can be understood to closely follow on from a general development in cybernetics where information is seen as

[24]On platform-based business models, see Annabelle Gawer, 'Platform Dynamics and Strategies: From Products to Services', in Annabelle Gawer (ed), *Platforms, Markets and Innovation* (Edward Elgar Publishing 2009).

[25]Jussi Parikka, 'On Seeing Where There's Nothing to See: Practices of Light Beyond Photography' in Thomas Dvorak and Jussi Parikka (eds), *Photography Off the Scale* (Edinburgh University Press 2020) (final draft) 8.

[26]Margaret J Radin, *Boilerplate: The Fine Print, Vanishing Rights, and the Rule of Law* (Princeton University Press 2013).

[27]Other terms for the general phenomenon of non-negotiable contracts include: adhesion contract, standard contract, take-it-or-leave-it contract, and shrinkwrap contract.

[28]Radin, *Boilerplate: The Fine Print, Vanishing Rights, and the Rule of Law* (n 26) and Margaret J Radin, 'Information Tangibility' in Ove Granstrand (ed), *Economics, Law and Intellectual Property: Seeking Strategies for Research and Teaching in a Developing Field* (Springer Science and Business Media 2003).

embodied independently from the human mind.[29] In this way, digital technologies as well as legal tools such as intellectual property rights and contracts increased the number of possibilities for commodifying information early on by making it possible to treat it as something tangible.[30]

Most likely, the importance of data flows in relation to autonomous vehicles will also manifest in an interest in controlling data that makes the connection between a vehicle and its surrounding space intelligible (as indicated in the quote by Parikka above). We already have a number of current examples to show that market actors are interested in data on how both people and cars move, e.g. the data provided by a number of exercise apps as well as GPS systems. The question of who will be able to control such data (and how) will therefore be of interest from the perspectives of intellectual property rights and data privacy, among others. The first insight gained by viewing these questions through a spatial property lens is that such data collection will have the possibility to work as an input that helps arrange space by providing information about how bodies move in space.[31] This marks a change from spaces where no data is collected and as such opens up new possibilities of control.

New encryption technologies could also have the consequence that data are kept increasingly secret and that information about the interaction between a vehicle and its surroundings is locked up as a result.[32] If this happens, it could be understood as a further shift in property logics whereby information in the interface between the private (i.e. autonomous vehicles controlled as property) and the public (i.e. things which citizens own in common) is increasingly in the hands of those who control the interface between autonomous vehicles and their environments. Such a shift leads us to the next part of this chapter, which addresses how spatial property theory can visualize how the pursuit of autonomous vehicles also recreates the materialities of the environments they move in in order to make them readable—and controllable.

4 Controlling Space's Materialities

The second aspect that is here visualized through spatial property is the way that space can be rematerialized through autonomous vehicles, possibly enabling a new form of control over this space as property. In media theory, the hybridization of vehicles and space has been addressed, among others, by Benjamin Bratton, who juxtaposes geography as a static form of measure with geolocation as a mediated practice embedded in the vehicle. He further points out that this mediation of space through the vehicle and geolocation services embedded in the vehicle can be understood as a new form of governance. This new logic unsettles both the owner

[29]See eg N Katherine Hayles, *How We Became Posthuman* (University of Chicago Press 1999).

[30]Radin, 'Information Tangibility' (n 28).

[31]Eg Philippopoulos-Mihalopoulos (n 7) 5.

[32]cf Jannice Käll, 'Blockchain Control' (2018) 29 Law & Critique 133.

of the vehicle and its place in space as well as who is in control of such governance. Furthermore, it addresses how such control is mediated, or codified, through visual interfaces.[33] As he puts it:

> When geography becomes geolocation, who or what truly occupies any given place? Its owner, its user, the platform that makes it useful to either? Again, how is one person governed when platforms of governance see her as a User at a particular layer of a whole more than as a formal citizen? What freedoms of movement and freedoms from movement can she claim? What constitutes a constitution when the terms of engagement with other publics, near and far, both human and nonhuman, are codified into visual interfaces—images that are also tools?[34]

From the perspective of spatial property, the realization of governance being embedded in smart or autonomous vehicles means the continuation of a logic discussed early on in terms of digitalization and control by Lawrence Lessig[35] and Jonathan Zittrain,[36] among others. Such a logic of governance implies that a number of convergences between law/governance, proprietary objects and coded environments are made visible. Even in a narrow sense, where intellectual property is understood as legally enacted rights to intellectual goods, the perspective advocated by Lessig and Zittrain implies that the construction of property as a legal right in itself extends to the governance of space. Lessig, e.g., addresses this effect in his famous remark that by coding certain properties, one can make certain actions impossible instead of just illegal. One of the examples that Lessig uses to illustrate this is how a person famous for creating beautiful poisonous plants in a virtual game was convinced by another player to make the poisonous effects disappear if flowers were stolen instead of bought from her. As Lessig shows, in virtual spaces, the coding of property objects in this way can be understood to transform (and as a result, extend) property power into a form that is inconceivable in an offline setting.[37] Zittrain further argues that the internet was from the beginning both a set of building blocks as well as a 'glue' holding the blocks together.[38] As I have mentioned above, this embedded governance of space through its material building blocks may be better enforced when advanced encryption technologies are added.[39]

Something else, however, is peculiar to the spatial governance embedded in autonomous vehicles as compared to spaces that are more fully digitized, such as the internet. The reason for this is that the vehicles as well as the spaces in which they move were equally dumb—or non-embedded in digital technologies—before their mutual shift to smartness in recent times. For the autonomous vehicle to become integrated into the spatial register, its capacity to read physical space requires a

[33]Benjamin H Bratton, *The Stacks: On Software and Sovereignty* (MIT Press 2015) 13.

[34]ibid.

[35]Lawrence Lessig, *Code and Other Laws of Cyberspace* (Basic Books 1999) 11-15.

[36]Jonathan Zittrain, 'The Generative Internet' (2006) 119 Harvard Law Review 1974.

[37]Lessig (n 35) and Zittrain (n 36).

[38]Zittrain (n 36).

[39]Also see: Käll, 'Blockchain Control' (n 32).

change to the material layer of both the vehicle and the space around it. One way that this new materialization is happening is that cities are being '[. . .] cut through by an extensive range of wireless signals between signal stations [. . .]'.[40] In this way, one can argue that the environment, in order for autonomous vehicles to read it, has to function as a site for seeing and sensing.[41] As Parikka puts it:

> we can now articulate how this camera-eye got stuck on the (autonomous) car, where it sees in ways that are not just seeing but modelling, mapping, measuring, predicting, and a range of other cultural techniques that pave the way for a wider set of infrastructural implications. In other words, the forms of seeing now introduced—whether through WiFi signals, lidar, radar or camera as measurements—are part of the operative ontologies that do not focus on the act of seeing at the site of the device or the body of the perceiver, but in the connected networks where multiple feeds are a part of the dynamic formation of an image in real-time.[42]

Bratton also points out that 'the integrated design of driverless cars includes navigation interfaces, computationally intensive and environmentally aware rolling hardware, and street systems that can stage the network effects of hundreds of thousands speeding robots at once'.[43] The way that LiDAR functions as a form of light scanning technology can subsequently be understood not only to materialize the environment in which the autonomous vehicle moves but to enable smart vehicles to sense and be sensed by their environment as pulses of light and sound as well as other technologies are used to map the city as 'one, intensive, complex landscape of dynamics and navigation'.[44] LiDAR technology participates in this sensing of the environment by sampling its surrounding at a rate in the range of 5–20 Hz, which is comparatively much lower than other sensors such as cameras (20–60 Hz) or WiFi adapters (100 Hz).[45] In the forthcoming text by Parikka cited above, he further suggests that WiFi in general, with its antennas and signals, can be understood as an effective sensor for detecting the outline of bodies.[46] He further points out that ScanLAB's art project Dream Life of Driverless Cars has been suggested to imply that smart vehicles transform cityscapes *and* visuality, images *and* data, movement *and* seeing movement.[47] Geoff Manaugh notably also describes how the use of 3D scanning mechanisms such as LiDAR sensors in autonomous cars make for a very specific navigational way of mapping the city as an ecology of flickering machines that capture 'extremely detailed, millimeter-scale measurements

[40] Parikka (n 25) 1.

[41] ibid.

[42] ibid 4, references omitted from quote.

[43] Bratton (n 33) 12.

[44] Parikka (n 25) 3.

[45] ibid 1.

[46] ibid.

[47] Geoff Manaugh, 'The Dream Life of Driverless Cars' *The New York Times* (New York, 11 November 2015) <www.nytimes.com/2015/11/15/magazine/the-dream-life-of-driverless-cars.html> accessed 10 January 2020.

of the surrounding environment [. . .]'.[48] Parallel to the development of autonomous vehicles utilizing the LiDAR system, Elon Musk's system for Tesla has furthermore been developed as a means to navigate the environment solely through machine learning.[49] In either case, however, the reading of the environment by the autonomous vehicle is created by a transmission and reception of information or images of the space surrounding the vehicle.[50]

This process of making the environment measurable furthermore connects to a shift in logics related to computation and control.[51] Following a theory of spatial property, changes in the environment to make a specific space readable affect which bodies can exist in this space. In the case of LiDAR, while changes to the space may not be visible for objects other than autonomous vehicles, they alter both the composition and readability of this space with the object of materializing the movements of autonomous vehicles. Through such measurement, the smart vehicle becomes a 'hub' or platform for data control that can be controlled through different traditional legal tools, such as intellectual property rights and contracts. Instead, the capacity to read the environment both shifts the space as such as well as makes the autonomous vehicle into a body with the capacity to hold up other bodies in space—both by securing and ignoring them. As illustrated in the next section, this latter stage of active participation in space can also be understood as endowing autonomous vehicles with the possibility to control the *interpretation* of space.

5 Controlling the Interpretation of Space

A final approach to considering how autonomous vehicles may become connected to a new form of spatial property is based on the normative power embedded in the way different forms of artificial intelligence (AI) interpret space. A first step towards conveying property in these terms is to understand that there are normative implications of AI. As such, this understanding deviates from the currently dominant perception of AI and various forms of automation as neutral operations leading to the general enhancement of otherwise passive or dull objects.[52] From the legal discipline, Hildebrandt, among others, has raised the issue that as with all digitalization,

[48]ibid and Parikka (n 25) 9.

[49]See eg Trent Eady, 'Tesla's Deep Learning at Scale: Using Billions of Miles to Train Neural Networks' (*Medium*, 7 May 2019) <https://towardsdatascience.com/teslas-deep-learning-at-scale-7eed85b235d3> accessed 10 January 2020.

[50]Parikka (n 25).

[51]Bratton (n 33); cf Donna J Haraway, *Simians, Cyborgs, and Women: The Reinvention of Nature* (Free Association Books 1991) 161-169.

[52]For a recent critical intervention into such debates, see eg Nick Dyer-Witheford, Atle Mikkola Kjosen and James Steinhoff, *Inhuman Power: Artificial Intelligence and the Future of Capitalism* (Pluto Press 2019).

the code is not neutral—that AI can in fact enable discrimination. In Hildebrandt's words:

> In an onli*fe* world that enables surreptitious pre-emptive targeting, the threat of prohibited discrimination differs in two respects from that in the world untouched by Big Data Analytics. First, it may not be easy to figure out that one is the subject of discrimination on the basis of a forbidden ground, because the decisions taken by smart technologies are largely invisible.[53]

In coming to recognize the relevance of such issues to autonomous vehicles, an important starting point is the notion that the detection of objects such as pedestrians and road signs is a key function of these vehicles' machine learning systems.[54] On the basis of this detection, the vehicle is taught which actions to pursue, such as when to brake or swerve, in order to mitigate damages, including fatalities. For example, Wilson, Hoffmann and Morgenstern write:

> Quickly identifying pedestrians has been a long-standing challenge in the Computer Vision community. From security systems to autonomous cars, Pedestrian Detection remains an important and crucial aspect of many Computer Vision models. Common challenges of Pedestrian Detection include: occlusion by other objects or people, changes in clothing, and diverse lighting conditions.[55]

Currently, the most famous example of the inadequacy of pedestrian detection in autonomous vehicles concerns an Uber Technologies, Inc. (Uber) test vehicle. The modified 2017 Volvo XC90, while operating with a self-driving system in computer control mode, struck a pedestrian on northbound Mill Avenue in Tempe, Maricopa County, Arizona, 18 March 2018. The Uber test vehicle was occupied by one vehicle operator.[56] As outlined in the preliminary report:

> Uber had equipped the test vehicle with a developmental self-driving system. The system consisted of forward- and side-facing cameras, radars, LIDAR, navigation sensors, and a computing and data storage unit integrated into the vehicle. Uber had also equipped the vehicle with an aftermarket camera system that was mounted in the windshield and rear window and that provided additional front and rear videos, along with an inward-facing view of the vehicle operator. In total, 10 camera views were recorded over the course of the entire trip.[57]

Furthermore, the report states that '[t]he self-driving system relies on an underlying map that establishes speed limits and permissible lanes of travel'.[58]

---

[53] Hildebrandt (n 11) 96.

[54] See eg Benjamin Wilson, Judy Hoffman and Jamie Morgenstern, 'Predictive Inequity in Object Detection' <https://arxiv.org/pdf/1902.11097.pdf> accessed 5 January 2020.

[55] ibid.

[56] National Transportation Safety Board, 'Preliminary Report Highway Hwy18mh010' 1 <www.ntsb.gov/investigations/AccidentReports/Reports/HWY18MH010-prelim.pdf> accessed 5 January 2020.

[57] ibid 2.

[58] ibid.

This case elucidates both of the above-mentioned ways a vehicle becomes embedded in space when scanning the city. In the crash report, it was furthermore addressed that one of the reasons for the crash was the fact that the system could not interpret the spatial characteristics of the human that was hit. The reason why the system failed to make an accurate interpretation in due time was that the person was jaywalking, something which had not been programmed as typical human behavior. Instead, the system classified the jaywalking human first as an unknown object, then as a vehicle and finally as a bicycle.[59] Possible further causes of the failure to interpret the pedestrian in this case are indicated by the crash report: videos from the crash show that the pedestrian was dressed in dark clothing and that the bicycle she walked with did not have any side reflectors. Furthermore, the report indicates that the victim tested positive in toxicology tests for marijuana and methamphetamine.[60] The characteristics described in the report appear to deviate from what is considered normal human behavior, including crossing the street at an unmarked, non-lit place, as well as from what is considered a normal human body, seeing that the substances revealed in the toxicology test are not understood to 'naturally' belong to the body.

Another example of how AI in autonomous vehicles interprets the bodies surrounding them was recently addressed in an article on machine learning (ML) vision systems in the above-cited article by Wilson, Hoffman and Morgenstern. In this article, they point to several examples of such systems displaying higher error rates for certain demographic groups than for others. Specifically, the article sets out to measure predictive imbalance for ML-guided vision systems related to driving-centric object detection. Their article asks in particular whether the detection of pedestrians differs depending on their respective skin tones. In conclusion, they propose that there are indications of a traceable inequality in how well the studied systems managed to detect pedestrians of different skin tones. They substantiate this claim by showing that standard models of object detection, trained on standard datasets, appear to exhibit higher precision for lower so-called Fitzpatrick skin types than for higher skin types—that is, for lighter versus darker skin tones. The machine learning systems assessed in the article were therefore found to discriminate between skin tones to the detriment of those with darker skin tones. It can be noted that, in regard to whether it was light outside, the study found no difference in terms of this type of discrimination (there was even a slight indication that the system better detected pedestrians of darker skin tones in the dark than in the light).[61]

A normative effect of how autonomous vehicles interpret data about their surroundings can also be found in the example above. Here, the characteristic of the pedestrian that the vehicle relies on to avoid a collision is skin tone instead of a certain standard of human movement, as in the actual lethal case involving Uber. Yet the way ML-guided vision systems differentiate between a pedestrian and other

---

[59]ibid 2-3.

[60]ibid 3-4.

[61]ibid.

objects in the environment can have similarly hazardous effects for those with darker skin tones (according to the scale used).

From the perspective of law, to echo Hildebrandt, when machine learning fails in this way to account for differences between skin tones, it implies that discrimination has been built into the technology. From the perspective of spatial property specifically, one may go further to suggest that this is not only a question of possible discrimination, but the effectuation of spatial governance by (AI systems embedded in) the autonomous vehicle. The processes that make the environment readable for autonomous vehicles are enforced by the power to interpret the environment embedded into different forms of artificial intelligence. As spatial theory informs us, making certain spaces visible and rendering others invisible partially determines what space ultimately comes into being and how.

The perspective on property as something that holds up bodies as space [illegible] a whole new intensity when the interpretative, normative qualities embedded in autonomous vehicles are made visible. The register of spatial property that can be addressed by this power to interpret and rank bodies could be framed as a form of affective power—affective, since it has the capacity to place and orient bodies in a specific way. In feminist theories such as the ones utilized by Keenan, there is also an understanding that the production of affect as something that orients bodies towards each other does not occur without an underlying logic. Instead, as mentioned above, a number of intersecting power regimes shape which bodies can reside in which space. Whiteness is one such power regime commonly addressed by these critical theories.[62] Another power regime addressed by similar perspectives on property is the entire divide between property and personhood as a classifier between human and non-human.[63] This implies that property as a power regime can be understood as an affective force as such since it is involved in holding up bodies as space. If machine learning discriminates based on skin color, this functions as an example of how the property object—the vehicle—entails the possibility of very literally holding up bodies of lighter skin tones while not doing so for bodies of darker skin tones. In a similar way, the normative ideas vested in what constitutes the human may be embedded into the systems that render space understandable for autonomous vehicles, as illustrated by the Uber case. To recap, ideas about which human behaviors are normal are embedded in the concept of the human in a particular society. These ideas may very well be embedded in power regimes that discriminate against certain bodies and behaviors in relation to others. In fact, all societies engage in sorting bodies according to different ideas about what constitutes belonging, whether by attributing subjectivity to some and not to others or in some other form. When interpretative power is embedded in autonomous vehicle systems, it can be understood as effectuating property in that these systems move or disentangle bodies

[62]See eg Sarah Ahmed, *Living a Feminist Life* (Duke University Press 2017) 43; Sarah Ahmed, 'A Phenomenology of Whiteness' (2007) 8 Feminist Theory 149.

[63]See eg Margaret Davies and Ngaire Naffine, *Are Persons Property? Legal Debates about Property and Personality* (Ashgate Publishing Limited 2002).

according to different standards. As a result, it is here suggested that the third layer of how autonomous vehicles arrange space is embedded in the affective power that they exercise through interpreting bodies—holding up some while disregarding others.

6 Conclusions: Governing Space Through Autonomous Vehicles—Why a Theory of Spatial Property Manages to Make Emerging Forms of Control Visible

In this chapter, my aim has been to study some of the unfolding interconnections between autonomous vehicles and space through the perspective of spatial property. To summarize, it has been argued that these interconnections can be explored through (at least) three emerging practices related to the way autonomous vehicles control or are connected to the spaces surrounding them. These practices have here been outlined as data commodification, control over space's materialities and control over the interpretation of space.

None of the forms of control that have here been visualized with reference to spatial property are new as such. For example, the commodification of data as an asset has for some time now functioned as a vector for platform-based business models online. As autonomous vehicles emerge as a new technology as well as a new area of the market, the same rationale is likely just extending into another era. As it does so, however, it also changes form. The reason for this is that because other characteristics of vehicles are commodities in their own right, it will be of interest to control new forms of data from a market perspective as well as for the sake of further developing the technologies involved. For example, where user data plays an important role in online business models (as they are often employed in personalized advertising), data in relation to a vehicle's spatiality, such as geo-location and geo-tracking, will become the more important asset to control in relation to autonomous vehicles. Furthermore, the service contracts for access to the vehicle will be different than contracts for access to subscription services, community platforms, etc. It is not unlikely that contracts will furthermore target spatial qualities in previously non-digital spaces and determine who/what will be able to access such qualities. As discussed by Rossana Ducato in this volume, an example of this kind of development can now be detected in relation to Uber's driving system, where the ratings given both by consumers and drivers decide (as laid out in the contract) who can or cannot have access to an Uber vehicle.[64] In the case of autonomous vehicles, such processes could be further automated and the limits or non-limits to such practices will have spatial effects. Thus, even the initial step of movement-related data becoming an asset in relation to autonomous vehicles can be understood to represent a practice of spatial property.

[64]Rossana Ducato, 'Private Ordering of Online Platforms in Smart Urban Mobility: The Case of Uber's Rating System', in this volume.

Second, this chapter illustrates that when technologies such as LiDAR and machine learning become embedded in smart vehicles, they also rematerialize the environments around them. Considering the LiDAR system specifically, it is apparent how the technology changes the way we understand the city—as a smart city—by scanning our surroundings (including ourselves) and thereby making them readable. This entails the ordering of space based on pulses of light and the production of a continuous flow of images ready to be processed so that the environment can be understood and navigated. In this case, the aspects of the spatiality of property can be read as a way of making the environment readable for the vehicle through different types of materialities. In the simplest form, this extension of governance takes place through the mapping out of spaces, creating new data and subsequently new forms of property control. However, as discussed by Lessig, among others, the implications of coded spaces are bigger than that, both in terms of property control and law. The reason for this is that when a space is coded, it can also be altered by the terms of the code. Which technologies are deployed as well as how and by whom will be important questions in deciding what degree of property control should apply to the spaces scanned by autonomous vehicles. Here, however, it is argued that coming to see and understand how spatial property control is involved in the process of making spatial interfaces readable—whether they are urban or not—is more fundamental at this stage.

The third and final form of spatial governance exhibited by autonomous vehicles that is here analyzed through the lens of spatial property concerns the power invested in AI systems to interpret bodies moving through their surroundings. The very fact that the systems embedded in autonomous vehicles have to classify the bodies surrounding them and decide how to react to them implies that normative ideas of which bodies to protect and which to disregard are learned and enacted by the vehicles. Returning here to the idea that property can be understood as that which holds up bodies in, and as, space, one can suggest that autonomous vehicles, in acting upon their interpretation of certain bodies, directly engage in the enactment of spatial property. From a critical perspective on space, this arranging of bodies furthermore needs to be read as a form of affective power that decides which bodies are treated in which way. In order to highlight an understanding of property in which some bodies are held up as space while others are not, I have pointed to the now famous Uber case where an autonomous vehicle system failed to recognize a human as a human. I have also pointed to research indicating that the standard ML systems at the time of the study were less successful at detecting pedestrians of darker skin colors. While this chapter is limited to theoretically outlining how this could be understood as a potential form of property control, what such an enactment of interpretative power implies in the worst-case scenario is that the power wielded through autonomous vehicles could have lethal effects. This in itself is not different from how property currently functions as a means to pursue certain interests as opposed to others. However, from the perspective of spatial property theory the unfolding development in how autonomous vehicles navigate their surrounding spaces can be understood as a potential new outlet for such control.

Part II
Business Perspective

Smart Urban Mobility: A Positive or Negative IP Space? A Case Study to Test the Role of IP in Fostering Digital Data-Driven Innovation

Giulia Priora and Caterina Sganga

Contents

Abstract Not all innovative processes rely on IP exclusive rights to incentivize and protect their content. While strategic considerations on the costs and convenience of IP enforcement generally play an important role, in specific sectors alternative norms and practices have proven more effective than exclusive rights in fostering progress by turning inclusivity into benefits, thus challenging IP protection at its core. At a first glance, the wide-ranging sector of digital data-driven innovations presents a twofold nature: on the one hand, they require remarkable investments, which likely call for a strict approach to IP rights; and on the other hand, they make interoperability and follow-up creations key factors of technological progress, thus valuing inclusivity in the enhancement of resource allocation and services.

Against this background, the paper aims to investigate the role and incentivizing potential of IP rights in the smart urban mobility context, which represents an

---

Giulia Priora is Postdoctoral Research Fellow in Comparative Private Law, Caterina Sganga is Associate Professor of Comparative Private Law, both at Sant'Anna School of Advanced Studies, Pisa, Italy.

G. Priora (✉) · C. Sganga
Sant'Anna School of Advanced Studies, Pisa, Italy
e-mail: giulia.priora@santannapisa.it; caterina.sganga@santannapisa.it

M. Finck et al. (eds.), *Smart Urban Mobility*, MPI Studies on Intellectual Property and Competition Law 29, https://doi.org/10.1007/978-3-662-61920-9_8

innovative sector of remarkable social impact and is rapidly on the rise. By applying the conceptual framework of legal and economic theories exploring the so-called 'IP negative spaces', this study highlights strengths and weaknesses of the exclusive rights paradigm in the promotion and management of innovative ideas for advancing urban planning and life in European cities.

1 Introduction: Locating the Intersection Between Smart Urban Mobility and Intellectual Property

The concepts of smart cities and, among the key components, of smart urban mobility (SUM) stem from the fertile soil of digital innovation, an environment under constant and rapid evolution that has great impact on our daily activities.[1] Although the debate on the relevant definitions is still lively,[2] the direction pursued is towards more efficient governance, virtuous practices and enhanced infrastructures in order to benefit society and the environment.[3] In particular, what distinguishes SUM innovations is the broad use of digital technologies for the collection and management of data,[4] the heavy reliance on intellectual capital and knowledge management schemes,[5] and the high volumes of investments required.[6]

Since the onset of the digital revolution, intellectual property (IP) law has acquired a central role as the regulatory backbone of modern innovation policies. The reasons behind its growing importance is to a significant extent the overlap with the above-mentioned characteristics of the evolving SUM sector, as IP law commonly tackles issues of protection of knowledge and information in its various possible forms, and of risky investments. In this light, IP promises to be a

[1]See Adriano Tanda and Alberto De Marco, 'Business Model Framework for Smart City Mobility Projects' (2019) 471 IOP Conference Series: Materials Science and Engineering 2.

[2]See, *inter alia*, Clara Benevolo, Renata P Dameri and Beatrice D'Auria, 'Smart Mobility in Smart City: Action Taxonomy, ICT Intensity and Public Benefits' in Teresina Torre, Alessio M Braccini and Riccardo Spinelli (eds), *Empowering Organizations: Lecture Notes in Information Systems and Organisation* (vol 11, Springer 2016); Andrea Caragliu, Chiara Del Bo and Peter Nijkamp, 'Smart Cities in Europe' (2011) 18 Journal of Urban Technology 2.

[3]See Benevolo, Dameri and D'Auria (n 2).

[4]Hans Schaffers and others, 'Smart Cities and the Future Internet: Towards Cooperation Frameworks for Open Innovation' in John Domingue (ed), *The Future Internet: Future Internet Assembly 2011: Achievements and Technological Promises* (Springer 2011) 431–434; Jesse Shapiro, 'Smart Cities: Quality of Life, Productivity, and the Growth Effects of Human Capital' (2006) 88 The Review of Economics and Statistics 324.

[5]See Renata Dameri and Francesca Ricciardi, 'Smart City Intellectual Capital: An Emerging View of Territorial Systems Innovation Management' (2015) 16 Journal of Intellectual Capital 861.

[6]Caragliu, Del Bo and Nijkamp (n 2).

meaningful component of the regulatory picture relevant to SUM innovation. The study of the conceptual intersection between this developing reality and the IP law paradigm remains, to date, underexplored. This paper aims to fill this gap by opening a window on the role of IP in the European digital innovative society.

2 The Problem of Incentives and Viable Perspectives to Address It

It can be argued that the intersection between the SUM sector and IP law fundamentally lies on two specific and intertwined problems, i.e. the problem of generating incentives to innovate and the problem of protectability of data. SUM innovations need to be incentivized primarily because the required technological infrastructures and know-how result in significant costs.[7] IP law fundamentally tackles the problem of incentives, as its leading justification relies on the utilitarian conception of exclusive rights as a necessary mechanism to promote human creativity and technological advancement.[8]

However, in the multi-faceted development of the digital environment, traditional IP rights started to prove ill-suited to protect innovations characterized by pure informational content,[9] thus leading to policy interventions towards the expansion of the scope and duration of existing entitlements and new forms of exclusivity.[10] Interestingly, in the scholarship, the problems IP law started facing in the online world also triggered the opposite reaction, prompting the question: is IP protection really necessary to stimulate innovation? The hypothesis arose that IP rights may be playing rather an *ex post* role, if at all, in some innovative processes.[11] Patent and trademark law have been mostly challenged in their structure and effects by

[7]For a detailed overview of the relevant costs see Schaffers and others (n 4) 435ff.

[8]Eg Niva Elkin-Koren and Eli Salzberger, *The Law and Economics of Intellectual Property in the Digital Age: The Limits of Analysis* (Routledge 2013) 57ff; Robert Merges, *Justifying Intellectual Property* (Harvard University Press 2011).

[9]Rochelle Dreyfuss, 'Does IP Need IP? Accommodating Intellectual Production Outside the Intellectual Property Paradigm' (2010) 31 Cardozo Law Review 1140; Yochai Benkler, 'Open Access and Information Commons' in Francesco Parisi (ed), *The Oxford Handbook of Law and Economics: Private and Commercial Law* (vol 2, Oxford University Press 2017).

[10]The expansion of IP protection has characterized the development of the discipline affecting both the duration and scope of IP protection, as summarized, among others, by Richard Posner, 'Intellectual Property: The Law and Economics Approach' (2005) 19 Journal of Economic Perspectives 2, 72ff.

[11]Eg Laura Murray, Tina Piper and Kirsty Robertson, *Putting Intellectual Property in Its Place: Rights Discourses, Creative Labor, and the Everyday* (Oxford University Press 2014); Jessica Silbey, *The Eureka Myth: Creators, Innovators and Everyday Intellectual Property* (Stanford University Press 2014).

highlighting how misuses and considerable costs of filing and litigation jeopardize the underlying incentive mechanism.[12] The role of copyright in creating a stimulus for creativity has also been questioned in a wide array of creative contexts.[13] The sectorial take of such studies has, on the one hand, enabled a thorough and context-sensitive assessment of the incentivizing role of IP rights, while, on the other, it has opened up room for criticism concerning the narrow scope of the inquiry.[14] Investigating the role of IP in the SUM sector not only adds to the realities covered by the scholarship, but it is also likely to shed light on cutting-edge innovative scenarios, which share core features with SUM, such as the data-driven nature and the environmental protection objective.

3 An Insightful Look Into the Knockoff Economy

The question whether the introduction of a law-crafted incentive to innovate is needed has evolved into the notion of an ‘IP negative space’.[15] This concept refers to a beneficial absence of IP protection in certain fields of invention and creativity, or—in other words—to spaces where, even without IP rights being enforced, value gets generated. As mentioned above, studies in this direction have addressed well-defined scenarios, which nevertheless allowed for wider theories to emerge. Among them, Raustiala and Sprigman introduced the notion of the ‘knockoff economy’.[16] The theory highlights how in the identified environments actors are not moved by the promise of exclusive entitlements over their works[17] and, subsequently, a highly permissible ‘copying’ culture gets generated. Innovators rely heavily on existing

[12]Eg Peter Picht, ‘Standard-Essential Patents: Limiting Exclusivity for the Sake of Innovation’ in Josef Drexl and Anselm Kamperman Sanders (eds), *The Innovation Society and Intellectual Property* (Edward Elgar 2019); Ansgar Ohly, ‘Free Riding on the Repute of Trade Marks: Does Protection Generate Innovation?’ in Josef Drexl and Anselm Kamperman Sanders (eds), *The Innovation Society and Intellectual Property* (Edward Elgar 2019); Kevin Emerson Collins, ‘Patent Failure: A Tragedy of Property’ <https://ssrn.com/abstract=1156434> accessed 1 March 2020; James Bessen and Michael J Meurer, *Patent Failure: How Judges, Bureaucrats, and Lawyers Put Innovators at Risk* (Princeton University Press 2008).

[13]See below Sect. 3; Diane Leenheer Zimmerman, ‘Copyright as Incentives: Did We Just Imagine That?’ (2011) Theoretical Inquiries into Law 12, 29.

[14]Eg Robert Merges, ‘Economics of Intellectual Property Law’ in Francesco Parisi, *The Oxford Handbook of Law and Economics: Private and Commercial Law* (vol 2, Oxford University Press 2017).

[15]See Elizabeth Rosenblatt, ‘A Theory of IP’s Negative Space’ (2011) 34 Columbia Journal of Law & the Arts 317; Dreyfuss (n 9).

[16]Kal Raustiala and Christopher Sprigman, *The Knockoff Economy: How Imitation Sparks Innovation* (Oxford University Press 2012).

[17]ibid 45.

works, using, imitating and building on them, thus carrying out what is called 'productive infringement'[18] and accepting the use of their own works by third parties, thus valuing the reciprocal advantage in borrowing from each other.[19] By this token, a close interconnection between inventions comes into being and the IP utilitarian justification is challenged at its core: not exclusive rights, but rather '*copying* spurs innovation'.[20]

At first blush, the SUM sector shows remarkable convergences with the concept of the knockoff economy. The motivations driving the actors involved generally differ from the expectation of exclusive rights and monetary gain, but are rather associated with a broader idea of benefit, which pivots on quality of life and reasonable use of resources. Moreover, the rise of the city itself—especially big city hubs—as a collaborative driver of innovation seems to match with the dimension of IP negative spaces, facilitating individuals to pool resources and energies together to find viable solutions to the problems they experience in their daily life.[21]

3.1 *The Features of IP Negative Spaces*

The existence of creativity and innovation outside the IP realm is a phenomenon that has already been noticed and described in the mid-1900s with regard to academic science,[22] and later on even in sectors beyond any suspicion, such as the English iron industry in the nineteenth century.[23] For almost two decades now, the critique against the efficiency of IP law in incentivizing and sustaining the cultural and technological progress has engaged economists, lawyers, management and social scientists. The free software movement is generally identified as the first successful example of a commons-based peer-production of innovation by users, not motivated

[18] Varada Balachandran, 'Negative Spaces of Intellectual Property - A Cursory Glance' (*The IP Site*, 31 March 2016) <http://blog.ciprnuals.in/?p=220> accessed 1 March 2020: 'Productive infringement is an innovation that builds closely on its forbear'.

[19] Raustiala and Sprigman, *The Knockoff Economy* (n 16) 58.

[20] ibid 7 (emphasis added).

[21] See Schaffers and others (n 4) 431–432, 442: '[C]ities are increasingly assuming a critical role as drivers of innovation in areas such as health, inclusion, environment and business [...] considered not only as the object of innovation but also as innovation ecosystems empowering the collective intelligence and co-creation capabilities of user/citizen communities for designing innovative living and working scenarios.'

[22] As in the case of Robert Merton, 'Science and Technology in a Democratic Order' (1942) 1 Journal of Legal and Political Sociology 115. Merton is cited as the precursory of the debate by Rebecca Eisenberg, 'Proprietary Rights and the Norms of Science in Biotechnology Research' (1987) 97 Yale Law Journal 177, 179 and by Dreyfuss (n 9) 1443–1444.

[23] Described in the work of Robert Allen, 'Collective Invention' (1983) 4 Journal of Economic Behavior & Organization 1.

by the attribution of proprietary rights over their intellectual creations and developing a product which is accessible, updated, and tailored to the needs.[24] Subsequent contributions have focused on the role played by so-called prosumers in the generation of creative content,[25] followed by case studies on creative sectors characterized by a widespread diffusion of copying as accepted social behavior which supports, instead of hindering, a thriving intellectual production. Examples range from stand-up comedy[26] to graffiti and street arts,[27] typefaces,[28] cuisine,[29] magic tricks,[30] fashion,[31] fan fiction,[32] musical genres and styles,[33] sport moves.[34] Studies of

---

[24]Yochai Benkler, 'Coase's Penguin, or Linux and the Nature of the Firm' (2002) 112 Yale Law Journal 370–372; Yochai Benkler, *The Wealth of Networks: How Social Production Transforms Markets and Freedom* (Yale University Press 2006).

[25]Eg Pamela Morrison, John Roberts and Eric von Hippel, 'Determinants of User Innovation and Innovation Sharing in a Local Market' (2000) 46 Management Science 1513.

[26]Dotan Oliar and Christopher Sprigman, 'There's No Free Laugh (Anymore): The Emergence of Intellectual Property Norms and the Transformation of Stand-Up Comedy' (2008) 94 Virginia Law Review 1787.

[27]Cathay Smith, 'Street Art: An Analysis under U.S. Intellectual Property Law and Intellectual Property's Negative Space Theory' (2013) 24 DePaul Journal of Art, Technology & IP Law 259; Enrico Bonadio, 'Street Art, Graffiti and Copyright' in Enrico Bonadio and Nicola Lucchi (eds), *Non-Conventional Copyright: Do New and Atypical Works Deserve Protection?* (Edward Elgar 2018).

[28]Arul Scaria and Mathews George, 'Copyright and Typefaces' in Enrico Bonadio and Nicola Lucchi (eds), *Non-Conventional Copyright: Do New and Atypical Works Deserve Protection?* (Edward Elgar 2018); Raustiala and Sprigman, *The Knockoff Economy* (n 16) 145–155.

[29]Emmanuelle Fauchart and Eric von Hippel, 'Norms-Based Intellectual Property Systems: The Case of French Chefs' (2008) 19 Organization Science 187; Christopher Buccafusco, 'On the Legal Consequences of Sauces: Should Thomas Keller's Recipes Be Per Se Copyrightable?' (2007) 24 Cardozo Arts and Entertainment Law Journal 1121.

[30]Jacob Loshin, 'Secrets Revealed: How Magicians Protect Intellectual Property Without Law' in Christine Corcos (ed), *Law and Magic: A Collection of Essays* (Carolina Academic Press 2007) 123ff.

[31]Kal Raustiala and Christopher Springman, 'The Piracy Paradox: Innovation and Intellectual Property in Fashion Design' (2006) 92 Virginia Law Review 1687.

[32]Rebecca Tushnet, 'Legal Fictions: Copyright, Fan Fiction, and a New Common Law' (1997) 17 Loyola of Los Angeles Entertainment Law Review 651.

[33]Tonya Evans, 'Sampling, Looping and Mashing . . . Oh My! How Hip Hop Music is Scratching More Than the Surface of Copyright Law' (2011) 4 Fordham Intellectual Property, Media and Entertainment Law Journal 843; Mark Schultz, 'Fear and Norms and Rock & Roll: What Jambands Can Teach Us About Persuading People to Obey Copyright Law' (2006) 21 Berkeley Technology Law Journal 651.

[34]Peter Mezei, 'Copyright Protection of Sport Moves' in Enrico Bonadio and Nicola Lucchi (eds), *Non-Conventional Copyright: Do New and Atypical Works Deserve Protection?* (Edward Elgar 2018); Scott Kieff, Robert Kramer and Robert Kunstadt, 'It's Your Turn, but It's My Move: Intellectual Property Protection for Sports "Moves"' (2009) 25 Santa Clara Computer and High Technology Law Journal 765, 766, 774–776; Raustiala and Sprigman, *The Knockoff Economy* (n 16) 126–136.

economic history have showcased similar patterns in now patent-dominated fields such as animal and plant breeding[35] and computer hardware.[36] These considerations show that IP negative spaces appear in two different forms.[37] Some creations, inventions or, more generally, information may be completely outside the scope of IP rights, or lay in "low-IP" zones, where the protection granted is limited and hard to get.[38] Others may be eligible for protection, but authors and inventors do not commonly resort to enforcement against infringements.[39] In both cases, creativity and innovation are present and thrive without relying on IP, but thanks to sector-specific social and business norms.

Despite their heterogeneity, the various scenarios share similar features, which scholars have tried to outline in an attempt to propose a general theory of what makes a creative or industry sector an IP negative space. Rosenblatt identifies four conditions that, when present, are likely to flag an IP negative space,[40] which are met when: (1) the incentive is given not by exclusivity, but by other types of rewards, not dependent on financial gain; (2) exclusivity hinders or harms subsequent innovation/creation; (3) there is high interest in free access from the public and from authors/inventor; and (4) authors/inventors are keener to invest in new innovation/creation rather than in IP enforcement.

If a creator is motivated by recognition, he/she will be willing to renounce to the benefit of exclusivity in order to decrease the cost of her work and foster access and dissemination.[41] Similarly, if the driver is the desire to belong to a community regulated by social norms that embrace a free sharing culture, creative works and inventions will be generated to contribute to the commons, and not on the basis of the promise of a future profit.[42] Incentives may also come from outside IP law, from

---

[35]Michael Heller and Rebecca Eisenberg, 'Can Patents Deter Innovation? The Anticommons in Biomedical Research' (1998) 280 Science 698.

[36]Peter B Meyer, *Episodes of Collective Invention* (Bibliogov 2013).

[37]Rosenblatt categorizes them in three areas, the third one covering products of uses that are exempted from IP infringement liability for they are covered by legislative exceptions. The category is not sector-specific and largely undefined, but for the inclusion of scholarly writing and medical techniques. See Rosenblatt (n 15) 335.

[38]Eg fashion and furniture design, typesets, recipes, perfumes, business method, sport moves and raw data fall within this category.

[39]As in the case, for instance, of programmers of open source software, academics, magicians, comedians, street art and tattoos artists.

[40]Rosenblatt (n 15) 322.

[41]See, *inter alia*, Thomas Eger and Marc Scheufen, *The Economics of Open Access* (Edward Elgar 2018) 10–11 highlighting how in academic and scientific production the drivers are scholars' curiosity and the 'recognition of priority of their research and the expected gain in reputation with their peers'. See also Daniela Simone, *Copyright and Collective Authorship: Locating the Authors of Collaborative Works* (Cambridge University Press 2019) 210–212: 'Credit is highly valued because of the reputational benefits that it might bring. [. . .] Scientific journals record much academic debate about which contributors in large collaborative projects deserve to be credited and the order in which they ought to be credited.'

[42]The peer-production sustaining the free software movement: Wikipedia and fan fiction is based on such mechanisms. See Yochai Benkler, 'Sharing Nicely: On Shareable Goods and the Emergence

the perspective of indirect, future gains: in the case of innovations which are inexpensive to produce, expensive to reverse-engineer and subject to quick obsolescence, for example, the inventor's competitive advantage derives predominantly from being the first comer, while obtaining and enforcing IP rights may be inefficient cost-wise.[43] By the same token, creations which achieve market success and increase their value thanks to network effects incentivize their makers to allow free uses—and thus forfeit exclusivity—in order to stimulate the adoption of the technology by a large number of customers, and to profit from the commercialization of related products at a later stage.[44]

While exclusivity and the fragmentation of IP ownership have the general effect of increasing the cost of new creations and inventions, naturally constraining their output, some sectors are more negatively affected by exclusivity than others, to the extent that legislative exceptions to IP rights are not enough to compensate and rebalance. This may depend on the higher risks of infringement and costs of enforcement compared to the profit deriving from the monopolistic position granted by IP, and on the relatively contained economic damages caused by the competitors' copycatting.[45] Creations featuring these characteristics, such as fashion design, recipes, perfumes, sport moves are usually more likely to become IP negative spaces.

The third condition identifies spaces that legislators carve out from IP laws in consideration of the strong public interest in maintaining certain creations and inventions in the public domain, or in excluding certain uses from infringement.[46] The legislative balance is based on the belief that, in spite of the missing or reduced exclusivity, other drivers will still sustain the production of knowledge and innovation, and/or the market will still grant a satisfactory income to the affected authors and inventors.

IP negative spaces are also likely to arise when authors and inventors are more prone to invest in the generation of new works than in obtaining protection and enforcing IP rights.[47] This may happen when the costs of applying and maintaining the exclusivity are too high compared to the actual value of the subject matter of

---

of Sharing as a Modality of Economic production' (2004) 114 Yale Law Journal 273, 321-322; Tushnet (n 32).

[43]Raustiala and Springman, 'The Piracy Paradox' (n 31) 1719-1729; Joost Poort, 'Borderlines of Copyright Protection: An Economic Analysis' in P Bernt Hugenholtz (ed), *Copyright Reconstructed. Rethinking Copyright's Economic Rights in a Time of Highly Dynamic Technological and Economic Change* (Wolters Kluwer 2018) 289–290.

[44]See Dan Burk and Mark Lemley, 'Policy Levers in Patent Law' (2003) 89 Virginia Law Review 1575, 1586-1588.

[45]See Collins (n 12); Bessen and Meurer (n 12).

[46]Rosenblatt (n 15) 349.

[47]Among the four features listed by Rosenblatt, this latter is highlighted in the literature with greatest emphasis, often in conjunction with a call for a forward-looking and inclusive approach to business. See Matthew David, *Sharing: Crime Against Capitalism* (Polity Press 2017) 83: 'In the fully digital economy, the best way to survive is to innovate, rather than to cling on to yesterday's success.'

protection, the ease (and costs) of enforcement, and the overall financial capabilities of the applicant. Examples range from the case of authors producing numerous small works, to creations having fast obsolescence, sectors featuring massive infringers or large numbers of non-infringing substitutes, or works the infringement of which is generally hard to prove, leading to high uncertainties on the outcome of potential litigations.

The four conditions may or may not be present at the same time and characterize, with different degrees, an entire sector or only part of it. The more conditions the sector features, the higher their degree of intensity and the more homogeneous their diffusion, the more the chances will be that creativity and innovation will flourish outside traditional IP schemes, and be hampered by the introduction of exclusivity rules. IP negative spaces may entail both solo production and networked peer-production as standard setting.[48] The same applies to open innovation platforms, where the development of new technologies and creations may be either fully conducted in a joint fashion or entail the reciprocal free sharing of know-how, skills, expertise and knowledge to support and foster individual production.[49] While individual creations and inventions take place following the creative norms of the sector involved and do not need specific conditions to be satisfied in order to take place, peer-production requires the common project to have particular characteristics in order to function well and reach satisfactory results.[50] In this light, it is essential to delve into the specific features and practices appropriate to the sector in order to explore the extent to which it flags the presence of an IP negative space, if at all.

3.2 Constituents of Innovation in Smart Urban Mobility Settings

SUM innovation presents three main constituents of its operation: (1) big data, (2) software infrastructures and interfaces, both in the form of traditional configurations and more sophisticated artificial intelligence algorithms, and (3) 'smart' transportation means and related accessory devices. The focus of this paper lies in the roots of innovation, as it inquires into the role of IP exclusive rights in incentivizing and sustaining new solutions to urban problems. In this sense, attention is paid to the project design, organizational practices and business models centered on the exploitation of data and software, whilst the engineering and manufacturing of smart

[48]Rosenblatt (n 15) 325.

[49]See Henry Chesbrough, *Open Innovation: The New Imperative for Creating and Profiting from Technology* (Harvard Business School Press 2003) 72–73.

[50]See Benkler, 'Coase's Penguin' (n 24) 375-376 identifying these features in modularity, heterogeneous granularity, and low-cost integration of the numerous contributions into a quality-controlled final product.

vehicles and devices is deemed a necessary, yet subsequent component flowing from the needs identified in the phase of SUM projects development.

3.2.1 (Big) Data

Data generated by users and their devices are key constituents of SUM innovation, and pillars for the development and functioning of its products and services.[51] As in any system leveraging the Internet of Things (IoT), data collected and processed by anybody for a specific purpose may be used by other market players for other purposes.[52] Smart cars register information to signal and predict the need for maintenance services, but can also collect data on road conditions, volume of traffic, viability changes, etc. Each data corpus may be aggregated to the data collected and processed by other devices, and used by municipalities to plan interventions, by intermediaries to offer traffic monitoring services, by public transportation providers to manage delays, envision alternative routes or deploy additional units, and by users to intelligently plan their itineraries. The greater the amount of data processed, the greater the reliability of the conclusions derived from their aggregation and analysis, and the larger the amount of information their correlations may provide and the number of questions it may answer.

Data used in SUM programs stem inevitably from different sources, some of them private, others public. A central role is played by user-generated data, which fundamentally contribute to the functioning of mobility services: suffice it to think of the information shared by users on locations, routes, traffic, possible disfunctions and, not less significantly, about their own preferences. Realizing the importance to grant access to public sector information (PSI) to businesses in order to foster innovation in the data economy, the EU legislator has already intervened with a Directive that aims at creating a level playing field to facilitate their commercial re-use.[53] The efficiency of sharing and cooperation against business models and policy options based on data propertization has also been clearly perceived by private actors, as proven by the skepticism they have shown in opposing regulatory proposals of the introduction of exclusive rights for data producers.[54] The results of

[51]Tanda and De Marco (n 1) 2.

[52]Similar observations can be found in Josef Drexl, 'Designing Competitive Markets for Industrial Data – Between Propertization and Access' (2016) Max Plank Institute for Innovation and Competition Research Paper No.16-13, 10 <https://papers.ssrn.com/sol3/papers.cfm?abstract_id=2862975> accessed 1 March 2020.

[53]Parliament and Council Directive EU 2019/1024 of 20 June 2019 on open data and the re-use of public sector information [2019] OJ L172/56. The importance of sharing and cooperation between the public and private sectors are well emphasized by the OECD, 'Data-Driven Innovation: Big Data for Growth and Well-Being' (2015) 402–408 <www.oecd.org/innovation/data-driven-innovation-9789264229358-en.htm> accessed 1 March 2020.

[54]The European Commission proposed in Commission, 'Building a European data economy' (Communication) COM (2017) 9 final 13 the introduction of a data producer's right to protect non-personal data generated within the EU from misappropriations by extra-EU companies. In the words of Guenther Oettinger, then heading DG CONNECT and thus leading the proposal, the

the online public consultation and specialized workshops held to discuss the policy options proposed by the European Commission (EC) in early 2017 have underlined the increasing dependency of companies on data produced by others, with three quarters of respondents sharing their data on the basis of contracts providing either open re-use conditions or payment of license fees.[55] At the same time, half of the respondents—particularly SMEs—have complained about problems experienced in accessing data held by competitors, and the totality of stakeholders supported the goal of making more data available for reuse to foster innovation and competitiveness.[56]

One common observation, however, is of key relevance and confirms earlier findings of the economic literature emphasizing the absence of evidence on market failures that would justify a regulatory creation of property rights.[57] Data holders, in fact, agree on the fact that the current regulatory ecosystem well protects their investment in data collection capabilities, and underlines how the data value chains and business models shaping the current data economy are so varied and fast evolving that crystallizing a one-size-fits-all legislative solution would entail greater risks than benefits.[58] On the contrary, freedom of contract, if sterilized of anti-competitive and opportunistic behaviors from intermediaries and other big players,[59] is perceived as more instrumental to the organic development of smart industries and their specific needs. Reinforcing the legal status of data is believed not to be conducive to any facilitation in the tradability of data, but rather to create legal uncertainty as to the allocation of exclusive rights and their scope, and to consequently raise transaction costs and other costs linked to the increased risk of litigation.[60]

---

economic importance of data was particularly visible in the automotive industry and for the development of self-driving automobiles, see Guenther Oettinger, 'Wem gehören die Daten?' *Frankfurter Allgemeine Zeitung* (14 October 2016) 19. On the industry rejection and its underlying reasons see Drexl (n 52) 5 and Heiko Willems, 'Trading in Data: An Industry Perspective' in Sebastian Lohsse, Reiner Schulze and Dirk Staudenmayer (eds), *Trading Data in the Digital Economy: Legal Concepts and Tools* (Nomos 2017) 323.

[55]As summarized in the European Commission, 'Synopsis Report of the Public Consultation on Building a European Data Economy' (European Comission) 4 <http://ec.europa.eu/information_society/newsroom/image/document/2017-36/synopsis_report_-_data_economy_A0EFA8E0-AED3-1E29-C8DE049035581517_46646.pdf> accessed 1 March 2020.

[56]ibid 6.

[57]Nestor Duch-Brown, Bertin Martens and Frank Mueller-Langer, 'The Economics of Ownership, Access and Trade in Digital Data' (2017) JRC Digital Economy Working Paper 2017-01 <https://papers.ssrn.com/sol3/papers.cfm?abstract_id=2914144> accessed 1 March 2020.

[58]See P Bernt Hugenholtz, 'Against Data Property' in Hanns Ullrich, Peter Drahos and Gustavo Ghidini (eds), *Kritika: Essays on Intellectual Property* (vol 3, Edward Elgar 2018) 48, noting how business models working with big data are constantly changing, and crystallizing entitlements in a property right when the object is a very risky policy option when the object of the right is such a moving target.

[59]For instance, with the application of FRAND rules to ensure fair access and re-use of data corpora.

[60]See European Commission, 'Synopsis Report' (n 55) 7.

The observations advanced by industrial stakeholders are in line with the concerns voiced by several scholars in response to the EC's proposal of introducing a data producer's right.[61] Aside from the legitimate systematic objections related to the problematic overlaps that the new exclusive right would have with other IP rights,[62] commentators have shed light on the incompatibility of a regulatory framework based on exclusivity with the main technical and economic features of business models based on big data. The '3 Vs' giving value to big data—volume, velocity and variety—are directly dependent on the different and large range, source and format of data analyzed in a dynamic and rapid fashion, and on the real-time information which may be extracted from them to provide smart products and services.[63] The traditional vertical value chain, where goods and services acquired value in their progression down the production and distribution chain until they reached the final consumer, is now substituted by dynamic value networks, where smart goods and services increase their value thanks to horizontal, real time and dynamic cooperation.[64] A propertized setting is hardly compatible with the needs such features pose. Similarly, the decision on where to allocate property rights would face the difficulty of defining and distinguishing the economic value to be attributed to the syntactic and semantic information contained in the data corpora, which are, respectively, the rough coded data, collected through the investment of the device producer, and the meaning that can be extracted from it, generally extracted by data analysts—two players which may or may not correspond.[65]

Big data analytics in general, and even more in the context of urban mobility, presents all the four characteristics of IP negative spaces. Despite the absence of strong exclusive rights, data analytics has not experienced any halt, nor have companies reduced their commitment to big data innovation. There is agreement on the fact that exclusivity would create a barrier to access, increase transaction costs, have chilling effects on sharing and cooperation, thus hindering innovation. Both market players—particularly SMEs—and the public have a strong interest in maintaining free access to data, and little or none of their investments are directed to

[61] See Drexl (n 52); Hugenholtz (n 58) 48.

[62] ibid.

[63] For a literature review and empirical assessment see Rob Kitchin and Gavin McArdle, 'What Makes Big Data, Big Data? Exploring the Ontological Characteristics of 26 Datasets' (2016) 3 Big Data and Society 1.

[64] See, *inter alia*, Nadine Côrte-Real, Tiago Oliveira and Pedro Ruivo, 'Assessing Business Value of Big Data Analytics in European Firms' (2017) 70 Journal of Business Research 379; Philipp Hartmann and others, 'Capturing Value From Big Data – A Taxonomy of Data-Driven Business Models Used by Start-up Firms' (2016) 36 International Journal of Operations & Production Management 1382; Daniel Chen, David Preston and Morgan Swink, 'How the Use of Big Data Analytics Affects Value Creation in Supply Chain Management' (2016) 32 Journal of Management Information Systems 4.

[65] Drexl (n 52) 15-16. On the three conceptual layers of big data see Herbert Zech, 'Data as a Tradeable Commodity' in Alberto De Franceschi (ed), *European Contract Law and the Digital Single Market, Implications of the Digital Revolution* (Intersentia 2017) 53–54.

protect their exclusivity on the data corpora individually produced, acquired and processed.

3.2.2 Software Infrastructures and Interfaces

Innovation in SUM also involves the development of algorithms used for big data analysis, in software managing the collection and storage of data, operating smart transportation systems and means in automated or semi-automated ways, offering friendly interfaces to users, and suggesting information on possible combinations of multiple mobility services. Most of these tools may find protection under software copyright and, in the case of computer-implemented invention—under patent law, with the exception of the functionality of a program, abstract principles, and underlying general algorithms, falling outside the scope of both IP rights.[66] Proprietary solutions have been developed by big players to secure portions of the market, especially in the automotive and transportation vehicles sectors, in order to recoup the high investments.

However, stakeholders converge in signaling the need for the development of open interoperability standards, particularly with regard to data formats, cloud security, data protection and application programming interfaces (APIs),[67] indicating how a strong enforcement of exclusive rights is detrimental to innovation, particularly when the most significant technological developments require cooperation and are boosted by network effects.[68] Interoperability and alignment to open standards are also in the interest of local governments, public research centers, public-private networks and entities carrying out publicly funded research, in light of the regulatory and financial constraints they are subject to, and of the risk management strategies they are required to implement. The acquisition, implementation and maintenance of proprietary software to run local urban mobility programs entails high costs and the risk of vertical hold-ups which these players are incentivized or compelled to minimize or avoid.[69] At the same time, in the development of urban mobility solutions, software programs do not represent core innovation, nor can they be easily licensed out in other sectors. This reduces the incentive to invest in

---

[66]As noted also by Josef Drexl and others, 'Data Ownership and Access to Data – Position Statement of the Max Planck Institute for Innovation and Competition of 16 August 2016 on the Current European Debate' (2016) Max Planck Institute for Innovation & Competition Research Paper No. 16-10, 5–6 <https://papers.ssrn.com/sol3/papers.cfm?abstract_id=2833165> accessed 1 March 2020.

[67]European Commission, 'Synopsis Report' (n 55) 7.

[68]Michelle Supper, 'Why Open Standards are the Key to Truly Smart Cities' (*SmartCitiesWorld*, 29 October 2018) <www.smartcitiesworld.net/opinions/opinions/why-open-standards-are-the-key-to-truly-smart-cities> accessed 1 March 2020.

[69]ibid: 'The issue of interoperability also extends beyond the city boundaries. What if the leaders in your city decide to install a proprietary technology stack that is incompatible with the systems in a neighboring city?'

obtaining, maintaining and enforcing exclusive rights, and particularly patents, making developers keener to invest in new innovation/creation rather than in IP enforcement.

In specific contexts, SUM interfaces and applications are built through peer-production mechanisms based on controlled open innovation platforms, where access is controlled on the basis of the participation in or affiliation with development projects. The reason behind the adoption of a hybrid, tempered form of openness derives from the fact that, while the incentive to create is indeed 'given not by exclusivity but by other types of rewards not dependent on financial gain', the programs to be developed do not present all the features that may allow a successful peer production. More specifically, while modularity is almost always present, heterogeneous granularity characterizes only user interfaces and common apps, but it is harder to find in algorithms for data analysis or software embedded in proprietary transportation means.

With due distinctions, SUM software presents all four characteristics of IP negative spaces. Despite the fragmented protection offered by IP rights, innovation in the field has not slowed down. Scholars point to the negative effects that more pervasive exclusive rights would create, and market players and the public value interoperability and affordability highly enough to prefer a low IP setting, the former limiting their investments in protection and rather directing the same sums towards research and development.

4 Smart Urban Mobility as an IP Negative Space? A Case Study

The focus on big data and software infrastructures as fundamental components of the project development in the SUM sector calls for further inquiry into the real practices in this innovative field. Europe boasts a significant number of trailblazing SUM projects.[70] Witnessing the lively developments and committed to its 2020 Climate Action Goals,[71] the European Union has shown an increasing interest and proactive role in promoting innovation in the sector, allocating funds and supporting venues of

[70]Numerous pilot initiatives and consolidated best practices have developed both in big and medium-sized cities across the region. See Antonio Garrido-Marijuan, Yana Pargova and Cordelia Wilson, 'The Making of a Smart City: Best Practices Across Europe' (EU Smart Cities Information System 2017) <https://smartcities-infosystem.eu/library/making-smart-city-best-practices-across-europe> accessed 1 March 2020; Rudolf Giffinger and others, 'Smart cities: Ranking of European Medium-size Cities' (*Europeansmartcities*, 2007) <www.smart-cities.eu/> accessed 1 March 2020.

[71]The policy plan being characterized by the goals of reduction of carbon emission and efficient use of energy resources. For an overview of the regulatory measures adopted so far, see European Commission, '2020 Climate & Energy Package' (*European Commission*) <https://ec.europa.eu/clima/policies/strategies/2020_en> accessed 1 March 2020.

cooperation and exchange.[72] Among them, in 2011, the Directorate General for Energy of the EC launched the so-called Smart Cities and Communities Initiative, which in 2012 stretched its wings encompassing the transportation and ICT sectors and becoming the European Innovation Partnership on Smart Cities and Communities (EIP-SCC).[73] The initiative aims to support the transitioning of around 300 European cities towards a 'smart' dimension,[74] the EC not being the sole sponsor of the projects developed by the participants.[75] The intent is, indeed, to foster private investments in smart city innovations.[76]

The EIP-SCC initiative represents a highly relevant scenario for the purpose of this paper, as it not only matches with its European focus, but also pays great attention to the SUM sector,[77] pooling together a wide array of stakeholders from municipalities to industry, small and medium-sized businesses, banks and universities,[78] thus encompassing a significant diversity of experiences. It is worth analyzing the initiative more closely both as an incubator for innovation and as a representative selection of European SUM realities. Such an investigation will be carried out benefiting from the information freely available online[79] and semi-structured interviews conducted with working group leaders and participants.

---

[72]Eg the International Conference 'Smart Mobility 2020: Innovative and Sustainable Urban Transport in Europe' held in Tallinn on 22-23 November 2017 was organized with the support of the 2017 Estonian Presidency of the Council of the European Union, see <https://europa.eu/newsroom/events/smart-mobility-2020-innovative-and-sustainable-urban-transport-europe_en> accessed 1 March 2020; the European Commission has granted funds for several initiatives, among which are the Urban Innovative Actions Initiative, the EU Smart Cities Information System and the European Network of Living Labs. See respectively <www.uia-initiative.eu/en> accessed 1 March 2020, <https://smartcities-infosystem.eu/> accessed 1 March 2020, <https://enoll.org/> accessed 1 March 2020.

[73]See Isabella Maschio, 'European Innovation Partnership on Smart Cities and Communities' (*European Commission*, 19 August 2020) <https://e3p.jrc.ec.europa.eu/articles/european-innovation-partnership-smart-cities-and-communities> accessed 1 December 2019; see also <https://eu-smartcities.eu/> accessed 19 August 2020.

[74]EIP-SCC, 'Explore, Shape, Deal. General Assembly 2018 Summary Report' (EIP-SCC 2018) 11–12 <https://eu-smartcities.eu/events/eip-scc-general-assembly-2018> accessed 1 March 2020.

[75]ibid 12, 18: Among the main sources of EU funds available in the sector are the EU Horizon 2020 Lighthouse program, European Structural and Investment Funds, and the 'sustainable infrastructure window' under InvestEU.

[76]It includes a matchmaking platform aimed at bringing projects and investors together. See <https://eu-smartcities.eu/> accessed 1 March 2020.

[77]In the consultations carried out by the Commission in 2011, public transport and urban mobility actions resulted as the second most supported area of intervention for EU initiative. See European Commission, 'Public Consultation on the Smart Cities and Communities Initiative' (Public Consultation Report 2011) <https://ec.europa.eu/energy/sites/ener/files/documents/public_consultation_report.pdf> accessed 1 March 2020.

[78]The most recent available data see the participation of 4,700 members from 31 countries and 370 commitments. See EIP-SCC, '6 European actions rolling out new, smarter and sustainable mobility solutions in European cities' Webinar presentation, 5 December 2017. For more information see <https://eu-smartcities.eu/clusters/11/description> accessed 1 March 2020.

[79]The subscription to the EIP-SCC database is open to everyone and the access to archived material (e.g. meeting reports, annual reports) is free.

4.1 Motivation to Innovate

Among the most characteristic features of the SUM sector is the wide-ranging variety of players, who interact and collaborate in developing and implementing projects, thus significantly affecting the patterns of incentives behind innovation.[80] On the one hand, the objectives to reduce traffic congestion, enhance environmental protection and the quality of life of citizens, and to encourage behavioral and policy change in European cities are pillars in the development of SUM initiatives.[81] On the other hand, economic opportunities and returns on investments are equally important components,[82] as concerns about the financing of, above all, small and medium-sized projects confirm.[83] These two sets of drivers of innovation do not reveal a neat divide between public and private players.[84] On the contrary, the emerging picture is [illegible],[85] which conceptually orbit around the key

[80]Interview with Anna Domenech, EIP-SCC Lead Intelligent Mobility for Energy Transition and Section Manager Nissan Europe (Budapest, 15 January 2020) (on file with authors): 'It depends a lot on who is answering the question [of incentive]: if you ask a city, it would tell you something very different from what a stakeholder in the automotive sector would tell you.'; interview with two members of Unit B4 Sustainable and Intelligent Transport at European Commission DG MOVE in charge of EIP-SCC and CIVITAS (Budapest, 10 January 2020) (on file with authors): 'It depends on the type of stakeholder. [. . .] There is a variety of possible incentives, they can be governmental, public-policy-oriented, or rather market-led.'

[81]Interview with Peter Lee, former member EIP-SCC and Principal Consultant BSI Group (Budapest, 19 December 2019) (on file with authors); interview with Ricardo Vitorino, Smart Cities R&I Manager EIP-SCC Intelligent Mobility for Energy Transition (Budapest, 13 January 2020) (on file with authors): 'Contribute to a smart and more sustainable society, improving the existing transportation options in smart cities and rewarding the most efficient and ecological alternatives.'

[82]Interview with Valerio Siniscalco, Sharing Cities Consortium Partner EIP-SCC Lighthouse Project (Budapest, 8 January 2020) (on file with authors): 'The generation of new economic opportunities, the possibility to open or access market segments.'; interview with Anna Domenech (n 80): 'Obviously, returns on investments and market positioning remain important objectives for industrial players.'

[83]EIP-SCC, 'General Assembly 2018 Report' (n 74) 8, 13: 'In particular, banks did not accept as a guarantee the cash flow of the project, since they rely on the traditional business model, which guarantees the investment with the value of the building. [. . .] difficulty to measure social and environmental benefits of the project in a quantitative and standardized way.'; EIP-SCC, 'Towards a Joint Investment Programme for European Smart Cities: A Consultation Paper to Stimulate Action' (EIP-SCC 2016) 2, 12, 17 <https://eu-smartcities.eu/sites/default/files/2018-06/EIP-SCC_TOWARDS%20A%20JOINT%20INVESTMENT-Paper.pdf> accessed 1 March 2020.

[84]Interview with Anna Domenech (n 80) 'Private sector stakeholders are also citizens, who like SUM projects because they will make their life easier [. . .], we all want better cities, more sustainable, easier to live in, so another thing important in the sector is to keep the company staff motivated.'

[85]See Table 2 Investors Engagement – types, motives and methods in EIP-SCC, 'Consultation Paper' (n 83) 17 listing, among others, the enhancement of city sustainability, efficiency of the public budget and optimization of risk management. See also interview with Graham Colclough, Chair Integrated Infrastructures and Processes Action Cluster EIP-SCC (Budapest, 16 December

purposes of economic profit, policy modernization, technological advancement and public health.

4.2 The Management of IP Rights and Exclusivity

One of the set priorities of the EIP-SCC initiative is to facilitate knowledge sharing.[86] To this end, the partnership has launched a platform, the so-called digital marketplace,[87] for the free exchange of information, events and financial opportunities to boost the amplification of intelligence and enhance the efficiency of project outputs by broadening the access to relevant knowledge.[88] Such a choice builds on a peculiar trend that is consolidating within the SUM sector and sees increasingly wider disclosure of project information and crowdsourcing as key factors of success.[89]

The typologies and specific characteristics of the information involved vary dramatically, thus complicating the inquiry into the management of intellectual capital in the SUM sector.[90] Embracing a broad perspective, three main trends stand out. First, the SUM sector seems to experience an increasing number of occasions allowing for the exchange of sector-relevant knowledge, mostly in the form of project networks, consortia, platforms, regular meetings and workshops, and public events.[91] This is epitomized, among others, by the rise of so-called living

---

2019) (on file with authors): 'You see a blend of different incentives and motives that drive different business models in the sector.'

[86]European Commission, 'Smart Cities' (*European Commission*) <https://ec.europa.eu/info/eu-regional-and-urban-development/topics/cities-and-urban-development/city-initiatives/smart-cities_en#european-innovation-partnership-on-smart-cities-and-communities> accessed 1 March 2020.

[87]See EIP-SCC, 'The Marketplace of the European Innovation Partnership on Smart Cities and Communities' (*EIP-SCC*, 2020) <https://eu-smartcities.eu/> accessed 1 March 2020.

[88]Nicos Komninos, 'Intelligent Cities: Variable Geometries of Spatial Intelligence' (2011) 3 Intelligent Buildings International 172.

[89]See Anne Faber and Florian Matthes, 'Crowdsourcing and Crowdinnovation' in Anne Faber, Florian Matthes and Felix Michel (eds), *Digital Mobility Platforms and Ecosystems: State of the Art Report* (TUM 2016) 37; Omer Uludag, Stefan Hefele and Florian Matthes, 'Platform and Ecosystem Governance' in Anne Faber, Florian Matthes and Felix Michel (eds), *Digital Mobility Platforms and Ecosystems: State of the Art Report* (TUM 2016) 14.

[90]Interview with Graham Colclough (n 85) sketching a taxonomy of relevant data (i.e. firewalled data, open data, commercial data, machine-to-machine data and social media data) and highlighting the problematic aspects of holistic approaches to them.

[91]Interview with members of the Sustainable and Intelligent Transport at European Commission in charge of EIP-SCC and CIVITAS (n 80): 'Exchange of good practices, communication and dissemination happen through workshops, regular meetings, conferences where we bring the actors together, cities and project developers.' Interview with Peter Lee (n 81): 'What is key is the willingness of all organizations to be a lot more involved, open and collaborative in the terms of how they operate.' Interview with Valerio Siniscalco (n 82): 'We attend almost monthly local and non-local meetings, workshops, conferences and other kind of gatherings with the purpose of

labs[92] and the decentralized rapid spreading of city hubs across Europe.[93] Second, within these collaborations, the degree of strategic information disclosed tends to be significant, encompassing best practices, business model strategies, project roadmaps and experience on benefits and encountered obstacles.[94] Third, against this increasingly collaborative background, the management of intellectual capital and the protection of IP rights are highly fragmented across SUM projects. This does not seem to stem from a complete unawareness or radical disinterest towards opportunities of IP protection,[95] but rather appears linked to inconsistent applications of standards, imbalances in strategic expert advice[96] and to a more substantial

sharing knowledge, experiences and best practices.' Interview with Ricardo Vitorino (n 81): 'Knowledge networks organizing workshops and think tanks, publishing white papers and organizing webinars.'

[92]Living labs being repositories of data, know-how, software interfaces and even prototypes of hardware enabling the free use of such resources with the aim 'to provide a useful third party laboratory environment to encourage innovation based on an open platform to support and provide new mobility concepts', Uludag, Hefele and Matthes, 'Platform and Ecosystem Governance' (n 89). See also Schaffers and others (n 4) 433; Grazia Concilio and Francesco Molinari, 'Living Labs and Urban Smartness: The Experimental Nature of Emerging Governance Models' in Andrea Vesco and Francesco Ferrero (eds), *Handbook of Research on Social, Economic, and Environmental Sustainability in the Development of Smart Cities* (IGI Global 2015).

[93]Interview with members of the Sustainable and Intelligent Transport at European Commission in charge of EIP-SCC and CIVITAS (n 80): 'The pattern is decentralization, [. . .] there is a connection among all of the layers [of information], like an octopus spreading around with its tentacles. And you have the trend of creating conferences, every city now wanting to create its own conference to create business partners, the European Commission, investors, funding agencies, etc. and we see more and more hubs created all over Europe.'

[94]Interview with Anna Domenech (n 80): 'All stakeholders are becoming more and more open to share information. Open innovation is now the trend and we are all quickly understanding the importance of sharing innovative information and that there is not so much risk as we perceived before. [. . .] The amount of information that you keep for yourself is becoming ever smaller.' Interview with Valerio Siniscalco (n 82): 'Companies tend to have a high degree of disclosure on information related to smart mobility projects as part of their business strategy.' Interview with Ricardo Vitorino (n 81): 'Case studies about the successes and lessons learnt with general audience, KPIs [Key Performance Indicators] about the implementation to support next deployments and projects with the city/service provider and public authority, roadmap about the products and solutions with potential customers and end users [are typically disclosed].'

[95]Interview with Anna Domenech (n 80): 'People entering SUM collaborative projects do ask about IPRs.' Interview with Ricardo Vitorino (n 81): '[Stakeholders are] highly interested [in IP protection], despite being one of the toughest area to learn insights. New players look for data about the result of projects from existing and past players, while keeping trade secrets and ensuring their management remains enclosed to protect their strategy.'

[96]Interview with Graham Colclough (n 85): 'People are not sufficiently informed about the financial value of what they own because it is complicated [. . .] and most of the industries involved cannot understand public value and public good.' Interview with Anna Domenech (n 80): 'What is missing in the sector is a forecast of monetization of IPRs, we do not know how to sell solutions.'

focus of all actors at play on the advancement of technology and policies than to the enforcement of exclusive entitlements.[97]

4.3 *Public Interest in Free Access and Inclusive Innovation*

The development of SUM projects in Europe has heavily relied on phenomena of replication from city to city.[98] Evidence of this pattern lies in the important role played by so-called lighthouse projects, usually developed in big metropolitan hubs, from which small and medium-sized urban realities take inspirations.[99] However, the replication of SUM initiatives has also proven to be, at times, unsustainable.[100] Urban areas across Europe differ greatly and this leads to structural obstacles slowing down the project implementation.[101] Even though city administrations tend to act in an individualistic manner, trying to preserve their uniqueness and protecting their benefit,[102] the response to such difficulties has not been towards isolation, but rather towards more sustainable models of resource aggregation. Such an approach differs from mere replication schemes, as it enhances collaborative practices, requires a more advanced co-planning among stakeholders and, above all,

---

[97] Interview with Peter Lee (n 81): ‘A pragmatic thought is that the costs of securing IP might actually outweigh the revenue that would be generated from licensing IPRs. [...] Even big universities that are partly set up with that in mind, to set up the IPRs, they sometimes struggle, so if a local authority hasn’t got a research university to work with, they are going to find it even more difficult to get their head around the issue and work out if it is really worth securing.’ Interview with Anna Domenech (n 80): ‘As we are mostly not developing our own technologies, but rather we suggest solutions based on a combination of existing technologies, we are not so much into investing in IPRs.’

[98] Interview with Valerio Siniscalco (n 82): ‘Scale-up and replication are crucial for the diffusion of innovative smart cities experiences.’ Interview with Anna Domenech (n 80): ‘Replication is part of the sector and it makes sense. I am hesitant towards it only to the extent I see a difference between advanced cities, which rely on high level technologies and are pioneers in smart mobility projects, and less advanced cities, which face serious problems in finding the financial resources to implement such projects.’ Interview with members of the Sustainable and Intelligent Transport at European Commission in charge of EIP-SCC and CIVITAS (n 80): ‘It is our wish not to finance one idea for one city, but rather to achieve benefit for the EU as a whole. Replication and the follower city concept are key for us. [...] If this concept is missing, there is no real European added value.’

[99] EIP-SCC, ‘General Assembly 2018 Report’ (n 74) 16, 21; Jorge Nunez Ferrer and others, ‘The Making of a Smart City: Replication and Scale-up of Innovation in Europe’ (EU Smart Cities Information System 2018) <https://smartcities-infosystem.eu/library/publications> accessed 1 March 2020.

[100] Han Vandevyvere and others, ‘Why May Replication (Not) Be Happening. Recommendation on EU R&I and Regulatory Policies’ (EU Smart Cities Information System 2018) <https://smartcities-infosystem.eu/library/publications> accessed 1 March 2020.

[101] ibid; EIP-SCC, ‘General Assembly 2018 Report’ (n 74) 18.

[102] EIP-SCC, ‘Consultation Paper’ (n 83) 12; interview with Graham Colclough (n 85); interview with Peter Lee (n 81).

a collective crafting of best practices to enable an effective and inclusive upscaling of SUM realities.[103]

5 Conclusion: A Lesson for the IP World

The study of the rapidly evolving SUM sector across Europe cannot depart from the contextual rise of the 'knowledge city' and 'sharing city' cultures, which signal a push towards an open and problem-solving idea of urban innovation.[104] Aspiring to fix the problem of incentives and to foster the progress of arts, science and technology, IP law aims to promote, among others, SUM innovative projects, yet not without resistance. The analysis has unveiled considerable elements which fit all the criteria distinguishing IP negative spaces. The key components at the roots of SUM innovations, i.e. big data and software infrastructures, feature characteristics which remarkably match the tendency towards a more open, inclusive and less propertized paradigm of IP protection. Moreover, practices that are consolidating across the European SUM realities follow a similar logic, bringing together a wide array of stakeholders and hence different motives, proactively supporting the decentralized dissemination of relevant knowledge and pursuing the public interest in opening the project results to replication and aggregation models.

In times of swift technological change and joint calls for regulatory intervention to protect public and private interests in the digitized environment, the configuration of the SUM sector vis-à-vis IP exclusive rights represents a meaningful perspective, which not only encourages to continue investigating the premises upon which IP law stands in real-life scenarios, but also serves as important input for the modernization and adjustment of policies in the era of data-driven innovation phenomena.

---

[103]ibid; EIP-SCC, 'General Assembly 2018 Report' (n 74) 8-10, 16: 'The participating cities have committed to work together to deliver innovative solutions for one of the Integrated Infrastructure cluster initiatives. [. . .] This is an important evidence point for aggregating demand, the application of standards, and the blending of funds from public and private sources.' Focusing on the inclusive approach towards the SME community, see EIP-SCC, 'Consultation Paper' (n 83) 23-24; interview with Peter Lee (n 81): 'For innovation it is a challenge: if the market doesn't grasp the innovation quick enough, an innovation can die. [. . .] So you do need these networks to sustain innovation and help reduce the risks.'

[104]Benevolo, Dameri and D'Auria (n 2): 'Knowledge city [. . .] regards the policies aiming at enforcing and valuing data, information and knowledge available and produced in city, especially through its cultural institutions such as universities, research centres, theatres and libraries, but also produced and used by companies, innovative districts, technological parks.' Aurelien Acquier and Valentina Carbone, 'Sharing Economy and Social Innovation' in Nestor M Davidson, Michèle Finck and John J Infranca (eds), *The Cambridge Handbook of the Law of the Sharing Economy* (Cambridge University Press 2018) 53.

Sharing or Platform Urban Mobility? Propertization from Mass to MaaS

Giancarlo Frosio

Contents

Abstract This chapter will discuss smart urban mobility within the context of the sharing economy. After a brief introduction on the history of urban mobility, it will look at the application of sharing economy models to smart urban mobility, such as ride-sharing, car- and bike-sharing programs and e-hailing services. The discussion will contextualize the evolution of peer mass production dynamics into Mobility-as-a-Service (MaaS). My focus is the fundamental data ownership and protection issues that will arise from mobility solutions consumed as services through centralized gateways and platforms. I criticize the neo-liberalist perspective that has gradually changed the sharing economy into the platform economy and argue that it brought about unfulfilled expectations and increasing inequalities. After moving this critique,

---

Giancarlo Frosio is Associate Professor, Center for International Intellectual Property Studies (CEIPI), University of Strasbourg, France; non-resident Fellow at the Stanford Law School Center for Internet and Society, U.S.A.; Faculty Associate, Nexa Center for Internet and Society, Polytechnic University, Turin, Italy.

G. Frosio (✉)
Center for International Intellectual Property Studies (CEIPI), University of Strasbourg, Strasbourg, France
e-mail: gcfrosio@ceipi.edu

M. Finck et al. (eds.), *Smart Urban Mobility*, MPI Studies on Intellectual Property and Competition Law 29, https://doi.org/10.1007/978-3-662-61920-9_9

I plead for the application of Ostrom's approach to commons to smart urban mobility and, in particular to MaaS. In conclusion, I argue that smart urban mobility should develop upon what I call a 3C model: commons, collaboration and crowdsourcing.

1 Introduction

From Elinor Ostrom's green pastures to Yochai Benkler's wealthy networks, the tragedy or comedy of the commons has now been taken to our metropolitan streets. Smart urban mobility, as sub-routine of the smart city, has been for some time now a glaring example of the emerging, over-hyped, sharing economy. It's yet another opportunity for society to test whether collaboration can hold the key to future social wealth, or possessive individualism will continue its relentless march.[1] The fundamental policy question is whether smart urban mobility will lean towards public interest or redeploy the mainstream neoliberal perspective where, as Morozov and Bria argue, 'cities hand over the management of public infrastructure and services to private companies both de-centralizing and de-personalizing the political sphere'.[2] I believe the latter would be a sub-optimal solution—although policy options are heavily constrained in an era of austerity. Neoliberal platform economy models have shown fundamental flaws by, for example, freeloading on users' personal data and lowering minimum wages.

After a brief account of the history of urban mobility, this chapter will introduce cooperation and cooperative models, which have been an emerging trend in the last 20 years, especially after the advent of the networked digital society. It will then consider the emergence of sharing economy models and cooperation in smart urban mobility, such as ride-sharing, e-hailing services, bike-sharing programs, and car-sharing services.

The discussion will contextualize the evolution of peer mass production dynamics into Mobility-as-a-Service (MaaS). The chapter will focus on fundamental data ownership, protection and transparency issues that will arise from mobility consumed as a service through centralized gateways and platforms. In this context, I criticize the neo-liberalist perspective where the sharing economy morphs into the platform economy. As I argue, the sharing economy's unfulfilled expectations actually brought about increasing inequalities and social injustice. Finally, I argue that Maas should lean toward liability rules rather than proprietary arrangements and develop upon collectivistic data ownership regimes and crowdfunded cooperative

---

[1]See Crawford Macpherson, *The Political Theory of Possessive Individualism: Hobbes to Locke* (Clarendon Press 1962).

[2]Evgeny Morozov and Francesca Bria, 'Rethinking the Smart City: Democratizing Urban Technology' (Rosa Luxemburg Stiftung 2018) <www.rosalux.de/fileadmin/rls_uploads/pdfs/sonst_publikationen/rethinking_the_smart_city.pdf> accessed 18 March 2020.

service provision models. Smart urban mobility should develop upon what I call a 3C model: commons, collaboration and crowdsourcing.[3]

2 Urban Mobility Gets 'Smart'

For the past two centuries, urban transportation has seen an almost endless stream of transit innovations.[4] After a quite uneventful use of horses, coaches and carriages for several centuries, things changed rapidly at the turn of the nineteenth century. The omnibus first appeared in Paris in 1828 and shortly thereafter in New York and Boston. It wasn't long before steam trains had linked major cities to their upper-class suburbs. In the 1830s the first horsecars on tracks were introduced. In London in 1860 the American entrepreneur G.F. Train opened a three line system of streetcars (also known as trams or trolleys) that were dependent on a small battery-powered electric motor.[5] In 1873, San Francisco featured the first cable cars and about two decades later they started being widely replaced by electric streetcars, which soon made their appearance almost everywhere in the world.[6] The electric streetcar was a game changer compared with horse drawn cars as it made urban mobility faster and more affordable for the working class.[7] The streetcar system allowed workers to live away from factories and pushed urban expansion with a considerable growth in mobility.[8] After reaching its peak in 1920s, the streetcar system proved to be financially unviable and subsequently declined rapidly due to low fares, over-expanded networks and multiple companies operating within the same city. Poor management of the streetcar system also lead to lasting changes in urban structure with massive growth, especially in the suburbs which grew faster than the center. In the 1920s the motorbus began to become a success and took over from streetcars in the following years.[9] In 1935, motorbuses replaced the streetcars that had operated for more than 100 years in downtown New York, and Paris also closed the last of its streetcar lines in the 1930s.[10] Meanwhile, nearly all systems converted to public ownership after being privately owned up to that point, with cities buying up streetcar and bus operations. Rapid transit began to emerge in the 1950s and became

[3]See Morozov and Bria (n 2) 42-43.

[4]See eg Martin Emanuel, *Frank Schipper and Ruth Oldenziel, A U-Turn to the Future: Sustainable Urban Mobility since 1850* (Berghahn Books 2020).

[5]See 'Streetcar', *Encyclopaedia Britannica* (29 October 2018) <www.britannica.com/technology/streetcar#ref281087> accessed 18 March 2020.

[6]ibid.

[7]See National Museum of American History, 'America on the Move' (National Museum of American History Behring Center) <https://americanhistory.si.edu/america-on-the-move> accessed 18 March 2020.

[8]ibid.

[9]See Streetcar (n 5).

[10]ibid.

fully operational in the 1970s. In parallel, from the end of World War II, the demand for cars steadily increased.[11] Governments have supported cars from the very beginning as a way to decentralize and get people away from the cities with public investment to improve roads and reduce congestion.[12]

This outline history of urban mobility immediately suggests how related policies impact heavily on social development.[13] Urban mobility has been a challenge from the very beginning. Urban growth, congestion, sub-optimal planning, pollution, environmental concerns, rising costs, global economic crisis have made the urban mobility puzzle a hard one to solve. However, the big data and AI revolution might come to the rescue. Smart urban mobility is the 'new black' when it comes to urban mobility. It might redress past inefficiencies as part of the global interconnected 'smart city' revolution.

Quayside, the world's most ambitious 'smart city' project led by Google in Toronto promises to fix everything from traffic congestion and rising housing prices to pollution.[14] A 'smart city' like Quayside would include a centralized identity management system for accessing all public services, driverless transportation, mixed-use spaces that change according to market demand, smart light posts and sensor-enabled waste separation.[15] 'Smart' urban mobility would be a critical component to the 'smart city'. Technologies such as autonomous driving, electric powertrains, and mobile data connectivity are emerging alongside new transportation services like ride-hailing, e-hailing and vehicle sharing to form integrated mobility systems.[16] In particular, micromobility or lightweight electric vehicles, such as electric scooters, electric skateboards, shared bicycles and electric pedal-assisted pedelec and bicycles, are taking the center stage in the urban mobility revolution.[17] This has also contributed to an apparent retreat of car sharing from major cities in the US and Europe.[18] As a solution to cover the 'last mile',

---

[11]See National Museum of American History (n 7).

[12]ibid.

[13]Peter Jones, 'The Evolution of Urban Mobility: The Interplay of Academic and Policy Perspectives' (2014) 38 International Association of Traffic and Safety Sciences (IATSS) Research 7.

[14]See Ava Kofman, 'Google's "Smart City of Surveillance" Faces New Resistance in Toronto' (*The Interceptor*, 13 November 2019) <https://theintercept.com/2018/11/13/google-quayside-toronto-smart-city> accessed 18 March 2020.

[15]ibid.

[16]See Shannon Bouton and others, 'Infrastructure for the Evolution of Urban Mobility' (Mckinsey 2017) <www.mckinsey.com/business-functions/sustainability/our-insights/infrastructure-for-the-evolution-of-urban-mobility> accessed 18 March 2020.

[17]See Bhagyalaxmi Madapur, Shilpa Madangopal and M N Chandrashekar, 'Micro-mobility Infrastructure for Redefining Urban Mobility' (International Conference on Research in Engineering and Technology, Barcelona, 12-14 December 2019) <www.dpublication.com/wp-content/uploads/2020/01/14-66.pdf> accessed 18 March 2020.

[18]See Claudio Bozza, 'Car sharing, la grande ritirata: Share Now (ex Car2go) lascia Firenze, Londra e New York' (*Corriere della Sera L'Economia*, 19 December 2019) <www.corriere.it/economia/consumi/19_dicembre_19/car-sharing-grande-ritirata-share-now-lascia-firenze-londra-new-york-1648451a-2248-11ea-8e32-6247f341a5cc.shtml> accessed 18 March 2020.

micromobility works with sharing services increasingly based on dockless or free floating business models—as opposed to docked or station-based—in which vehicles can be left anywhere or within a geo-fenced area.[19] Sharing services—that do not require vehicles to be individually owned, transported or stored—have led to the growth of micromobility practices.[20] Micromobility start-ups have seen $5.7 billion in investment since 2015 with large percentage of this money targeting China.[21] The shared micromobility market is expected to be worth between $300 billion and $500 billion by 2030.[22]

Smart urban mobility—and micromobility—will be electric, autonomous, shared, platformed and integrated. 'Smart cities' and 'smart urban mobility' promise all this and much more, including strong data collection and protection headaches.[23]

3 Sharing Economy and Cooperation

The character of urban transportation and mobility is dramatically changing, in part because of the explosive growth of Shared-Use Modes (SUM) of travel such as ridesourcing or e-hailing, bikesharing, carsharing and, more recently, electronic scooter-sharing.[24] SUM in urban mobility belongs to a broader development, which have been taking place for the last 20 years. Boosted by technological innovation, collaboration is regaining its natural role in human interactions. Recent empirical research found that rather than the *homo economicus*, we are 'a cooperative species'.[25] Men are complex entities that cannot be explained only through economic incentives; instead, several other factors come into play, among them altruism. In his recent book *Together*, social scientist Richard Sennett emphasizes the role of collaboration in human life and reminds readers that 'cooperation

---

[19]See, eg, Susan Shaheen and Adam Cohen, 'Shared Micromoblity Policy Toolkit: Docked and Dockless Bike and Scooter Sharing' (2019) UC Berkeley Transportation Sustainability Research Center Report <https://escholarship.org/uc/item/00k897b5> accessed 18 March 2020.

[20]Grant McKenzie, 'Urban Mobility in the Sharing Economy: A Spatiotemporal Comparison of Shared Mobility Services' (2020) 79 Computers, Environment and Urban Systems 101418.

[21]See Kersten Heineke and others, 'Micromobility's 15,000-mile checkup' (Mckinsey 2019) <www.mckinsey.com/industries/automotive-and-assembly/our-insights/micromobilitys-15000-mile-checkup#> accessed 18 March 2020.

[22]ibid.

[23]See Kofman (n 14).

[24]See Kirstin Anderson-Hall and others, 'Governing Micro-Mobility: A Nationwide Assessment of Electric Scooter Regulations' (Transportation Research Board 98th Annual Meeting, Washington DC, 13-17 January 2019) <https://trid.trb.org/view/1572811> accessed 18 March 2020.

[25]See Sam Bowles and Herbert Gintis, *A Cooperative Species: Human Reciprocity and Its Evolution* (Princeton UP 2013). See also Adam Smith, *Theory of Moral Sentiments* (1759).

precedes individuation: cooperation is the foundation of human development, in that we learn how to be together before we learn how to stand apart'.[26]

From Ridley Scott's collaborative YouTube movie 'Life in a Day', to virtual choirs,[27] to volunteer astronomers looking for new galaxies in the Galaxy Zoo, taxonomists classifying images from collections of herbarium specimens in the 'Herbaria@home' project,[28] or millions of users enlisting in the SETI@Home project to search for signs of extra-terrestrial life—online collaborations have projected granular individual contributions in the kaleidoscopic multiplier of the Net.[29] Similarly, collaborative authorship and social editing in Wikipedia and wiki environments have become increasingly influential models for content creation and dissemination, so that commentators are now talking about 'wikinomics' or 'wikiborg'.[30]

Sharing is a contagious process insofar as it has rapidly exploded on a previously unimaginable scale.[31] It moves to more and more areas of our lives. Recent research highlights the rise of collaborative consumption.[32] Swapping, sharing, bartering, trading, and renting have been reinvented through technology and peer-to-peer communities. Collaborative consumption is rising in enormous marketplaces such as eBay and Craigslist, and emerging sectors such as peer-to-peer money lending (Zopa), 'swap trading' (Swaptree), car sharing (Zipcar), ridesharing (Zimride), apartment sharing (Airbnb), skills sharing (Skillshare), time sharing (TaskRabbit), land sharing (Landshare), kid clothes sharing (thredUP), or anything else you may need (Sharesomesugar).[33]

---

[26]See Richard Sennett, *Together: The Rituals, Pleasures, and Politics of Cooperation* (Yale UP 2012).

[27]See Eric Whitacre, 'About the Virtual Choir' (*Eric Whitcare*) <http://ericwhitacre.com/the-virtual-choir> accessed 18 March 2020. (Virtual Choir is a choral music performance created by piecing together 3,746 videos from a community of singers from 73 countries around the world).

[28]See Botanical Society of the British Isles, 'Herbaria@home: Recording Historical Biodiversity' <http://herbariaunited.org/atHome/> accessed 18 March 2020.

[29]See Mark Cooper, 'From Wifi to Wikis and Open Source: The Political Economy of Collaborative Production in the Digital Information Age' (2006) 5 Journal on Telecommunications & High Technology Law 125.

[30]See Don Tapscott and Anthony Williams, *Wikinomics: How Mass Collaboration Changes Everything* (Atlantic Books 2008). See also Shun-ling Chen, 'Collaborative Authorship: From Folklore to the Wikiborg' [2011] University of Illinois Journal of Law, Technology & Policy 131. For a discussion of Wikipedia and wiki environments as a sharing economy and a cultural commons, see Michael Madison, Brett Frischmann and Katherine Strandburg, 'Constructing Commons in the Cultural Environment' (2010) 95 Cornell Law Review 657, 657.

[31]See Lawrence Lessig, *Remix: Making Art and Commerce Thrive in the Hybrid Economy* (Bloomsbury 2008) 143-176 (discussing sharing economies).

[32]See Rachel Botsman and Roo Rogers, *What's Mine is Yours: the Rise of Collaborative Consump tion* (Harper Business 2010).

[33]All these collaborative consumption platforms can be found online. They are mentioned as an example of the wide variety of platforms already available. Some of them might not be operating any longer by the time this chapter will be published.

In cyberspace, human intelligence has become collective through user-generated mass collaboration,[34] which—as several authors have noted—may produce social and economic enrichment to a far greater extent than in the past.[35] Yochai Benkler defined the high generative capacity of online commons as the 'wealth of networks'.[36] In the 'Wealth of Networks', Benkler writes: '[r]adical decentralization of intelligence in our communications network and the centrality of information, knowledge, culture, and ideas to advanced economic activity are leading to a new stage of the information economy— the networked information economy'.[37] Benkler qualified the concept by saying that

> [w]hat characterizes the networked information economy is that decentralized individual action—specifically, new and important cooperative and coordinate action carried out through radically distributed, nonmarket mechanisms that do not depend on proprietary strategies—plays a much greater role than it did, or could have, in the industrial information economy.[38]

The wealth of networks lies in networked peer production that it is highly generative because it is modular, granular, and cheap to integrate the results. To borrow Reichman's categories, new forms of innovation allow, throughout the net, small grains of information and innovation to be transformed into distributed and collective forms of intelligence.[39] As Benkler put it,

> [t]he networked environment makes possible a new modality of organizing production: radically decentralized, collaborative, and nonproprietary; based on sharing resources and outputs among widely distributed, loosely connected individuals who cooperate with each other without relying on either market signals or managerial commands. This is what I call 'commons-based peer production'.[40]

According to Benkler, the networked information economy improves individual capacities in three ways. First, individuals can do more for and by themselves. Second, the networked information economy enhances individuals' capacity to do more in loose commonality with others, without being constrained to organize their

---

[34]See Pierre Levy, *L'Intelligence Collective: Pur Une Anthopologie Du Cyberspace* (Editions La Découverte 1995).

[35]A large quantity of literature has been produced on mass collaboration in the networked information society. See eg Clay Shirky, *Cognitive Surplus: Creativity and generosity in a Connected Age* (The Penguin Press 2010); Charles Leadbeater, *We-Think: Mass Innovation, Not Mass Production* (Profile Books 2009); Tapscott and Williams (n 30); Clay Shirky, *Here Comes Everyone: The Power of Organizing Without Organizations* (Penguin 2008); David Weinberger, *Everything Is Miscellaneous: The Power of the New Digital Disorder* (Henry Holt 2008); Cass Sunstein, *Infotopia: How Many Minds Produce Knowledge* (OUP 2006).

[36]See Yochai Benkler, *The Wealth of Networks: How Social Production Transforms Markets and Freedom* (Yale UP 2007).

[37]ibid 32.

[38]ibid 3.

[39]See eg Jerome H Reichman, 'Of Green Tulips and Legal Kudzu: Repackaging Rights in Subpatentable Innovation' (2000) 53 Vanderbilt Law Review 1743.

[40]Benkler (n 36) 60.

relationship through a price system or in traditional hierarchical models. Finally, it improves the capacity of individuals to do more in formal organizations that operate outside the market sphere.[41] In this context, Reichman argues that property rules applied to small grains of innovation create 'legal kudzu'.[42] Therefore, small grains of innovation are best brought together in a contractually reconstructed commons, governed by liability, rather than property rules.[43]

Large scale cooperative behaviour and gift exchange that was previously limited to rarefied groups is now possible, thanks to technological advances.[44] Initially, the large scale cooperative behaviour emerged and evolved in software communities[45] and in academia.[46] Benkler describes open source software as the 'quintessential instance of commons based peer production'.[47] However, these cooperative and participative behaviours have spread far beyond those initial rarefied communities. From open source, we have been moving to open culture.[48] Open networks and networked peer collaboration have transformed markets by enabling amateurs to innovate.[49] David Bollier described this process as a 'viral spiral' by which internet users come together to build digital tools and share content on self-created online

---

[41]ibid 8-9. See also Benkler Yochai and Helen Nissenbaum, 'Commons-Based Peer Production and Virtue' (2006) 14 Journal of Political Philosophy 394. Cf Steven Weber, *The Success of Open Source* (Harvard UP 2004) 1.

[42]See Reichman (n 39).

[43]For a review of the notion of contractually constructed commons, see Jerome Reichman and Paul Uhlir, 'A Contractually Reconstructed Research Commons for Scientific Data in a Highly Protectionist Intellectual Property' (2003) 66 Law & Contemporary Problems 315. See also Lawrence Lessig, *The Future of ideas: The Fate of The Commons in a Connected World* (Vintage Books 2002); Madison, Frischmann, and Strandburg (n 30); Molly Van Houweling, 'Cultural Environmentalism and the Constructed Commons' (2007) 70 Law & Contemporary Problems 5.

[44]See Lewis Hyde, *The Gift: Creativity And The Artist In The Modern World* (Vintage Books 2007) (describing creativity exchange among artists); Robert Merton, *The Sociology Of Science: Theoretical And Empirical Investigations* (Norman Storer ed, University of Chicago Press 1973) 273-275, 339 (exploring norms of sharing among scientists).

[45]See Benkler (n 36) 63-68; Yochai Benkler, 'Sharing Nicely: On Shareable Goods and the Emergence of Sharing as a Modality of Economic Production' (2005) 114 Yale Law Journal 273; Yochai Benkler, 'Coase's Penguin, or, Linux and The Nature of the Firm' (2002) 112 Yale Law Journal 369, 374.

[46]See Madison, Frischmann and Strandburg (n 30).

[47]Benkler (n 36) 63.

[48]See Lee Davis, 'Should the Logic of 'Open Source' Be Applied to Digital Cultural Goods? An Exploratory Essay' in Helle Porsdam (ed), *Copyright and Other Fairy Tales: Hans Christian Andersen and the Commodification of Creativity* (Edward Elgar Publishing Ltd 2006) 129. See also Primavera De Filippi and Félix Tréguer, 'Expanding the Internet Commons: The Subversive Potential of Wireless Community Networks' (2015) 6 The Journal of Peer Production <http://peerproduction.net/issues/issue-6-disruption-and-the-law/peer-reviewed-articles/expanding-the-internet-commons-the-subversive-potential-of-wireless-community-networks/> accessed 18 March 2020 (discussing the phenomenon of decentralization in telecommunications networks and the revival of grassroots (wireless) community networks).

[49]See Stefan Thomke and Eric Von Hippel, 'Customers as Innovators: A New Way to Create Value' (2002) 80 Harvard Business Review 74.

commons.[50] Individual experimentation, sub-cultures, and a community of social trust created Linux, Wikipedia, Facebook, YouTube, and major political websites.

4 Neoliberalism Meets the Sharing Economy: The Platform Economy

In truth, the potential of the 'sharing economy' and mass cooperation have remained partially unfulfilled. Neoliberalism took over the expectations of the 'sharing economy' through its 'platformization'.[51] Neoliberalist economic doctrines shaped the twentieth century and their influence extended in the twenty-first century. Neoliberalist law and economics scholars have launched a crusade to expose the evil of the commons.[52] They constantly pushed for increasing propertization of intellectual assets. The evil of not propertizing would lie in underuse and suboptimal resource management. Since Harold Demsetz, economists have viewed property rights as a desirable tool to internalize the full social value of people's actions and therefore maximize the incentive to engage in those actions.[53] An influential article written by Garret Hardin in 1968 described the evil of not propertizing as the tragedy of the commons.[54] The subject of Hardin's essay was the carrying capacity of the commons and its limits. Hardin identified the tragedy of the commons in the environmental dysfunctions of overuse and underinvestment found in the absence of a private property regime. Hardin made it clear that any commons open to all, ungoverned by custom or law, will eventually collapse.[55]

The fear of the tragedy of the commons propelled more property rights to incentivise assets' creation and management, including information and cultural assets. Once digitization provided new, massive value for information assets,

[50]See David Bollier, *Viral Spiral: How the Commoners Built a Digital Republic of Their Own* (New Press 2009).

[51]See Vera Demary, 'The Platformisation of Digital Markets' (2015) Institut der Deutschen Wirtschaft (IW) Policy Paper 39 <www.iwkoeln.de/studien/iw-policy-papers/beitrag/vera-demary-the-platformization-of-digital-markets-257401.html> accessed 18 March 2020; David Nieborg and Thomas Poell, 'The Platformisation of Cultural Production: Theorizing the Contingent Cultural Commodity' (2018) 20 New Media & Society 4275.

[52]See Scott Gordon, 'The Economic Theory of a Common-Property Resource: The Fishery' (1954) 62 Journal of Political Economy 124; and Anthony Scott, 'The Fishery: The Objectives of Sole Ownership' (1955) 63 Journal of Political Economy 116 (introducing an economic analysis of fisheries that demonstrated that unlimited harvesting of high-demand fish by multiple individuals is both economically and environmentally unsustainable). See also Chander Anupam and Madhavi Sunder, 'The Romance of the Public Domain' (2004) 92 California Law Review 1331, 1332-1333 (discussing the move toward propertization).

[53]See Harold Demsetz, 'Toward a Theory of Property Rights' (1967) 57 American Economic Review 347.

[54]See Garrett Hardin, 'The Tragedy of the Commons' (1968) 162 Science 1243.

[55]ibid.

enclosure and 'information feudalism' followed as a natural application of the dominant economic paradigm.[56] As Elinor Ostrom and her colleague Charlotte Hesse argued '[i]nformation that used to be "free" is now increasingly being privatized, monitored, encrypted, and restricted. The enclosure is caused by the conflicts and contradictions between intellectual property laws and the expanded capacities of new technologies'.[57] The commodification of information was propelled by the ability of new technologies to capture resources previously unowned and unprotected in what amounts to a new, digital, land grab.[58]

While the new economics of commons-based peer production democratized innovation,[59] they underperformed in terms of value creation. As Bodó Balázs puts it, 'the rise of the platform economy [. . .] was the failure of the commons based peer production movement, because it refused to think about value.'[60] On one side, flexibility, decentralization, cooperative [illegible] and customization out-performed corporate bureaucracies that were unwilling to experiment, because it was thought to be too risky and costly. However, on the other side, heavily centralized, hierarchical, hyper-capitalistic, market-based solutions were much more effective in extracting and redistributing value from the shared, distributed resources, than the communities that produced them under the naive dream of building a commons.[61] In a decade or so, these communities have been assimilated within platform economy models as in the case of YouTube, SSRN, etc.

This unhappy turn has created plenty of negative externalities. The platform economy has left behind social values, including fundamental rights, competition, and democracy.[62] This unhappy turn was also made possible by what has been termed 'privacy myopia'. According to Professor Fromkin, individuals have been

---

[56]See Peter Drahos with John Braithwaite, *Information Feudalism: Who Owns the Knowledge Economy?* (Earthscan Publications 2002); James Boyle, 'The Second Enclosure Movement and the Construction of the Public Domain' (2003) 66 Law & Contemporary Problems 33, 45-46.

[57]Charlotte Hess and Elinor Ostrom, 'Ideas, Artifacts, and Facilities: Information as a Common-Pool Resource' (2003) 66 Law & Contemporary Problems 112.

[58]See Charlotte Hess and Elinor Ostrom, 'Introduction: An Overview of the Knowledge Commons' in Charlotte Hess and Elinor Ostrom (eds), *Understanding Knowledge as a Commons: From Theory to Practice* (MIT Press 2007) 12.

[59]See Eric von Hippel, *Democratizing Innovation* (MIT Press 2005) 2 (noting that '[o]pen, distributed innovation is 'attacking' a major structure of the social division of labor'). See also Robert Cunningham, 'The Separation of (Economic) Power: A Cultural Environmental Perspective of Social Production and the Networked Public Sphere' (2010) 11 Journal of High Technology Law 1 (noting that social production 'affords the possibility of harnessing the critical liberal function of separating (economic) power' by diversifying the modes of production).

[60]Bodó Balázs, 'Was the Open Knowledge Commons Idea a Curse in Disguise?: Towards Sovereign Institutions of Knowledge' (2019) SSRN Research Paper 3502119 <https://ssrn.com/abstract=3502119 or https://doi.org/10.2139/ssrn.3502119> accessed 18 March 2020.

[61]ibid.

[62]See Sofia Ranchordás and Catalina Goanta, 'The New City Regulators: Platform and Public Values in Smart and Sharing Cities' (2019) Computer Law & Security Review <https://doi.org/10.1016/j.clsr.2019.105375> accessed 18 March 2020.

surrendering their privacy bit by bit by giving away their data too often and too cheaply.[63] Multiple jurisdictions—with the exceptions of the European Union—have endorsed policy strategies that lead to the unstoppable growth of businesses that have been thriving on data appropriation thanks to 'privacy myopia'.

5 Data Integration: From Mass Production to MaaS

User-generated data is the goldmine that the platform economy has been relentlessly exploiting. The value created by networked user-based mass production has been internalised by centralized capitalistic endeavours that maximized profits thanks to business models free-riding on external naturally occurring digital raw materials. In the streets and roads of the smart city, mass production morphs into MaaS or Mobility-as-a-Service. In MaaS, mobility provided as a service replaces personally-owned modes of transportation by combining transportation services from public and private transportation providers.[64] MaaS will integrate plenty of innovative new mobility service providers, including ride-sharing and e-hailing services, bike-sharing programs, scooter sharing systems and car-sharing services as well as on-demand bus services,[65] while sharing a vast amount of data and integrating it into big data patterns.[66] The MaaS Alliance describes Mobility as a Service as

> the integration of various forms of transport services into a single mobility service accessible on demand. To meet a customer's request, a MaaS operator facilitates a diverse menu of transport options, be they public transport, ride-, car- or bike-sharing, taxi or car rental/lease, or a combination thereof. For the user, MaaS can offer added value through use of a single

[63]See Michael Fromkin, 'The Death of Privacy?' (2000) 52 Stanford Law Review 1461, 1502-1503.

[64]See eg Roni Utriainen and Markus Pöllänen, 'Review on Mobility as a Service in Scientific Publications' (2018) 27 Research in Transportation Business & Management 15; Peraphan Jittrapirom and others, 'Mobility as a Service: A Critical Review of Definitions, Assessments of Schemes, and Key Challenges' (2017) 2(2) Urban Planning 13; Maria Kamargianni and Melinda Matyas, 'The Business Ecosystem of Mobility-as-a-Service' (Proceedings of the 96th Transportation Research Board Annual Meeting, Washington DC, 8-12 January 2017) <https://discovery.ucl.ac.uk/id/eprint/10037890/> accessed 18 March 2020. See also Göran Smith and David Hensher, 'Towards a framework for mobility-as-a-service policies' (2020) 89 Transport Policy 54 <www.sciencedirect.com/science/article/abs/pii/S0967070X19307504> accessed 18 March 2020.

[65]See Glenn Lyons, Paul Hammond and Kate Mackay, 'The Importance of User Perspective in the evolution of MaaS' (2019) 121 Transportation Research Part A: Policy and Practice 22 (providing a taxonomy of MaaS integration, which underlines different levels of service provision to the user).

[66]See Christian Bussmann, Magdalene Piec and Andreas Gutweniger, 'Data Sharing in the Age of Mobility as a Service' (*Detecon*, 28 March 2019) <www.detecon.com/en/knowledge/data-sharing-age-mobility-service> accessed 18 March 2020.

application to provide access to mobility, with a single payment channel instead of multiple ticketing and payment operations.[67]

Through a unified gateway or app that creates and manages the trip, users can pay per trip or a monthly fee with a single account.[68] The gateway will serve also as a journey planner showing transportation means available for moving from location A to location B, while choosing the preferred trip based on cost, time, and convenience.[69] All bookings for completing the trip would be performed as a unit. Basically, multiple modes of transport will be integrated into seamless trip chains, with bookings and payments managed collectively for all legs of the trip. According to Kamargianni et al. three main elements that are needed within MaaS systems to provide users with seamless journeys, including ticket and payment integration (when one smart card allows to access all transportation modes and one account can be charged for using the services), mobility package (which users can pre-pay for a combination of mobility services), and ITC integration (when a single application can be used to access information about the transportation modes).[70]

The integration of services and transport modes will be led by data integration and analysis. In offering services, MaaS gathers data from hundreds of billions of public and private transport journeys per year.[71] There are multiple sources of data coming into play, including private, passive, community and self-quantification data.[72] Data are typically held by governments, governmental organizations and local communities and include census, transport data and energy use figures.[73] Private data may include proprietary information held by private firms or individuals.[74] Passive data are 'ambient data' passively collected without being specifically relevant to the activities of the collecting agency, such as internet search histories or mobile phones' location traces.[75] Community data refer to unstructured data that can be analyzed and structured so that meaningful patterns can be inferred. They can be captured for

---

[67]MaaS Alliance, 'What is MaaS?' <https://maas-alliance.eu/homepage/what-is-maas/> accessed 18 March 2020.

[68]Sergio Guidon, 'Transportation Service Bundling: For Whose Benefit? Consumer Valuation of Pure Bundling in the Passenger Transportation Market' (2020) 131 Transportation Research Part A: Policy and Practice 91.

[69]See Maria Kamargianni, Weibo Li and Melinda Matyas, 'A Comprehensive Review of "Mobility as a Service" Systems' (Transportation Research Board 95th Annual Meeting, Washington 2016) <https://pdfs.semanticscholar.org/ebbb/5ce87cca2547d5bd1d073563af43a5da90c0.pdf?_ga=2.13831615.904933516.1584459187-470961107.1583238027> accessed 18 March 2020.

[70]See Maria Kamargianni and others, 'A Critical Review of New Mobility Services for Urban Transport' (2016) 14 Transportation Research Procedia 3294.

[71]See International Association of Public Transport (UITP), 'Public Transport Trends 2019' *(UITP,* 2019) <www.uitp.org/public-transport-trends> accessed 18 March 2020.

[72]See Gerard George, Martine Haas and Alex Pentland, 'Big Data and Management' (2014) 57 Academy of Management Journal 321.

[73]ibid.

[74]ibid.

[75]ibid.

example, as part of social interactions, such as online reviews/ratings, or social media feeds.[76] Self-quantification data are revealed by individuals through self-monitoring, such as through the use of personal fitness trackers.[77]

The data can be used for multiple purposes. On the one hand, collected and processed data help people's journeys become more efficient.[78] On the other, the same data allows public authorities—as well as private service providers—to make informed decisions when considering improvements in transit systems.[79] In particular, data analysis based around modern urban mobility trends will determine public transport scheduling and transport system upgrading.[80] However, while geotagged and location-enabled data are critical to the development of the MaaS ecosystem, location data collected from personal devices can be used to created detailed traces of MaaS users' behaviour.[81]

6 Property Rights vs Personality Rights

Of course, data protection, appropriation and ownership remain critical issues in an era of 'surveillance capitalism'.[82] 'MaaS surveillance' would be a tightly related concept as 'MaaS services are predicated upon the sharing of personal travel information (vehicle availability, origins, destinations, financial information, social network data, etc.)'.[83] In Europe, for example, the General Data Protection Regulation (GDPR) has the potential to significantly impact on the further implementation of MaaS.[84] Under GDPR, travel information may be considered personal, subject to the regulations and restrictions this categorisation implies. An emerging conundrum is whether data such as those integrated in MaaS should continue to be treated as

---

[76]See Caitlin Cottrill and others, 'Tweeting Transit: An Examination of Social Media Strategies for Transport Information Management During a Large Event' (2017) 77 Transportation Research Part C: Emerging Technologies 421.

[77]See George (n 72).

[78]Barbara Lenz and Dirk Heinrichs, 'What Can We Learn from Smart Urban Mobility Technologies?' (2017) 16 IEEE Pervasive Computing 84, 84-86.

[79]ibid 84-86.

[80]ibid.

[81]See Yves-Alexandre De Montjoye and others, 'Unique in the Crowd: The Privacy Bounds of Human Mobility' (2013) 3(1376) Scientific Reports 1; Gennady Andrienko and others, 'Report from Dagstuhl: the Liberation of Mobile Location Data and its Implications for Privacy Research' (2013) 17(2) ACM SIGMOBILE Mobile Computing Communications Review 7.

[82]Shoshana Zuboff, *The Age of Surveillance Capitalism* (Profile Books 2019). See also Tim Wu, *The Attention Merchants: The Epic Struggle to Get Inside Our Heads* (Atlantic Books 2017).

[83]See Caitlin Cottrill, 'MaaS surveillance: Privacy considerations in mobility as a service' (2020) 131 Transportation Research Part A: Policy and Practice 50.

[84]ibid; Jittrapirom and others (n 64).

personality rights, like in most EU jurisdictions, or should be construed as property rights.

Since European courts have acknowledged a right to informational self-determination, data protection rights have been recognized the status of fundamental rights, worthy of constitutional protection. The term informational self-determination was first used in the context of a German constitutional ruling relating to personal information collected during the 1983 census.[85] The German term is *informationelle Selbstbestimmung*. On that occasion the German Federal Constitutional Court ruled that:

> [. . .] in the context of modern data processing, the protection of the individual against unlimited collection, storage, use and disclosure of his/her personal data is encompassed by the general personal rights of the German constitution. This basic right warrants in this respect the capacity of the individual to determine in principle the disclosure and use of his/her personal data. Limitations to this informational self-determination are allowed only in case of overriding public interest.[86]

The right of informational self-determination is a critical achievement in empowerment of users' rights. It was embedded in Art. 12(b) of the Data Protection Directive by the rule that allows a data subject to request 'rectification, erasure or blocking of data the processing of which does not comply with the provisions of this Directive, in particular because of the incomplete or inaccurate nature of the data.'[87] The right of informational self-determination empowers individuals against data processing entities—such as advertisers, insurers, online platforms, transport services, and data brokers—by guaranteeing the 'authority of the individual in principle to decide for himself whether or not his personal data should be divulged or processed'.[88] The German Court vested this right with constitutional value. In recent times, this fundamental right has been qualified as a right to human dignity that serves as a foundation for the right to privacy.[89] The recently enacted General Data Protection Regulation makes specific reference to the fact that rules [for processing in the context of employment] 'shall include suitable and specific measures to

---

[85]BVerfGE 65, 1 of 15 December 1983 (Volkszählungs-Urteil) translated in English by Eibe Riedel in (1984) 5 Human Rights Law Journal 94. See also Eibe Riedel, 'New Bearings in German Data Protection: Census Act 1983 Partially Unconstitutional' (1984) 5 Human Rights Law Journal 67; Gerrit Hornung and Christoph Schnabel, 'Data Protection in Germany I: The Population Census Decision and the Right to Informational Self-determination' (2009) 25 Computer Law & Security Report 84; Antoinette Rouvroy and Yves Poullet, 'The Right to Informational Self-Determination and the Value of Self-Development: Reassessing the Importance of Privacy for Democracy' in Serge Gutwirth and others (eds), *Reinventing Data Protection?* (Springer 2009) 45-76.

[86]BVerfGE 65, 1 (n 85).

[87]Parliament and Council Directive 95/46/EC of 24 October 1995 on the protection of individuals with regard to the processing of personal data and on the free movement of such data [1995] OJ L 281/31 (Data Protection Directive) art 12.

[88]Riedel (n 85) 69.

[89]See Luciano Floridi, 'On Human Dignity as a Foundation for the Right to Privacy' (2016) 29 Philosophy and Technology 307. See also Orla Lynskey, *The Foundations of EU Data Protection Law* (OUP 2015).

safeguard the data subject's human dignity, legitimate interests and fundamental rights.'[90]

In contrast, the UK legal tradition has endorsed the essence of this right but framed it within a property, rather than a human right perspective. In doing so, UK courts noted that 'if information is my private property, it is for me to decide how much of it should be published'.[91] This propertarian approach to data ownership and management has been recently gaining momentum, possibly overtaking the well-established fundamental right approach that was described earlier.

7 Data Propertization

Building upon neoliberal perspectives, proposals towards data propertization have been increasingly challenging a long-standing construction of data protection rights as personality rights. Meanwhile, data propertization would also challenge the traditional dichotomy idea/expression in copyright law, according to which data—and ideas—would not qualify as protectable expression and therefore would be outside the scope of the copyright monopoly.[92]

Relentless data propertization comes as a result of the so called 'datafication' of society.[93] Datafication 'is a contemporary phenomenon which refers to the quantification of human life through digital information, very often for economic value'.[94] According to Mayer-Schönberger and Cukier, 'to datafy a phenomenon is to put it in quantified form so that it can be tabulated and analyzed'.[95] Datafication and data propertization reflect the tension inherent in the 'digital dilemma'[96] that Stuart Brand has summarised as follows: 'information wants to be free, because it has become so cheap to distribute, copy, and recombine—too cheap to meter. It wants to be expensive because it can be immeasurably valuable to the recipient. That tension will not go away ...'.[97] Just like any other phenomenon, urban mobility can be 'datafied'. In particular, the success of MaaS rests in its 'datafication' and the value

---

[90]See Parliament and Council Regulation (EU) 2016/679 of 27 April 2016 on the protection of natural persons with regard to the processing of personal data and on the free movement of such data, and repealing Directive 95/46/EC [2016] OJ L119/1 (General Data Protection Regulation GDPR) art 88.

[91]*McKennitt v. Ash* [2006] EWCA Civ 1714, s 55 (Lord Justice Buxton).

[92]See eg Bernt Hugenholtz, *Auteursrecht op informative* (Kluwer 1989).

[93]Ulises Mejias and Nick Couldry, 'Datafication' (2019) 8(4) Internet Policy Review 1 <https://policyreview.info/concepts/datafication> accessed 18 March 2020.

[94]ibid.

[95]Viktor Mayer-Schönberger and Kenneth Cukier, *Big Data: A Revolution That Will Transform How We Live, Work and Think* (John Murray 2013) 78.

[96]National Research Board, *The Digital Dilemma: Intellectual Property in The Information Age* (National Academy Press 2000).

[97]Stuart Brand, *The Media Lab: Inventing the Future at MIT* (Penguin Books 1986) 86.

that can be extracted from it. The dilemma becomes whether value for society at large can be better extracted through data propertization or open access models and data protection based on personality rights.

In this context, there is an increasing push for data propertization and new *sui generis* rights.[98] In a recent interview, the WIPO Director Francis Gurry said that 'we will see intellectual property moving to areas like data.'[99] A recent example of a possible model for data propertization might follow from the former Democratic US presidential candidate Andrew Yang. He proposed a policy named 'data as a property rights', which would grant users ownership of their own data.[100] Users would have seven rights recognized that match more or less the same rights granted to EU citizens under the GDPR and EU data protection regulations. These are the right to be informed as to what data will be collected, and how it will be used; the right to be informed if ownership of your data changes hands; the right to be told if a website has data on you and what that data is, the right to download all data in a standardized format to port to another platform; the right to be informed of any data breaches including your information in a timely manner; the right to opt out of data collection or sharing; and the right to be forgotten and to have all data related to you deleted upon request.[101] However, in this proposal, unlike the personality rights recognized under EU law, these rights can be voluntarily waived and shared with companies as long as 'a share of the economic value generated from [the] data' is internalized by the users.[102]

In 2017, at the IT trade fair CeBit, Angela Merkel reflected on the need for regulation and EU harmonization over data ownership in the context of automotive mobility, where by 'using the data of the user it is possible to produce new products and applications'.[103] Not long afterwards, Alexander Dobrindt, the German Federal Minister of Transport and Digital Infrastructure, proposed a new law under the title 'Data Sovereignty for the individual'. The first principle of this proposed law declared that data should have the same legal status as material commodities, so

[98] See eg Jeffrey Ritter and Anna Mayer, 'Regulating Data as Property: A New Construct for Moving Forward' (2018) 16 Duke Law & Technology Review 220, 226. For a review of an earlier debate (long before the advent of the platform economy) about data propertization in the US, see Pamela Samuelson, 'Privacy as Intellectual Property' (1999) 52 Stanford Law Review 1125 (arguing against property on personal information).

[99] See Francis Gury, 'IP Horizon 5.0 Conference' (*Twitter*, 14 October 2019) <https://twitter.com/EU_IPO/status/1183694801071423489> accessed 18 March 2020.

[100] See Andrew Yang, 'Policy, Data as a Property Right' (Yang 2020) <www.yang2020.com/policies/data-property-right> accessed 18 March 2020. See also Kevin Chen, 'Yanging and Hanging onto Our Own Data' (*BTLJ Blog*, 30 December 2019) <https://btlj.org/2019/12/yanging-and-hanging-onto-our-own-data> accessed 18 March 2020.

[101] ibid.

[102] ibid.

[103] Ritter and Mayer (n 98) 228 fn 19.

that they can be allocated as 'property' to a natural person or a legal entity.[104] Further, the proposal would consider property assignment by stating that the right to dispose of data belongs to the person who created the data. In particular, 'for vehicle data, for example, [the property over the data should be assigned] to the owner who bought the vehicle'.[105] These principles would be coupled by an 'open provision of non-personal mobility data in order to use the associated potential for traffic planning and intelligent traffic control'.[106] In addition, transparency should be enhanced by a data ID for all services and products such as motor vehicles that provides 'information about the scope and frequency of data collection and about the use and disclosure of the data'.[107]

Meanwhile, the Directive 2019/770 on certain aspects concerning contracts for the supply of digital content and digital services seems to have construed data as counter-performance in consumer contracts,[108] signifying 'a paradigm shift in the law of personal data'.[109] Article 3(1) of the Directive states, on one hand, that the Directive applies 'to any contract where the trader supplies or undertakes to supply digital content or a digital service to the consumer and the consumer *pays or undertakes to pay a price*'.[110] On the other hand, the same provision states that the Directive applies also 'where the trader supplies or undertakes to supply digital content or a digital service to the consumer, and the consumer *provides or undertakes to provide personal data* to the trader',[111] equating 'personal data' to 'payment of a price' as 'quid pro quo' in contracts for the supply of digital content or services to consumers. However, the final text of the Directive avoids the wording of the initial proposal mentioning 'personal data as counter-performance' to make clear that 'the European legislature does not encourage a further commercialisation of

[104]See Bundesministerium für Verkehr und Digitale Infrastruktur (BMVI), 'Wir Brauchen Ein Datengesetz in Deutschland! [We Need a Data Law in Germany!]' <www.bmvi.de/SharedDocs/DE/Artikel/DG/datengesetz.html> accessed 18 March 2020.

[105]ibid.

[106]ibid.

[107]ibid. See also Boris Otto and others, 'Industrial Data Space: Digital Sovereignty Over Data' (Fraunhofer 2016) <www.fraunhofer.de/content/dam/zv/en/fields-of-research/industrial-data-space/whitepaper-industrial-data-spaceeng.pdf> accessed 18 March 2020 (discussing the Industrial Data Space (IDS) research project funded by the German Federal Ministry of Education and Research, which would like to ensure similar 'digital sovereignty of data owners').

[108]Parliament and Council Directive (EU) 2019/770 of 20 May 2019 on certain aspects concerning contracts for the supply of digital content and digital services [2019] OJ L 136/1 (Digital Content Directive) art 3(1).

[109]Axel Metzger, 'A Market Model for Personal Data: State of the Play under the New Directive on Digital Content and Digital Services' in Lohsse Sebastian, Schulze Reiner and Staudenmayer Dirk (eds), *Data as Counter Performance: Contract Law 2.0?* (forthcoming). See also Axel Metzger, 'Data as Counter-Performance: What Rights and Duties do Parties Have?' (2017) 8 Journal of Intellectual Property, Information Technology and Electronic Commerce Law (JIPITEC) 2; Axel Metzger and others, 'Data-Related Aspects of the Digital Content Directive' (2018) 9 JIPITEC 90.

[110]Digital Content Directive (n 108) art 3(1) (emphasis added).

[111]ibid (emphasis added).

personal data'.[112] In addition, the Recital 24 of the Directive stresses apparently that very point by noting that 'while fully recognising that the protection of personal data is a fundamental right and that therefore personal data cannot be considered as a commodity, this Directive should ensure that consumers are, in the context of such business models, entitled to contractual remedies'.[113]

Some courts have started applying more decisively this novel construction of 'personal data'. The Roman administrative Court, for example, has recognized personal data as an economic value.[114] According to the court, Facebook was wrong to assume that the protection of personal data is only related to fundamental rights.[115] Instead, the exploitation of personal data may also represent a value which is susceptible of economic exploitation and can serve as a 'quid pro quo' in a contractual sense.[116] For this reason, Facebook was to be sanctioned for stating that signing up was for free and there was no counter-performance for the consumers when, instead, Facebook processing users' data for commercial purposes was a contractual 'quid pro quo' and a counter-performance.[117]

8 A 3-C Model for Smart Urban Mobility

The negative externalities of data propertization have lain exposed for some time now. First, there are fundamental considerations regarding the competing positive externalities of information and data commons for market efficiency. Nobel laureate Joseph Stiglitz stressed this point by noting that:

> [i]t is imperative to understand the ways in which the production and distribution of knowledge differs from that of goods like steel and cars. [...]. The fact that knowledge is, in central ways, a public good and that there are important externalities means that exclusive or excessive reliance on the market may not result in economic efficiency.[118]

Restricting access to information would increase the inefficiency of the market because perfect information makes the perfect market.[119] A market that commodifies

[112]Metzger, 'A Market Model for Personal Data: State of the Play under the New Directive on Digital Content and Digital Services' (n 109) 2.

[113]Digital Content Directive (n 108).

[114]See Tribunale Amministrativo Regionale Lazio, *Facebook v Altroconsumo* [2020] No. 5288/ 2018.

[115]ibid.

[116]ibid.

[117]ibid.

[118]Joseph Stiglitz, *Public Policy for a Knowledge Economy* (World Bank Department for Trade and Industry and Center for Economic Policy Research 1999) 25.

[119]See Sanford Grossman and Joseph Stiglitz, 'On the Impossibility of Informationally Efficient Markets' (1980) 70 American Economic Review 393.

information excessively will be less efficient in allocating resources since key information to facilitate that allocation will be more difficult to find.

Second, data propertization seems inconsistent with the traditional IP incentive/innovation balance: that fundamental notion according to which follow-on creativity and innovation is based on unburdened and open reuse of basic knowledge and information. Data fall outside the scope of intellectual property rights because 'the general rule of law is, that the noblest of human productions—knowledge, truths ascertained, conceptions, and ideas—become, after voluntary communication to others, free as the air to common use'.[120]

Third, in certain contexts, business models based on open access approaches might produce considerable economic and social value,[121] while property rules might be especially inefficient. From Yochai Benkler's 'wealth of networks' to Reichman's 'legal kudzu', scholarship has shown the emerging value of open models. In particular, in light of Calabresi and Melamed's liability rules' framework,[122] Reichman argues that property rules applied to small grains of innovation create 'legal kudzu'.[123] Therefore, small grains of innovation are best together in a contractually reconstructed commons, governed by liability, rather than property rules.[124]

Finally, as Couldry and Mejias argue, society might be entering an era of 'data colonialism', which 'paves the way to a new stage of capitalism [. . .] the capitalization of life without limit'.[125] Although apparently counter-intuitive, by promoting alienability and monetization of personal data, data propertization might push 'predatory extractive practices of historical colonialism with the abstract quantification methods of computing'.[126] Once property rights are based on data, users with no bargaining power will transfer them as part of cheap deals as counter-performance

[120]*International News Service v Associated Press*, 248 US 215, 250 (1918) (Justice Louis Brandeis, dissenting).

[121]The research carried out by Brett Frischmann points exactly in this direction, see generally Brett Frischmann, *Infrastructure: the Social Value of Shared Resources* (OUP 2012); Brett Frischmann, 'An Economic Theory of Infrastructure and Commons Management' (2005) 89 Minnesota Law Review 917.

[122]See Guido Calabresi, 'Some Thoughts on Risk Distribution and the Law of Torts' (1961) 70 Yale Law Journal 499; Guido Calabresi and Douglas Melamed, 'Property Rules, Liability Rules and Inalienability: One View of the Cathedral' (1972) 85 Harvard Law Review 1089.

[123]See Reichman (n 39).

[124]For a review of the notion of contractually constructed commons, see Reichman and Uhlir, 'A Contractually Reconstructed Research Commons for Scientific Data in a Highly Protectionist Intellectual Property' (n 43). See also Lawrence Lessig, *The Future of ideas: The Fate of The Commons in a Connected World* (Vintage Books 2002); Madison, Frischmann, and Strandburg (n 30); Van Houweling (n 43).

[125]Nick Couldry and Ulises Mejias, 'Data Colonialism: Rethinking Big Data's Relation to the Contemporary Subject' (2019) 20 Television and New Media 336, 336.

[126]ibid 337.

for services they already receive for free.[127] Actually, a McKinsey & Co's study found that customers might be far less concerned with data ownership than the automakers expected.[128] For example, if the driver owns the data, automakers will provide discounts upon car purchases inclusive of the transfer of the data that the vehicles are generating. Again, users will be transferring data ownership in exchange for a discount on the latest digital cockpit or navigator. This will arguably push platform economy models, oligopolistic market dominance and consumer exploitation.

Rather than through data propertization and platform economy models, smart urban mobility should develop upon what I call a 3C model: commons, collaboration and crowdsourcing.[129]

8.1 Commons

Fundamental literature has highlighted that no economic theory of intellectual property and commons management supports the prediction of the tragedy of the commons.[130] According to empirical research, there seem to be sustainable options along the road to propertization. Nobel laureate Elinor Ostrom powerfully advocated the cause of the commons against the mantra of propertization. Ostrom's works showed the inaccuracies of Hardin's tragedy of the commons.[131] Empirical studies, which Ostrom has spearheaded, have shown that common resources can be effectively managed by groups of people under suitable conditions, such as appropriate

[127]cf Pamela Samuelson (*Twitter:* @PamelaSamuelson, 30 December 2019) <https://twitter.com/PamelaSamuelson/status/1211725833704026113> accessed 18 March 2020, Tweet: 'Well intentioned idea to create property rights in data, but profoundly misguided. This idea will backfire. To get services, you'll be asked to transfer them, & then exploiters will own' (noting that the concern is that a well-intentioned idea might easily backfire: to get services, users will be asked to transfer the data which exploiters will then own).

[128]See Dominik Wee and others, *Competing for the Connected Customer: Perspectives on the Opportunities Created by Car Connectivity and Automation* (McKinsey & Co 2015).

[129]See Morozov and Bria (n 2) 42-43. See also Giancarlo Frosio, *Reconciling Copyright with Cumulative Creativity: the Third Paradigm* (Edward Elgar 2018) 331-371 (where I propose a similar framework in the context of digital content creation).

[130]See Yochai Benkler, 'A Political Economy of the Public Domain: Markets in Information Goods vs The Marketplace of Ideas' in Rochelle Dreyfuss, Diane L Zimmerman, and Harry First (eds), *Expanding the Boundaries of Intellectual Property: Innovation Policy for the Knowledge Society* (OUP 2001) 270-272.

[131]See Elinor Ostrom, *Governing the Commons: The Evolution of Institutions for Collective Action* (CUP 1990); Elinor Ostrom, Roy Gardner, and James Walker, *Rules, Games, and Common-Pool Resources* (University of Michigan Press 1994); Elinor Ostrom, *The Drama of the Commons* (National Academies Press 2002).

rules, good conflict-resolution mechanisms, and well-defined group boundaries.[132] Under suitable conditions and proper governance the tragedy of the commons becomes 'the comedy of the commons'.[133] Commons might work under appropriate management rules that stimulate value creation.

In the context of smart cities and urban mobility, there might be even a more markedly changing approach towards commons-based sharing models. Property's role in the sharing economy is gradually decreasing in importance, which pushes for a mobile and flexible vision of engaging with possessions.[134] Meanwhile, decentralization might be re-emerging. Platforms might be losing their innovative impetus, while the new now comes from the fringes. In this regard, even the Financial Times praised Barcelona's Decode project treating data as commons.[135] Decode—a EU-backed consortium of fifteen partners—is meant to let people regain control of their data, while providing 'tools that put individuals in control of whether they keep their personal information private or share it for the public good'.[136] Decode would like to create an alternative, decentralized data ecosystem, where municipalities like Barcelona and Amsterdam treat their residents' data as a public good—or public infrastructure—that should be made available 'for broader communal use' by the local community in particular.[137] Decode aims specifically at providing countermeasures to the increasingly centralized digital economy, which 'relies on the manipulation and commercial exploitation of personal information by very few Big Tech Giants'.[138] Barcelona, for example, is taking data from Vodafone and handing it back to its own citizens. Vodafone is now contractually obliged to hand back data collected from the public, which is published on the city open data portal in an anonymized form.[139]

---

[132] See Hesse and Ostrom (n 58) 11; Susan S Hanna, Carl Folke, and Karl-Gören Mäler (eds), *Rights to Nature: Ecological, Economic, Cultural, and Political Principles of Institutions for the Environment* (Island Press 1996); Daniel Bromley and others (eds), *Making the Commons Work: Theory, Practice and Policy* (International Center for Self-Governance Press1992); Robert Andelson (ed), *Commons without Tragedy: The Social Ecology of Land Tenure and Democracy* (Center for Incentive Taxation 1991).

[133] See Carol Rose, 'The Comedy of the Commons: Custom, Commerce, and Inherently Public Property' (1986) 53 University of Chicago Law Review 711.

[134] See Shelly Kreiczer-Levy, *Destabilized Property: Property Law in the Sharing Economy* (CUP 2019).

[135] See Financial Times, 'Protecting Data Privacy Needs Constant Evolution' (*FT*, 30 December 2019) <www.ft.com/content/9a3bb14c-2255-11ea-b8a1-584213ee7b2b> accessed 18 March 2020.

[136] Decode, 'What is DECODE?' <https://decodeproject.eu/what-decode> accessed 18 March 2020.

[137] Ibid.

[138] Decode, 'DECODE gives back Data Sovereignty to Citizens' <https://tools.decodeproject.eu> accessed 18 March 2020.

[139] Amy Lewin, 'Barcelona's Robin Hood of Data: Francesca Bria' (*FT Sifted*, 16 November 2018) <https://sifted.eu/articles/barcelonas-robin-hood-of-data-francesca-bria> accessed 18 March 2020.

Rather than propertized—and transferred to capitalistic centralized online conglomerates as part of cheap bargains—anonymized urban mobility data should be pooled in public data banks[140] for community viewing under the understanding that rights management of the dataset would be under community control, and that use of the data must always produce public value for the community. In what has been termed as 'smart commons or a smart approach to the commons', the public should have a central role in advancing and maintaining urban commons in the smart city.[141] Decentralization of 'smart commons' is key to its sustainable management. Communities will serve as representative proxies for users, providing the bargaining power that individual users would be inherently lacking, in addition to a broader vision to promote public interest uses that might foster progress. As part of a so called 'citizen sensing' approach—that develops and uses lightweight technologies with local communities to collect, share and act upon data—communities will also become more aware of how they can tackle local issues.[142]

City data commons can be integrated with city data marketplaces such as the City Data Exchange in Copenhagen.[143] This explorative project examined the possibilities of creating a marketplace for the exchange of data between public and private organizations.[144] City data marketplaces would incentivise corporate data holders to collect and share data to develop data-oriented solutions to urban problems like traffic congestion.[145] Integration between city data commons and city data marketplace could be based on liability rules rather than proprietary arrangements, according to Calabresi and Melamed's liability rules framework and Reichman's

[140]Cf Kenneth Laudon, 'Markets and Privacy' (1996) 39 Communications of the Association for Computing Machinery 92, 92 (proposing the establishment of a regulated National Information Market, where individuals 'establish information accounts and deposit their information assets and informational rights in a local information bank'). See also Kenneth Laudon, 'Extensions to the Theory of Markets and Privacy: Mechanics of Pricing Information' in *Privacy and Self-Regulation in the Information Age* (US Department of Commerce, National Telecommunications and Information Administration 1997).

[141]Paolo Cardullo, 'Smart Commons or a "Smart Approach" to the Commons?' in Paolo Cardullo, Cesare Di Feliciantonio and Rob Kitchin (ed), The Right to the Smart City (Emerald Publishing Limited 2019) 85-98.

[142]See Mara Balestrini and others, 'A City in Common: A Framework to Orchestrate Large-scale Citizen Engagement around Urban Issues' in Gloria Mark and Susan Fussell (eds), *CHI '17: Proceedings of the 2017 CHI Conference on Human Factors in Computing Systems* (2017) 2282–2294.

[143]See Copenhagen Solutions Lab, 'City Data Exchange' <https://cphsolutionslab.dk/en/news/city-data-exchange> accessed 18 March 2020.

[144]ibid.

[145]See Gowri Sankar Ramachandran and Rahul Radhakrishnan, Bhaskar Krishnamachari, 'Towards a Decentralized Data Marketplace for Smart Cities' (IEEE International Smart Cities Conference (ISC2), Kansas, 16-19 September 2018) <https://ieeexplore.ieee.org/document/8656952/citations#citations> accessed 18 March 2020 (exploring how a decentralized data marketplace could be created using blockchain and other distributed ledger technologies).

contractually reconstructed commons approach.[146] Under this framework, all parties would be entitled to take and reuse data from the data marketplace, so long as they equally share all their data as well. All parties will, then, share with the community a portion of the revenue coming from products and services developed by using the pooled data, according to pre-determined percentages and standards. Private businesses could use large clusters of users' urban mobility data for developing global services, but local communities might internalize part of the value created by the data for local projects. Meanwhile, local communities could also use data available in city data marketplaces for their own uses that, when profitable, will also produce a revenue stream for businesses pooling data.

8.2 *Cooperation*

Cooperation—decentralized and user-based—stands as an additional feature that smart urban mobility should deploy in order to overcome platform economy negative externalities and embrace a pure collaborative sharing economy models.[147] Platform cooperativism adopts alternative organizational models to classical digital platforms, like Uber, Lyft or Deliveroo and aims at 'building a digital economy we own'.[148] Rather than separating and isolating providers and consumers, cooperative platforms enable 'the propensity of providers and consumers to engage in collective actions and become the protagonist of the platform activity'.[149] A cooperative platform allows both providers and consumers to join the business project, share resources equally, and be part of a community. Rather than just serving as a 'matching system' as in the case of traditional platform applications acting as a

[146]See Jerome Reichman, Paul Uhlir and Tom Dedeurwaerdere, *Governing Digitally Integrated Genetic Resources, Data, and Literature: Global Intellectual Property Strategies for a Redesigned Microbial Research Commons* (CUP 2015) (discussing similar strategies applied to microbial commons).

[147]See Koen Frenken, 'Political Economies and Environmental Futures for the Sharing Economy' (2017) 375(2095) Philosophical Transactions of the Royal Society 1 <https://royalsocietypublishing.org/doi/10.1098/rsta.2016.0367> accessed 18 March 2020 (arguing that there are three future scenarios for governing the sharing economy: (1) platform capitalism, which is characterized by the integration of various sharing-economy initiatives into a super-platform that follows neoliberal development; (2) platform redistribution, which is state-based distribution for public interest and uses principles of social justice; and (3) platform cooperativism as a grassroots movement that uses collective ownership and management principles).

[148]See Trebor Scholz, *Platform Cooperativism: Challenging the Corporate Sharing Economy* (Rosa Luxemburg Stiftung 2016) 1.

[149]See Francesca Martinelli and others, 'Platform Cooperativism in Italy and in Europe' (2019) CIRIEC Working Paper 27 <www.zbw.eu/econis-archiv/bitstream/handle/11159/4013/WP2019-27.pdf> accessed 18 March 2020. See also Trebor Scholz, 'Platform Cooperativism vs. the Sharing Economy' in Nicolas Douay and Annie Wan (eds), *Big Data & Civic Engagement* (Planum Publisher 2017).

digital intermediary for organizing and managing providers activities according to users' needs,[150] platform cooperatives 'allow workers to exchange their labor without manipulation by an intermediary, as they are managed by members in a democratic fashion while supporting the development of digital commons'.[151]

LaZooz, for example, is a community-owned transport platform that would like to decentralize real-time ridesharing, while relying on blockchain technology to achieve its objectives.[152] It replaces Bitcoin's proof of work method with 'proof of movement' generating new tokens called 'zooz'. As soon as driving commences, community members—divers, coders or funders—can start earning 'zooz' tokens, which can be also used for paying for rides. The LaZooz community-led rewards system is meant to empower the community and allow it to take control.[153] Good examples of cooperative ridesharing can also be found in Indonesia.[154]

Of course, the challenge for local platform cooperativism is economies of scale that make it seem impossible to compete with Uber like services and their several billion dollars in VC-backing to inflate an anticompetitive bubble. However, the solution would be within reach as long as 'smart commons' manage properly decentralization processes by developing integrated portals for access to multiple cooperative platform mobility services. Regional, national and local public authorities must develop integrated portals where the offerings of cooperative platforms can be chosen as part of MaaS journey planners. Actually, the MaaS model fits well with the goal of enhanced visibility and access to local cooperative platform solutions as a replacement to global centralized capitalistic platform models. Once cooperative platform services are integrated in MaaS gateways, they will be able to compete on a more equal standing with Uber and the like.

8.3 Crowdfunding

Digital crowdfunding is an increasingly popular tool to raise money online.[155] It allows communities to fund projects that are expected to provide benefits to those

---

[150]See eg Nick Srnicek, *Platform Capitalism* (Polity Press 2017).

[151]Morozov and Bria (n 2) 43.

[152]See LaZooz <http://lazooz.org> accessed 18 March 2020.

[153]See Morozov and Bria (n 2) 44.

[154]See Suci Lestari Yuana, 'Framing the sharing economy: A media analysis of ridesharing platforms in Indonesia and the Philippines' (2019) 212 Journal of Cleaner Production 1154-1165.

[155]For a general overview of crowdfunding and literature review, see Alexandra Moritz and Jorn Block, 'Crowdfunding: A Literature Review and Research Directions' in Dennis Brüntje and Oliver Gajda (eds), *Crowdfunding in Europe: State of the Art in Theory and Practice* (Springer 2016) 25-53.

communities. On Kickstarter and similar platforms[156] such as Crowdfunder or Ulule, people can pledge for an economic goal, which is set up in advance by the project developer.[157] Crowdfunding lets innovators and creators offer different tiers through which backers can help fund a project, in the hope of reaching a funding threshold.[158] Usually, the money changes hands only after the threshold is met.[159] However, crowdfunding platforms may apply an 'all or nothing' or a 'keep it all' model.[160] In the latter case, the funds collected are handed over to the campaigner, regardless of whether the project goal is met or not.[161] Other crowdfunding platforms, such as Bountysource, allow for a continuous funding model, rather than one-time donation, for those innovators such as software developers making content on a regular basis.[162]

Crowdfunding platforms like Goteo and Startnext emphasise sustainability and public welfare projects, obliging all projects to define their social responsibilities.[163] These platforms would like to push for a more ethical and collaborative society with special emphasis on environmental sustainability. They fall within the emerging category of 'civic crowdfunding', a practice applied to civic schemes which aims at developing a wide range of public interest projects, from social and environmental innovation to urban commons.[164] Crowdfunding rail, for example, is a train service catering to the real demand of passengers, based on multiple variants of so-called 'crowd ticketing', where each investor purchases an advance ticket which can be used flexibly without restrictions.[165] 'Civic crowdfunding' promotes empowerment

---

[156]See Jonathan Bone and Peter Baeck, 'Lessons from four years of running the UK's first crowdfunding platform directory' (Nesta, 15 December 2017) <www.crowdingin.com> accessed 18 March 2020.

[157]See Kickstarter, 'About' <www.kickstarter.com/about> accessed 18 March 2020.

[158]ibid.

[159]ibid.

[160]Moritz and Block (n 155).

[161]ibid.

[162]ibid.

[163]See Goteo <https://en.goteo.org> accessed 18 March 2020 and Startnext <www.startnext.com> accessed 18 March 2020.

[164]See Bruno Ávila Eça de Matos, 'Crowdfunding Urban Infrastructure: Qualitative and Geospatial Analysis' (Master thesis, Buffalo University 2016) 27-44 (describing several case studies in multiple jurisdictions). See also Rodrigo Davies, 'Civic crowdfunding as a marketplace for participation in urban development' (The Internet, Policy & Politics Conference, Oxford 2014) <http://blogs.oii.ox.ac.uk/ipp-conference/sites/ipp/files/documents/IPP2014_Davies.pdf> accessed 18 March 2020; Daniel Brent and Katie Lorah, 'The Economic Geography of Civic Crowdfunding' (2019) 90 Cities 122.

[165]See Varsha Saraogi, 'Crowdfunding Rail: Five Projects From Around the World' (Railway Technology, 9 December 2019) <https://www.railway-technology.com/features/crowdfunding-rail-five-projects-from-around-the-world> accessed 18 March 2020 Jiawei Gui, 'An Advanced Simulation and Optimization for Railway Transportation of Passengers: Crowdfunding Train' in Li Xiang and Xu Xiaofeng (eds), *Proceedings of the Sixth International Forum on Decision Sciences* (Springer 2020) 283.

and engagement of local communities as in the case of Spacehive, a ‘United Kingdom-based crowdfunding platform for projects aimed at improving local civic and community spaces’.[166] Similar ‘civic crowdfunding’ platforms are Voor je buurt in the Netherlands, Co-city in France and Ioby in the USA.[167]

Although still an alternative finance model, crowdfunding’s potential is obvious, especially in supporting local communities’ urban projects. The crowdfunding market has more than doubled in size in the last 3 years, growing to €7560.8 million in 2020.[168] It is expected to grow to €10,614.7 million by 2023.[169] Unsurprisingly, given its strong tradition of grassroot financing and communitarian sense of appurtenance, China shows by far the highest crowdfunding transaction value worldwide with a total of €6243 million in 2020.[170] For example, funding for the upcoming e-bike urban mobility revolution in China comes mostly from crowdfunding.[171] This might play a role in China’s leadership in smart shared urban mobility innovation and serve as supporting evidence for a wider promotion of crowdfunding as a financing model in smart urban mobility.

9 Conclusions

Moving from mass to MaaS, social and technological development struggles to disentangle itself from the dominant neoliberal discourse about propertization. Whether it is the green pastures of the sixteenth century enclosed British commons or the asphalt of the smart city’s mobility routes, long-standing misperceptions resurface to challenge the sustainability of commons-based solution. It is a fundamental Western struggle that finds its origin in the deformation of Romantic individualism into ‘possessive individualism’[172] and pits the individual against the community. Rather than relying on ‘information fiduciaries’,[173] the time has come

[166] See Spacehive <www.spacehive.com> accessed 19 March 2020.

[167] See Voor je buurt <https://voorjebuurt.nl> accessed 19 March 2020, Co-city <https://co-citoyens.fr> accessed 19 March 2020 and Ioby <https://ioby.org> accessed 19 March 2020.

[168] See Statista, Crowdfunding <www.statista.com/outlook/335/100/crowdfunding/worldwide> accessed 19 March 2020.

[169] ibid.

[170] ibid.

[171] See Dennis Zuev, *Urban Mobility in Modern China: The Growth of the E-bike* (Palgrave Macmillan 2018) 97-110.

[172] See Crawford Macpherson, *The Political Theory of Possessive Individualism: Hobbes to Locke* (Clarendon Press 1962).

[173] See Jack Balkin, ‘Free Speech in the Algorithmic Society: Big Data, Private Governance, and New School Speech Regulation’ (2018) 51 University of California Davis Law Review 1149, 1160-63; Jack Balkin, ‘Information Fiduciaries and the First Amendment’ (2016) 49 University of California Davis Law Review 1183. See contra David Pozen and Lina Khan, ‘A Skeptical View of Information Fiduciaries’ (2019) 133 Harvard Law Review 49.

to take back our data—but as a community, rather than as individuals. While cheap individualized monetization of personal data serves no other purpose than further empowering capitalistic global monopolies, pooling data in a commons under local community management and for community benefit—together with local 'platform cooperativism' and 'civic crowdfunding' finance models—might pave the way to smart urban mobility's growth.

Collaborative Platforms and Data Pools for Smart Urban Societies and Mobility as a Service (MaaS) from a Competition Law Perspective

Björn Lundqvist and Erion Murati

Contents

Abstract In smart urban settings, all devices and service providers monitor, collect and exchange data whilst device producers and service providers store, distribute, analyse and re-use data on a grand scale. If firms would like to combine such data, they need to give each other access by sharing, trading or pooling the data. On the one hand, the industry-wide pooling of data could increase the efficiency of certain services and contribute to the innovation of other services, e.g. whole transport networks that are available on one platform, or Mobility as a Service (MaaS). On the other hand, firms that pool business data may use the data not to advance their services or products but to collude, to exclude competitors or to abuse their market position. Indeed, by combining their data and collaborating they can gain market power and hence the ability to violate competition law. Platforms can also hoard data and design the data architecture so as to become system leaders in vertical value

Björn Lundqvist is Associate Professor of Law Stockholm University, Stockholm, Sweden.

Erion Murati is PhD Fellow at the MaaS Project, University of Hamburg, Law Faculty Hamburg, Germany.

B. Lundqvist (✉)
Stockholm University, Stockholm, Sweden
e-mail: Bjorn.Lundqvist@juridicum.su.se

E. Murati
Hamburg University, Hamburg, Germany
e-mail: erion.murati@studium.uni-hamburg.de

M. Finck et al. (eds.), *Smart Urban Mobility*, MPI Studies on Intellectual Property and Competition Law 29, https://doi.org/10.1007/978-3-662-61920-9_10

chains, exclusively obtaining all data from various sources and creating a silo or ecosystem. This chapter will discuss a new platform configuration regarding transport services. The platform is being developed and discussed according to the notion of MaaS. MaaS is a new transport paradigm that integrates existing and new mobility services as well as public and private transport services into one single digital platform, providing customised door-to-door transport and offering personalised trip planning and payment options. The development of integrated multimodal information systems and integrated payment solutions has enabled the MaaS concept to unfold. We will analyse the MaaS concept from a competition law perspective, asking whether the concept might be in violation of EU Competition Law, specifically Arts. 101 and 102 TFEU.

1 Introduction

The chapter discusses phenomena resulting from the development of the digital economy, in particular platforms and data pools related to Mobility as a Service (MaaS), a new transport paradigm which integrates existing and new mobility services as well as public and private transport services into one single digital platform, providing customised door-to-door transport and offering personalised trip planning and payment options. From a legal perspective, the only legal definition of integrated mobility services currently available at the EU level can be found in the recent Finnish Act on Transport Services, which deals specifically with MaaS platform providers. According to the Act, integrated mobility services refer to the 'formation of travel chains and other service packages in return for remuneration by combining the mobility services offered by different service providers, excluding travel packages or combined travel arrangements falling within the scope of the Act on Travel Service Combinations'.[1] Thus, the term is used when organisations agree to combine their transport services in a given geographic area via a platform. MaaS set-ups and platforms may become a normal feature in the future as transport modes, devices, services, products and individuals become interoperable and connected. Yet it is necessary to assess whether this new business practice is a good match for existing EU competition rules, i.e. in line with the competition law doctrine for research and development (R&D) collaborations, standard-setting, patent pools, exchange of information and collusion. Moreover, their vertical organisation will need to be analysed from an EU competition law perspective. The chapter asks whether the EU Commission should adopt new guidelines specifically focusing on

[1] See Ministry of Transport and Communications of Finland, *Act on Transport Services 320/2017* (amendments up to 731/2018 included) (Finnish Act on Transport Services) s 2 n 5 <www.finlex.fi/en/laki/kaannokset/2017/en20170320_20180731.pdf> accessed 30 March 2020.

platforms in general and MaaS in particular or whether the existing EU competition doctrine is sufficient.

It is important to first note that the proper development of smart urban services and data pools will require a collective spirit of collaboration as well as some new technical solutions for the digital economy. For example, the inclusion of both private self-driven cars and app-driven, MaaS-oriented public transport on city streets can only work sufficiently if public and private transport providers, car manufacturers, road construction firms, repair maintenance shops, leasing firms, self-driven car service providers, etc. can pool their respective services and digital information. For this to happen, collaborative technical standards need to be developed so as to enable data interoperability,[2] which has not yet taken place.[3] In addition, it has also become apparent that to achieve seamless access to data it is necessary not only to adopt appropriate technical standards, practices and architecture but also to develop legal frameworks that facilitate the use of and access to data.[4]

According to Göran Smith et al.,[5] the notion of MaaS has rapidly become an important concept in the personal transport sector, propelled by global trends such as digitalisation and servitisation.[6] Several pilot demonstrations of MaaS and MaaS-related services have been performed, for example UbiGo in Sweden, SMILE in

[2]The interoperability of data has been defined in academia as 'the ability to transfer and render useful data and other information across systems, applications or components'. See Urs Gasser, 'Interoperability in the Digital Ecosystem' (ITU 2015) <www.itu.int/en/ITUD/Conferences/GSR/Documents/GSR2015/Discussion_papers_and_Presentations/Discussionpaper_interoperability.pdf> accessed 4 March 2020.

[3]See, for example, the issue with accessing in-vehicle data from vehicle manufacturers. Bertin Martens and Frank Mueller-Langer, 'Access to Digital Car Data and Competition in Aftersales Services' (JRC EU Commission 2018) <https://ec.europa.eu/jrc/sites/jrcsh/files/jrc112634.pdf> accessed 31 March 2020.

[4]Different bodies of law—copyright, patent, privacy, confidentiality and contract law—will be relevant to the collection, storage and dissemination of data. See Anne Fitzgerald, Kylie Pappalardo and Anthony Austin, 'Understanding the Legal Implications of Data Sharing, Access and Reuse in the Australian Research Landscape' in Brian Fitzgerald (ed), *Legal Framework for e-Research: Realising the Potential* (Sydney University Press 2018) 161-188.

[5]Göran Smith, Jana Sochor and MariAnne Karlsson, 'Public-private Innovation: Barriers in the Case of Mobility as a Service in West Sweden' (2019) 21 Journal Public Management Review 116.

[6]Sonja Heikkilä, 'Mobility as A Service: A Proposal for Action for the Public Administration Case Helsinki' (Master Thesis, Aalto University 2014) <https://aaltodoc.aalto.fi/handle/123456789/13133> accessed 31 March 2020.

Austria, Jelbi[7] and MVG[8] in Germany and Whim in Finland.[9] In general, there is very limited information on the impact of these pilots. Still, the UbiGo pilot illustrated the potential to shift modal share away from private car use toward servitised transport modes.[10] It has been suggested that integrated journey planning and payment systems as well as multimodal service packages are fundamental features of MaaS. As a consequence, the development of MaaS demands that public transport authorities and private transport services cooperate more intensively, combining their services and sharing data across organisational borders. Further, MaaS introduces a new role in the value chain, 'MaaS operator', which assembles the offerings of several transport service providers[11] (e.g. PTAs, rental car companies, city-bike businesses, etc.), designs the MaaS products and sells them to end-users.[12] Indeed, MaaS is an interesting example of a smart urban mobility initiative that relies on a platform and a pool of current ('nowcasting') data to function. Such services may become more common in the interoperable urban environment of the future.

MaaS services will greatly benefit society, and while the chapter focuses on the risks involved in such services, their benefits may be included in the analysis of whether or not these collaborations have anticompetitive effects. MaaS platforms

[7]Trafi, 'Trafi & BVG'S All in One Mobility App Jelbi Goes Live in Berlin' (*Traffi*, 11 June 2019) <www.trafi.com/site/press-release/trafi-bvgs-all-in-one-mobility-app-jelbi-goes-live-in-berlin> accessed 22 March 2020.

[8]See Trafi, 'MVG and Trafi to Launch Mobility as a Service Solution in Munich' (*Medium*, 11 June 2019) <https://medium.com/trafi/mvg-and-trafi-to-launch-mobility-as-a-service-solution-in-munich-9a2c0f0ada9e> accessed 22 March 2020.

[9]Maria Kamargianni, Weibo Li and Melinda Matyas, 'A Comprehensive Review of "Mobility as A Service" Systems' (Transportation Research Board 95th Annual Meeting, Washington DC, 10-14 January 2016).

[10]Jana Sochor, Helena Strömberg and MariAnne Karlsson, 'Implementing Mobility as a Service: Challenges in Integrating User, Commercial, and Societal Perspectives' (2015) 2536 Transportation Research Record: Journal of the Transportation Research Board 1; see also, Jana Sochor, MariAnne Karlsson and Helena Strömberg, 'Trying Out Mobility as a Service: Experiences from a Field Trial and Implications for Understanding Demand' (2016) 2542 Transportation Research Record: Journal of the Transportation Research Board 57.

[11]Markku Tinnilä, 'Towards Servitization of Mobility: Mobility as a Service' (2016) 8 International Journal of Research in Business and Technology 958.

[12]The MaaS platform is the IT structure used by the MaaS operator to provide the final service of mobility to end-users. The MaaS platform is split into two elements, the front-end and the back-end, both of which are made up of components developed by the IT providers. The front-end is the customer-facing element. It is a digital interface such as a mobile and/or web application which customers interact with to purchase and use MaaS products. The back-end is the internal support element that enables the delivery of MaaS. It is a collection of components which perform integral functions such as data import, data storage, journey planning, optimisation, ticketing, payment and communication. The MaaS platform provider is the company responsible for providing the MaaS platform. This could be the MaaS operator or a third party responsible for just the technological elements. See Maria Kamargianni and others, 'The MaaS Dictionary' (MaaSLab, University College London 2018) <https://28716f27-42ea-4260-ac26-48e00a153449.filesusr.com/ugd/a2135d_d6ffa2fee2834782b4ec9a75c1957f55.pdf> accessed 31 March 2020.

increase the risk of firms colluding because such platforms provide them with access to each other's price levels and sensitive business data. In a MaaS ecosystem, data can be accessed, traded and shared (or rather pooled). However, data pooling, where this includes competitively sensitive information, may constitute a breach of competition law.[13] Moreover, there is a risk that too much transparency can enable firms to tacitly collude and lessen investment into R&D, among other things. Firms pooling commercial data may share relevant business and competitive information regarding e.g. price, output and new product developments. The pooling of such data can facilitate collusion between competitors. Moreover, pricing algorithms may be connected to MaaS platforms, which could facilitate elaborate unilateral pricing schemes and thus lead to pricing discrimination or excessive pricing.[14]

A dominant MaaS platform or a combination of MaaS silos/platforms may also act as a barrier to entry for other transport service providers. Indeed, access to the dominant MaaS platform or one of the relevant MaaS platforms in an oligopolistic market structure may become indispensable to be able to provide transport services in the future. Exclusion of competitors, potential competitors or third parties may indeed be facilitated through the vertical structure of the MaaS platforms.

Notwithstanding these risks, we argue in the chapter that smaller firms collectively creating independent platforms and pooling transport data may be the remedy to a more acute competition problem. As it is currently set up, the legal system around data and the internet seems to benefit the system leaders—the gatekeepers—of the virtual ecosystems being developed around e-platform 'silos'. Amazon, Google, Microsoft and the like are great assemblers of data since they control the data of their respective e-ecosystems. They indeed hold the most traffic and travel data, and the concentration of data among a few internet giants may be a 'bigger' problem for competition than transport-specific firms pooling their data.

Furthermore, in reference to the Internet of Things (IoT), we are seeing the development of system leaders and platforms. Car manufacturers, for example, may become future system leaders in the approaching IoT era. In the IoT era, all things (devices) will include embedded sensors both in their mechanical parts and their human interfaces. Cars, for example, will become platforms. Data will be collected from several sensors embedded in different parts of the vehicle, and a wide range of service providers, original equipment manufacturers (OEMs), after-sale service providers as well as leasing companies and vehicle loan providers will want to get access to the data generated in the car by the parts or services they have

[13]See Kiran Desal, 'Sharing Data: the 4D Competition Law Model to Determining Data Value Available' (*EY Law*, June 2019) <www.eylaw.be/2019/06/04/sharing-data-the-4d-competition-law-model-to-determining-data-value/#_ftn2> accessed 18 March 2020.

[14]In addition, data protection rules may be violated when large sets of data are combined, which in turn may cause antitrust rules to be triggered. See further on the Facebook investigation being conducted by the German Competition Authority, 'Bundeskartellamt Initiates Proceeding Against Facebook on Suspicion of Having Abused its Market Power by Infringing Data Protection Rules' (*Bundeskartellamt*, 2 March 2016) <www.bundeskartellamt.de/SharedDocs/Meldung/EN/Pressemitteilungen/2016/02_03_2016_Facebook.html> accessed 13 July 2018.

provided. MaaS providers could also be interested in receiving information from cars and vehicles when calculating trips for individuals. Relevant information regarding traffic on specific stretches, the condition of the road, etc. could be information collected by cars or smart tires that is valuable to MaaS providers when establishing the route of a customer. However, already today we see that car manufacturers can design the data architecture of a vehicle such that it ensures their exclusive access to its data. This gives them a monopoly in the market for data originating from their brand of cars.[15] Furthermore, cities are interested in such mobility data. In 2018, for example, Los Angeles (L.A.) launched an open-source data standard and software system designed to hold sway over ridesharing operators. Known as the 'mobility data specification'[16] or MDS, the platform collects information from discrete vehicle trips in near real time and lets the city communicate back to operators. Right now, it is only being used by 'micromobility' companies. In order to keep its sidewalks clear of stray dockless scooters and bikes, L.A. requires operators to send the start and stop locations of individual vehicle trips back to City Hall within 5 s in addition to the routes they have travelled within the past 24 h. Eventually, all kinds of current and future transportation forms—from ride-hailing and car-sharing to delivery drones and autonomous vehicles—could fall under the omniscient gaze of the MDS platform. By gathering these data points as well as trip times and whether vehicles are on or off, it is possible to manage the size and dispersal of licensed private fleets and ultimately control where they travel, take off and land. But the project has a powerful detractor: Uber. The ride-hailing giant has refused to share the data[17] that L.A. seeks from its Jump e-bikes, claiming it would infringe upon riders' privacy rights, and its lawyers assert that the architects of the MDS platform have an ulterior motive, namely 'collect[ing] vast quantities of valuable, private, sensitive data so that they can find ways to monetize it and so they can ultimately control the physical movement of bikes, scooters and cars on the streets'.[18] Indeed, this risk of location data privacy becomes more sensitive on MaaS platforms due to the connection and sharing of various data via application programming interfaces (APIs) and the possibility of real-time monitoring of users' routes.[19]

In light of the above-mentioned issues, this chapter elaborates on the issue of MaaS and the applicability of EU competition law. While the applicability of EU

[15]See Martens and Mueller-Langer (n 3).

[16]See Laura Bliss, 'A Controversial Scooter Data Tracking Program Gains Traction' (*CITYLAB*, 23 August 2019) <www.citylab.com/transportation/2019/08/scooter-ride-mobility-data-privacy-laws-ecpa-los-angeles/596446/> accessed 17 March 2020.

[17]Laura Bliss, 'Uber's Beef With L.A. Is Bigger Than Data' (*CITYLAB*, 29 October 2019) <www.citylab.com/transportation/2019/10/uber-lawsuit-data-privacy-scooter-tracking-los-angeles/600985/> accessed 17 March 2020.

[18]Laura Bliss, 'This City Was Sick of Tech Disruptors: So It Decided to Become One' (*CITYLAB*, 21 February 2020) <www.citylab.com/transportation/2020/02/los-angeles-transportation-data-mobility-scooter-mds-uber/606178/> accessed 17 March 2020.

[19]See Erion Murati and Manjola Hënkoja, 'Location Data Data Privacy on MaaS under GDPR' (2019) 2 European Journal of Privacy Law & Technologies 115.

competition law to the digital economy and to single firms' assembling of data has been discussed academically, the issue of MaaS collaborations and platform building has not yet been widely researched. This chapter is an attempt to address this void. We analyse various MaaS concepts, collaborations and ecosystems from the perspective of Arts. 101 and 102 Treaty on the Functioning of the European Union (TFEU). We argue that MaaS collaborations may come in many different forms. While some raise doubts as to whether they are anticompetitive, others seem clearly efficient and pro-competitive. We purport that the EU Commission, national competition authorities and courts may find guidance in the application of EU competition law to patent pools, R&D and standard-setting collaborations. On the other hand, there is still room and a clear need for guidelines from the EU Commission in reference to platforms and extensive digital collaboration between industry participants.

The structure of the chapter is as follows. First, it briefly outlines the MaaS concept. The benefits and drawbacks of MaaS collaborations that have been identified above are then further elaborated on. Third, the chapter addresses the application of EU competition law to these forms of platforms and collaborations. Here, the chapter draws on the experience of competition law cases dealing with other forms of joint ventures such as standard-setting agreements, R&D collaborations and technology (patent) pooling. In the end, the authors evaluate the applicability of the current EU competition law framework to MaaS collaborative practices.

2 The MaaS Concept

MaaS is a new transport paradigm that integrates existing and new mobility services into a single digital platform, providing customised door-to-door transport and offering personalised trip planning and payment options. The development of integrated multimodal information systems[20] and integrated payment[21] solutions have enabled the unfolding of the MaaS concept, defined for the purpose of the chapter as a 'digitally supported distribution model bundling several transport options together, and enabling users to plan their trips, select the transport option that best suits their needs, and finally book and pay for it via an app'.[22] Thus, the rise of MaaS relies heavily on access to user data, open APIs of transport providers and the interoperability of the systems.[23]

[20]This enables users to access and compare specific travel information in real time from different transport providers and therefore pick the solution that best fits their mobility needs.

[21]This enables users to access various transportation solutions with a single means of ticketing, which could be a card (smart card) or a dedicated app.

[22]Matthias Finger and Maxime Audouin (eds), *The Governance of Smart Transportation Systems* (Springer 2019) 5.

[23]For a discussion of interoperability, see Mariateresa Maggiolino and Laura Zoboli 'Smart Mobility and Technological Compatibility from an Antitrust Perspective' in this volume.

The MaaS concept was officially introduced to the public at the 2014 Intelligent Transport Systems (ITS) European Congress in Helsinki with a video demonstration entitled 'Could mobility be viewed as service?'[24] In 2016, the EU Horizon 2020 programme financed IMOVE and MaaS4EU projects in order to stimulate European development towards MaaS with a total budget of 25 million euros. In the meantime, Sweden and Finland have acted as global pioneers of MaaS. For instance, the 2014 pilot of UbiGo in Gothenburg (SE) is often referred to as the first in real-life conditions[25] and the 2016 launch of Whim in Helsinki (FI) drew international recognition to the concept.[26] In both countries, the public sector has had a hand in MaaS developments. For instance, an expert group was tasked with drafting a road map for the diffusion of MaaS in Sweden, including how the national government could support the development. This resulted in funding for a development programme[27] entitled 'Combined Mobility as a Service in Sweden' (*Kombinerad mobilitet som tjänst i Sverige*, KOMPIS).

Proponents argue that MaaS should become the new transport paradigm since it addresses many of society's greatest challenges in transport, promising to improve environmental sustainability, reduce congestion and increase accessibility.[28] They offer a set of justifications for why to develop MaaS. Firstly, they suggest that by reducing private car use,[29] MaaS has the potential to address the negative externalities of personal transport and combat problems such as congestion, parking, noise, transport-related injuries and deaths, local pollution and carbon gas emissions. Secondly, MaaS is a user-centric concept, providing the user with access to a variety

[24]Ministry of Transport and Communications of Finland, 'Could Mobility Be Viewed As Service?' (*YouTube*, 17 June 2014) <www.youtube.com/watch?v=ZQieTU7_5xo> accessed 31 March 2020.

[25]Jana Sochor and others, 'The Added Value of a New, Innovative Travel Service: Insights from the UbiGo Field Operational Test in Gothenburg Sweden' (International Conference on Mobility and Smart Cities, Rome, 27-28 October 2014) <https://doi.org/10.1007/978-3-319-19743-2_26> accessed 31 March 2020.

[26]See MaaS Global, 'Whim, the World's First All-Inclusive Mobility Service, Promises to Change Urban Travel Forever' (*Whim*, 13 June 2016) <https://whimapp.com/whim-the-worlds-first-all-inclusive-mobility-service-promises-to-change-urban-travel-forever/> accessed 12 March 2020.

[27]For more information about the programme, see KOMPIS, 'Det Här Är KOMPIS' <https://kompis.me/> accessed 31 March 2020.

[28]POLIS, 'Mobility as a Service: Implications for Urban and Regional Transport' (*POLIS*, September 2017) <www.polisnetwork.eu/document/mobility-as-a-service-implications-for-urban-and-regional-transport/> accessed 11 March 2020; MaaS Alliance, 'White Paper: Guidelines & Recommendations to Create the Foundations for a Thriving MaaS Ecosystem' (MaaS Alliance, 4 September 2017) <https://maas-alliance.eu/wp-content/uploads/sites/7/2017/09/MaaS-WhitePaper_final_040917-2.pdf> accessed 12 March 2020.

[29]See Göran Smith, Jana Sochor and MariAnne Karlsson, 'Mobility as a Service: Development Scenarios and Implications for Public Transport' (2018) 69 Research in Transportation Economics 592. More specifically, experts believe that at first urban and suburban families will get rid of their secondary cars; only at a later stage will they bid farewell to their primary car as well.

of transport options through a single information, booking and payment service.[30] The added values for MaaS users may be cost saving,[31] convenience, choice[32] and customisation. Thirdly, proponents suggest that MaaS can increase accessibility to personal transport services by improving and extending the transport service ecosystem.[33] Indeed, the MaaS vision is 'to see the whole transport sector as a cooperative, interconnected ecosystem, providing services reflecting the needs of customers'.[34] Finally, MaaS could impact a variety of sectors beyond transport, including health.[35] In a nutshell, MaaS has the potential to deliver a wide range of direct and indirect benefits, such as seamless journeys, better travel planning, incentivised trip making, best fare options, fewer episodes of poor air quality and freed-up road space. These potential benefits align with the goals of EU transportation policy, and MaaS could operate as a vector towards their realisation.[36]

According to a House of Commons report on MaaS,[37] the MaaS ecosystem is made up of users; MaaS platform providers, who design and offer the MaaS platform (typically a smartphone app, i.e. software/hardware) and create packages based on customer demands; data providers,[38] who share and use data that is crucial to MaaS; and a range of transport operators. MaaS is an interesting data pooling concept. From a technological perspective,[39] a MaaS provider positions itself on two different fronts. On one hand, the MaaS provider basically integrates data such as routes,

---

[30]Paul Hammond, Kate Mackay and Glen Lyons, 'The Importance of User Perspective in the Evolution of MaaS' (2019) 121 Transportation Research Part A: Policy and Practice 22.

[31]A potentially decisive reason for using MaaS is cost savings. For example, MaaS may be cheaper than owning one's own car or holding an annual public transport pass.

[32]MaaS offers freedom of choice, which does not just involve different modes of transport (e.g. a bus or an e-bicycle) but a range of vehicles on offer (e.g. an electric city car or a family car).

[33]Andrea Melis and others, 'Integrating Personalized and Accessible Itineraries in MaaS Ecosystems Through Microservices' (2018) 23 Mobile Networks and Applications 167.

[34]Sampo Hietanen, 'Mobility as a Service: The New Transport Model?' (2014) 12 (2) Eurotransport 27.

[35]It was asserted that MaaS can provide potential health benefits, for example, less stress associated with multi-modal travel, more physical activity through increased demand for active modes, less pollution through a reduction in congestion and private car use and more social interactions through increased accessibility. See Jane Krantz, 'Mobility-as-a-Service from a Health Perspective: Exploratory Research Into the Potential Health Impact of MaaS' (Master thesis, Delft University of Technology 2018) 9 <https://repository.tudelft.nl/islandora/object/uuid%3A6f2faefb-9f80-49db-b226-9accf97f0105> accessed 31 March 2020.

[36]See Commission, 'The European Green Deal' (Communication) COM (2019) 640 final.

[37]UK Transport Committee, 'Mobility as a Service Inquiry' (UK Parliament, 19 December 2018), <www.parliament.uk/business/committees/committees-a-z/commons-select/transport-committee/inquiries/parliament-2017/mobility-as-a-service-17-19/> accessed 11 March 2020.

[38]Besides transport operators, the data providers include the MaaS provider and user as well as potential external actors, e.g. the weather forecasting or traffic management authorities.

[39]In this case, the authors referred especially to the MaaS Whim app, but the same logic is valid for other MaaS providers. See Maxime Audoin and Matthias Finger, 'The development of Mobility-as-a-Service in the Helsinki Metropolitan Area: A Multi-level Governance Analysis' (2018) 27 Research in Transportation Business & Management 24.

pricing information or real-time position. On the other hand, the provider also has access to the APIs of different transport operators, which allows it to provide or purchase tickets for users of the MaaS platform in order to provide them with a one-stop-shop for package deals on door-to-door transport.

APIs represent a set of processes that govern the interactions between different web-based services,[40] together constituting what is referred to as the back-end (also called the data platform or data layer), where the MaaS provider operates. The MaaS provider also takes care of building the front-end, or the app (i.e. Whim, Jelbi, etc.) that is connected to the back-end, which is the major customer interface. The customer interface provides the user with the ability to purchase mobility, receive personalised and contextualised information that is relevant to real-time travel decisions and provide feedback to the MaaS provider. To summarise, MaaS platforms allow the supply side (the suppliers) to meet the demand side (the customers), creating a triangular structure that is based on relations between (1) the platform and the supplier, (2) the platform and the consumer and (3) the supplier and the customer. From a legal point of view, this triangular structure is the fundamental aspect of the MaaS concept.

Following the MaaS Alliance 'White paper' on MaaS, there are four main requirements and preconditions for the MaaS ecosystem to succeed. The first precondition is a 'single market for MaaS'. In order to build real multi-option market platforms and to make seamless multi-modal transport a reality, the service providers should provide each other access to essential information in a computer-readable format, including routes, timetables, stops, ticketing, payment system interfaces, accessibility information and a real-time data connection to the vehicles. The ecosystem should be open for varied service providers to establish their business, without an exclusive position for any particular operator.[41] The second precondition is 'user experience'. End-users are the focus of the 'service' in MaaS, and all other elements (i.e. technology, policy, business models) are enablers. The third precondition is 'data openness'. In terms of technology, the critical points for MaaS are interoperability, roaming and harmonised standards. An essential prerequisite for the effective deployment of a MaaS ecosystem is an open middle-layer platform to connect the transportation service providers with the MaaS.

The last prerequisite for establishing MaaS services on a European scale is a 'regulatory framework'. Transport regulation is based on historical and conventional conceptions; with the boom of digital services, such assumptions and categories may have to be adjusted. Therefore, the first step towards a digital transport system is to

---

[40] David König and others, 'Technology for MaaS' (2017) Conference of European Directors of Roads: Mobility As A Service for Linking Europe (MAASiFiE Project) 21 <www.researchgate.net/publication/317416475_Deliverable_5_Technology_for_MaaS_MAASiFiE_project_funded_by_CEDR> accessed 31 March 2020.

[41] See MaaS Alliance, 'White Paper: Guidelines & Recommendations to Create the Foundations for a Thriving MaaS Ecosystem' (MaaS Alliance, 4 September 2017) <https://maas-alliance.eu/wp-content/uploads/sites/7/2017/09/MaaS-WhitePaper_final_040917-2.pdf> accessed 20 March 2020.

harmonise data and the enforcement of secure real-time access to data as well as to ensure clarity regarding the liability of parties with principal control over the data. Reliable data, which serves as a basis for advanced and up-to-date travel information services, is one of the main prerequisites to MaaS uptake and attractiveness, creating more predictable travel chains and inducing people to leave their cars at home.

The first known regulatory effort to boost the fulfilment of preconditions for MaaS services and the openness of data took place in Finland with the adoption of the Act on Transport Services[42] in April 2017. The data provisions entered into force on 1 January 2018 and all the other provisions on 1 July 2018. The Act's aim is to enable the introduction of new technologies, digitalisation and new business concepts in the transport sector. In turn, this should promote the provision of transport services that better meet user needs. It obliges both private and public passenger transport service providers to give access to essential data related to mobility services and contains provisions on the interoperability of ticketing and payment systems. This results in the widest possible accessibility to transport services and also facilitates the efficient combination of services.

Audoin gives two reasons for why[43] the Finnish Transportation Act can be understood as a regulatory push towards employing MaaS. Firstly, the Act is seen as a MaaS enabler in that it forces all transport service providers to open essential data such as routes, timetables, stops and fares in a computer-readable format. Secondly, it lays down provisions for the technical interoperability of ticketing systems by requiring all public transport providers to open their single ticket APIs for third-party resale and use.[44]

Following the Finnish example, France has also adopted a new legal framework to enhance the use of new mobility means (i.e. MaaS, ACV, Carpooling, e-scooter etc.). The French mobility orientation law (*La loi d'orientation des mobilités* or 'LOM') was adopted on 24 December, 2019. This large text, whose primary objective is to improve travel throughout the country, is a victory for sustainable mobility in that it supports new forms of mobility as alternatives to single car ownership. The objectives set forth in the law are both ambitious and varied. In particular, two major steps are being taken to facilitate the expansion of MaaS's concept: first, the LOM requires that public and private mobility data be made available and that ticketing options be expanded to move towards more intermodality; second, with the establishment of the new guidelines requiring each Organising Authorities of Mobility (AOM) to create an information system which

[42]See Finnish Act on Transport Services (n 1).

[43]See Audoin and Finger (n 39) 6.

[44]The second part of the Finnish Act on Transport Services (n 1) was approved (amendment n 301/2018) in 2018. The concept of acting on someone else's behalf, forcing public transport operators to also open up seasonal ticket APIs, was introduced in Sect. 2.

provides a complete overview of a user's mobility options within their locality or region, a major step is being taken to facilitate the expansion of MaaS.[45]

The MaaS concept is nominally based on the idea of open data, but this is only partially true. According to the European data portal definition,[46] open data can be defined as 'data that can be freely used, modified, and shared by anyone for any purpose subject, at most, to measures that preserve provenance and openness'. In other words, open data is data that can be accessed, shared, used and reused without any barriers for any type of (re)user.[47] However, according to MaaS Alliance,[48] forced data sharing, as stipulated in the Finnish Transport Service Act, does not necessarily equal free data. Instead, data sharing and exchange models should be conducted at arm's length between partners that are free to negotiate terms and conditions. The Finnish Code stipulates an obligation for public transport service providers to open their ticket APIs to third-party sellers. Meanwhile, Section 4 states that providers should grant 'access to information and information systems offered through the open interfaces on fair, reasonable and non-discriminatory terms'. The Finnish legislator has adopted the FRAND principle to guide the calculation of the remuneration that private users should transfer to the public sector transport providers for accessing and utilising their payment system APIs. Moreover, only transport stakeholders (i.e. MaaS providers, taxi apps, bus operators, etc.) are allowed to benefit from the data access right under Finnish transport law.

However, the Transport Act does not prevent transport operators or MaaS providers that aim to gain access to the data from collaborating through data access agreements. Data access agreements, *inter alia*, identify the data to be accessed; identify the party, person/s or class of persons who are permitted to access the data; often restrict the access rights to the contract party, i.e. neither the right nor data accessed under the agreement can be transferred to third parties; limit the purposes for which the data may be used; contain a disclaimer that the provider is not responsible for any inaccuracies in the data; and provide for the termination of the agreement in case of a failure to comply with the terms and covenants of the agreement. For example, an access agreement may provide that the data can be accessed and used for non-commercial purposes only or that if a user engages in commercial uses of the data, they must transfer a fee to the provider representing a proportion of the revenues obtained.[49] The obligation stipulated in the Finnish Act to

---

[45]See the French Mobility Orientation law, LOI n° 2019-1428 du 24 décembre 2019 d'orientation des mobilités; see also Urban Mobility, 'Your Guide to the French Mobility Orientation Law' (*Urban Mobility Company*, 27 March 2020) <https://urbanmobilitycompany.com/content/daily/your-guide-to-the-french-mobility-orientation-law> accessed 2 April 2020.

[46]See European Data Portal, 'Open Data in a Nutshell' (European Union 2018) <www.europeandataportal.eu/en/providing-data/goldbook/open-data-nutshell> accessed 4 March 2020.

[47]See Murati and Hënkoja (n 19) 120.

[48]MaaS Alliance, 'Data Makes MaaS Happen' (MaaS Alliance, November 2018) <https://maas-alliance.eu/wp-content/uploads/sites/7/2018/11/Data-MaaS-FINAL-after-plenary-1.pdf> accessed 4 March 2020.

[49]See Fitzgerald and others (n 4) 167.

share or make data accessible originates from the EU Regulation (n. 1926/2017) on providing multimodal travel information services. The Regulation requires both private and public transport service providers to grant access to travel data at any time in a machine-readable format through the National Access Point (NAP).[50] Those NAPs will gather travel and traffic data from all type of transport from both private and public entities within and, eventually, outside the borders of an EU Member State. The type of static travel data to be made available through the NAPs are detailed in Annex I of the Regulation. The Regulation stipulates that firms have a right to access transport data at any time. However, access to payment data services (i.e. APIs), as granted by the Finnish and French mobility laws, is not granted under this EU Regulation. Therefore, a new EU Regulation/Directive is required to render open/accessible these data to MaaS platform providers. From a user's perspective, the benefits of that would be an easy access to various means of transport around EU and the chance to have roaming in mobility (similar to telecommunication sector), cutting mobility costs. For instance, once a user has a MaaS app or had acquired a MaaS mobility package in Helsinki and currently he is in vacation in Vienna, the Whim app, owned by MaaS Global in Finland, offers the possibility not only to have access and buy Vienna's mobility means but also to use the same mobility package acquired in Helsinki.

While it is widely expected that the public sector will support open data policies, the private sector is generally more hesitant to enable data sharing. Many private-sector mobility providers see a competitive advantage in keeping data proprietary. Where interoperable and integrated systems already exist, the technology of these systems is proprietary and cannot be accessed by other service providers.[51] For any type of service, it is necessary to make a distinction between the sharing of data for information purposes[52] on the one hand and for distribution purposes (i.e. reselling tickets on MaaS platforms) on the other. For distribution, an agreement is necessary.

Distribution agreements are also necessary due to the fact that for rail and air transport dynamic pricing practices are often used, which means that the price changes based on demand, the date of departure and various other factors. The distribution of tickets requires an agreement with the private service provider.[53] This

---

[50]See Parliament and Council Regulation (EU) 2017/1926 of 31 May 2017 supplementing Directive 2010/40/EU with regard to the provision of EU-wide multimodal travel information services [2017] OJ L 272/1.

[51]See Valdani Vicari & Associati Economics and Policy, 'Study on Market Access and Competition Issues Related to MaaS' (*MaaS Alliance*, June 2019) <https://maas-alliance.eu/maas-alliance-commissioned-study-to-clarify-the-legal-framework-and-roles-of-public-and-private-parties/> accessed 5 March 2020.

[52]The notion has also been taken into account by Regulation 1926/2017 (n 50) on providing multimodal travel information, which considers that only information data can be requested to be published by the National Access Points (NAPs).

[53]Recently, a decision of the Paris Commercial Court prevented the online travel agent Lastminute.com from selling Ryanair tickets without the consent of the airline and using information on its website for commercial purposes (screen scraping); see AFP, 'French Court Condemns lastminute.com for 'Parasitism' of Ryanair Website' *The Local* (Paris, 6 April 2018) <www.thelocal.fr/20180406/french-court-condemns-lastminutecom-for-parasitism-of-ryanair-website> accessed 5 March 2020.

would imply that the general rule is that transport service providers may exclude third parties from the use of their database to provide a journey planner or other travel service.

The problem of the right to access data does not arise anymore in Finland, given the Code's provisions for creating 'data commons' in reference to transport data. Moreover, the interoperability of the public ticketing systems, which is made possible by requiring all public transport providers to open their single ticket APIs, provides the possibility for MaaS platforms to reserve and purchase tickets for their customers, creating MaaS package deals. (See Chapter 2, Section 1, 2 and 2a of the Finnish Code).[54] Public transport operators are actually obliged to contract with MaaS providers.

While some research has focused on technical impediments, especially the lack of open, interoperable, and trusted interfaces for data, most attention has, arguably, been on organizational and relational challenges. MaaS builds on the integration of offerings from several transport service providers. Thus, MaaS is an intrinsically collaborative venture—sharing data—that requires new business ecosystems to emerge in order to bring MaaS offerings to end users. Business models that are viable for all the organizations in the emerging MaaS pools, and that cater for MaaS offerings that contribute to policy goals, are yet to be proven. Similarly, a lack of suitable processes for, and experience in, managing collaborative innovation has been found to make it difficult for key stakeholders to agree on shared goals for MaaS and to divide responsibilities.[55]

In light of the above, a MaaS service may look different in different jurisdictions. Indeed, there is no EU-wide definition of MaaS. The different MaaS set-ups described above, however, have some common features: a combined transport service that the respective individual transport service providers cannot facilitate on their own. They can only provide parts of the MaaS service. Meanwhile, if the set-up is a joint MaaS platform, they need to agree on a price mechanism (and API access) for the combined service and make a commitment to share up-to-date and instant data regarding where their individual service means are available and how many service units should be available on the platform. The venture must also presumably include some kind of explicit or implicit agreement on how to share the revenues from the MaaS platform. Moreover, other relevant competitive data possibly need to be provided so that the algorithm of the MaaS platform can provide a travel route which best serves the interests of individual customers (the user experience).

[54]See Finnish Act on Transport Services (n 1).

[55]Göran Smith and others, 'Governing Mobility-as-a-Service: Insights from Sweden and Finland' in Matthias Finger, Maxime Audouin (eds), *The Governance of Smart Transportation Systems* (Springer 2019) 169-188.

However, the MaaS concept can also be realised by a stand-alone platform provider that distributes transport services provided by different firms in a more vertical arrangement. In this case, different firms (both private and public) connect to a platform (an app) and there is less transparency with regard to price and service/product development between the different transport service suppliers.

While both crude MaaS collaborations outlined above hold great potential, they also harbour great risks from the point of view of competition law. They are joint concepts based on the notion of coopetition, through which prices and supply can align; at the same time, they may represent market power and enable the exclusion of new entrants and transport service suppliers. Indeed, whether they are anticompetitive or not depends on how the MaaS service platform is set up and how the data is handled.

3 Competition Law

3.1 MaaS from a Competition Law Perspective

From a competition law perspective, the MaaS concept is something akin to a joint venture or a joint vehicle where the participating firms pool information regarding travel and transport while also offering the possibility of a one-stop-shop for door-to-door transport services. It resembles a local, jointly controlled travel agency but opens the possibility for one platform to become the most important hub in the MaaS ecosystem by collecting and pooling data. Such data-driven business models can trigger network effects and potentially cause the market to tip in favour of one dominant platform.

As will be developed below, platforms and pools where parties share and agree on relevant strategic and competitive information (e.g. price lists, future output prediction and possibly new innovations in reference to routes) should be considered potential risks for anticompetitive behaviour according to Art. 101(1) TFEU, though there is still the possibility that they qualify for an exemption under Art. 101 (3) TFEU. We may also put in this category cases with facilitators, firms that provide the service of facilitating collaboration regarding price or output.[56] However, joint ventures which are able to provide services which the individual providers cannot provide by themselves may very well fall outside Art. 101(1) TFEU altogether or at least be available for an exemption under Art. 101(3) TFEU. Data pools facilitating interoperability between firms, devices, products such as connected cars and

[56]See e.g. Case C-74/14 *'Eturas' UAB and Others v Lietuvos Respublikos konkurencijos taryba* EU:C:2016:42.

individuals may provide new forms of services and transport systems.[57] Indeed, pools containing information for the development of new transport services could be regarded as benign technical development cooperations and considered as an analogy of R&D collaborations, standard-setting efforts or, to some extent, patent pools. The MaaS concept can open the door to innovations and new designs for smart city transport.

The 'difficult' data collaborations would be the pools containing customer (i.e. firm or consumer) information and output information, i.e. possible 'production output' for different members or even where they locate their output geographically. MaaS platforms for transport services may be transparent regarding where individual transport service units (the vehicles) are located, which can actually serve as a hidden mechanism to prevent several different competing transport service units from entering the same geographical area (which could decrease price levels with respect to the joint algorithm). Moreover, connecting a MaaS platform to other pooled information such as the income level and home address of the users could create a powerful tool for price discrimination. The platform would be able to identify what price an individual purchaser might accept. While the platform might need this to create the best user experience, such data may give firms an incentive to use hyper-nudging[58] or even perfect discriminatory pricing.[59] MaaS platforms utilising these possibilities may at first glance be considered anticompetitive. At the same time, however, they may be at the forefront of the development of new and better products and services. They might create better and more efficient ways to commute and travel.

As will be discussed below, for MaaS platforms that have acquired some kind of market power, Art. 102 TFEU will be applicable. Article 102 TFEU may be triggered for similar reasons, and Art. 101 TFEU would be available for collaborative MaaS platforms. Indeed, the combination of data in the MaaS pool—holding strategic competitive information such as routes, timetables, stops, customer preferences and history and fares in a computer-readable format—with high presence in the connected transport markets might be questionable from a competition law perspective. MaaS platforms that are considered market leading or dominant might

[57]If such data pools are open access on fair, reasonable and non-discriminatory (FRAND) terms, they may very well fall outside Paper 101 TFEU altogether, similarly to the open access standard-setting agreements that fall inside the standard-setting safe harbour.

[58]Nudging implies using data-driven, sophisticated personal persuasion. Nudging often refers to one of three strategies: (i) if the deferral is mainly the result of simple procrastination or inertia, using scarcity appeals such as limited time offers; (ii) if it is about fear of making the wrong choice (regret aversion), offering a guarantee; and (iii) if the deferral is due to confusion or choice overload, helping customers by simplifying their decision making. Alain Samson, 'Big Data Is Nudging You' (*Behavioral Economics*, 30 August 2016) <www.behavioraleconomics.com/big-data-is-nudging-you/> accessed 13 July 2018.

[59]Perfect price discrimination occurs when a firm charges the maximum price for every unit sold (consumed). A firm that is able to charge the maximum possible price for each unit captures all available consumer surplus for itself. See Economics Online: for students of Economics, 'Price Discrimination' (*Economics Online*) <https://economicsonline.co.uk/Business_economics/Price_discrimination.html> accessed 15 July 2018.

abuse their dominant position to try to get a competitive advantage. A dominant MaaS platform can exclude competition by denying entry to the platform for suppliers, or its provider can use the platform to vertically integrate or exclude specific suppliers of transport services on the downstream transport markets. Simultaneously, with respect to dominant MaaS providers, the competitive analysis needs to take into consideration their role in facilitating innovations and efficiencies. Both the potentials risks and benefits will be discussed below.

The competition law analysis must also discuss the obligation stipulated in the Finnish Transport Act to share or make data accessible, inspired by the EU Regulation (n. 1926/2017) on providing multimodal travel information services that are accurate and available across borders. The Regulation provides something akin to 'data commons' in reference to some transport data. The static and dynamic travel and traffic data listed in the Regulation and the corresponding metadata shall be accessible on a non-discriminatory basis for exchange and reuse within the Union through the national or common access point (NAPs) and within a timeframe that ensures the timely provision of travel information services. They shall be accurate and up to date. The Regulation even stipulates that criteria used for ranking travel options of different transport modes or combinations thereof, or both, shall be transparent and not be based on any factor directly or indirectly relating to the user identity or, if any, the commercial consideration related to the reuse of the data and shall also be applied on a non-discriminatory basis to all participating users. Thus, the regulation creates an obligation for Member States to create common open pools regarding extensive yet basic transport data. That is a significant obligation for both public and private transport providers to provide the basic raw material (data) to the benefit of private MaaS enablers and other platforms. Entry to the MaaS concept is open for newcomers. Indeed, the MaaS providers may, and most likely will, pool more information than listed in the Regulation; for example, data concerning local arrangements and even individual customers may be pooled. Yet in reference to the transport data encompassed by the Regulation, such data must be considered anti-competitive and part of the public domain for it to be pooled or shared.

3.2 *Hub-and-Spoke Arrangements in the Online Context*

While a large share of the debate tends to focus on dominance, platforms also raise competition concerns regarding collusion (colluding algorithms) or restrictive vertical agreements, which can be a problem even in the absence of dominance. Hub-and-spoke arrangements are triangular schemes that involve economic players operating at different levels of the supply chain, thus containing both horizontal and vertical elements.[60] In EU competition law, hub-and-spoke arrangements are

[60]See OECD, 'Hub-and-spoke Arrangements: Note by the European Union' (OECD 2019) <https://one.oecd.org/document/DAF/COMP/WD(2019)89/en/pdf> accessed 31 March 2020.

mentioned in the section of the Horizontal Guidelines related to information exchange. Paragraph 55 of the Horizontal Guidelines states that '[i]nformation exchange can take various forms. Firstly, data can be directly shared between competitors. Secondly, data can be shared indirectly through a common agency (for example, a trade association) or a third party such as a market research organisation or through the companies' suppliers or retailers.'[61] The Horizontal Guidelines thus recognise two main scenarios for indirect data exchanges: one in which the hub is a third party or common agency and another in which the hub is an upstream supplier or a downstream customer. Hub-and-spoke arrangements are also briefly referred to in the Vertical Guidelines. Paragraph 224 of the Vertical Guidelines, which concerns retail price maintenance (RPM), states that

> by eliminating intra-brand price competition, RPM may also facilitate collusion between the buyers, that is, at the distribution level. Strong or well organised distributors may be able to force or convince one or more suppliers to fix their resale price above the competitive level and thereby help them to reach or stabilise a collusive equilibrium.[62]

The Vertical Guidelines thus focus on the scenario in which the hub is an upstream supplier.

Hub-and-spoke arrangements often relate to price, supply intentions or business strategies. In hub-and-spoke arrangements, collusion is achieved through the hub, which acts as the facilitator and sometimes also as the enforcer of anticompetitive horizontal conduct.[63] In the online platform context, a platform operator might take the role of both facilitator and enforcer of anticompetitive practices, coordinating the behaviour of suppliers and retailers operating via its platform. With regard to the use of algorithms as price-fixing tools, it is possible to distinguish between various situations:[64] the use of algorithms to implement a pre-existing agreement between colluding parties; the use of a hub-and-spoke algorithm to regulate a platform that carries the products of various companies (as in the *Eturas* case); and unrelated companies in the same market using predictable agent algorithms to track each other and hence to reach similar or same price levels. While competition authorities have found infringements in the first two situations,[65] the third might constitute tacit

---

[61] See Commission, 'Guidelines on the applicability of Article 101 of the Treaty on the Functioning of the European Union to horizontal co-operation agreements Text with EEA relevance' [2011] OJ C 11/1, para 55.

[62] See Commission, 'Guidelines on Vertical Restraints' [2010] OJ C 130/1.

[63] See OECD (n 60) 4-5.

[64] Ariel Ezrachi and Maurice E Stucke, 'Artificial Intelligence & Collusion: When Computers Inhibit Competition' [2017] University of Illinois Law Review 1775. See also Manon van Roozendaal, 'Algorithms: Teenage Troublemakers of EU Competition Law: A Closer Look at Algorithms as the New Price-Fixing Tool in EU Competition Law' (European Law Institute 2018) <www.europeanlawinstitute.eu/fileadmin/user_upload/p_eli/YLA_Award/Submission_ELI_Young_Lawyers_Award_Manon_van_Roozendaal_2018.pdf> accessed 31 March 2020.

[65] The implementing algorithm was found to infringe in the United States in *United States v David Topkins*, No 15 CR 201 (NDC April 6, 2015) and the administrator pricing model in the European Union in *Eturas* (n 56).

coordination or what economists define as tacit collusion, which might not qualify as an infringement of Art. 101 TFEU. However, members of academia claim that such creations should give rise to antitrust intervention.[66]

Subsequently, whether a hub-and-spoke arrangement is a restriction by object or by effect does not in principle depend on whether or not the collusion is achieved through a third party but rather on the nature of the information exchange and the legal and economic context in which the information exchange takes place. The assessment would therefore be similar to that of collusion achieved through direct contacts.[67] Hub-and-spoke arrangements presuppose at least two information exchanges: one between spoke A and hub B and another between hub B and spoke C. Such vertical information exchanges, even when relating to strategic information, may often be legitimate and thus legal business practices. The difficulty, therefore, is to identify the situations in which such legitimate practices amount in reality to an illegal horizontal agreement or concerted action. It is therefore of particular importance to assess the context behind the information exchanges between spoke A and hub B and between hub B and spoke C. This assessment is case-specific and has to take into account the level of awareness of the spokes regarding the information exchanges between other spokes and the hub and whether they have distanced themselves from the behaviour of the hub. This raises the question as to the requisite standard of proof for horizontal collusion in such cases and notably whether it is necessary to show that the spokes are aware that the information they exchange with the hub is being passed on to other spokes.

The European Court of Justice's recent jurisprudence suggests that full knowledge of the anticompetitive conduct may not be necessary. In the preliminary ruling on *VM Remonts*,[68] the CJEU held that, in principle, an undertaking may be held liable for a concerted practice on account of the acts of an independent service provider if, *inter alia*, the undertaking was aware of the anticompetitive objectives pursued by its competitors and the service provider and intended to contribute to them by its own conduct, or if that undertaking could reasonably have foreseen the anticompetitive acts of its competitors and the service provider and was prepared to accept the risk which they entailed.

From the perspective of the discussion above, the *John Deere* case[69] is also interesting in that it concerned the United Kingdom Agricultural Tractor Registration Exchange, which employed a system in which competitors frequently shared

---

[66]See Ezrachi and Stucke (n 64).

[67]See OECD (n 60) 4-5.

[68]Case C-542/14 *SIA 'VM Remonts' (formerly SIA 'DIV un KO') and Others v Konkurences padome* EU:C:2016:578.

[69]Case C-7/95 P *John Deere v Commission* EU:C:1998:256 [1998] ECR I-03111; preceding case law: Case T-35/92 *Deere v Commission* EU:T:1994:259 [1994] ECR II-00957; Joined Cases C-89/85, C-104/85, C-114/85, C-116/85, C-117/85 and C-125/85 to C-129/85 *Ahlström Osakeyhtiö and Others v Commission* EU:C:1993:120 [1993] ECR I-01307; Case C-8/08 *T-Mobile Netherlands and Others v Raad van bestuur van de Nederlandse Mededingingsautoriteit* EU:C:2009:343 [2009] ECR I-04529.

large amounts of specific data regarding the sale of tractors. Even though the information did not state (directly) every sale made during a specific time period, given the detailed nature of the data it was possible to identify the details of individual tractor sales. For this specific reason, *John Deere* has been distinguished from later cases, e.g. *Wirtschaftsvereinigung Stahl v Commission*.[70] Possibly, the *John Deere* case can also be distinguished with regard to data pools containing customers' information. The collection of (personal) data from potential customers in order to map their behaviour and nudge individual consumers to make specific purchases at an individually set price does not imply that the data pool is sharing price information between competitors. The pool may contain 'only' the raw data about individual consumers' general and specific purchasing behaviour for making the relevant algorithmic calculation, which does not directly imply an exchange of specific prices.[71] Indeed, the customer-relevant information might be kept at the system administrator (MaaS platform) level exclusively and not shared with the transport service providers.

Another relevant judgment in this regard was given in the *Eturas* case (Case C-74/14[72] judgment of 2016), which was the first time the CJEU addressed a digital platform with a joint price function, in this case a platform on which Lithuanian travel agencies sold their products. The CJEU decided on a preliminary ruling concerning the decision of the Lithuanian Competition Council to impose fines on Eturas and 30 travel agencies for applying a common cap on discounts applicable to services provided through the Eturas online booking platform. The facts of the *Eturas* case raise questions as to the existence of competition infringement by way of a tacit arrangement between the administrator of an online travel booking system and the individual travel agencies (TAs) selling through the system. In other words, what makes the case particularly interesting is that the alleged coordination would have taken place via an online travel booking system (E-TURAS, owned by Eturas) used by more than 30 travel agents in Lithuania.

The facts and the situation in the main proceedings may be briefly described as follows:[73] Eturas is the proprietor and administrator of an online travel booking platform (E-TURAS) for TAs. Having obtained a platform licence, each TA is provided with a uniform layout for their online booking services. The licence does not include pricing provisions. The TA is also provided with an electronic password-secured account that contains a mailbox for booking system notifications (messages). In August 2009, the administrator of the booking platform circulated an email (entitled 'Vote') inquiring about limiting the online discount level from 4% to

[70] Case C-441/97 P *Wirtschaftsvereinigung Stahl and Others v Commission* EU:C:2000:643 [2000] ECR I-10293.

[71] The question of whether such a solution complies with the data protection framework remains beyond the scope of this paper.

[72] *Eturas* (n 56).

[73] See Katri Havu and Neža Zupančic, 'Case Comment: Collusion and Online Platforms in Eturas' (2016) 11 Competition Law Review 255.

1–3%. The correspondence was not sent to all the TAs using the system. Two days later, the administrator sent a system notification about a newly adopted discount cap (3%). Apparently, it was not obvious to the recipients who else received the notification. In addition, a technical restriction was imposed that limited online discounts to the new level. This signified that if a discount was set above the cap, it was automatically reduced back to the 3% discount rate. Although this restriction did not preclude any TA from granting additional discounts to its individual customers, the TAs were required to take additional technical steps in order to do so.

In 2012, after investigating whether the TAs using the E-TURAS system had coordinated their discounts, the national competition authority (NCA) found that 30 TAs as well as Eturas were involved in anticompetitive behaviour in breach of Art. 101(1) TFEU and corresponding national provisions. The anticompetitive practice was considered to have started on the date of the 3% discount cap message. According to the NCA's reasoning, the TAs could reasonably expect that other users were subject to the same 3% cap, which indicated that the agencies had reached tacit or implied consent on their common behaviour.[74] Liability could have been avoided by expressing an objection. Eturas, not active in the same market as the TAs, was considered to have played the role of a facilitator.

An annulment action was partially upheld and fines were reduced, but both the authority and the companies appealed before the Administrative Supreme Court, which referred two questions to the CJEU. In essence, the referring court inquired whether the mere dispatch of a message on a discount cap should lead to a presumption that the addressees knew or should have known of its content and whether it should be inferred from this that, unless they voiced opposition, they may be liable for participating in a concerted practice. Furthermore, the referring court asked about the factors that must be considered to establish participation in a concerted practice.[75]

In his Opinion, which the Court mainly followed, Advocate General (AG) Szpunar stated that the national court could find it probable that the undertakings became aware of the message.[76] Furthermore, a concerted practice could be established between undertakings that became aware of the system notification and continued using the system without sufficient public distancing from the anticompetitive practice.[77] Sufficient public distancing, in the AG's opinion, entailed opposition to as many members of the concertation as possible and notifying the

[74]See Alfonso Lamadrid, 'Eturas on the Scope of "Concerted Practices" and on Technological Collusion' (*Chillin'Competition Blog*, 22 January 2016) <https://chillingcompetition.com/2016/01/22/ecjs-judgment-in-case-c-7414-eturas-on-the-scope-of-concerted-practices-and-on-technological-collusion/> accessed 5 March 2020.

[75]See Havu and Zupančic (n 73) 258.

[76]See *Eturas* (n 56) Opinion of AG Szpunar EU:C:2015:493, paras 55-57. The AG emphasised that the evaluation of evidence is a matter of national law.

[77]ibid paras 71 and 10.

administrator as well as informing the site users. In case this was not effective, reporting to the competition authority was appropriate.[78]

As to the first question—whether proof that a message was sent is enough to presume the awareness of the recipient—the CJEU starts off by recalling the principles that companies are to determine their behaviour autonomously and that 'passive modes of participation' (i.e. complicity/facilitation) are also caught by Art. 101 (referring here to the recent judgment in *Treuhand*).[79] The Court nevertheless explains that, whereas there is a presumption that companies take into account the info exchanged with others for determining their behaviour (33, citing the infamous *T-Mobile case*), the question posed by the national court is not really about that; rather, it concerns an evidential issue[80] which remains a matter of the national law, provided that the principles of effectiveness and uniformity are respected. The principle of effectiveness requires that national rules on evidence do not render the application of EU law impossible or excessively difficult, accordingly, it requires that not only direct evidence but also indicia be valid to prove an infringement.[81]

However, if, as in the case at issue, the national court has doubts as to whether the travel agents became or must have become aware of the content of the system notification, then the presumption of innocence applies, in the sense that the mere sending of the notification cannot be in itself enough to infer awareness of its content.[82] It could nonetheless be used in combination with other objective and consistent indicia to establish a rebuttable presumption of awareness. According to the judgment, the national court should not make it excessively difficult for the companies to rebut this presumption; for instance, the travel agencies concerned must have the opportunity to rebut the presumption that they were aware of the content of the message at issue in the main proceedings as from the date of that message's dispatch, for example by proving that they did not receive that message or that they did not look at the section in question or did not look at it until some time had passed since that dispatch.[83]

Subsequently, as to the second question, the CJEU recalls that a 'concerted practice' implies not only an element of concertation but also an ensuing behaviour on the market and a causal link between the two. Therefore, another important element in assessing hub-and-spoke arrangements is the link between the information exchanges and the actual market conduct. In this regard, it should be recalled that there is a presumption that the undertakings participating in concerted arrangements and remaining active on the market take account of the information exchanged with their competitors when determining their conduct on that market. The CJEU recalled that an undertaking may rebut the presumption that it participated

[78]ibid para 92.

[79]*Eturas* (n 56) paras 27-28.

[80]ibid paras 33-34.

[81]ibid paras 35-37.

[82]ibid paras 38-39.

[83]ibid paras 40-41.

in a concerted practice by proving that it publically distanced itself from that practice or reported it to the administrative authorities.[84] With regard to 'public distancing', the Court observes that in a case like this, in which it is impossible to identify all addressees of the message, it cannot be required that a company distances itself in the eyes of all other addressees and takes the view that a 'clear and explicit objection' addressed to the system administrator would be enough to rebut the presumption.[85]

With regard to the other means of rebutting the presumption of having participated in a concerted practice, the Court states that, in circumstances such as the ones at issue, the causal link could be rebutted by showing that the company systematically applied a discount exceeding the cap in question.[86]

The Interesting Implications of *Eturas*

In light of the *Eturas* case, undertakings that share platforms with competitors will now have to carefully craft protocols to avoid possible liabilities. *Eturas* highlights a hazard of managing cooperation through an online platform and demonstrates that such platforms can facilitate unlawful cooperation amongst platform users even without any direct contact. Although far from the archetypal 'behind closed doors' cartel meeting, the *Eturas* decision demonstrates how information technology can distort markets in the digital space. Businesses using online platforms will need to ensure that online communication channels are effectively monitored to avoid inferences of collusion. Users should also be aware of the steps necessary to rebut any presumption of collusion. Thus, not only can the public distancing requirement be applied in a digital environment, but most of all it means the requirement can be applied in a situation where there was probably no anticompetitive meeting at all. The *Eturas* decision is consistent with the 2015 judgment in *AC-Treuhand* v *Commission* (C-194/14), which recognised the liability of intermediaries for facilitating anticompetitive practices.[87] Platform operators and administrators should therefore take particular care not to include anticompetitive restrictions in their terms and conditions to reduce the risk of liability for facilitating collusion between users—the defence of lack of knowledge would certainly not be available to the party which initiated the terms.[88] Indeed, in a MaaS collaboration, different transport providers should preferably set their own prices unilaterally while the system administrator (the MaaS platform provider) should provide the algorithm for calculating the joint price.

[84]ibid para 46.

[85]ibid paras 47-48.

[86]ibid paras 49.

[87]ibid paras 28.

[88]See Sophie Lawrance and Marc Linsner, 'Eturas: Any Conclusions on Platform Collusion?' (*Kluwer Competition Law Blog*, 19 January 2017) <http://competitionlawblog.kluwercompetitionlaw.com/2017/01/19/eturas-conclusions-platform-collusion/?print=print> accessed 5 March 2020.

However, questions remain open, particularly in regard to system administrators.[89] For instance, in para. 48 the CJEU accepts that distancing may be done only vis-á-vis the 'system administrator'. But in that case, what obligations fall upon the system administrator? Could the forwarding of messages between different transport providers be benign or is it anticompetitive? How transparent can the MaaS platform provider be vis-à-vis the transport service providers? Would a 'suggestion' or 'recommendation' of price levels—for calculating prices on a competing MaaS platform—be benign? What about the service in itself? Indeed, the MaaS platform makes prices for specific routes more transparent between transport providers.

Aside from online platform operators acting as facilitators of horizontal collusion, another specific hub-and-spoke scenario in the online context is horizontal coordination through third-party algorithms (or rather independent algorithms). The large availability of data and the reduction of costs associated with data processing and AI have made algorithmic pricing more frequent in online markets. As noted by the Commission in a previous note to the OECD,[90] algorithms increase the risk of parallel behaviour (tacit collusion[91]) since firms can use software to automatically monitor competitors' prices almost in real time and adapt prices accordingly. Algorithms can be also used to implement pre-existing price fixing agreements between competitors (explicit collusion) by agreeing on a particular pricing formula to set price levels and avoid giving unnecessary discounts. A growing concern in relation to algorithmic pricing is the use of common third-party algorithm providers by competitors to adopt the same algorithmic formulas or data pools to determine price levels. In practice, as software pricing develops and becomes cheaper and accessible to a larger number of businesses, companies contract business intelligence services from IT companies to integrate advanced pricing systems in their supply chain. When various industry players (the spokes) use the same third-party provider of algorithmic software (the MaaS platform or hub) to exchange commercially sensitive information in order to determine market prices and/or react to market changes, they could be violating Art. 101(1) TFEU.[92]

The collection of and access to data is a critical step in automatic price-setting processes since data is the most crucial input of algorithmic software. In order to collect relevant data, IT companies normally use 'web scraping', which consists in gathering publicly available information such as competitors' prices and product categories through automatic collection methods on the internet. This data is

---

[89]See Lamadrid (n 74).

[90]Cf OECD, 'Algorithms and Collusion: Competition Policy in the Digital Age' (OECD 2017) <www.oecd.org/daf/competition/Algorithms-and-colllusion-competition-policy-in-the-digital-age.pdf> accessed 6 March 2020.

[91]The damaging influence that tacit collusion can have on a market is that it becomes less attractive for competitors to lower their prices and engage in price wars. In order for such decisions to attract customers, time is needed. Algorithms, by making decisions in less than a second, essentially take away this element, leading to prices being kept artificially high and resulting in distorted market conditions.

[92]See OECD (n 60) 7.

subsequently aggregated and fed into the algorithmic software to obtain price recommendations. However, when third-party providers enter into multiple contracts with competing companies, they can both gain access to a large pool of confidential, commercially sensitive information such as individual pricing and enhance or nudge the development of differentiated prices depending on the customer and specific travel route or on internal product data that is obtained directly from contractors. While using publicly available data to feed algorithmic software is legal, the aggregation of sensitive information through a pricing tool offered by a single platform to which various competitors have access could amount to horizontal collusion. From a legal perspective, the use of a third-party provider to coordinate market behaviour by means of a common pricing algorithm would likely constitute an infringement of Art. 101(1) TFEU. In addition, the exchange of information on future pricing intentions through a third-party provider would typically constitute a restriction of competition by object. Currently, however, tacit coordination or collusion might fall outside the scope of Art. 101 TFEU. It does not qualify as an 'agreement' since there is no concurrence of wills between the parties, and even firms in an oligopolistic market structure may intelligently adapt their business conduct and model to the conduct or model of their competitors.[93] Attempts were raised to qualify tacit collusion as 'concerted practices', but these were eventually quashed by the oligopoly defence. Independent parallel pricing behaviour on its own was not enough to conclude collusion and, in this very specific setting, was deemed to be the result of rational behaviour.[94] As already indicated above, the main issue in the assessment of such conduct is the determination of the level of knowledge of each of the spokes about the anticompetitive coordination taking place through algorithmic price-setting.

As will be discussed below, MaaS collaborations and platforms will likely come to benefit from Art. 101(3) TFEU. MaaS collaborations that only include

[93]Cf Case C-48/69 *ICI v Commission* EU:C:1972:70, 655 para 66.

[94]Consolidated Version of the Treaty on European Union - Part Three: Union Policies and Internal Actions - Title VII: Common Rules on Competition, Taxation and Approximation Of Laws - Chapter 1: Rules on competition - Section 1: Rules Applying to Undertakings - Article 101 (ex Article 81 TEC) [2008] OJ C115/88, failing art 101, attempts were made to categorise this under art 102 TFEU. Consolidated Version of the Treaty on European Union - Part Three: Union Policies and Internal Actions - Title VII: Common Rules on Competition, Taxation And Approximation Of Laws - Chapter 1: Rules on competition - Section 1: Rules Applying to Undertakings - Article 102 (ex Article 82 TEC) [2008] OJ C115/89, approaching this group behaviour from art 102 TFEU would not be novel. The Commission has shown an interest in this in the past. At one point, the Court even ruled that it was possible for independent companies in the relevant market to have a collective dominant position which they could abuse. This conclusion also required some economic link, interdependence or ensured parallelism between the participants in the collective dominant position. However, the Commission has since lost its interest in such an approach, meaning that there is, as of yet, no conclusion for such an approach. It is not unthinkable, however, for the Commission to take up the baton once again when algorithms become more and more influential. See Nicolas Petit, 'The Oligopoly Problem in EU Competition Law' in Ioannis Liannos and Damien Geradin (eds), *Research Handbook in EU Competition Law* (Edward Elgar Publishing 2013) 259-349.

non-competing transport service providers may even fall outside 101(1) TFEU altogether.

To summarise, from the perspective of Art. 101 TFEU, the use of online platforms creates digital environments that might facilitate interactions between business users even without direct contact, as platform operators can easily organise and enforce coordination between undertakings using their platform (i.e. facilitate infringements by imposing operational restrictions on the system which prevent undertakings from offering lower prices or other advantages to final consumers). Dominant third-party platforms that facilitate MaaS services on an arm's length basis vis-à-vis suppliers and customers may be judged under Art. 102 TFEU, while collaborative practices could be pursued under Art. 101 TFEU if there is evidence demonstrating sufficient knowledge among the spokes that their commercially sensitive information would be passed on to other spokes. Platform operators that coordinate the horizontal anticompetitive practice by acting as a hub could also be held responsible for their conduct as a facilitator. Finally, as discussed above, the rise of MaaS relies heavily on access to user data, open APIs of transport providers and the interoperability of the systems.[95] Thus, since data are the key factor of MaaS, establishing clear and fair rules for the control of information is crucial in order to avoid platform collusion in MaaS ecosystems.

3.3 Vertical Competition Restraints in MaaS Ecosystems

Besides the risk of platform collusion, another problematic competition issue is vertical integration on online platforms. The Commission's enforcement action following the publication of the final report of the e-commerce sector inquiry[96] focused on vertical restraints occurring in online distribution. In a MaaS ecosystem, MaaS platforms, whenever operating as private undertakings, will optimise revenue for themselves while trying to satisfy customers. Thus, the MaaS provider can play a dual role: facilitating market access and competing at the same time with suppliers. This can lead to platforms unfairly promoting their own services to the disadvantage of these suppliers. In other words, like Amazon and Google, a MaaS provider can function as both an intermediary and a reseller. The phenomenon known as self-preferencing or leveraging, performed by system leaders who use a platform to capture more value on downstream or upstream markets, can also be conducted in a MaaS setting. Vertical integration implies that the platform provider starts creating its own goods or services for distribution through its platform in order to make an additional profit on those sales. After such vertical integration, the platform actually

[95]For a discussion of why smart mobility needs semantic compatibility, see Mariateresa Maggiolino and Laura Zoboli, 'Smart Mobility and Technological Compatibility from an Antitrust Perspective' in this volume.

[96]Commission, 'Final report on the E-commerce Sector Inquiry' COM (2017) 229 final.

competes with certain suppliers, which creates an incentive to exclude them. This exclusion can be carried out explicitly through the delisting of certain suppliers from the platform[97] or by granting more favourable treatment to its affiliated division (supplying under better conditions, supplying higher quality products), or vice versa. Thus, the platform operator uses its control over the ecosystem to favour its own goods and services.[98]

For instance, now that Google has its own specialised services (e.g. comparison shopping and flights), consumers are pointed in that direction. After 7 years of investigation, the Commission issued its decision in the *Google Search* case in 2017.[99] It decided that Google had abused its market dominance as a search engine by giving an illegal advantage to another Google product, its comparison shopping service. According to the decision, Google systematically gave prominent placement to its own comparison shopping service while demoting rival comparison shopping services in its search results. In other words, Google used its control of the platform (the search engine) to favour its own service (comparison shopping). In this scenario in a MaaS ecosystem, the MaaS provider not only matches and integrates various transport modes but also introduces its own, for example bike or car fleets. Therefore, the MaaS platform will suggest the cheapest, fastest, most reliable or most ecological route to get from A to B while at the same time seeking to optimise its own revenue. For example, a train ride may be more ecological than a bus ride, but it may take a few more minutes; similarly, an Uber ride may be faster than a metro ride, but the MaaS platform may get a better deal with the metro service provider. In any case, MaaS platforms—like any other digital platform for that matter—will influence, if not determine, consumer choices. These choices will be programmed into the algorithms that suggest or even select the mobility options for the users. What is programmed into these algorithms will remain non-transparent as these algorithms constitute the very competitive advantage of the MaaS platform, not to mention that they are at the heart of the MaaS platform's business model. Thus, platforms and their underlying algorithms do not need to be regulated for the sake of regulating but because they interfere with public policies. For example, if a national, regional or local government wants to promote public transport over private transport because it aims to reduce CO_2 emissions but the MaaS platform continues to systematically offer the cheapest and most CO_2-intensive route, public policymakers will find it difficult, if not impossible, to implement their policy.[100]

[97]More often, however, this exclusion proceeds through a subtle combination of commission rates imposed on the supplier and the ranking of results presented to the consumer. See Friso Bostoen, 'Neutrality, Fairness or Freedom?: Principles for Platform Regulation' (2018) 7(1) Internet Policy Review 4.

[98]See Pablo Ibáñez Colomo, 'Discriminatory Conduct in the ICT Sector: A Legal Framework' in Gintarė Surblytė (ed), *Competition on the Internet* (Springer 2015) 66-67.

[99]See *Google Search (Shopping)* (Case AT.39740) Summary of the Commission Decision 2017/4444 [2018] OJ C9/11.

[100]See Matthias Finger, 'Algorithms as Public Policy: How to Regulate Them?' (2019) 21 (4) Network Industries 10, 12.

Hence, this competition conflict arises out of the fact that MaaS providers work for multiple principals (i.e. transport suppliers). It is the number of principals that creates the possibility that during the users' search for a given destination, the MaaS platform provider may favour its own transport services or some principals over others through algorithmic discrimination because they offer higher commissions and are thus more profitable for its agency business. In this context, MaaS provider is similar to the position of a travel agent in being able to achieve different levels of commission in promoting and enabling the sale of potentially competing properties for different principals where one property would generate higher revenue due to, for example, higher sales price, higher commission rate or even due to the fact the travel agent provide the travel service.[101] However, whether a MaaS provider is abusing its (dominant) position in these circumstances must be assessed on a case-by-case basis.

On the other hand, in the case of platform collusion in a MaaS ecosystem, if a MaaS provider acts as an independent agent[102] of his transport suppliers, this might have relevant legal consequences. In particular, the implication of this finding for EU competition law is that agreements between MaaS platforms and their suppliers which contain restrictions of competition on the relevant market (i.e. transportation) cannot be scrutinised under the prohibition of anticompetitive agreements due to the 'single economic entity' doctrine.[103] The doctrine treats agreements between agents and their principals as taking place within one and the same undertaking, which renders Art. 101 TFEU inapplicable following the requirement that an agreement must take place between separate undertakings for the provision to be applicable. Thus, there is a potential 'platform gap' in the application of competition law to agreements between platforms and suppliers.[104]

---

[101]See Pinar Akman, 'Online Platforms, Agency, and Competition Law: Mind the Gap' (2019) 43 Fordham International Law Journal 209, 288.

[102]The determining factor in defining an agency agreement for the application of art 101(1) is the financial or commercial risk borne by the agent in relation to the activities for which it has been appointed as an agent by the principal. See judgment of the Court of First Instance in Case T-325/01 *Daimler Chrysler* v *Commission* EU:T:2005:322, [2005] ECR II-3319; judgments of the Court of Justice in Case C-217/05 *Confederación Española de Empresarios de Estaciones de Servicio* v *CEPSA* EU:C:2006:784, [2006] ECR I-11987; and Case C-279/06 *CEPSA Estaciones de Servicio SA* v *LV Tobar e Hijos SL* EU:C:2008:163, [2008] ECR I-6681.

[103]Article 102 TFEU is still applicable, see Case 66/86 *Ahmed Saeed Flugreisen v Zentrale zur Bekampfung unlauteren Wettbewerbs* EU:C:1989:140, para 35 and the *Interbrew* case in Commission, 'XXVIth Report on Competition Policy' (European Union 1996) para 53 <https://ec.europa.eu/competition/publications/annual_report/1996/en.pdf> accessed 1 April 2020.

[104]See Pinar Akman (n 101). See also Pinar Akman, 'A Competition Law Assessment of Platform Most-Favored-Customer Clauses' (2016) 12 Journal of Competition Law and Economics 781, 806, where Akman argued that proceedings and decisions against Booking.com, for example, should have been pursued on the basis of TFEU art 102 prohibiting the abuse of a dominant position (assuming that the conditions of that article would have been fulfilled) rather than on the basis of art 101 because Booking.com is the agent of the hotels and their agreements fall outside the scope of art 101.

It should be noted that many MaaS operators will probably enter licence agreements and other agreements with transport service providers that might cause the agency set-up to still fall inside Art. 101 TFEU.[105] The operator may also benefit from the application of Art. 101 TFEU when it combines its agency arrangement by vertically integrating and acting as an independent transport service provider in competition with its principles.[106] When a MaaS operator conducts market-specific investments for transport service providers and their business models, Art. 101 TFEU can also become applicable. These are investments specifically required for the type of work for which the agent has been appointed by the principals, that is, investments which are required to enable the agent to conclude and/or negotiate the type of contract the transport service companies provide to the market. Such investments are usually sunk, which means that upon leaving that particular field of activity the investment cannot be used for other activities or sold other than at a significant loss. Indeed, this may also cause the MaaS collaboration to fall inside Art. 101 TFEU. Moreover, according to the vertical guidelines—and the *Eturas* and *AC-Treuhand* cases seem to acknowledge this doctrine—an agency agreement may also fall within the scope of Art. 101(1) TFEU, even if the principals bear all the relevant financial and commercial risks, where the agent, e.g. a MaaS operator, facilitates collusion. That could be the case, for instance, when a number of principals use the same agents while collectively excluding others from using these agents or when they use the agent to collude on marketing strategy or prices or to exchange sensitive market information between the principals.[107] Indeed, it is likely that the Court or the EU Commission would scrutinise these MaaS collaborations under Art. 101 TFEU.

The risk of unfair competition in MaaS ecosystems can be limited by ensuring that the different treatment complies with the principle of equality (i.e. that the different treatment serves a legitimate aim), that it is based on objective criteria, that it is necessary to achieve the legitimate aim and that it does not go further than is required for the achievement of that aim (proportionality). This is the EU interpretation of the principle of equality.[108]

---

[105]Under competition law the designation of the intermediary as an 'agent', 'commission agent', 'licensee' or 'independent dealer' is less material than an economic analysis of the relationship between the agent and the principle.

[106]Case 40/73 *Suiker Unie v Commission* EU:C:1975:78 [1975] ECR 1663, paras 544-547.

[107]Guidelines on Vertical Restraints (n 61) para 20.

[108]See Caroline Cauffman, 'The Commission's European Agenda for the Collaborative Economy: (Too) Platform and Service Provider Friendly?' (2016) Maastricht European Private Law Institute (M-EPLI) Working Paper 07/2016, 9 <https://papers.ssrn.com/sol3/papers.cfm?abstract_id=2883845> accessed 1 April 2020.

3.4 Analysis of MaaS Under Competition Law

Commissioner Vestager previously addressed data pooling, stating that sometimes ‘bigger is better’ and combining companies’ data into a single, big pool might provide insights that could not otherwise be obtained independently. As examples, connected car businesses and bookstores were mentioned.[109] She seems, therefore, to perceive data pooling as a pro-competitive behaviour or at least to suggest that it does not raise a presumption of antitrust harm. In this way, she appears to promote the sharing of data across the whole industry for the development of technology, i.e. for innovation or R&D. However, she also stresses the need to use the Horizontal Guidelines[110] for reference when pooling data, as sharing information may also be considered anticompetitive.[111]

According to Vestager, one way to [illegible] is by sharing information anonymously. Companies could send their data to a platform and get back aggregated data with no indication of what company it comes from. That would still provide companies with the information they need to facilitate more efficient production, ‘it just wouldn’t undermine competition’.[112] She continues,

> [o]r companies might limit the type of information they share. So car companies might decide not to share information that would tell rivals too much about their technology. Online shops might share data without saying when products were bought, or for how much. And, companies also need to be sure that pooling data doesn’t become a way to shut rivals out of the market. It’s one thing to decide who you want to cooperate with. But that decision shouldn’t deny the others a chance to compete.[113]

Moreover, the German Federal Cartel Office (*Bundeskartellamt*) accepts that cooperations between companies in the collection and pooling of data can generate efficiencies and pro-competitive effects, especially in the context of connected industry applications and the IoT. However, according to the *Bundeskartellamt*, cooperations between competitors exchanging and pooling competitively sensitive data could facilitate collusion, hamper access to data for third parties and establish market entry barriers. Whilst there is no general prohibition of such cooperations, in the competitive assessment, cooperations between competitors would be more difficult to justify than cooperations between non-competing companies operating on different market levels.[114]

---

[109]Margrethe Vestager, ‘Big Data and Competition’ (Speech at the EDPS-BEUC Conference on Big Data, Brussels, 29 September 2016) <https://wayback.archive-it.org/12090/20191129222113/https://ec.europa.eu/commission/commissioners/2014-2019/vestager/announcements/big-data-and-competition_en> accessed 13 July 2018.

[110]Guidelines on Horizontal Co-operation Agreements (n 61) 1-72, para 55.

[111]Vestager (n 109).

[112]ibid.

[113]ibid.

[114]Bundeskartellamt, ‘Big Data und Wettbewerb Schriftenreihe “Wettbewerb und Verbraucherschutz in der Digitalen Wirtschaft”’ (*Bundeskartellamt*, October 2017) <www.

The Horizontal Guidelines explicitly recognise that cooperation between competitors can lead to substantial economic benefits, in particular if competitors share risks, save costs, increase investments, *pool know-how* (author's emphasis), enhance product quality and variety and launch innovation more quickly. Generally, and looking specifically at information exchange, R&D collaboration and standard-setting, the exchange of data may fall under several categories or chapters of the Horizontal Guidelines. The general rules regarding information sharing are only of interest when analysing whether the collaboration is a disguised cartel or facilitates collusion or other forms of pricing abuses such as price discrimination.[115]

The Horizontal Guidelines assume that standard-setting agreements or R&D collaborations are pro-competitive. Only in specific circumstances may these agreements give rise to restrictive effects on competition. This can occur through three main channels, namely reducing price competition, hindering the emergence of innovative technologies and excluding or discriminating against certain companies by preventing their effective access to the technology, in this case data.[116] The R&D block exemption reflects this and stipulates a risk for R&D collaborators, namely that the entire collaboration falls outside the exemption should any member of the collaboration be excluded from the R&D result, i.e. the data created by the collaboration.[117]

Thereafter, the Horizontal Guidelines define safe harbours. Regarding standards, the Guidelines state that where participation in standard-setting is unrestricted (i.e. where open access is used) and the procedure for adopting the standard in question is transparent, standardisation agreements which contain no obligation to comply with the standard and provide access to the standard on fair, reasonable and non-discriminatory (FRAND) terms will normally not restrict competition within the meaning of Art. 101(1) TFEU.[118] Interestingly, this safe harbour is applicable regardless of the market share of the parties to the standard-setting agreement or the level of penetration of the standard. Logically, it may also influence the application of Art. 102 TFEU.

MaaS platforms, especially when they are the joint project of transport suppliers, are both a joint pool for data and a joint transport venture for marketing a unique door-to-door transport service. Indeed, MaaS services could be regarded as services which the individual transport service providers and members of the joint venture could not provide independently. In line with the statements of DG Vestager, the

---

bundeskartellamt.de/SharedDocs/Publikation/DE/Schriftenreihe_Digitales/Schriftenreihe_Digitales_1.pdf?__blob=publicationFile&v=3> accessed 13 July 2018.

[115]Guidelines on Horizontal Co-operation Agreements (n 61) 1-72, para 55, paras 65 ff.

[116]ibid paras 262 ff.

[117]Article 3(2); Commission Regulation (EU) 1217/2010 of 14 December 2010 on the application of Article 101(3) of the Treaty on the Functioning of the European Union to certain categories of research and development agreements OJ L 335/36, 36 ff (defined as the R&D block exemption or 2010 R&D block exemption).

[118]Guidelines on horizontal co-operation agreements (n 61) para 280. See also the certification case, Joined Cases T-213/95 and T-18/96 *SCK and FNK v Commission* EU:T:1997:157.

MaaS platforms in that setting should also be presumed pro-competitive. Data pooling in general and MaaS platforms in particular may very well be assessed similarly to R&D, specialisation collaboration or other pro-competitive joint ventures, depending on the rules for the collaboration. The joint pricing and transport mechanism, i.e. the algorithm, is indispensable for the MaaS concept to work. The starting point of both the MaaS collaboration as a whole and the individual transactions is the data pool holding the necessary raw data for the algorithm, while the joint commercialisation of the result through the service provided on the platform would be subsequent, implying that the competition law analysis should focus on the data pool.[119]

Depending on the members, it is likely that the datasets provided by firms to the MaaS platform will overlap due to multi-homing. Multi-homing signifies that several of the firms collaborating under a pool are likely to provide the same or similar data, e.g. regarding the traffic or their customers. The data provided will thus be neither unique nor essential for the pool objective. This is in stark contrast with patent pools, where the parties are often required to only provide essential and non-substitutable patents to prevent cartels from developing.[120] Would this imply that data pools should be able to harbour data that represents competing alternatives, i.e. substitute non-essential data? It depends on the competitive relationship of the members. The underlying idea behind drawing a legal distinction between essential and non-essential patents and between substitutable and non-substitutable patents in patent pools is that the firms providing technology to the patent pool should not provide competing technologies. When competing technologies enter the patent pool it becomes something very similar to a cartel because the parties providing the competing technologies are likely competitors themselves. A similar logic could be transferred to data pools, such that pools which do not facilitate the collaboration of competitors might be considered benign or even pro-competitive. MaaS platforms and collaboration could be judged in a similar fashion.

When analysing data pools and collaborative platforms, we could include a general principle for establishing a safe harbour. If the contributing parties to the joint venture (for MaaS, the transports service providers) are not competitors, then the platform and similar arrangements should be regarded as vertical collaborations between complementary service providers, not horizontal agreements between competitors. If so, such collaborations could be seen as falling outside Art. 101(1) TFEU or presumed eligible for exemption under 101(3) TFEU if they can show that the service provided by the MaaS platform cannot be set up by the transport service providers individually and if the market presence of the MaaS platform is less then dominant. In these cases the MaaS collaboration should be considered a pro-competitive joint venture that includes both a data pool and a platform providing the door-to-door joint service for a price agreed upon by the members through the application of a price algorithm. Indeed, the only anticompetitive harm to be

[119]Guidelines horizontal co-operation agreements (n 61) 1-72, paras 13-14.

[120]ibid paras 245 ff.

prevented and neutralised in this setting would occur if the MaaS collaboration began to utilise business strategies that induced network effects. This would promote the tipping of the relevant market. Such behaviour could include the platform's prevention of multi-homing of the information contained in the data pool or prevention of the transport service providers from offering their services on competing MaaS platforms. Possibly, the MaaS platform also needs to be open for newcomers that provide complementary transport services.

MaaS platforms which encompass competing suppliers on certain alternative routes can also be exempted under Art. 101(3) TFEU if they can show that efficiencies and consumer benefits resulted from the MaaS service that outweigh the potential anticompetitive effects.

Moreover, if the MaaS operator purchases and redistributes transport services provided by various transport service providers, the distribution agreements in the context of integrated ticketing in a MaaS ecosystem may be able to escape the application of Art. 101 TFEU based either on the application of (1) the Vertical Block Exemption Regulation (VBER),[121] as long as they meet the conditions set therein and their market share does not exceed certain thresholds, or (2) an individual exemption, if the requirements of Art. 101(3) TFEU are met.

Were the relevant market for the MaaS platform to tip, the platform could be obliged under competition law to exclude transport service providers whose competitors outside the platform would otherwise be excluded from the relevant markets; the platform could also be obliged to welcome all suppliers, i.e. new transport service providers, if there is no risk of violating Art. 102 TFEU. A dominant MaaS platform may prevent maverick firms from entering the market because such firms would then need to be a member of this MaaS platform and in turn give up possible strategic competitive information.[122]

An important issue to discuss is whether the competition authorities should interfere with what market, technology or industry the data pool monitors. How wide and deep can the parties go in their effort to collect and share data? This is a

---

[121]Commission Regulation (EU) 330/2010 of 20 April 2010 on the application of Article 101(3) of the Treaty on the Functioning of the European Union to categories of vertical agreements and concerted practices [2010] OJ L 102/1.

[122]Pools are set up by complex contracts that explicitly or implicitly imply four agreements. First, there is a clear pool agreement whereby the contributors of patents agree on (i) the definition of the technology (often identical to how the technology is defined under a technology standardisation agreement) and (ii) the terms (e.g. royalty rates) on which downstream product manufacturers should get access to the essential intellectual properties. Second, patent pools include standard licensing agreements from the pool to third-party licensees. Third, implicitly or explicitly, there is also an agreement to exchange licences between the patent providers (pool builders) that are also active in the downstream product markets. Thus, there is a horizontal aspect between firms that both contribute patents and take out licences from the pools, compared to the otherwise vertical set-up of patent pools. Fourth, implicitly, pooling may include an agreement on the further development of technology through grant-back clauses or cross-licensing covenants for future innovations and patents. See e.g. Björn Lundqvist, *Standardization under EU Competition Rules & US Antitrust Laws: The Rise and Limits of Self-Regulation* (Edward Elgar 2014) 229 ff.

difficult issue to solve. Commissioner Vestager seems to imply that the decision of what data is to be pooled under a joint venture could be subject to the scrutiny of competition law. However, in the area of standard-setting, competition authorities have refrained from examining what technology is being standardised; similarly, the parties decide on the technology for the patent pool while the patents being pooled should be essential for the chosen technology. Perhaps, by analogy, competition authorities should refrain from assessing what data is being collected and shared as long as the data pool is not a veil for a cartel and the data collected is essential to provide the service the data pool is connected to.

We can expect that at least the terms of access, including the licence, will be subject to the founders' agreement. For example, they need to decide whether all firms accessing the pool also have a duty to provide their entire transport services and data or whether they need to hold some capacity outside the platform. Indeed, even though the joint MaaS venture should be considered benign from a competition law perspective, the ancillary terms of the agreement on access to the platform need to be scrutinised so as to avoid anticompetitive effects.

It could be recommended to the Commission to consider using the knowledge acquired with respect to patent pools and standard-setting agreements when elaborating the principles and specific terms for data and platform collaborations. Notwithstanding the requirements discussed above, some general principles or good 'procedural rules' for establishing benign data pools between non-competitors and creating a safe harbour for data pools could be outlined as follows:[123]

(i) in light of the objective of the data pool, only datasets essential for that objective should be transferred (copied) and included in the pool;
(ii) pool members should be allowed to grant individual access (licences) to their individual datasets;
(iii) to benefit from the safe harbour, or if the pool represents market power (i.e. is dominant), the pool must be open to any newcomer, i.e. third parties wanting to access the pool;
(iv) grant-back data clauses, applicable to all parties to the pool, must be limited to essential data;
(v) access to the joint collaboration and data in the pool must be granted under fair and non-discriminatory terms;
(vi) the original pool members should enter standard access agreements with the pool;
(vii) royalties obtained by the pool should not represent a significant part of the final prices of the end-product/service;
(viii) remuneration for the individual transport services provided should be separated from the royalties obtained by the pool itself and benefit the transport providers on a case-by-case basis;

---

[123]For a similar list, see Björn Lundqvist, 'Competition and Data Pools' (2018) 7 Journal of European Consumer and Market Law 146-155.

(ix) any party to the pool should be allowed to exit the pool with his or her essential dataset at any given point in time;
(x) the pool must utilise standard, widely used technology for data storage and transfer;
(xi) all parties should erect firewalls to prevent competitively sensitive information from reaching each other and to keep it confidential; and finally,
(xii) the pool might be required to offer access to sub-segments of its data to a specific category of producers should that data reflect or represent relevant product or service markets.

If the principles of R&D collaborations and standard-setting were used for data pools, data pools would thus be treated leniently under EU competition law, both under Arts. 101 and 102 TFEU, whilst the risk of anticompetitive exclusionary effects could still materialise. It is thus important that large data pools for a given industry or market offer open access in order to fall outside Arts. 101 and 102 TFEU. Such data pools could be connected to relevant open access technical standards and APIs. Should a dominant MaaS platform be closed to newcomers, it could be scrutinised under Art. 102 TFEU.

Finally, it should be stressed that interoperability lies at the heart of the digital market and data pooling.[124] In general, firms try to achieve interoperability or compatibility by increasingly connecting their products to smart systems and technology as well as to data.[125] This inevitably puts limits on competition policy. To create the virtual infrastructure or interoperability of smart cities, the pool procedure needs to be an open venture where firms negotiate and collaborate on design, business model and technology while continuing to compete. Indeed, the MaaS concept implies that the service providers will be conducting collaborative R&D.[126] They will develop the MaaS concept together. Such a procedure will create the 'best' MaaS service and the best transport services downstream, whereas other procedures for creating the 'best' technology and products (such as competition) may create suboptimal results considering that a de facto technology or a firm with greater possibilities to collect and access data can become a monopolist as a result of network effects.[127] As discussed, promoting data pools might counterbalance the tendency for network-driven markets to tip to the benefit of one firm.

---

[124] See Mariateresa Maggiolino and Laura Zoboli, 'Smart Mobility and Technological Compatibility from an Antitrust Perspective' in this volume book.

[125] Claudia Tapia, *Industrial Property Rights, Technical Standards and Licesing Practices (FRAND) in the Telecommunications Industry* (Carl Heymanns Verlag 2010) 7 with references.

[126] Josef Drexl, 'Anti-competitive Stumbling Stones on the Way to a Cleaner World: Protecting Competition in Innovation without a Market' (2012) 8 Journal of Competition Law & Economics 534.

[127] It has been claimed that the old war between VHS and Betamax standards led to an outcome where the lesser quality standard (VHS) still won and became the global standard. However, others claim that VHS on the whole represented a better product and technology. See e.g. Julian Christ and André Slowak, 'Why Blue-Ray v HD-DVD is not VHS v BETAMAX: The Co-evolution of Standard Setting Consortia' (2009) Forschungszentrum Innovation und Dienstleistung (FZID)

In light of the above, the inclusion of several firms in the data pool can prevent monopolies both on the data level as well as on the downstream product market to the benefit of oligopolies or more competitive markets. Indeed, data pooling as well as collective standard-setting procedures may have clear pro-competitive effects.

4 Concluding Remarks: The Need for Guidance

The Horizontal Guidelines and the TT Guidelines are soon to be updated. When the Commission makes such a revision, it would be beneficial if the Horizontal Guidelines were amended specifically to address the issues of data pooling and platform collaborations. Clearer guidance is needed both for the creation of safe harbours and to identify the finer details of possible violations of Arts. 101 and 102 TFEU. Moreover, the TT Guidelines should be amended to include rules on data in patent pools or on the combination of data and patent pools.

It should be acknowledged that there is little case law to use for writing data collaboration guidelines; however, they could be based on insights from legal scholarship as well as the CJEU's case law on information sharing in data pools. Moreover, the broad guidelines regarding R&D collaborations, patent pools and standard-setting could provide further inspiration.

The MaaS concepts introduced above may very well fall inside Art. 101 (1) TFEU, especially if they imply that the platform sets one price for several potentially competing transport services without remaining open to all newcomers. However, Art. 101(3) TFEU may still be applicable given the great efficiencies and consumer benefits offered by MaaS systems. The MaaS concept therefore needs to be addressed by the Commission.

A more difficult nut to crack is the situation where all relevant data belongs to a system leader, that in fact is the hub for the data flowing in the system from users to the system leader (a data hub and spoke set-up). Should the system leader indeed hold an essential dataset, the eleven principles stated above could also apply to this de facto data pool. At the very least, exclusive agreements or agreements that open up the possibility to discriminate between data users so as to enable leveraging or the exclusion of competitors should be seen as outside the notion of competition on the merits. Google Maps or Apple Maps' agreements with suppliers and subcontractors that stipulate exclusive access may be in violation of Arts. 101 or 102 TFEU.

Discussion Papers Universität Hohenheim 5/2009, 4 ff with references <http://opus.uni-hohenheim.de/volltexte/2009/366/pdf/fzid_dp_2009_05_Slowak_Christ.pdf> accessed 1 April 2020.

Smart Mobility and Technological Compatibility from an Antitrust Perspective

Mariateresa Maggiolino and Laura Zoboli

Contents

Abstract The development of smart mobility faces two main issues: data sharing and technological interoperability, which can be summed up by the expression 'semantic interoperability'. This chapter focuses on technological interoperability, using the antitrust experience as a benchmark to identify guidelines for possible interventions of public authorities in the market. To do so, the chapter addresses both the different characterisations that antitrust law gives to incompatibility (predatory innovation, refusal to share interoperability codes, technical tying) and the main tool that firms can employ to create incompatibility: standard setting organisations (SSOs).

Mariateresa Maggiolino is Director of Master of Arts in Law and Associate Professor in Commercial Law, Bocconi University, Milan, Italy.

Laura Zoboli is Assistant Professor in European Economic Law, Faculty of Management, University of Warsaw, Warsaw, Poland.

M. Maggiolino
Bocconi University, Milan, Italy
e-mail: mariateresa.maggiolino@unibocconi.it

L. Zoboli (✉)
University of Warsaw, Warsaw, Poland
e-mail: lzoboli@wz.uw.edu.pl

M. Finck et al. (eds.), *Smart Urban Mobility*, MPI Studies on Intellectual Property and Competition Law 29, https://doi.org/10.1007/978-3-662-61920-9_11

1 Why Smart Mobility Needs Semantic Compatibility

Currently, the so-called 'Internet of Things' could be said to consist of many isolated 'Intranets of Things'. These are closed vertical systems where data is created, used, and kept locked in, and where a single technology is used.[1] In this regard, smart cities represent an excellent testing ground, because they comprise a wide range of service providers and their respective stakeholders, who all have to work together and interact with each other, to provide services in telecommunications, transportation, healthcare, security, finance and so forth.[2] In the case of smart mobility, each stakeholder owns a dataset, which is meant to be used with its own application to deliver its own service. In other words, smart mobility entails a complex distributed network, which hosts multiple stakeholders' mobility-related services, applications and devices.[3] The case of electric vehicles (EV) provides an interesting example of this. Different cars need to communicate with the smart parking and charging infrastructure[4] to provide EV users with reliable and real time data about battery condition and availability of charging points. This is particularly critical if one considers that recharging EVs requires more time than the refuelling of combustion engines and that therefore charging slots (which may also be in limited amount) are occupied for much longer than traditional petrol stations. Furthermore, a smart mobility framework may need data concerning traffic control, city planning, air pollution monitoring, street lighting control, and smart parking, among other things.

However, the lack of interoperability among the various technologies employed is proving quite an obstacle.[5] On closer inspection it seems this deficiency may occur on two levels, namely data interoperability and technological interoperability, which each pose different challenges. In the first case, the focus lies on understanding if and how the datasets produced by the various stakeholders are structured in such a way to allow interaction with one another, and whether the service providers are actually interested in supporting such sharing. In the second case the question is whether the technologies employed are able to effectively communicate among themselves, and

---

[1]Shuai Zhao, Le Yu and Bo Cheng, 'An Event-Driven Service Provisioning Mechanism for IoT (Internet of Things) System Interaction' (2016) 4 IEEE Access 5038.

[2]Jeremy Robert and others, 'Open IoT Ecosystem for Enhanced Interoperability in Smart Cities—Example of Métropole De Lyon' (2017) 17 Sensors 2849.

[3]Mervi Hämäläinen and Pasi Tyrväinen, 'Improving Smart City Design: A Conceptual Model for Governing Complex Smart City Ecosystems' in Andreja Pucihar and others (eds), *Bled 2018: Proceedings of the 31th Bled eConference. Digital Transformation: Meeting the Challenges* (University of Maribor Press 2019).

[4]Anastasiia Karpenko and others, 'Data Exchange Interoperability in IoT Ecosystem for Smart Parking and EV Charging' (2018) 18 Sensors 4404.

[5]José M Hernandez-Munoz and others, 'Smart Cities at the Forefront of the Future Internet' [2011] The Future Internet Lecture Notes in Computer Science 447.

whether the relevant stakeholders will allow that communication. In other words, smart mobility requires semantic interoperability.[6]

The successful implementation of smart mobility systems, then, relies on two pre-conditions.[7] The first of these is the development and implementation of horizontally-oriented open systems based on data sharing.[8] This, in turn, requires a proper strategy for integrating heterogeneous data sources, to ensure that the overall smart mobility system is able to adopt well-informed decisions.[9] As a consequence, by employing the newly-available data, smart city environments would witness both the creation of new services and an increase in the effectiveness of current applications (and in the number of service providers involved).[10] For such a strategy to be feasible, however, the various technologies in place need to communicate among themselves, which brings us to the second—perhaps more fundamental—pre-condition: technological compatibility. Technology aside, one should not forget that the development and maintenance of a smart mobility system also relies on sustainable partnerships and cooperation strategies among the main stakeholders, to ensure adequate and efficient access to resources.[11]

In this chapter, we shall focus on technological compatibility. In particular, in Sect. 2, we will consider why firms may either promote, or hinder it. In turn, this will inform our analysis on antitrust law in Sect. 3, and in particular on how it may intervene against incompatibility and in support of compatibility. Specifically, Sect. 3.1 discusses an ongoing competition law investigation within the smart mobility

[6]Amelie Gyrard and Martin Serrano, 'Connected Smart Cities: Interoperability with SEG 3.0 for the Internet of Things' (30th International Conference on Advanced Information Networking and Applications Workshops (WAINA 2016), Crans-Montana, Switzerland, 23-25 March 2016).

[7]For a general definition of *interoperability* and an analysis of all its layers (technological, data, institutional and human interoperability), see Urs Gasser, 'Interoperability in the Digital Ecosystem' (2015) Berkman Klein Center for Internet & Society Research Publication No. 2015-13 <https://papers.ssrn.com/sol3/papers.cfm?abstract_id=2639210> accessed 1 February 2020. Furthermore, in connection to the concept of compatibility see, Richard J Gilbert, 'Symposium of Compatibility: Incentives and Market Structure' (1992) 40 The Journal of Industrial Economics 1; Nicholas Economides, 'Desirability of Compatibility in the Absence of Network Externalities' (1989) 79 American Economic Review 1165; Carmen Matutes and Pierre Regibeau, 'A Selective Review of the Economics of Standardization. Entry Deterrence, Technological Progress and International Competition' (1996) 12 European Journal of Political Economy 183; Michael L Katz and Carl Shapiro, 'Product Compatibility Choice in a Market with Technological Choices' (1986) 38 Oxford Economic Series 146; Joseph Farrell and Garth Saloner, 'Installed Base Compatibility: Innovation, Product Preannouncement, and Predation' (1986) 76 The American Economic Review 940; Joseph Farrell and Garth Saloner, 'Standardization, Compatibility and Innovation' (1985) 16 Rand Journal of Economics 70.

[8]See on this aspect Björn Lundqvist and Erion Murati, 'Collaborative Platforms and Data Pools for Smart Urban Societies and Mobility as a Service (MaaS) from a Competition Law Perspective', in this volume.

[9]Karpenko and others (n 4).

[10]ibid.

[11]Hans Schaffers and others, 'Smart Cities and the Future Internet: Towards Cooperation Frameworks for Open Innovation' [2011] The Future Internet Lecture Notes in Computer Science 431.

world. Finally, in Sect. 4 we will conclude by discussing the reasons for policy makers to support compatibility.

2 Why Firms Promote or Hinder Technological Compatibility

Generally, the stronger the technological compatibility within a certain market, the better the chances for small firms and new entrants to access and thrive in that market itself. This feeds back to these small firms tending to make their own technologies interoperable with those of other players. If the products and services sold in a market belong to a system or to a *family*, such as that of a smart city, until (if ever) the system is monopolised, *all* players will pursue a mix and match strategy,[12] because they have no interest in being cut off from the system, and profit from spill-overs and synergies with others.[13] In other words, the possibility of exploiting positive externalities thanks to direct network effects incentivises firms to adopt compatible technologies.[14]

Consumers, on their part, benefit from accessing a system with many interoperable components for the added value that this interconnection brings to the table. For example, they may prefer driving a smart car connected to the city's smart grid rather than an incompatible car that is less adaptable, as it does not communicate with traffic and lighting control systems, etc. Moreover, they are able to choose those specific system's components that better meet their needs.[15] Technical compatibility allows consumers to enjoy full network benefits, because they are not forced to buy the overall service from a single supplier, and a differentiated choice is able to match the various consumers' requirements effectively.

That said, there are market scenarios where firms actually hinder compatibility, a fact that in itself shows that incompatibility may be a strategic choice.[16] First, this

[12]Carmen Matutes and Pierre Regibeau, 'Mix and Match Product Compatibility without Network Externalities' (1988) 19 Rand Journal of Economics 221; and, for a literature survey, see Stanley M Besen and Joseph Farrell, 'Choosing How to Compete: Strategies and Tactics in Standardization' (1994) 8 Journal of Economic Perspective 117.

[13]Daniel F Spulber, 'Unlocking Technology: Antitrust and Innovation' (2008) 4 Journal of Competition Law & Economics 915.

[14]Nicholas Economides and Lawrence J White, 'Networks and Compatibility: Implications for Antitrust' (1994) 38 European Economic Review 651; Michael L Katz and Carl Shapiro, 'Technology Adoption in the Presence of Network Externalities' (1986) 94 Journal of Political Economy 822; Michael L Katz and Carl Shapiro, 'Network Externalities, Competition, and Compatibility' (1985) 75 American Economic Review 424.

[15]Paul Klemperer, 'Network Effects and Switching Costs: Two Short Essays for the New Palgrave' [2006] <https://papers.ssrn.com/sol3/papers.cfm?abstract_id=907502> accessed 1 February 2020.

[16]Timothy F Bresnahan, 'Network Effects in the Microsoft Case' (2001) SIEPR Discussion Paper No. 00-51 <www.researchgate.net/publication/246927385_Network_Effects_and_Microsoft> accessed 1 February 2020.

may happen when a firm wants to prevent its competitors from learning about its own technology, because such knowledge could both neutralise its competitive advantage and grant competitors the opportunity to displace or work around it easily.[17] This is most likely to happen when the company enjoys an already well-established market position.

Second, by preventing technological compatibility with its own structure, a company can lock-in its own consumers to then extract their surplus. Switching costs[18] may discourage consumers from leaving a specific service provider within a smart mobility system if their contents and apps cannot communicate with, or be moved to, another service provider's platform. Therefore, a lack of compatibility binds customers to a specific platform, dissuading them from switching to other service providers.[19]

Third, a firm may deliberately create incompatibility to protect its own market position. In this sense, *being* incompatible is a strategy in its own right. In particular, if a firm is dominant and integrated across different markets, it may decide to introduce technological incompatibility[20] because it allows the implementation of

---

[17]See the literature on trade secrets, e.g. Michael A Epstein and Stuart D Levi, 'Protecting Trade Secret Information: A Plan for Proactive Strategy' (1988) 43 The Business Lawyer 887; John C Steidman, 'Trade Secrets' (1962) 23 Ohio State Law Journal 4; William F Crittenden, Victoria L Crittenden and Allison Pierpont, 'Business Trade Secrets: Managerial Guidance for Competitive Advantage' (2015) 58 Business Horizons 607, 613; Paul David, 'Intellectual Property Institutions and the Panda's Thumb: Patents, Copyrights, and Trade Secrets in Economic Theory and History' in Mitchell B Wallerstein, Mary E Mogee and Roberta A Schoen (eds), *Global Dimensions of Intellectual Property Rights in Science & Technology* (National Academy Press 1993).

[18]It should be noted that the switching costs associated with internet and mobile experiences are considered lower than those associated with activities with a substantial hardware base. And this is becoming increasingly true as we are moving from PC-based to mobile-based internet. See Aaron S Edlin and Robert G Harris, 'The Role of Switching Costs in Antitrust Analysis: a Comparison of Microsoft and Google' (2013) 15 Yale Journal of Law & Technology 169.

[19]Joseph Farrell and Paul Klemperer, 'Coordination and Lock-In: Competition with Switching Costs and Network Effects' in Mark Armstrong and Robert H Porter (eds), *Handbook of Industrial Organization* (vol 3, North Holland 2007). Jean-Pierre Dubé, Günter J Hitsch and Peter E Rossi, 'Do Switching Costs Make Markets Less Competitive?' (2009) 46 Journal of Marketing Research 435.

[20]Indeed, interoperability may be the preferred strategy until the achievement of dominance. Economides argues that the existence of different competitive characteristics is a motive to prefer incompatibility to compatibility: firms that have the same size and are similar in other competitive characteristics prefer the latter, cf Economides (n 7). Farrell, Monroe and Saloner argue that firms may prefer incompatibility with cost, or quality, heterogeneity, cf Joseph Farrell, Hunter K Monroe and Garth Saloner, 'The Vertical Organization of Industry: Incompatibility versus Compatibility' (1998) 7 Journal of Economics and Management Strategy 143. Katz and Shapiro state that if one firm has a distinctly superior overall package, including its product offering, its installed base, and its reputation, that firm is likely to prefer incompatibility and may in fact spend resources to block compatibility, cf Michael Katz and Carl Shapiro, 'Systems Competition and Network Effects' (1994) 8 Journal of Economic Perspectives 93, 110. See, also, Vincenzo Denicolò, 'Compatibility and Bundling with Generalist and Specialist Firms' (2000) 2 The Journal of Industrial Economics 177.

a 'defensive leverage strategy.'[21] Let us consider a scenario where consumers are used to enjoying a full-range of goods—including products and services coming from both the primary and secondary markets. A firm that dominates the primary market and that faces competition in secondary ones may have a strong incentive to prevent competitors from entering those secondary markets, with the ultimate goal of protecting its primary market. Incompatibility serves this purpose well because it deprives competitors of a foothold in the secondary market from where they could leap into the primary one. In other words, incompatibility works as a barrier, or as a tool to increase rivals' costs, because it requires those competitors who would be able to satisfy consumers with a full-range of goods to enter both the primary and secondary markets at the same time.

Incompatibility as a Tool to Create Ecosystems

So far, our discussion mirrors the problems that many 'traditional'[22] and digital[23] antitrust cases have already faced. However, incompatibility could be used to pursue a new strategy that is peculiar to the digital world, where companies may develop mono-brand ecosystems.[24]

A digital ecosystem is understood as a group of interconnected information technology resources that function as a unit thanks to interoperability. In addition, from a commercial standpoint, a digital ecosystem is an environment where consumers may find all the products and services that they need from a single company.

---

[21]Traditional antitrust law teaches that incompatibility can be explained by taking into consideration two different strategies: not only the defensive leverage one, mentioned in the text but also price discrimination. Via incompatibility, indeed, the products sold in the secondary markets may work as metering devices to distinguish the consumers who price a lot the primary product from the consumers who price it just a few. Nevertheless, to work as a metering device, a product needs to be perishable, as toners for printing machines and blades for razors. At the moment, it is hard to think about a software that becomes perishable because of its use. True, there is obsolescence. However, regardless of whether it is natural or artificial, it regards every copy of the software, not depending on the use of that specific copy.

[22]*Transamerica Computer Company, Inc. v. IBM*, 698 F.2d 1377 (9th Circ. 1983); *California Computer Products, Inc. and Century Data System, Inc., v. IBM*, 613 F.2d 727 (9th Circ. 1979); *United States v. Microsoft Corp.*, 253 F3d 34 (DC Circ. 2001). *Microsoft* (Case COMP/C-3/37.792) Commission Decision 2007/53/EC [2004] OJ L32/23.

[23]*Kickflip, Inc. v. Facebook, Inc.*, 999 F.Supp.2d 677 (D.C. Del. 2013); *Charlotte Smith v eBay*, Lexis 74121 (U.S. Dist. 2012); *In re eBay Seller Antitrust Litigation*, 433 Fed. Appx. 504 (9th Circ. 2011); *Joseph v Amazon.com, Inc.*, 46 F. Supp. 3d 1095 (W.D.Wash. 2014); *Booklocker.com v. Amazon.com, Inc.*, 650 F.Supp. 2d 89 (D.C. Maine 2009); *The Apple iPod iTunes Antitrust Litigation*, 75 F. Supp. 3d 1271 (California N.D. 2014).

[24]Michael G Jacobides and others, 'What Does a Successful Digital Ecosystem Look Like?' (*Boston Consulting Group*, 2019) <www.bcg.com/publications/2019/what-does-successful-digital-ecosystem-look-like.aspx> accessed 1 February 2020; Omar Valdez-De-Leon, 'How to Develop a Digital Ecosystem: a Practical' (2019) 9 Technology Innovation Management Review 8; Michael G Jacobines, Carmelo Cennamo and Annabelle Gawer, 'Industries, Ecosystems, Platforms, and Architectures: Rethinking our Strategy Constructs at the Aggregate Level' <www2.uwe.ac.uk/faculties/BBS/BUS/Research/CENTIENT/ESRC%20seminar%204%20-%20UWE,%20Bristol/Michael%20G%20Jacobides.pdf> accessed 1 February 2020.

Consider, for example, Apple's ecosystem composed of the iPhone, iPad, Mac, Apple TV, Apple Watch, AirPods and, recently, HomePod.[25] A consumer who buys one of these products is encouraged to also acquire the others. So, if you download a song via Apple Music on your iPhone, you have it at your disposal on all your other Apple devices without any further action. Arguably, families of devices or 'ecosystems' create a sense of consistency and ease in a consumer's life. People who buy an iPhone are likely to then consider getting a smartwatch, and the Apple Watch can only be used together with an Apple iPhone and will not communicate with the products of other manufacturers. Other big-tech companies have achieved high degrees of diversification by entering weakly related—or at times totally unrelated—new markets. For example, Amazon transformed its core business from selling books online to providing a wide range of goods, payment services, cloud computing, and even started producing and distributing movies and television series. Google expanded from its search engine and advertising services to include location services, operating systems, mobile and personal computing devices, and cloud services. Facebook introduced photo and video social networking with Instagram, messaging with WhatsApp, virtual reality with Oculus VR and is now considering the launch of a cryptocurrency, Libra.

Thus, if we see an ecosystem as a *family* of products, we can understand why a firm would be interested in making its own ecosystem incompatible with those of its competitors. Ecosystems increase differentiation and soften competition.[26] They allow companies to shift the focus of competition away from products to ecosystems themselves, which brings the possibility of excluding products that do not belong to the company's ecosystem. This incompatibility raises entry barriers for innovating entrants and strengthens market power via increased differentiation.

In particular, on the supply side, these companies then enjoy important economies of scope in the development of digital products and services. A company does indeed benefit from shareable inputs that can be used or re-used for different outputs, as it happens when Apple uses its in-house range of processors in its iPhones and iPads. However, the key point about digital ecosystems is that the output of code programming can be scaled up rather quickly, as it is applicable to any conceived product or service. This makes it relatively easy to leap from one digital product/service to another.[27]

---

[25]On the specific case of the Apple ecosystem, see Jeff Carlson and Dan Moren, *The Connected Apple Family: Discover the Rich Apple Ecosystem of the Mac, iPhone, iPad, and Apple TV* (Peachpit Press 2014).

[26]For an overview of the competitive complexities arising from a digital conglomerate, see Marc Bourreau and Alexandre de Streel, 'Digital Conglomerates and EU Competition Policy' [2019] <https://papers.ssrn.com/sol3/papers.cfm?abstract_id=3350512> accessed 1 February 2020.

[27]Another example is a smart home which can allow the minimization of energy consumption by the coordination of the different components, while guaranteeing user comfort, cf Christian Reinisch, Mario J Kofler and Wolfgang Kastner, 'ThinkHome: A Smart Home as Digital Ecosystem' in IEEE, *2010 4th IEEE International Conference on Digital Ecosystems and Technologies (DEST 2010)* (IEEE 2010).

On the demand-side, companies exploit consumption synergies derived by consumers when adopting product ecosystems.[28] Consumers can positively value purchasing different products or services from the same seller and can enjoy a full-range user experience.[29] Such consumption synergies may be of different types. They may derive from bundling (for example, if consumers value receiving a single bill). They may also involve lower transaction costs (e.g. lower search costs for individual products). Consumption synergies from linkage within an ecosystem arise from shared functionalities between products within the ecosystem. One should not forget, however, that demand-side (consumption) synergies differ from supply-side synergies (economies of scope) in that consumers may not uniformly value consumption synergies.[30] For example, consumers may have different opportunity costs of time, some higher some lower, and thus they will perceive different benefits from one-stop shopping.

Besides, digital companies are always greedy for data from diverse sources, with the intention to combine them and glean a variety of information from them. Ecosystems, via differentiation, support this strategy by collecting data that describes consumers' different preferences and habits.[31] Furthermore, ecosystems result from the attempt of big companies to tug and chase each other on different markets and to develop different innovations.[32]

However, there are cases when even a company like Apple may prefer compatibility over incompatibility. This usually happens when a company is not dominant in the market or niche in question. For example, Apple provides its personal computers with word processor (Pages) whose documents are synced across all users' available Apple devices, such as other Apple computers, iPhones, etc. But in this case users are still able to export their documents in a format that is compatible with Microsoft's Word, merely because otherwise they would be rather useless, with Apple's share of this particular market being just a small fraction when compared with Microsoft's.

[28] Bourreau and de Streel (n 26) 7.

[29] Nicolas Petit, 'Technology Giants, the Moligopoly Hypothesis and Holistic Competition: A Primer' [2016] <https://papers.ssrn.com/sol3/papers.cfm?abstract_id=2856502> accessed 1 February 2020.

[30] Zhijun Chen and Patrick Rey, 'A Theory of Conglomerate Mergers' [2015] <https://editorialexpress.com/cgi-bin/conference/download.cgi?db_name=EARIE42&paper_id=224> accessed 1 February 2020.

[31] Petit (n 29).

[32] ibid.

3 The Reaction of Antitrust Law

When it comes to the role of EU antitrust law toward technological incompatibilities, we should remember that antitrust law is neutral. It should never be thought of as a tool to favour the interoperability between technologies *ex ante,* but only to assess *ex-post* whether incompatibility has harmed the well-functioning of the market by impairing its natural evolution.[33] With this in mind we will consider the main scenarios that antitrust law could face concerning firms' conducts that interfere with technological compatibilities relevant to the smart mobility framework.

The most basic scenario is the one in which a company producing a component of the smart mobility system has become so dominant in its relevant market that its own technology is a *de facto* standard. In this scenario, other players are forced to follow its standard in order to maintain compatibility. Nevertheless, it may happen that the company creates incompatibility and, therefore, excludes its rivals from the relevant market. Here, antitrust law should rule on dominance, according to Art. 102 of the Treaty on the Functioning of the European Union (TFEU), since a firm can abuse of its dominance by creating technological incompatibility or by reducing the existing technological compatibility. In this context, it is important to clarify that the same abusive conduct could be qualified in different ways. In other words, any time a unilateral conduct creates incompatibility we could consider the possibility of a violation of Art. 102 TFEU, with a series of infractions that could be envisaged.

First, suppose that the company managing the smart mobility grid launches a new version of it and makes it less compatible with third parties' applications (products or services) by changing its interface. In such a case, there could be grounds for accusing the company of pursuing a predatory innovation strategy,[34] because the dominant firm is adopting an innovation with the sole scope of introducing an incompatibility which would limit competition without benefiting consumers. The predatory nature of the conducts depends on the fact that the dominant firm is not improving its own product, but has chosen this conduct only to create a technological incompatibility. Therefore, the innovation introduced could be qualified as a sham innovation which is justified only by the negative effects produced on the

[33]Mariateresa Maggiolino, 'The Regulatory Breakthrough of Competition Law: Definitions and Worries', in Josef Drexl and Fabiana di Porto (eds), *Antitrust as Regulation* (Edward Elgar 2015).

[34]Janusz A Ordover and Robert Willig, 'An Economic Definition of Predation: Pricing and Product Innovation' (1981) 91 Yale Law Journal 8; Richard J Gilbert, 'Holding Innovation to an Antitrust Standard' (2007) 3 Competition Policy International 47; Joseph G Sidak, 'Debunking Predatory Innovation' (1983) 83 Columbia Law Review 1121, 1135; Carlos Acuña-Quiroga, 'Predatory Innovation: A Step Beyond? Understanding Competition in High-technology Markets' (2001) 15 International Review of Law, Computers & Technology 7; Mariateresa Maggiolino, *Intellectual Property and Antitrust: A Comparative Economic Analysis of US and EU Law* (Edward Elgar 2011) 115; Thibault Schrepel, 'Predatory Innovation: The Definite Need for Legal Recognition' (2017) 21 SMU Science & Technology Law Review 19.

competition.[35] However, the hypothesis of a predatory innovation is residual and mainly theoretical, especially in the European Union.

Second, suppose that the new version of the smart mobility grid is not a sham innovation and that the rivals of the company require the company managing the smart mobility grid to share the interoperability codes governing the interface. In general terms, to protect its own incentive to innovate, the dominant firm is not obliged to share its technical specifications.[36] But there are some exceptions that allow a public authority to force the *de facto* standard holder to share its technical specifications with its competitors. Such an activity would require a demanding process for guaranteeing profits for the standard-setter, an operation whose costs might outweigh the benefits.[37] In other words, forcing the interconnection through regulation and antitrust tools, with certain conditions, may incur in a consumer welfare loss.[38] Antitrust law could decide not to intervene on the technological change introduced to create incompatibility, but to impose technological compatibility on the basis that the information necessary to develop interoperability within a smart mobility system is an *essential facility*.[39] Indeed, under the refusal-to-deal doctrine, a number of conditions need to be established in order to prove that the refusal is unlawful. These are market dominance; harm to competition and absence of objective justifications, when there was a pre-existing business relationship between the parties[40] (or, as an alternative, the essential nature of the claimed resource, if there were no pre-existing business relationships).[41] In the specific case where the claimed resource is protected by an intellectual property right, the plaintiff must meet an additional condition, i.e. demonstrate that the refusal prevents

[35]Gilbert (n 34); Pablo Ibanez Colomo, 'Restrictions on Innovation in EU Competition Law' [2016] EL Rev 41; Richard J Gilbert, 'Looking for Mr. Schumpeter: Where Are We in the Competition-Innovation Debate' in Adam B Jaffe, Josh Lerner and Scott Stern (eds), *Innovation Policy and the Economy*, vol 6 (University of Chicago Press 2006).

[36]The economic literature shows that innovation is likely to be affected via interoperability-centric measures: fostering interoperability could provoke a decrease in investments in developing innovation as well as intellectual property protected new technologies; see Turgut A Beydogan, 'Interoperability-Centric Problems: New Challenges and Legal Solutions' (2010) 18 International Journal of Law and Information Technology 301. Wolfgang Kerber, 'Competition, Innovation and Competition Law: Dissecting the Interplay' in Bernd Meyring, Damien Gerard and Eric Morgan de Rivery (eds), *Dynamic markets, Dynamic competition and Dynamic Enforcement* (Bruylant 2018).

[37]Soon-Yong Choi and Andrew B Whinston, 'Benefits and Requirements for Interoperability in the Electronic Marketplace' (2000) 22 Technology in Society 33.

[38]Spulber (n 13).

[39]Maggiolino, *Intellectual Property and Antitrust* (n 34) 133.

[40]Joined Cases 6/73 and 7/73 *Istituto Chemioterapico Italiano SpA and Commercial Solvents Corporation v. EC Commission* [1974] ECR 225.

[41]Case C-7/97 *Oscar Bronner GmbH & Co. KG v Mediaprint Zeitungs- und Zeitschriftenverlag GmbH & Co. KG, Mediaprint Zeitungsvertriebsgesellschaft mbH & Co. KG and Mediaprint Anzeigengesellschaft mbH & Co. KG* [1998] ECR I-7791.

a technical development.[42] Therefore, the recurrence of the essential facility doctrine requirements should be verified on a case-by-case basis. This hypothesis is much more likely to be pursued within the EU rather than predatory innovation.

Third, the company changing the smart mobility grid could launch a new version together with new applications which displace those of rivals and are combined with the new grid. In such a case, the creation of incompatibility by a dominant firm operating in a smart mobility system could also be abusive in the form of a *technical tying*, that is, putting together products that were separated which results in technical incompatibility. In other words, a dominant company physically integrates its (previously separated) products, generating a lack of interoperability.[43] Therefore, antitrust law would intervene on the tying conduct.[44] In order to prove the existence of an unlawful tying, the following conditions should be matched: dominance; the existence of two separated markets; coercion; harm to competition; and absence of an objective justification.[45] The detection of an abuse of a dominant position by tying is as common as the essential facility scenario within the EU dimension.

Fourth, consider a totally different scenario where firms operating in a smart mobility framework naturally move in the direction of establishing technological interoperability. In this context, the setting of standards could cover a leading role in achieving the interoperability, with different forms of partnerships (private-private or public-private) possible. The standardisation process usually relies on the market players via standard-setting efforts—for example, by identifying features that should be compatible for the benefit of all those that take part in the process. It could also happen that firms which are part of a smart mobility system decide to establish a standard-setting organisation (SSO) to create standards and, as a consequence, technological compatibility. Indeed, all competing suppliers should be authorised to participate and, therefore, the superior supplier should share the benefits of its investment to produce industry standards.[46]

This standard-setting among firms operating in the smart city framework would entail a partnership and, for its own nature, it would not guarantee that such a

---

[42]Joined Cases C-241/91 and 242/91 P *Radio Telefis Eireann and Others v Commission (Magill TV)* [1995] ECR I-743; Case C-418/01 *IMS Health GmbH & Co. OHG v NDC Health GmbH & Co. KG* [2004] ECR I-5039; Case T-201/04 *Microsoft Corp v Commission* [2007] ECR II-3601.

[43]Case T-201/04 *Microsoft Corp v Commission* [2007] ECR II-3601.

[44]Andrea Amelio and Bruno Jullien, 'Tying and Freebies in Two-sided Markets' (2012) 30 International Journal of Industrial Organization 436; Dennis W Carlton and Michael Waldman 'Theories of Tying and Implications for Antitrust' (2005) Johnson School Research Paper Series 24-06 <https://papers.ssrn.com/sol3/papers.cfm?abstract_id=809304> accessed 1 February 2020; Jay Pil Choi and Chrisodoulos Stefanidis 'Tying, Investment, and the Dynamic Leverage Theory' (2001) 32 RAND Journal of Economics 52; Jay Pil Choi, 'Tying and Innovation: A Dynamic Analysis of Tying Arrangements' (2004) 114 Economic Journal 83. More specifically, on software, see Qiang Yu, 'Technically Tying Applications to a Dominant Platform in the Software Market and Competition Law' (2015) 36 ECLR 160.

[45]See the part of Microsoft decision concerning Windows Media Player, cf Case T-201/04 *Microsoft Corp v Commission* [2007] ECR II-3601.

[46]Beydogan (n 36).

coordinated effort would not provoke anti-competitive effects on the market. In all the stages of the SSO its participants should respect antitrust rules and—since a standard constitutes an agreement between companies—should not adopt conducts in violation of Art. 101 TFEU.[47] SSOs cannot be exclusionary, except for technical and quality-driven reasons: they cannot monopolise a technology which becomes a standard by preventing whoever is interested in using that technology from having access to the SSO. In addition, the SSO cannot become a place where competitors exchange sensitive information and thereby a disguised forum for collusion.[48]

3.1 The Recent **Google-Enel** *Case*

In the context of smart mobility, on 8 May 2019 the Italian Competition Authority (Autorità Garante della Concorrenza e del Mercato) started an investigation against Google for an alleged abuse of dominance[49] in the market for licensable smart mobile operating systems.[50] Specifically, Google owns the operating system for Android smartphones and tablets, around which it has built an ecosystem for smart devices that includes the Android Auto extension, which enables some apps and smartphone functions (e.g. calls or messages) to display on a car's screen, and to be accessed via car controls and voice commands. In addition, Google has developed and maintains Google Maps, which provides not only static information on places (maps) and directions on how to reach destinations of interest, but also real-time information on traffic, shops and utilities in a given area, as well as booking services through agreements with third-party operators.

---

[47]Ruben Schellingerhout, 'Standard-Setting from a Competition Law Perspective' (2011) 1 Competition Policy Newsletter 3. Concerning the Consolidated Version of the Treaty on the Functioning of the European Union [2012] OJ C326/47 (TFEU), art 101(3), see Communication of the Commission, 'Guidelines on the applicability of Article 101 of the Treaty on the Functioning of the European Union to horizontal co-operation agreements' [2011] OJ C11/01.

[48]Choi and Whinston (n 37); Mark A Lemley, 'Antitrust and the Internet Standardization Problem' (1996) 28 Connecticut Law Review 1041.

[49]In its decision *Google Android* (Case AT.40099) Commission Decision 2019/C 402/08 [2018] OJ C402/19, the European Commission concluded that through its control of the Android operating system, Google holds a dominant position in the market for licensable smart mobile operating systems. This is due to the fact that Google has a market share of more than 95% and the existence of entry barriers, also related to the network effects (the greater the number of end users of the Android operating system, the greater the number of developers of compatible apps). The Commission has also assessed that at the level of end-users (who decide which device to buy and/or whether to switch from one operating system to another), Apple devices do not exercise influence over those devices, <https://europa.eu/rapid/press-release_IP-18-4581_en.htm> accessed 1 February 2020.

[50]<www.agcm.it/dotcmsdoc/allegati-news/A529_avvio%20istrutt_omi.pdf> accessed 1 February 2020.

Enel has developed the Enel X Recharge app, which offers various functions related to the recharging of electric vehicles. Among its functions, the Enel X Recharge app allows the booking of car recharging points—as mentioned, a particularly critical feature, as recharging requires significantly longer times than refuelling. Enel X Recharge app was developed according to the guidelines provided by Google for compatible apps with Android Auto. In particular, user-app interaction can only take place with voice commands to ensure safe driving conditions.

In July 2018, Enel began developing the integration of Enel X Recharge into Android Auto and, on September 2018, Google refused to move forward with this integration. According to Enel, by unjustifiably refusing Enel's request to integrate the Enel X Recharge app into Android Auto, Google would be abusing its dominant position in the market for licensable smart mobile operating systems. In Enel's view, the scope of such a conduct would be to exclude a competitor's app from offering services to end-customers, so as to protect and consolidate the business model of Google Maps and its role as a single point of access to users and as a funnel for the data flow generated by their activities. This conduct is likely to significantly undermine the competitive dynamics in terms of the level of services offered, the breadth and variety of the offer, and innovation and diversity of business models, thus limiting consumers' choice and hindering the emergence of a merit-based competition. At the moment, the Italian Competition Authority is still carrying out an investigation, the deadline for which is set for 30 May 2020.[51]

To discuss Google's conduct as a drive toward greater incompatibility (see Sect. 2 above), we could consider that this strategy is likely to undermine the development of a digital service of *vertical* nature (i.e. dedicated to a specific purpose—in this case the provision of information and functions for recharging electric vehicles). Google is indeed strengthening a tool of *horizontal* nature, Google Maps, which aggregates a plurality of functions and services that Google previously acquired from the market and then integrated. A driver of an EV who starts using Google Maps—which currently is not compatible with EnelX Recharge app—will most likely become a locked-in Google customer and will not consider using EnelX services, as she would incur a switching cost. More generally, any new utility on the EV market that lacks compatibility with Google Maps will see its chances of being used by Google customers decrease. Then again it is hard to guess the nature of Google's anticompetitive strategy (if any such strategy actually exists): it could be that, by limiting Enel, it shelters its alleged dominant position in the market for operating systems. For example, it could be that Google wants to sell Android at a very low price, while extracting monopoly profits from the consumers in the applications market—but only the facts may support such a theory of harm.

In light of the competition law categories already framed (see Sect. 3), the challenge for the Italian competition authority will be to assess whether such conduct is unlawful, according to Art. 102 TFEU. To this end, the authority should first prove Google's dominance, though the relevant market is hard to define for this case as it

[51]ibid letter e, last page.

could be the market for operating systems for devices, operating systems for smart cars, or that of interactive maps. Second, the authority should prove that Google's refusal to deal with Enel forecloses competition, that is, it prevents Enel from reaching out for consumers. This evidence will depend on whether Enel has alternative channels to distribute its EnelX Recharge app or not. In order to exclude the existence of further channels for Enel, it should be demonstrated that the exclusion from Google's ecosystem translates into an exclusion from the overall market, which would be the case if Google's operating system was an essential facility. Third, the Italian authority should verify whether there are objective justifications for Google's refusal.

In this preliminary stage of the investigation, as a matter of speculation, two hypotheses can be elaborated regarding the reasons underpinning Google's strategy. First, Google fears that Enel, via the Google-compatible software that it has already developed, will challenge Google dominance and its own technology, at least in a niche such as geo-localisation systems, software for smart cars, and so forth. Second, Google may be interested in pursuing a strategy that involves removing rivals from the secondary market to shift there the market power it already holds in the primary market. The ultimate goal of this would be the selling of primary products (operating systems) at a cheap price, while charging monopolistic profits on the secondary products (applications). Actually, even in lack of dominance, this could be a good strategy for working toward a monopoly. Indeed, it would allow Google to acquire a large consumer base thanks to its cheap operating system, without running the risk of losing profits (because it could then apply high prices for applications to the now locked-in consumers).

4 Conclusions

In this chapter, we have tried to show how the creation of a smart city and, therefore, the development of a smart mobility grid requires a deep reflection on the issue of technological interoperability.

If an administrator, for example, were to entrust the development of the city grid to a company via an exclusive agreement, without imposing any interoperability obligation, this administrator would run two risks. First, the means of transportation in her city might not communicate with those in her region or other locations—if these have not adopted the same technology. Second, the administrator might find herself to be bound to the company indefinitely, perhaps due to unmanageable switching costs.

Of course, antitrust law could intervene in this context, via the application of Art. 102 TFEU, to force the company developing the grid to make its technology interoperable with those of others. However, this intervention would be lengthy and costly, and it would probably have an uncertain outcome, as with most legal matters that are breaking new ground. Therefore, without prejudice to future antitrust actions, an administrator should require a company to ensure that its smart mobility grid is interoperable, especially in the case of exclusive agreements. In other words, this is a situation where *ex ante* and regulatory intervention would be preferable to an *ex post* adjudication intervention.

In the same way, if the administrator wanted to involve several companies in the creation or development of the smart mobility grid, she would better translate into regulatory terms what the antitrust law suggests in relation to standard setting organisations (see Sect. 3 above). That is, she should take care of the need to develop a technology whose interoperability is based solely on technical and quality reasons. Public regulation would therefore appear to be the most appropriate tool to foster the establishment of industry-wide (public or private) technological standards while ensuring the presence of an adequate anti-collusion framework—which should be strong, naturally, but not so overzealous regarding the standard-setting activities themselves.

As an alternative to command-and-control regulation, the public administration could incentivise the adoption of standards by providing private players with relevant guidelines that identify the preferred interoperability and standardisation models (that is, those that in abstract terms would not produce anti-competitive effects). Guidelines dealing specifically with the smart mobility framework would definitely favour the needed interoperability in the field.[52] Overall, by incentivising interoperability, public authorities would provide consumers with a superior product or service.

[52]Antonio Garrido-Marijuan, Yana Pargova and Cordelia Wilson, 'The Making of a Smart City: Best Practices Across Europe' (EU Smart Cities Information System 2017) <www.smartcities-infosystem.eu/sites/default/files/document/the_making_of_a_smart_city_-_best_practices_across_europe.pdf> accessed 1 February 2020.

Efficient Mobility: Lessons on Dynamic Pricing and Sustainable Passenger Service

Martin Fries

Contents

Abstract The Internet of Things is increasingly delivering high-precision mobility data. This makes it possible to fine-tune the use of scarce mobility goods and services and thus achieve higher system efficiency. In the future, it will be feasible to put a price tag on even the smallest traffic areas and auction them off to the highest bidder. This will enable congestion-free driving, search-free parking, and a trouble-free switching from road to rail and vice versa. Many contractual decisions will be made automatically on the basis of previously determined preferences, without the individual noticing anything. At the same time, the increase in data created in this system will also lead to new manipulation potential. The intelligent legislator will try to make the opportunities of the Internet of Things possible while at the same time limiting the associated risks.

Martin Fries, PD Dr., is Lecturer at the Ludwig-Maximilians-Universität, Munich, Germany.

M. Fries (✉)
Ludwig-Maximilians-Universität, Munich, Germany
e-mail: martin.fries@jura.uni-muenchen.de

M. Finck et al. (eds.), *Smart Urban Mobility*, MPI Studies on Intellectual Property and Competition Law 29, https://doi.org/10.1007/978-3-662-61920-9_12

1 Introduction

Recent data protection regulation has not stopped the economy from developing more and more sophisticated ideas on how to collect large amounts of data and use that data in order to tailor products and services to the needs of individuals. The crucial promise of a data-driven economy is the aspiration to increase system efficiency and thus maximize societal welfare. However, a system fueled with data is subject to considerable vulnerabilities which, with an increasing degree of system automation, appear all the more urgent.

Where products and services can be almost endlessly supplied, as in the field of electronic commerce, data-driven sales lead to higher consumption triggered by individually targeted advertisements and price discrimination. In contrast, where the goods provided are scarce like in public networks, which can be enlarged only in a slow and complicated process of forming public opinion and obtaining majority approval, the challenge is to design rights distribution processes that stick with the core principles of effective data protection, genuine self-determination, and allow for equal opportunities in realizing private autonomy.

Against this background, this contribution explores the impact of big data on the use and distribution of mobility goods using various examples of modern mobility options (Sect. 2). Afterwards, the article takes a look at questions of contract law and namely deals with the intricacies of law interacting with data-driven code (Sect. 3). The following section deals with rather fundamental legal questions beyond contract law relating to the interplay of law and code in a networked society (Sect. 4). The final section concludes with an outlook on the current need for action with regard to long-term sustainable mobility (Sect. 5).

2 Big Mobility Data and Efficiency Gains Through Auction Structures

What kind of mobility data should be expected to be available in the near future? How will this kind of data help to increase system efficiency?

2.1 Increasing Amounts of Mobility Data

The most obvious bottleneck of population mobility is scarce driving space. As of today, unhindered driving on the streets of big cities and on many highways is only possible at nighttime. This is true not only for central Europe but also for the coastal metropolitan areas of the United States and in Eastern Asia. The reason for this phenomenon is not only excessive demand of driving space and inappropriate driving style but also insufficient distribution of cars on the available roads, inflexible driving priority regulation, and insufficient knowledge of the extent of road use.

At the same time, the increasing percentage of data-sending cars and passenger devices allow for very precise predictions on the current supply and demand of driving space.[1] A large portion of this data is already generated today due to the fact that navigation services such as Google Maps or Apple Maps are connected to a number of drivers sufficient to report current and predict future usage of streets. However, only a small percentage of drivers currently base their decisions on these services, and those who do so do not maximize collective welfare but only pursue their own individual utility which, because of the structural dilemma of the game, eventually leads to a non-efficient overall outcome.

The observations for the use of parking spots are very similar to the situation regarding scarce driving space. In many conurbations there is far too little parking space available. On the one hand, this leads to massive expenditure of time in the search for a parking space and, on the other hand, it causes recoil effects on the available road space, i.e. when parking space search traffic congests roads. Data on available parking spots is not yet available on the large web mapping services; however, it is already collected by many local parking systems and bundled by innovative service providers displaying the formerly scattered data within one application.[2] Systematically making use of that data could easily optimize the use of public parking areas. The same idea is also applicable to battery charging spots, which, due to public funding, are rarely over-demanded at the moment, but will also become a scarce resource in the foreseeable future.[3]

---

[1]Increasingly, it is not the free decision of car manufacturers, but a legal requirement that vehicles can send and receive data. For example, Parliament and Council Regulation (EU) 2015/758 of 29 April 2015 concerning type-approval requirements for the deployment of the eCall in-vehicle system based on the 112 service and amending Directive 2007/46/EC [2015] OJ L123/77, arts 4ff requires car manufacturers to equip vehicles with an automatic emergency call system and thus to establish some sort of a permanently available communication option with State-run institutions. Aside from that, Parliament and Council Regulation (EU) 2019/631 of 17 April 2019 setting CO2 emission performance standards for new passenger cars and for new light commercial vehicles, and repealing Regulations (EC) No 443/2009 and (EU) No 510/2011 [2019] OJ L111/13, art 7 requires the EU Member States to collect carbon dioxide emission data from new cars in the near future.

[2]See, eg, the apps provided by *Easypark* (<https://easypark.de/en> accessed 16 July 2020), *parkingpay* (<https://parkingpay.ch> accessed 16 July 2020), and *ParkNow* (<https://www.your-now.com/de/our-solutions/park-now> accessed 16 July 2020).

[3]Exemplary proposals for the technical implementation of these ideas can be found at Aditya Vikram Agarwal, Navneet Verma and Sanjeev Kumar, 'Intelligent Decision Making Real-Time Automated System for Toll Payments' in Basant Tiwari and others (eds), *Proceedings of International Conference on Recent Advancement on Computer and Communication: ICRAC 2017* (Springer 2018) 223; Segun I Popoola and others, 'A Cloud-Based Intelligent Toll Collection System for Smart Cities' in Pushpak Bhattacharyya and others (eds), *Smart and Innovative Trends in Next Generation Computing Technologies* (Springer 2018) 653.

2.2 Sale of Rights to the Highest Bidder

The inefficient overuse of free and public goods is well-known to economists as the *tragedy of the commons*.[4] The standard solution here is the creation of property rights or usage rights of similar kind. With regard to public driving and parking space, this idea could not be implemented so far because regulation basically does not work out at a micro level. In contrast, the artificial shortage and sale of public goods is well known in the field of public transport, where people usually have to pay money to be allowed to travel.[5] In the field of road traffic, this is still the absolute exception. In many countries, costly road sections such as tunnels or bridges or individual motorway sections may be subject to a charge. Even where this is the case, however, the sale of driving rights is usually not intended as a reaction to a specific shortage situation but takes place in a rigid format that has little to do with the situation-dependent control of traffic flows. Exceptions prove the rule.[6]

Whereas unlimited release of road space was almost inevitable as long as the actual usage of driving space could hardly be monitored, the situation fundamentally changes when taking into account that today it is possible to observe traffic flows in real time and flexibly steer them according to the respective situation. Where sufficient traffic data is available, it is a simple calculation task for a traffic coordinator to distribute the available space in a way that maximizes efficiency.[7] Such a coordinator will model the distribution of driving rights as an auction in which those who win bid the most because—according to economic theory[8]—they get the most out of it. The number of driving rights sold will be determined by the permeability of the respective street. At intersections with varying intensity of road use, smart traffic lights help to keep the traffic flowing.[9]

---

[4]Garrett Hardin, 'The Tragedy of the Commons' (1968) 162 Science 1243.

[5]The exception proves the rule. The Estonian capital Tallinn is one of the rare examples where public transportation has been free for local residents since 2013.

[6]In Singapore, since 1998, motorists are charged a toll on their account, the amount of which depends on the time of day when they drive which route. Several European cities have since followed this example. A detailed analysis of the Oslo toll cordon is provided by James Odeck and Morten Welde, 'Economic Evaluation of Intelligent Transportation Systems Strategies: the Case of the Oslo Toll Cordon' (2010) 4 IET Intelligent Transport Systems 221.

[7]See, eg, Ram Singh, 'Economic Efficiency', *Encyclopedia of Law and Economics* (living edition, 2018) <https://link.springer.com/referenceworkentry/10.1007/978-1-4614-7883-6_206-1> accessed 16 July 2020, with further references.

[8]The theory neglects unequal wealth, which would ideally be compensated at the level of income and wealth taxation. If this approach is not followed, it is possible to multiply the offers made in the auction by an inverse income or wealth factor.

[9]In theory, auction processes could even be extended to the driving style. For example, if a driver going 130 mph has a higher space-time-consumption than someone driving at 70, she could be allowed to do so at a proportionate higher price.

In such a system, cars and buses with a higher number of occupied seats are, without a high-occupancy vehicle lane[10] or assignment of special bidding privileges, awarded priority driving as they will usually outbid single drivers in the auction process. People for whom rapid mobility is not so important are referred to slower alternate routes or to off-peak times in this system. The restriction of their mobility seems justified in view of the gain in rapid mobility for the winners of the auction. At the same time, every individual has the freedom to secure travel rights through higher bids. And the organizer of the transport infrastructure is free to improve the scarce network in order to increase general mobility. Of course, resources should only be invested to the extent that one can expect them to be recouped later through the auctioning of travel rights.

The situation regarding parking space is slightly different, as in recent years parking was made much more costly in many city centers. Thus, it is already not unusual that temporary space usage rights are sold at a price that increases with higher demand.[11] However, due to a lack of flexibility even the current parking system is far from being efficient. The use of data on usual and current use of parking space still bears a huge potential to minimize parking space search traffic. And again, an excess demand of parking space can easily be managed by auctioning off parking rights to the highest bidder. In the same way, battery charging spots can be auctioned to the neediest individual or car.

2.3 *Consequences for the Overall Mobility System*

The economization of public transport spaces associated with the use of data-driven auction structures extends far beyond road traffic. Similar structures can be implemented in public or semi-public means of transport like rental cars, buses, subways, trains, and aircraft. Of course, the providers of these means of transport already set ticket prices depending on the respective demand. However, many of them still use pricing systems that are far too rigid and thus far removed from efficiency. For example, most subway tickets follow an extreme flat-rate pricing approach according to which there is no difference between travelling 1 or 10 miles, no surcharge from the fourth ride of the day, and no distinction between going as the sole passenger or as one out of 300. For a long time, the monopolists and oligopolists driving this system had little incentives to gather more data for a more sophisticated

[10]Such a special lane for vehicles is well-known, eg, in Norway, California and Canada. Some central European States provide separate bus lanes with a similar goal. The economic problem with such lanes is, however, an often obvious underuse, as these lanes remain unused for most of the time.

[11]This is especially true for large US cities like Los Angeles, San Francisco and Washington, D.C. For details of the conceptual framework, see Shobhit Shanker and Syed Masud Mahmud, 'An Intelligent Architecture for Metropolitan Area Parking Control and Toll Collection' [2005] IEEE Proceedings 723.

pricing approach. However, with the advent of smartphone tickets and electronic check-in procedures, the signs for a more differentiated and overall fairer traffic organization system are meanwhile quite promising.[12]

A data-driven approach to set public transportation ticket prices would also bear consequences for the competition between different means of transport. A well-informed switch from road to rail and bus and vice versa seems much more realistic where the price tags adhering to the respective transport options approximately reflect the associated costs. The model also allows for effective consideration of ecological needs because externalities[13] can be accounted for by means of ecotaxes imposed depending on how much carbon dioxide is released by a certain means of transport.[14]

3 The Contract Law of New Mobility

How can new forms of data handling and pricing in a modern mobility-driven world be reflected by contract law? There are considerable challenges with regard to contract design, contract performance, and the breach of contractual obligations.

3.1 Contract Design in the Digital Sphere

The flexible design of mobility offers comes along with crucial features that modern contract law must be able to deal with appropriately. An important aspect is that the mobile individual cannot oversee every detail and every spontaneous change in pricing in a flexible mobility service contract. This leads to the fact that the concrete layout of the mobility option ultimately taken up is spontaneously selected by a software solution according to the situation. The contractually bound individual will neither necessarily experience this software decision in real time nor be able to understand it afterwards without considerable effort.

One way of overcoming these difficulties in concluding contracts is to shadow the natural person with a fictitious electronic person who, like a legal person, could independently conclude contracts and be liable with her assets for any breaches of contractual obligations.[15] It is questionable, however, what advantages would be

---

[12]One of the early adopters of distance-related prices was the Californian train operator Caltrain which implemented a tag-on-tag-off procedure to calculate travel fares already ten years ago.

[13]See Ronald H Coase, 'The Problem of Social Cost' [1960] The Journal of Law & Economics 1.

[14]For details, see below Sect. 5.

[15]See Committee on Legal Affairs, *Report with recommendations to the Commission on Civil Law Rules on Robotics* (2015/2103(INL), 2017) <https://www.europarl.europa.eu/doceo/document/A-8-2017-0005_EN.html> accessed 16 July 2020. A similar, even more decisive proposal was made

associated with such an e-person compared to the already widely recognized construct of a legal person. The need for regulation is particularly doubtful if a natural person would have to be liable anyway for each e-person.[16]

Above all, however, the applicable law already contains viable possibilities to conclude contracts with the help of electronic agents. For example, every transaction on the online auction platform eBay is concluded via automatic bidding agents who conclude a contract under certain conditions on a route specified by the bidder. The auctioning of mobility options would not differ significantly from this from the point of view of contract law. Like in the eBay example, road users would offer an individually determined amount for a right to drive on a motorway which is temporarily narrowed due to a construction site. Those whose bids are not successful would, depending on their preferences, be allocated either a less popular time or a different route or even a different mode of transport.

The comparison with eBay also answers the question of the transparency of the *essentialia negotii* in the run-up to the conclusion of the contract, which is of great importance for contract law. For a system of flexible mobility options, it seems to be quite sufficient if the mobility user can view the criteria for pricing in good time. A legislative regulation with respect to surprising price developments would be desirable, however, as Art. 5 of the European Council Directive 93/13/EEC on unfair terms in consumer contracts has no effect on pricing itself.

3.2 Contract Performance

The more mobility contracts make the choice of route and means of transport dependent on spontaneous circumstances in the individual case, the greater the importance of data sources, oracles and contract performance software. Legal theory on smart contracts has quite unanimously carved out that, even if a contract was translated into software, the rules stipulated in the classical contract still legally prevail.[17] However, given the actual power of the code, frictions between contract and software will hardly be legally dealt with in practice. This might make the legislator think about defining rules for a proper design of contract performance software in order to avoid strong players orchestrating an unfair allocation of goods that is usually not altered through legal claims.

quite some time ago by Steffen Wettig and Eberhard Zehender, 'A Legal Analysis of Human and Electronic Agents' (2004) 12 AI & Law 111.

[16]Gerhard Wagner, 'Robot liability' [2019] Working Paper No 2 des Forschungsinstituts für Recht und digitale Transformation <http://www.rewi.hu-berlin.de/de/lf/oe/rdt/pub/working-paper-no-2> accessed 16 July 2020, with further references.

[17]Max Raskin, 'The Law and Legality of Smart Contracts' (2017) 1 Georgetown Law Technology Review 304; Alexander Savelyev 'Contract Law 2.0: "Smart" Contracts as the Beginning of the End of Classic Contract Law' (2017) 26 Information & Communications Technology Law 116.

Specifically, for software managing mobility services, this means that legislators could have a say on which data sources may be fed into the software, who has sovereignty over the data provided, and to which assessments and controls the data may be subject. Legislation could also determine which obligations of the contracting parties must be reflected in the code and how the pricing criteria are to be made visible to end customers.

3.3 *Breach of Contract*

When designing contract performance software, particular attention should always be paid to dealing with breaches of duty by both contracting parties. What are the payment obligations of the high-bidding end customer if she gets stuck in a traffic jam despite smart traffic management? To what extent should the provider be liable for the promised success, i.e. the arrival at the destination at a certain point in time? And what sanctions in the form of fines or even a vehicle ban are linked to driving on routes that have not been cleared for the person concerned, for example, because she did not bid high enough in the auction of driving rights?

At this point, the tasks of contract law include, on the one hand, respecting and safeguarding the freedom of any individual to creatively design contracts and, on the other hand, protecting end users from an unbalanced design of contract performance software to their disadvantage. There is no doubt that, in a matter like this one, contract law is increasingly becoming a sort of law on appropriate software design. In the coming years, legal science will have to examine in detail what legal course seems appropriate for this.

4 Legal Challenges in a Networked Society

Even with the technicalities of contract law solved, a number of fundamental open topics remain that legal science has to discuss in the years to come. This concerns questions of price discrimination and data protection as well as issues of pricing transparency and the problem of increasing software dependency.

4.1 *Price Discrimination and Data Protection*

A pricing system based on individual preferences can take into account not only the individual willingness to pay but also other personal circumstances beyond the specific traffic situation when setting prices. Any personal information from the usage data of a vehicle, the payment data of a bank, or the cookies of a browser could be used as a starting point for such personalized pricing. For example, the system may make wealthy people or people with poor payment habits pay comparatively high prices. In return, persons with high maintenance obligations or good payment habits could receive correspondingly reduced prices.

The promise of this kind of price discrimination would be increased consumption for poorer individuals and a higher level of efficiency in the market. At the same time, such an adaptation of the auction system would amount to different taxation of different categories of persons, without any discernible connection to the traffic situation. Moreover, it is questionable whether price differentiation on the basis of personal data complies with fundamental rights and obligatory rules of data protection.

The European Union has pointed out in a number of legal acts including the General Data Protection Regulation No. 2016/679 and the JHA Directive No. 2016/680 that personal data is regarded as a non-commodity which should not be traded in business[18] and that only under exceptional circumstances may it be accessed by public authorities without the consent of the person concerned. A data-driven system of traffic space allocation, however, would not work without private individuals making available at least their location data to some clearing organization, which then calculates the appropriate price and assigns driving or parking rights.[19]

There is broad agreement that proper data protection requires such a clearing institution to immediately delete the respective personal data when the rights assignment is over. Such an institution must not be allowed to save a data history of private individuals without their genuine and explicit consent even if such use of data would allow for more precise traffic predictions. Thus, price discrimination is not simply impermissible under current European law but is nevertheless subject to high standards of data protection law that are difficult to meet, particularly in relation to consumers.

The assessment is not significantly different if prices are differentiated with regard to directly traffic-related reasons. There are quite a number of traffic-related criteria that could be taken into account when setting a price tag on the use of scarce traffic space. A pricing mechanism could, for example, account for ecological aspects like the current passenger-vehicle ratio, for social aspects like the individual driving style, or for special priorities that might be given to civil servants or elderly people. Even if the relationship to the current traffic situation is closer here, the exploitation of personal data and the associated legal challenges remain.

[18]If, however, *non-personal* data is concerned, the legislative approach is quite the opposite, as the regulatory aim of the EU is the maximum free flow of data; see, eg, the Parliament and Council Regulation (EU) 2018/1807 of 14 November 2018 on a framework for the free flow of non-personal data in the European Union [2018] OJ L 303/59.

[19]As to the compatibility of this approach with Parliament and Council Regulation (EU) 2016/679 of 27 April 2016 on the protection of natural persons with regard to the processing of personal data and on the free movement of such data, and repealing Directive 95/46/EC (General Data Protection Regulation) [2016] OJ L119/1 (GDPR), art 22, see Michèle Finck, 'Smart Contracts as a Form of Solely Automated Processing Under the GDPR' (2019) 9 International Data Privacy Law 1.

Aside from that, one should bear in mind that these kinds of privileges not only raise difficult fairness issues[20] but essentially are an expression of a paternalistic approach that weakens the orientation to individual preferences associated with a pure auction system. Instead of assigning privileges, a liberal and efficiency-oriented approach would rather subsidize road users who enjoy some sort of priority so that they keep the choice of what they do. In this respect, individual willingness to pay remains the only relevant criterion for the allocation of traffic space usage rights. Even with this system design, there are data protection challenges, but these are at least comparatively easy to solve.[21]

4.2 Pricing Transparency

A pricing approach that is solely based on the individual's willingness to pay is comparably simple. However, the transparent presentation of the price drivers remains a challenge. For example, if the decision when to buy electricity for which price is deferred to an algorithm and a parking spot is automatically reserved by the smart car itself, the individual loses control over individual contracting decisions to a notable extent. It is doubtful whether this kind of black box contracting can be simply justified by the fact that the details of contracts are ignored anyway by most people. After all, the example of eBay shows that the contract law of today can already deal with these kinds of agreements. With regard to the freedom of action of those affected, it will be necessary here to demand that the determinants of price formation be made transparent in such a way that consumers interested in them can easily recognize them and, on this basis, correctly predict the payment obligations that will be incurred.

Anyone who bids for traffic space will then know that there is a minimum bid accounting for road maintenance and the like, and that the price increase is dependent on how many other people have decided to bid for the same spot. By setting a maximum bid, every driver keeps control of her expenditures. Unlike in a traditional system, where each travel or parking permit is purchased in advance at a fixed price, the perception margins in a flexible system are greater than the billing periods: road users will not reconsider at every intersection whether they should turn right at a high cost or left at a lower cost, but will leave this decision largely to the software. For reasons of transparency, however, there are no objections to this, as long as the pricing criteria are known and the participants can stop using traffic areas at any time.

[20] Details provided by Robert Brauneis and Ellen P Goodman, 'Algorithmic Transparency for the Smart City' (2017) 20 Yale Journal of Law & Technology 103, 122ff.

[21] Bart Custers and others, 'Data on the Move: Privacy of Road Pricing' (2010) 63 The Journal of Navigation 51.

4.3 *Software Dependencies*

Last but not least, any increase in system efficiency achieved through high-level data analysis comes along with a significant increase in dependency from high-quality data input and well-functioning traffic management software. Even a traffic system triggered to maximum efficiency can break down when there is a severe malfunction in the algorithm. This calls for the creation of redundancies and partially decoupled systems, which might come at a considerable price but, at the same time, insure people against a scenario of traffic anarchy that might bear unforeseeable consequences far beyond public traffic areas.

The associated challenge of investing in hedging mechanisms should not be underestimated. Many people are susceptible to hyperbolic discounting[22] and systematically underestimate the value of a running information system. Even if they know the importance of modern information intermediaries in the abstract, people tend to get easily used to the dependency as the new normal and will experience considerable disillusionment once the system they have become fond of shows unexpected failures.

Experience to date suggests that these risks will ultimately not be able to stop the triumphal march of algorithms. This is precisely why legislators should make an early effort not to leave traffic control software to its own devices. After all, where traffic *lights* regulate traffic today, the old traffic *signs* have been left standing for good reason.

5 Outlook: No Way Around Low-Emission Traffic

An efficient mobility system makes a decisive contribution to the welfare of society as a whole. The efficiency postulate is often misunderstood as a call for the unsparing capitalization of certain areas of life and additional privileges to wealthy social classes. But that is not the point: efficiency in the economic sense means a better ratio of resource consumption and social benefits.[23] At a time when excessive use of resources and excessive pollution are by far the most pressing policy needs,[24] this objective should better be unanimously supported.

There are frequent objections to making traffic flows more flexible and fluid, arguing that this would only make car traffic in particular more attractive, which

[22]For details on this phenomenon, see Robert H Strotz, 'Myopia and Inconsistency in Dynamic Utility Maximization' (1955-56) 23 The Review of Economic Studies 165; David Laibson, 'Golden Eggs and Hyperbolic Discounting' (1997) 112 The Quarterly Journal of Economics 443.

[23]See above n 6.

[24]From the multitude of statistics see only <https://climate.nasa.gov/vital-signs/carbon-dioxide/> accessed 16 July 2020 and <https://data.worldbank.org/topic/climate-change> accessed 16 July 2020.

would ultimately only exacerbate the problem. However, it is not convincing to want to resolve the ecological externalities of mobility by blocking certain traffic arteries, which in turn are harmful to the environment. Here, too, a look at economic theory proves helpful: it is the task of the legislator to internalize negative external effects for the benefit of society.[25]

With regard to the considerable CO_2 pollution of the environment caused by air and car traffic, this means that emissions have to be taxed at least at the level of their environmental impact, e.g. through a substantial[26] fuel tax which is not subsequently neutralized by other tax concessions.[27] Such a tax would contain an automatic incentive to refrain from journeys that are only attractive for the individual because the associated pollution burden is distributed across the entire population. In addition, such a tax would provide an incentive to use low-emission means of transport and to use them as fully as possible to reduce per capita emissions. In view of the urgent goal of prompt and significant CO_2 reduction, this approach would be far more effective than the rather timid efforts currently being made by the EU to collect and control the CO_2 consumption of new cars via the manufacturers.[28]

A concept of long-term sustainable mobility therefore needs both: on the one hand, intelligent traffic control through a flexible pricing system and, on the other hand, an unyielding taxation system that recoups the ecological damage caused by careless mobility. Time is running out.

[25]Andrew Torre, 'Externalities', *Encyclopedia of Law and Economics* (living edition, 2014) <https://link.springer.com/referenceworkentry/10.1007/978-1-4614-7883-6_40-1> accessed 16 July 2020, with further references.

[26]Recent research from British Columbia proves the economic prediction that timid carbon taxes have hardly any measurable effects; Felix Pretis, 'Does a Carbon Tax Reduce CO2 Emissions? Evidence from British Columbia' [2019/2020] Working Paper <https://ssrn.com/abstract=3329512> accessed 16 July 2020.

[27]Such neutralization effects have been observed in various European countries; see Boqiang Lin and Xuehui Li, 'The Effect of Carbon Tax on per Capita CO2 Emissions' (2011) 39 Energy Policy 5137. See, eg, § 9(1) No 4 of the German Income Tax Act (EStG) which establishes a tax privilege for commuters which will be increased from 2021 to offset the burden of a new carbon dioxide tax (that is already insufficient in itself).

[28]Parliament and Council Reg (EU) 2019/631, art 7 setting CO_2 emission performance standards for new passenger cars and for new light commercial vehicles.

Part III
Citizens' Perspective

Location Data as Contractual Counter-Performance: A Consumer Perspective on Recent EU Legislation

Zohar Efroni

Contents

Abstract This chapter analyses recent developments in the area of digital consumer law in the EU while focusing on the 'data as counter-performance' quandary and its application to location data. The immense technological and economic significance of location data in smart urban spaces renders them a relevant subject for inquiry in the context of ongoing legal efforts to protect consumers who grant permission to use their location data in exchange for digital goods and services.

This work has been funded by the Federal Ministry of Education and Research of Germany (BMBF) under grant No. 16DII111 ('Deutsches Internet-Institut'). Zohar Efroni, Dr., LL.M., is Research Group Lead at the Weizenbaum Institute for the Networked Society in Berlin, Humboldt University Law Faculty, Berlin, Germany.

Z. Efroni (✉)
Weizenbaum Institute for the Networked Society, Humboldt University Law Faculty, Berlin, Germany
e-mail: zohar.efroni@rewi.hu-berlin.de

M. Finck et al. (eds.), *Smart Urban Mobility*, MPI Studies on Intellectual Property and Competition Law 29, https://doi.org/10.1007/978-3-662-61920-9_13

1 Introduction

The classic problem of how to get from point A to point B in the most efficient and convenient way demands new solutions in our digital time and age, especially in modern cities, which are home to 70% of the EU population.[1] Technological solutions are predominantly based on the generation, collection and extensive use of electronic data. To name just one example, 'mobility as a service' (MaaS) stands for a technology-based platform solution in an urban setting that heavily relies on multiple mobility data sources.[2] Location data play a key role not only in MaaS platforms but also in many other data-driven solutions, technologies, products and business models that shape life in the hyper-connected environment powered by the growth of smartphones. The promise of location-based services and personalised mobility solutions for consumers is considerable, and so are the challenges and risks they pose to individual interests.

A recent privacy incident that has captured much media attention is illustrative. Apple's iPhone 11 Pro was reported to have continued collecting location data even when the user set the iPhone not to collect such data.[3] Namely, the phone continued pinging its GPS modules despite users' deliberate choice to disable this function.[4] In this way, contrary to users' expectations and possibly to Apple's own privacy policy, it was impossible to completely turn off location-based system services simply by individually switching off location services for all applications and system services. Rather, users needed to turn off all global location services in the device settings.

Apple replied to the allegation by explaining that the matter was rooted in the 'ultra wideband technology' embedded in the device.[5] This technology endows the

---

[1]EU Commission, 'Urban Mobility Package' (*European Commission*, 26 August 2020) <https://ec.europa.eu/transport/themes/clean-transport-urban-transport/urban-mobility/urban-mobility-package_en> accessed 26 August 2020.

[2]See eg Warwick Goodall and others, 'The Rise of Mobility as a Service: Reshaping how Urbanites Get Around' (2017) 20 Deloitte Review 112-129. In this review, MaaS is described as a model which, at its core, relies on a digital platform that integrates end-to-end trip planning, booking, electronic ticketing and payment services across all modes of transportation, public or private, ibid 114. For further analysis and the regulative dimensions of MaaS, see Yanying Li, 'The Role of Public Authorities in the Development of Mobility-as-a-Service', in Matthias Finger and Maxime Audouin (eds), *The Governance of Smart Transportation Systems: Towards New Organizational Structures for the Development of Shared, Automated, Electric and Integrated Mobility* (Springer 2019).

[3]Kate O'Flaherty, 'Apple's iPhone 11 Pro Collects Location Data, Even When Told Not To' (*Forbes*, 4 December 2019) <www.forbes.com/sites/kateoflahertyuk/2019/12/04/apple-iphone-11-iphone-11-pro-location-privacy-issue> accessed 21 February 2020.

[4]ibid: An IT security expert showed how GPS data are also collected when individual location services are disabled in the iPhone 11 Pro's settings. This happened even when users set their location services toggle to 'Never'.

[5]Zack Whittaker, 'Apple Says its Ultra Wideband Technology is Why Newer iPhones Appear to Share Location Data, Even When the Setting is Disabled' (*TechCrunch*, 5 December 2019) <https://techcrunch.com/2019/12/05/apple-ultra-wideband-newer-iphones-location> accessed 21 February 2020.

device with spatial awareness to identify other ultra wideband devices nearby. One application of this technology is enabling file sharing between devices via AirDrop.[6] Apple added that the management of ultra wideband compliance and its use of location data are done entirely on the device and that the company is not collecting user location data.[7] Still, the revelation was not particularly flattering for a company that takes pride in its comparatively strict privacy and security standards.[8]

The location data that mobile devices collect fuel giant, global and in some cases thinly regulated markets, which often operate and prosper entirely unnoticed by those who own the devices. A series of articles in *The New York Times* picked up the topic. As part of The Privacy Project, reporters obtained a file containing more than 50 billion location pings from over 12 million US citizens as they moved through several major cities such as Washington, San Francisco and Los Angeles.[9] The newspaper attained the data from a commercial location data company—one of dozens of its kind—that collects precise location data by utilising software included in mobile phone applications. The online article illustrates via the use of interactive heatmaps and analytics techniques how much can be learned about people simply by following their movement traces over time, and how easy it can be to obtain and use such data in the absence of effective regulation.[10] The report shows further how omnipresent surveillance is and how penetrative it can be. A US advertising executive was quoted as describing the location data industry there as 'the Wild West'.[11]

[6]Apple explained: 'Ultra wideband technology is an industry standard technology and is subject to international regulatory requirements that require it to be turned off in certain locations [...]. iOS uses Location Services to help determine if an iPhone is in these prohibited locations in order to disable ultra wideband and comply with regulations.', ibid.

[7]ibid: According to Apple, a new, dedicated toggle option for this feature will be included in upcoming iOS updates.

[8]See Apple's Privacy Governance Statement explaining its cross-functional approach to privacy governance, <www.apple.com/legal/privacy/en-ww/governance> accessed 21 February 2020: 'At Apple we design our products and services according to the principle of privacy by default and collect only the minimum amount of data necessary to provide our users with a product or service. We also deploy industry-leading consent mechanisms to allow our customers to choose whether to share data such as their Location, Contacts, Reminders, Photos, Bluetooth Sharing, Microphone, Speech Recognition, Camera, Health, HomeKit, Media & Apple Music and Motion & Fitness Data with apps.'

[9]Stuart A Thompson and Charlie Warzel, 'Opinion – The Privacy Project: Twelve Million Phones, One Dataset, Zero Privacy' *The New York Times* (19 December 2019) <www.nytimes.com/interactive/2019/12/19/opinion/location-tracking-cell-phone.html> accessed 21 February 2020.

[10]The report notes: 'You've probably never heard of most of the [data brokerage] companies—and yet to anyone who has access to this data, your life is an open book. They can see the places you go every moment of the day, whom you meet with or spend the night with, where you pray, whether you visit a methadone clinic, a psychiatrist's office or a massage parlor.', ibid.

[11]Stuart A Thompson and Charlie Warzel, 'Opinion – The Privacy Project: Smartphones are Spies. Here's Whom They Report To' *The New York Times* (20 December 2019) <www.nytimes.com/interactive/2019/12/20/opinion/location-tracking-smartphone-marketing.html> accessed 21 February 2020.

Shortly before this chapter went to print, a global crisis overshadowed all the problems location data have elicited so far, and for that matter, it dwarfed all other national, regional and global problems as well: As of July 15th 2020, the novel coronavirus (SARS CoV-2) has caused over thirteen million infection cases and over half a million deaths worldwide. In order to slow down its expansion rate and bring the spread of the pandemic under control, an early identification of infected individuals as well as all other individuals who have been in contact with them is considered critical: Knowing the mobility patterns of positively tested individuals during the relevant period, cross referencing this data with the location data (typically generated by smartphones) of all the persons who were in close physical contact with them, and then, based upon matches, taking preventive measures such as sending direct SMS warnings, ordering quarantine and isolation, conducting pinpointed testing, etc., is considered by many a promising [illegible] strategy to contain the disease.

This current example comes to briefly demonstrate both the enormous utility location data may have and the potential for misuse. In times of crisis such as these, the harm to privacy rights and even to the integrity of the political system in some democracies as a whole often go unnoticed. Less people ponder now whether a massive and unchecked collection of location data by the government as part of the measures it takes against a health disaster of this dimension is justified, proportionate and in conformity with fundamental rights.

In emergency situations, as in normal times, utilising location data is particularly prevalent in modern urban environments, in which mobility becomes ever 'smarter' and in which movement patterns can be ascertained and exploited in more accurate, sophisticated and pervasive manners.[12] With this observation in mind, the aim of this chapter is twofold. The first part (Sect. 2) seeks to sketch the main issues triggered specifically by *location* data and the application of EU data privacy and data protection law to evolving commercial scenarios. This part argues that assessing the problem requires a broad perspective that, besides law, includes technological and economic aspects of newly evolving ecosystems. The three spheres are often intertwined: technological advancements offer new solutions to familiar problems, and moreover, they offer entirely new behavioural options and choices (that might ultimately create new problems). The potential added value for consumers stimulates economic activity and business models designed to monetise technological innovation and enhance consumption. All this happens within a legal environment that might impose restrictions on technology and commerce and where regulative adjustments might be called for.

The second part (Sect. 3) focuses on risks and opportunities for consumers who are willing to trade their (location) data specifically for digital goods and services. Providing the data often relates directly to benefiting from more personalised, finely tuned and, in the end, useful technological solutions. In light of the rising trend often

[12] See Jonathan Andrew, 'Challenges to Locational Privacy: The Transformation of Urban Mobility', in this volume.

described as (consumer) data commodification,[13] the second part endeavours to provide initial insights into the problem of location data that economically—and potentially also legally—function as a counter-performance, particularly after the enactment of Directive (EU) 2019/770, which addresses the topic.

2 Location Data: Conceptual, Technological and Economic Perspectives

2.1 Conceptual and Definitional Perspectives

2.1.1 General Observations

Location data is a term often used in the context of digital technology and economy but which is less often explained or treated as a unique type of data that creates a unique set of problems.[14] In order to somewhat narrow the scope of the present discussion, it appears reasonable to begin by limiting it to machine-readable data, i.e. data that are generated, stored, analysed, aggregated, enriched, edited, manipulated, transmitted, etc. by the use of digital machines and devices. Next, it is clear that location data in our context go beyond the colloquial meaning of a category of machine-readable data that essentially indicate a physical location in space (often referred to as 'geolocation'[15]); non-spatial information can also reveal the location of an individual.[16]

In addition, technologies that collect and utilise spatial coordinates very often match it with temporal data, namely timestamps associated with pings of physical locations. The timestamps are an integral element of the data from a technological

---

[13]See eg Stacy-Ann Elvy, 'Commodifying Consumer Data in the Era of the Internet of Things' (2016) 59 Boston College Law Review 424; McKinsey & Company, 'Monetizing Car Data: New Service Business Opportunities to Create New Customer Benefits' (*Advanced Industries*, September 2016) <www.mckinsey.com/~/media/McKinsey/Industries/Automotive%20and%20Assembly/Our%20Insights/Monetizing%20car%20data/Monetizing-car-data.ashx> accessed 21 February 2020.

[14]One exception is a paper by Keßler and McKenzie in which the authors argue that, at least in the context of privacy, 'spatial is special' since information about an individual's location is substantially different from other kinds of personally identifiable information. See Carsten Keßler and Grant McKenzie, 'A Geoprivacy Manifesto' (2018) 22 Transactions in GIS 3, 5ff.

[15]See eg the definition of 'Geolocation' in Wikipedia <https://en.wikipedia.org/wiki/Geolocation> accessed 21 February 2020.

[16]See Keßler and McKenzie (n 14) 10. Sources of non-spatial public or otherwise shared data can reveal the location of an individual by inferring it from information on stated interests, social activities and temporal behaviours.

perspective.[17] Hence, some academics[18] and actors in the business-technology sector[19] use the term spatio-temporal data to more precisely describe the data being collected and processed for analytics, functionality, mobility and other purposes. Moreover, fully capturing the essence and value of location data includes not only an indication of physical location at a certain time but also information about the direction and speed they may encapsulate.[20]

Location data hence provide the basis for *mobility data*,[21] a concept that is intimately related to the common understanding of smart mobility. In turn, smart mobility was defined on one occasion as 'collecting, managing, and analysing (fusing) various data sources related to different aspects of residents' movement in order to better understand and improve the way people move.[22] It follows that smart mobility crucially depends on high quality mobility data on a massive scale and from multiple sources.

Spatio-temporal data can be said to create an interface layer between the presence and behaviour of a person in cyberspace and the presence and behaviour of that person in real space. Beyond the deductive force of such data (knowing the physical location of a person at a certain time can disclose personal preferences, tastes, behaviours and social connections),[23] the data interface layer highlights a problem

[17]For further discussion, see Jonathan Andrew, 'Location Data and Human Mobility: An Evaluation of a Dissonance that Frames Data Protection and Privacy Rights' (PhD Thesis, European University Institute 2018) 32 <https://cadmus.eui.eu/handle/1814/51585> accessed 21 February 2020.

[18]ibid 280-281: 'the term "location data" [. . .] fails to connote a core dimension of the data inhered i.e. the temporal data. A more appropriate nomenclature would be that of 'spatio-temporal data.'

[19]See eg Hasso-Plattner-Institut, 'Spatio-Temporal Data Analysis' (*Hasso-Plattner-Institut*) <https://hpi.de/plattner/projects/spatio-temporal-data-analysis.html> accessed 21 February 2020 (references to development projects in the area of time-stamped data analytics); omni.sci, 'Spatio-temporal Definition' (*omni.sci*) <www.omnisci.com/learn/resources/technical-glossary/spatial-temporal> accessed 21 February 2020.

[20]See eg Uber's statement that '[i]n order to calculate speeds we use two data inputs: (a) GPS locations of vehicles over time, and (b) map data that represents the street network on which vehicles travel', in 'Uber Movement: Speeds Calculation Methodology' <https://movement.uber.com/_static/56b3b1999eb80fadffbeb9bebe9888a7.pdf> accessed 21 February 2020. The PECR in the UK define in s 2(1) location data as specifically including the direction of travel and the time the location information was recorded, <www.legislation.gov.uk/uksi/2003/2426/contents/made> accessed 21 February 2020.

[21]See eg Mohamed Maouche, Sonia Ben Mokhtar and Sara Bouchenak, 'HMC: Robust Privacy Protection of Mobility Data against Multiple Re-Identification Attacks' (2018) 2(3) Proceedings of the ACM on Interactive, Mobile, Wearable and Ubiquitous Technologies 1, 2. In applying various models, raw location traces are associated with semantic information to yield mobility patterns.

[22]Billy Pik Lik Lau and others, 'A Survey of Data Fusion in Smart City Applications' (2019) 52 Information Fusion 357, 365. In this article, the authors propose that the smart human mobility domain can be divided into three sub-domains: (1) Smart Location-Based Services, (2) Human Mobility Understanding and (3) Smart Transportation Systems, ibid 365-366.

[23]Data logs about past locations combined with social and other data can tell third parties much about the person's personality, background, preferences and habits. They also have predictive force: based on past location data and an analysis of recurring patterns, informed assumptions can be made

that can be described as the vanishing boundaries between living and operating in these two ostensibly distinct and yet increasingly intertwined spaces.[24]

The location component not only triggers the question of (which) space but also the question of *what* or *whom*. Location data are machine generated. With various levels of accuracy, they ascertain the location of a device—not a natural person. Attributing the location to a specific individual is necessarily based on assumptions, correlations, statistical calculations and often on additional data sets and information that establish the presumed nexus to an individual.[25] It can be reasonably assumed, for instance, that the location of a smartphone at a certain time and the location of the person registered as its owner are one and the same. Based on device location data alone, however, a certain degree of uncertainty always remains.

2.1.2 Legal Definitions

Location data are potentially subject to data protection and data privacy laws. Though the main legal data protection instrument in the EU—the GDPR[26]—mentions location data by name in its definition of 'personal data',[27] it neither defines this term nor provides a detailed explanation. The ePrivacy Directive,[28] which aims to guarantee the confidentiality of communications over publicly available electronic communication networks and services, defines location data as meaning 'any data

regarding the physical location of the person at a future point in time. See eg Ourania Kounadi, Bernd Resch and Andreas Petutschnig, 'Privacy Threats and Protection Recommendations for the Use of Geosocial Network Data in Research' (2018) 7 Social Sciences 191.

[24]For the argument that software, through its ability to do work in the world, transduces space, see Rob Kitchin and Martin Dodge, *Code/Space: Software and Everyday Life* (MIT Press 2011). For a legal analysis of virtual reality and augmented reality aspects, see Mark Lemley and Eugene Volokh, 'Law, Virtual Reality, and Augmented Reality' (2018) 166 University of Pennsylvania Law Review 1051. See also Jannice Käll, 'Governing Smart Spaces through Autonomous Vehicles', in this volume.

[25]*United States v. Jones*, 565 U.S. 400 (2015). The location of a suspect in a criminal investigation was determined based on GPS location data from a vehicle registered to his wife and on information showing that the wife turned the car over to the suspect for his exclusive use.

[26]Parliament and Council Regulation (EU) 2016/679 of 27 April 2016 on the protection of natural persons with regard to the processing of personal data and on the free movement of such data, and repealing Directive 95/46/EC (General Data Protection Regulation) [2016] OJ L119/1 (GDPR).

[27]GDPR, art 4(1).

[28]Parliament and Council Directive 2002/58/EC of 12 July 2002 concerning the processing of personal data and the protection of privacy in the electronic communications sector (Directive on privacy and electronic communications) [2002] OJ L201/37 (ePrivacy Directive), as amended, *inter alia*, by Parliament and Council Directive 2009/136/EC of 25 November 2009 amending Directive 2002/22/EC on universal service and users' rights relating to electronic communications networks and services, Directive 2002/58/EC concerning the processing of personal data and the protection of privacy in the electronic communications sector and Regulation (EC) No 2006/2004 on cooperation between national authorities responsible for the enforcement of consumer protection laws [2009] OJ L337/11 (the so-called 'cookie Directive').

processed in an electronic communications network or by an electronic communications service, indicating the geographic position of the terminal equipment of a user of a publicly available electronic communications service'.[29] Recital 14 of this Directive is somewhat more detailed in providing that:

> Location data may refer to the *latitude, longitude and altitude* of the user's terminal equipment, to the *direction of travel*, to the level of accuracy of the location information, to the identification of the network cell in which the *terminal equipment is located at a certain point in time* and to the time the location information was recorded (emphasis added).

The ePrivacy Directive distinguishes between 'location data' and 'traffic data', with the latter defined as 'any data processed for the purpose of the conveyance of a communication on an electronic communications network or for the billing thereof'.[30]

Based on these definitions, the Directive further distinguishes between the protection scheme and compliance requirements pertaining to 'traffic data' on the one hand and 'location data other than traffic data' on the other. Regarding the latter category, Art. 9(1) of the ePrivacy Directive provides, *inter alia*, that '[w]here location data other than traffic data, relating to users or subscribers of public communications networks or publicly available electronic communications services, can be processed, such data may only be processed when they are made anonymous, or with the consent of the users or subscribers to the extent and for the duration necessary for the provision of a value added service'.

Accordingly, location data only sometimes qualify as traffic data—it depends on whether the data processing goes beyond the mere purpose of enabling the transmission of communication.[31] This structure, and specifically the lack of sufficient coherence in the distinction between location data that qualify as traffic data and location data that do not as well as the separate sets of rules that apply to each category, has been criticised.[32] Realising these deficiencies, Art. 29 Working Party (predecessor of the European Data Protection Board) recommended merging the provisions of Art. 6 and Art. 9 of the ePrivacy Directive, suggesting furthermore that

---

[29] ePrivacy Directive, art 2(c).

[30] ePrivacy Directive, art 2(b).

[31] Recital 35 of the ePrivacy Directive provides: 'In digital mobile networks, location data giving the geographic position of the terminal equipment of the mobile user are processed to enable the transmission of communications. Such data are traffic data covered by Article 6 of this Directive. However, in addition, digital mobile networks may have the capacity to process location data which are more precise than is necessary for the transmission of communications and which are used for the provision of value-added services such as services providing individualised traffic information and guidance to drivers. The processing of such data for value added services should only be allowed where subscribers have given their consent. Even in cases where subscribers have given their consent, they should have a simple means to temporarily deny the processing of location data, free of charge.'

[32] See eg Andrew, 'Location Data and Human Mobility' (n 17) 62-68.

both traffic data and location data are 'metadata' of increasing informational value that should be subject to a harmonised consent-based regime.[33]

This approach was adopted in the Commission's proposal for the ePrivacy Regulation,[34] which, once enacted, would repeal the ePrivacy Directive and drop the distinction between traffic data and location data—including their respective definitions.[35] At the same time, the ePrivacy Regulation Proposal would introduce an explicit distinction between the content of electronic communications and metadata. Recital 2 of the ePrivacy Regulation Proposal explains:

> The content of electronic communications may reveal highly sensitive information about the natural persons involved in the communication, from personal experiences and emotions to medical conditions, sexual preferences and political views, the disclosure of which could result in personal and social harm, economic loss or embarrassment. *Similarly, metadata derived from electronic communications may also reveal very sensitive and personal information.* These metadata includes the numbers called, the websites visited, *geographical location*, the time, date and duration when an individual made a call etc., allowing precise conclusions to be drawn regarding the private lives of the persons involved in the electronic communication, such as their social relationships, their habits and activities of everyday life, their interests, tastes etc.[36]

This approach reflects the understanding that both location data and traffic data fall under the concept of 'metadata', a designation that nonetheless is not contradictory to the very sensitive personal information they may contain. The Proposal maintains a different distinction manifested in new definitions of 'electronic communications content'[37] and 'electronic communications metadata'.[38] Accordingly, data on the location of the device generated in the context of providing electronic communications services and the date, time, duration and type of communication qualify as electronic communications metadata. After noting the great importance users attribute to the confidentiality of their communications and their wish to control the use of electronic communications data for purposes other than conveying the communication, Recital 17 of the Proposal provides:

---

[33]Article 29 Data Protection Working Party, 'Opinion 03/2016 on the evaluation and review of the ePrivacy Directive (2002/58/EC)' (2016) WP240, 13-16.

[34]Commission, 'Proposal for a Regulation of the European Parliament and of the Council concerning the respect for private life and the protection of personal data in electronic communications and repealing Directive 2002/58/EC (Regulation on Privacy and Electronic Communications)' COM (2017) 10 final.

[35]ibid art 4 of the Proposal, titled 'Definitions', no longer contains separate definitions for location data and traffic data.

[36]ibid recital 2 (emphasis added).

[37]ibid art 4(3)(b): '"Electronic communications content" means the content exchanged by means of electronic communications services, such as text, voice, videos, images, and sound.'

[38]ibid art 4(3)(c): '"Electronic communications metadata" means data processed in an electronic communications network for the purposes of transmitting, distributing or exchanging electronic communications content; including data used to trace and identify the source and destination of a communication, data on the location of the device generated in the context of providing electronic communications services, and the date, time, duration and the type of communication.'

> Therefore, this Regulation should require providers of electronic communications services to obtain end-users' consent to process electronic communications metadata, which should include data on the location of the device generated for the purposes of granting and maintaining access and connection to the service. *Location data that is generated other than in the context of providing electronic communications services should not be considered as metadata.* Examples of commercial usages of electronic communications metadata by providers of electronic communications services may include the provision of heatmaps; a graphical representation of data using colors to indicate the presence of individuals. To display the traffic movements in certain directions during a certain period of time, an identifier is necessary to link the positions of individuals at certain time intervals. This identifier would be missing if anonymous data were to be used and such movement could not be displayed (emphasis added).

This statement clarifies that location data collected in contexts other than providing electronic communications services[39] would fall outside the scope of the Regulation. If the same data, however, qualify as personal data under the GDPR, the latter instrument applies and users' consent might still be required. In the latest iteration and proposed amendments to the text of the ePrivacy Regulation Proposal, introduced by the EU Parliament in late 2019,[40] an additional Recital (17aa) was proposed:

> Metadata such as location data can provide valuable information, such as insights in human movement patterns and traffic patterns. Such information may, for example, be used for urban planning purposes. Further processing for such purposes other than for which the metadata where initially collected may take place without the consent of the end-users concerned, provided that such processing is compatible with the purpose for which the metadata are initially collected, certain additional conditions are met and safeguards are in place, including, where appropriate, the consultation of the supervisory authority, an impact assessment by the provider of electronic communications networks and services and the requirement to genuinely anonymise the result before sharing the analysis with third parties. As end-users attach great value to the confidentiality of their communications, including their physical movements, such data cannot be used to determine the nature or characteristics on an end-user or to build a profile of an end-user, in order to, for example, avoid that the data is used for segmentation purposes, to monitor the behaviour of a specific end-user or to draw conclusions concerning the private life of an end-user. For the same reason, the end-user must be provided with information about these processing activities taking place and given the right to object to such processing.[41]

Overall, the EU legal scheme and recent trends regarding location data are conscious of the increasing utility of location data and the importance of safeguarding users' privacy and data protection interests, regardless of the specific technology applied. Both the GDPR and the ePrivacy Regulation Proposal advance a

---

[39]For a definition of 'electronic communications service', the Proposal refers to art 2(4) of Parliament and Council Directive (EU) 2018/1972 of 11 December 2018 establishing the European Electronic Communications Code [2018] OJ L321/36.

[40]Council of the European Union, Proposal for a Regulation of the European Parliament and of the Council concerning the respect for private life and the protection of personal data in electronic communications and repealing Directive 2002/58/EC (Regulation on Privacy and Electronic Communications), 13808/19, Brussels, 8 November 2019.

[41]ibid recital 17aa.

technology-neutral approach to their respective subject matters.[42] In parallel, the conceptual and definitional distinction between content and metadata remains, as does the reliance on anonymisation to reduce risks to privacy interests.

2.2 *Technological Perspectives*

A myriad of devices and technologies used by urbanites collect, process and exchange location data at a considerable volume, frequency and scale. Location-based services generally aim to obtain the accurate position of individuals—both indoors and outdoors—in order to provide services such as route planning and navigation and to facilitate travel efficiently and comfortably. Global Positioning Systems (GPS) are considered the dominant technology for outdoors positioning as well as the most accurate and reliable, but other technologies are also prevalent, such as WiFi-based localisation cell tower triangulation.[43] Technologies used for localisation indoors include WiFi (WLAN), internal measurement unit (IMU), radio frequency ID tags (RFID), Bluetooth, GSM and FM.

Research has identified three principal domains in which technology is advancing rapidly, penetration into consumer markets is considerable and location data provide increasing functionality: smartphones, connected cars and the Internet of Things (IoT).[44] In all of these domains, various location technologies are in use, and the positioning data generated are often infused with other information sources such as geographic information system (GIS) data or real traffic data.

Some technologies are specifically tailor-made for smartphones, e.g. applications with location-based check-in services that enable individuals to share their activity-related choices. In particular, social media applications equipped with check-in functions (such as Facebook or Twitter) provide a vast amount of relevant data that help to determine activity patterns in the context of urban mobility. Among other purposes, such data allow researchers and analytics experts to ascertain individual mobility patterns with growing precision and granularity.[45]

---

[42]GDPR, recital 15; ePrivacy Regulation Proposal, recital 14.

[43]Lau and others (n 22) 365-366.

[44]The distinction between the three domains is by no means clear-cut. This classification, however, is not material for the arguments in this chapter and is offered for convenience only. cf European Data Protection Supervisor (EDPS), 'TechDispatch #3: Connected Cars' (*EDPS*, 20 December 2019) <https://edps.europa.eu/data-protection/our-work/publications/techdispatch/techdispatch-3-connected-cars_en> accessed 21 February 2020. This report classifies connected cars as an IoT category and describes the modern car as a 'computer on four wheels'.

[45]Samiul Hasan, Xianyuan Zhan and Satish V Ukkusuri, 'Understanding Urban Human Activity and Mobility Patterns Using Large-scale Location-based Data from Online Social Media' in Yu Zheng, Steven E Koonin and Ouri E Wolfson (eds), *UrbComp '13: Proceedings of the 2nd ACM SIGKDD International Workshop on Urban Computing* (Association for Computing Machinery 2013).

The potential of location data is obviously not limited to social media applications with check-in functions. Mobile phone traces can be used for various purposes, ranging from urban transportation modelling and research[46] to the creation of personal profiles and targeted advertising by commercial entities[47] as well as areas beyond commerce such as criminal investigations.[48] Researchers have noticed that companies also use ultrasonic side channels on mobile devices, usually without the customers being aware of it, in order to determine physical locations and content consumption habits and to follow their movements with applications that permanently 'listen' through the device's built-in microphone to ultrasonic beacons in the background.[49]

Due to the extremely broad use of smart mobile devices for performing daily tasks in urban settings, the location points of a growing number of such devices (and by extension, of their users) are being [illegible] processed, calculated and transmitted. Researchers determined that it is now dramatically easier to track the location of a huge number of mobile devices, 'leading to a wealth of information about the mobility of humans, vehicles, devices, and practically anything that can be fitted with a mobile computing device'.[50] And the density of sensors, signals and reception points—particularly in the city—contributes to the aggregation of very precise, high-quality location data.[51]

Developments in the area of consumer IoT also demonstrate an increasing reliance on location,[52] and the penetration of IoT into more areas of private and social life contributes to an explosion in the volume, variety, accuracy and quality of

---

[46]Francesco Calabrese and others, 'Understanding Individual Mobility Patterns from Urban Sensing Data: A Mobile Phone Trace Example' (2013) 26 Transportation Research Part C: Emerging Technologies 301. This study concludes that mobility phone traces represent a reasonable proxy for individual mobility and can provide useful insights into inter-urban mobility patterns under certain conditions.

[47]Taylor Peterson, 'Location Data 101: A Primer for Marketers' (*Marketing Land*, 19 August 2019) <https://marketingland.com/location-data-101-a-primer-for-marketers-265395> accessed 21 February 2020.

[48]*Carpenter vs. United States*, 585 U.S. ___,1-2 (2018). Cell Site Location Information (CSLI) retained by cellular networks was used by investigators to ascertain the location of the suspect at the time of the crime.

[49]Daniel Arp and others, 'Privacy Threats through Ultrasonic Side Channels on Mobile Devices' in *2017 IEEE European Symposium on Security and Privacy (EuroS&P)* (IEEE 2017) 35–47.

[50]Eran Toch and others, 'Analyzing Large-scale Human Mobility Data: a Survey of Machine Learning Methods and Applications' (2019) 58 Knowledge and Information Systems 501, 502.

[51]*Carpenter vs. U.S.* (n 48) 2: 'The greater the concentration of cell sites, the smaller the coverage area. As data usage from cell phones has increased, wireless carriers have installed more cell sites to handle the traffic. That has led to increasingly compact coverage areas, especially in urban areas.'

[52]See 'Location Data: IoT Applications and Benefits' (*IoT for all*, 12 October 2018) <www.iotforall.com/location-data-iot-applications-and-benefits/> accessed 21 February 2020: 'Location data is how many modern businesses make sense of their processes, their products and/or services, and how people interact with all of the above. It enables businesses to track assets across oceanic black holes. It allows them to map customer journeys seamlessly. It is the tool they use to optimize the routes of swarms of vehicles weaving through smart cities.'

processable data.[53] IoT location data are particularly accurate, which also renders them a particularly valuable, multipurpose source for commercial players, among others.[54] Researchers have begun to take notice of the possible impacts and risks involved in analysing data sets from IoT devices combined with smart city infrastructure in the context of digital forensics,[55] among other areas. It would not be exaggerated to say that location data are the lifeblood of smart mobility, and IoT devices are one critical source for such data.

Clearly, connected cars, assisted driving technologies and autonomous vehicles (collectively 'connected cars') are another important source.[56] Modern automobiles also become smarter[57] and more connected thanks to numerous in-car sensors, on-board computing capacities and an internet connection to external sources. According to one account, connected cars are equipped with on-board computers and embedded mobile broadband as well as dozens of sensors and around 40 microprocessors collecting telematics and driver data. These can produce and then upload to the cloud up to 25 GB of data with every driving hour.[58] A considerable portion of this data qualifies as location data or is part of the mobility data the car generates.

As indicated by researchers, both the technologies that generate the data and technology-based analytics models (including AI) open up an extremely broad range of use cases for such data:

> Mobility data have been used to answer questions such as how people travel between cities and what the patterns are of their daily commute, as well as to predict socioeconomic trends, find relationships in online social networks, identify people's weight and health status, discover employment patterns, and follow the spread of infectious diseases [...]. Models of mobility were used in designing public transportation systems, in taxicab allocation, and in performing crowd-sourcing tasks. In addition, the analysis of mobility patterns leads to a

---

[53]Katarzyna Kryla-Cudna, 'Consumer contracts and the Internet of Things' in Vanessa Mac, Eric Tjong Tjin Tai and Anna Berlee (eds), *Data Science and Law* (Edward Elgar 2018) 83-86.

[54]cf Andrew, 'Challenges to Locational Privacy' (n 12) 7-8. See also, Andrew, 'Location Data and Human Mobility' (n 17) 179ff. Here the developments in the IoT area are described as a 'paradigm shift' in the significance of location data from a legal perspective.

[55]Michael M Losavio and others, 'The Internet of Things and the Smart City: Legal Challenges with Digital Forensics, Privacy and Security' (2018) 1 Security and Privacy <https://onlinelibrary.wiley.com/doi/epdf/10.1002/spy2.23> accessed 21 February 2020.

[56]For simplicity, the term 'connected cars' is used while being conscious of the various levels of vehicular automation and connectivity. See eg the explanation of the five automation levels from 1 (driver assistance) to 5 (full automation, driverless car) on the BMW website <www.bmw.com/en/automotive-life/autonomous-driving.html> accessed 21 February 2020.

[57]See eg Sylvia Zhang, 'Who Owns The Data Generated By Your Smart Car?' (2018) 32 Harvard Journal of Law & Technology 299, 302. This study applies a broad definition to smart car to include any personal vehicle that has connectivity to the Internet, other devices, or surrounding vehicles or infrastructure, and is equipped with external or internal sensors and a method of recording data.

[58]Gabriel Seiberth and Wolfgang Gründiger, 'Data-Driven Business Models in Connected Cars, Mobility Services & Beyond' (2018) BVDW Research No. 01/18, 21 <www.bvdw.org/fileadmin/user_upload/20180509_bvdw_accenture_studie_datadrivenbusinessmodels.pdf> accessed 21 February 2020 (citing Jorge L Balcells, 'Datacentres: In the Driving Seat of the Connected Car Revolution' (*IoT Tech News*, 16 December 2016) <www.iottechnews.com/news/2016/dec/16/datacentres-driving-seat-connected-car-revolution/> accessed 21 February 2020).

> growing field of commercial applications by mobile communication service providers [...] as well as by several companies that have already started to provide location-based services analyzing mobile phone location traces.[59]

2.3 Economic Perspectives

There is a close bond between the useful things technology makes possible and the commercial endeavours that monetise and design business models around them. Given the sheer wealth of information advanced technologies and analytics methods currently offer, the economic significance of location data can hardly be overstated.[60] The data have an enormous commercial value for companies that provide a wide range of products and services and sometimes become a key resource for the firm's value proposition. As mentioned in a recent study, data can become *the product* (as compared to merely enhancing or augmenting an existing product), with location-based services being an archetypical example.[61]

As a result, personal data are being increasingly commodified,[62] that is, they are being traded and handled by market participants as a valuable commodity.[63] To name one prominent example, companies such as HERE provide a plethora of services based on the understanding that 'the world [...] is increasingly powered by location data and technology, enabling people and objects to live, move and interact faster, safer and in a more efficient way than ever before'.[64] HERE, in which major automotive players currently hold significant shares, provides products and solutions that are centred around the idea that location, described as the 'data layer of everything', is the one element that is critical to enabling an 'autonomous world'.[65] The HERE Open Location Platform is described as being able to create exhaustive data pools (with data gathered from car sensors, smart city systems and/or other IoT platforms) and thereby offer the opportunity to develop advanced location-based services.[66]

---

[59]Toch and others (n 50) 502 (citations omitted).

[60]For a recent account on valuation of data in data-driven markets, see Dan Ciuriak, 'Unpacking the Valuation of Data in the Data-Driven Economy' (Notes for Remarks at the NYU Conference on Global Data Law, New York, 26-27 April 2019) <https://papers.ssrn.com/sol3/papers.cfm?abstract_id=3379133> accessed 21 February 2020.

[61]Seiberth and Gründiger (n 58) 6-7.

[62]See eg Sebastian Sevignani, 'The Commodification of Privacy on the Internet' (2013) 40 Science and Public Policy 733–739.

[63]ibid: Sevignani refers to commodification as 'the process of making things exchangeable on markets, either actually and/or discursively by framing things as if they were exchangeable'.

[64]See statement on HERE's website <www.here.com/vision> accessed 21 February 2020.

[65]ibid.

[66]Seiberth and Gründiger (n 58) 36.

HERE is not alone in discovering the economic potential of commercialising high-quality location data on a massive scale. It competes with other players in an ecosystem where the automotive industry and smart mobility are building on AI-based solutions and where business, innovation, markets and the economy at large are 'data-driven'.[67] In China, Navinfo is striving to become 'the digital brain of intelligent driving with ultraprecise location information and automotive-grade semiconductors for Advanced Driver Assistance Systems (ADAS) and autonomous driving'.[68] In the realm of location-based services, Foursquare, the company that, as per its own statement, 'invented the check-in', now has a product (Pilgrim SDK) that embeds foreground and background location awareness into smartphone applications in order to provide contextual content in real time.[69] According to an online report from 2018, this company generated over 3 billion visits a month from 105 million locations globally.[70] Such enormous amounts of location data—in some cases the product that carries the entire business model of commercial enterprises—are being successfully and creatively converted into revenue.

A wide range of business models have emerged in the location data ecosystem, including platform, service, hardware and software providers that initially collect the data from consumers; data brokers that specialise in buying and selling data sets in secondary data markets;[71] and data-driven technology companies that invent sophisticated methods and models to analyse and extract more insights and commercially valuable information from Big Data. Consequently, new markets emerge in which businesses and users directly and explicitly trade personal-level location information.[72] In other words, business models in which consumers 'pay' with their data are on the rise, and consumer protection law is confronted with completely new situations and problems.

---

[67]See Commission, 'Towards a Thriving Data-Driven Economy' COM (2014) 442 final.

[68]Seiberth and Gründiger (n 58) 12.

[69]See Foursquare website <https://enterprise.foursquare.com/products/pilgrim> accessed 21 February 2020.

[70]Jordan Crook, 'Foursquare is Finally Proving its (Dollar) Value' (*Tech Crunch*, 19 January 2018) <https://techcrunch.com/2018/01/19/foursquare-is-finally-proving-its-dollar-value> accessed 21 February 2020.

[71]See Mathew Crain, 'The Limits of Transparency: Data Brokers and Commodification' (2016) 20 New Media and Society 88-104.

[72]McKinsey & Company (n 13) 13ff. Survey results regarding car data show that consumers are increasingly willing to share data but that they also expect a fair value in return.

3 Recent EU Legislation in the Area of Digital Consumer Protection

3.1 Background

In December 2015, the European Commission published two proposals for directives that would regulate certain aspects concerning contracts for the supply of digital content[73] and for the online sale of goods.[74] The proposals triggered a lively debate that continued during the various phases of legislation,[75] with the European Parliament and the Council of the EU proposing significant changes to the original proposals along the way.[76] At the conclusion of the trilogue negotiations in March

[73]Commission, 'Proposal for a Directive of the European Parliament and of the Council on certain aspects concerning contracts for the supply of digital content' COM (2015) 634 final (hereinafter referred to as 'COM-DCD').

[74]Commission, 'Proposal for a Directive of the European Parliament and of the Council on certain aspects concerning contracts for the online and other distance sales of goods' COM (2015) 635 final.

[75]See eg Reiner Schulze, Dirk Staudenmayer and Sebastian Lohsse (eds), *Contracts for the Supply of Digital Content: Regulatory Challenges and Gaps*: *Münster Colloquia on EU Law and the Digital Economy II* (Nomos 2017); European Law Institute (ELI), *Statement on the European Commission's Proposed Directive on the Supply of Digital Content to Consumers COM (2015) 634 final* (ELI 2016). Many commentators, especially in Germany, have participated in the debate. A partial list includes Philipp Hacker, 'Daten als Gegenleistung: Daten als Gegenleistung. Rechtsgeschäfte im Spannungsfeld von DS-GVO und allgemeinem Vertragsrecht' [2019] Zeitschrift für die gesamte Privatrechtswissenschaft 14; Niko Härting, 'Digital Goods und Datenschutz – Daten sparen oder monetarisieren? Die Reichweite des vom DinhRL-E erfassten Geschäftsmodells' (2016) 11 Computer und Recht 735; Axel Metzger, 'Data as Counter-Performance – What Rights and Duties do Parties Have?' (2017) 8 Journal of Intellectual Property, Information Technology and E-Commerce Law 2; Andreas Sattler, 'Personenbezogene Daten als Leistungsgegenstand – Die Einwilligung als Wegbereiter des Datenschuldrechts' (2017) 72 Juristenzeitung 1036; Martin Schmidt-Kessel and others, 'Die Richtlinienvorschläge der Kommission zu Digitalen Inhalten und Online-Handel: Teil 1' [2016] Zeitschrift für das Privatrecht der Europäischen Union 2; Martin Schmidt-Kessel and others, 'Die Richtlinienvorschläge der Kommission zu Digitalen Inhalten und Online-Handel: Teil 2' [2016] Zeitschrift für das Privatrecht der Europäischen Union 54; Louisa Specht, 'Daten als Gegenleistung – Verlangt die Digitalisierung nach einem neuen Vertragstypus?' (2017) 72 Juristenzeitung 763; Gerald Spindler, 'Verträge über digitale Inhalte – Anwendungsbereich und Ansätze – Vorschlag der EU-Kommission zu einer Richtlinie über Verträge zur Bereitstellung digitaler Inhalte' (2016) 19 Multimedia und Recht 147; Gerald Spindler, 'Verträge über digitale Inhalte – Haftung, Gewährleistung und Portabilität – Vorschlag der EU-Kommission zu einer Richtlinie über Verträge zur Bereitstellung digitaler Inhalte' (2016) 19 Multimedia und Recht 219; Friedrich Graf von Westphalen, 'Richtlinienentwurf der Kommission betreffend die Bereitstellung digitaler Inhalte und das Recht des Verbrauchers auf Schadensersatz' [2016] Betriebsberater 1411; Friedrich Graf von Westphalen and Christiane Wendehorst, 'Hergabe personenbezogener Daten für digitale Inhalte – Gegenleistung, bereitzustellendes Material oder Zwangsbeitrag zum Datenbinnenmarkt?' [2016] Betriebsberater 2179.

[76]For the draft of the Digital Content Directive, see Council, 'Proposal for a Directive of the European Parliament and of the Council on certain aspects concerning contracts for the supply of

2019, the texts of both directives received their final form,[77] followed by the official publication of the directives shortly thereafter.[78]

The debate in recent years has circled around several issues,[79] including (1) coverage of situations in which the consumer provides data as counter-performance instead of a price for digital content and services and (2) the inclusion of embedded digital content under the protection scheme of the directives (in the current texts of the directives such embedded digital content is referred to as 'goods with digital elements'). Framework questions such as the explicit inclusion of 'personal data' as counter-performance and the simultaneous application of the GDPR triggered an extensive discussion. Another question circled around protection to consumers that 'passively' provide personal data instead of a price.

The general aim of the resulting directive concerning digital goods and services (DCSD) is to fully harmonise certain requirements concerning contracts between traders and consumers for the supply of digital content or services (Recital 11 DCSD). It is explicitly designed to harmonise

> rules on the conformity of digital content or a digital service with the contract, remedies in the event of a lack of such conformity or a failure to supply and the modalities for the exercise of those remedies, as well as on the modification of digital content or a digital service.[80] Recitals 12 through 17 lay out a fairly long list of matters in which Member States are not strictly bound by the DCSD. These matters include national rules on the formation, validity, nullity or effects of contracts; the legal nature or classification of the contract; remedies for 'hidden defects'; and claims against any third party that is not the trader. The debate regarding the proper reach of the DCSD did not focus specifically on location data. The remainder of this chapter seeks to fill this gap.

---

digital content (First reading) – General approach' 9901/17 ADD 1, 2015/0287 (COD), 01.06.2017 (hereinafter referred to as 'Council-DCD'); European Parliament, 'Report on the proposal for a directive of the European Parliament and of the Council on certain aspects concerning contracts for the supply of digital content (COM(2015)0634 – C8-0394/2015 – 2015/0287(COD))' A8-0375/2017, 27.11.2017 (hereinafter referred to as 'EP-DCD').

[77]See Nikolina Sajn, 'Contracts for the Supply of Digital Content and Digital Services' (PE 635.601, March 2019) <www.europarl.europa.eu/RegData/etudes/BRIE/2019/635601/EPRS_BRI(2019)635601_EN.pdf> accessed 21 February 2020.

[78]Parliament and Council Directive (EU) 2019/770 of 20 May 2019 on certain aspects concerning contracts for the supply of digital content and digital services, OJ L136/1 (hereinafter referred to as 'DCSD'); Parliament and Council Directive (EU) 2019/771 of 20 May 2019 on certain aspects concerning contracts for the sale of goods, amending Regulation (EU) 2017/2394 and Directive 2009/22/EC, and repealing Directive 1999/44/EC, OJ L136/28 (hereinafter referred to as 'SGD').

[79]These issues received an earlier treatment *inter alia* in Axel Metzger and others, 'Data-Related Aspects of the Digital Content Directive' (2018) 9 Journal of Intellectual Property, Information Technology and E-Commerce Law 90.

[80]DCSD, recital 11.

3.2 Data as Counter-Performance

3.2.1 Recognition in the DCSD

The initial Commission's proposal (COM-DCD) included a provision that extended the scope of the Directive to cases where the consumer actively provides, in exchange for digital content, counter-performance other than money in the form of *personal data or any other data*.[81] After much debate over this issue (including a critical opinion issued by the European Data Protection Supervisor[82]), the Directive now sets forth that consumers who provide *personal data* in exchange for digital content or digital services in principle should benefit from the protections therein.[83] This provision is subject to two exceptions: (1) when the personal data are provided by the consumer is exclusively processed by the trader for the purpose of supplying the digital content or digital services, or (2) for allowing the trader to comply with legal requirements to which the trader is subject—and in both cases, the trader does not process that data for any other propose.[84]

3.2.2 Normative Priority of EU Data Protection and Privacy Law

The DCSD now states generally that in the case of any conflict, the GDPR overrides provisions under the DCSD.[85] The same applies to conflicts with the e-Privacy Directive (Directive 2002/58/EC).[86] This priority rule is helpful at least on a formal level for resolving questions of parallel application.[87] It should help domestic legislatures and courts with the task of applying a certain legal regime in case of discrepancies. Such discrepancies are likely in light of the conceptual and practical overlaps between data protection/privacy law (protecting the individual as a data subject/user) and consumer protection law (protecting potentially the same individual as a consumer). This bright-line rule represents the general understanding that neither contract law in general nor specific consumer protection regulations should

---

[81]COM-DCD, art 3(1) and recitals 13, 14.

[82]EDPS, 'Opinion 4/2017 on the Proposal for a Directive on certain aspects concerning contracts for the supply of digital content' (EDPS 14 March 2017) <https://edps.europa.eu/sites/edp/files/publication/17-03-14_opinion_digital_content_en.pdf> accessed 21 February 2020.

[83]Note that the DCSD (as opposed to the COM-DCD) no longer includes the phrase 'counter-performance' in connection with personal data provided by the consumer. It further omitted the phrase 'in exchange', which referred in the COM-DCD directly to the phrase 'a consumer actively provid[ing] counter-performance other than money in the form of personal data or any other data'.

[84]DCSD, art 3(1).

[85]DCSD, art 3(8).

[86]ibid.

[87]cf Carmen Langhanke and Martin Schmidt-Kessel, 'Consumer Data as Consideration' (2015) 6 EuCML 218, 219ff. Here it is suggested that two 'layers' of consumer protection apply in such cases.

derogate from the level of protection persons enjoy under data protection and privacy law. More precisely, Art. 3(8) DCSD provides that consumer protection under the DCSD should be 'without prejudice' to the data protection body of law.

3.2.3 'Passively Provided' Data

Early proposals suggested a distinction between actively and passively provided data in data-as-counter-performance scenarios. Whereas the COM-DCD referred only to data that are *actively* provided by the consumer,[88] the Council's draft would have allowed Member States to extend the application of the directive to passively provided data as well.[89] Both the Council and the EU Parliament refrained from using the term 'actively' within their respective amendments to Art. 3 of the DCD draft. The Council's draft kept the emphasis on actively provided data while excluding collected metadata (such as IP addresses) or automatically generated content (such as information collected and transmitted by cookies).[90] By comparison, the Parliament's draft (EP-DCD) would allow for the inclusion of data that is provided passively (e.g. personal data collected by the trader such as IP addresses).[91] The option of excluding passively provided data from the scope of Art. 3 DCSD has been criticised on several grounds,[92] including the fact that the distinction between actively and passively provided data could turn fuzzy in certain situations.[93] Ultimately, the phrase 'actively provide[s]' was removed from the final text.

Especially relevant to location data is Recital 25 DCSD, which indicates that 'metadata' are not covered by the DCSD unless Member States specifically extend the application of this Directive to such situations.[94] It follows that data which qualify as 'metadata' will trigger protection only if the exchange of such data against digital content/services is specifically recognised under domestic law as a

---

[88]COM-DCD, recital 14: 'As regards digital content supplied not in exchange for a price but against counter-performance other than money, this Directive *should apply only* to contracts where the supplier requests and the consumer *actively* provides data' (emphasis added).

[89]Council-DCD, art 3(1) at n 15.

[90]ibid at n 15.

[91]EP-DCD, recital 14. This Recital also mentioned as covered by the directive 'the name and e-mail address or photos, provided directly or indirectly to the trader, for example through individual registration or on the basis of a contract which allows access to consumers' photos'. ibid.

[92]See eg Metzger and others (n 79) 96, paras 26-28; Spindler, 'Verträge über digitale Inhalte – Anwendungsbereich und Ansätze' (n 75) 149-159; Hacker (n 75) 166.

[93]cf Graf von Westphalen and Wendehorst (n 75) 2180-2181.

[94]DCSD, recital 25: 'This Directive should also not apply to situations where the trader only collects metadata, such as information concerning the consumer's device or browsing history, except where this situation is considered to be a contract under national law [...]. However, Member States should remain free to extend the application of this Directive to such situations, or to otherwise regulate such situations, which are excluded from the scope of this Directive.'

'contract'.[95] At the same time, Recital 24 DCSD clarifies generally that the conclusion of the contract and the provision of the data do not have to happen simultaneously or at any specific proximity of time in order for the DCSD to apply.[96] This Recital includes the ongoing collocation of data that users upload or create in the course of using the digital content/service, which might, under a certain interpretation, also encompass 'passive' data provision situations.[97]

Alas, the DCSD does not provide a definition for the term 'metadata'.[98] The examples of metadata it mentions—namely, 'information concerning the consumer's device or browsing history'—do not offer a conclusive answer. One important area in which this ambiguity is relevant is the case of cookies. It has been argued, for instance, that cookies that collect data such as browsing history (hence 'metadata' that the consumer, strictly speaking, neither uploads nor creates) in exchange for digital goods or services is a situation excluded from DCSD.[99] Another area that comes to mind, of course, is location data.

3.2.4 Application to Location Data

Given that only *personal* data can count as counter-performance,[100] location data would qualify if (a) it is considered 'personal data' under the GDPR and if (b) the data are not exclusively processed by the trader for the purpose of supplying the digital content or digital services.[101] As to the first condition, in light of the GDPR's

---

[95] cf Axel Metzger, 'A Market Model for Personal Data: State of the Play under the New Directive on Digital Content and Digital Services' in Sebastian Lohsse, Reiner Schulze and Dirk Staudenmayer (eds), *Data as Counter Performance – Contract Law 2.0? Münster Colloquia on EU Law and the Digital Economy V* (Nomos, 2020) (forthcoming) 3-4 <www.rewi.hu-berlin.de/de/lf/ls/mzg/pub/metzger-markets-for-data-oct-2019-preprint.pdf> accessed 21 February 2020.

[96] DCSD, recital 24: 'The personal data could be provided to the trader either at the time when the contract is concluded or at a later time, such as when the consumer gives consent for the trader to use any personal data that the consumer might upload or create with the use of the digital content or digital service.'

[97] For more discussion, see Zohar Efroni, 'Gaps and Opportunities: The Rudimentary Protection to "Data-Paying Consumers" under New EU Consumer Protection Law' 57(3) Common Market Law Review 799-830 (2020).

[98] For a comprehensive treatment and argument that metadata is more than merely 'data about data', see Jeffrey Pomerantz, *Metadata* (MIT Press 2015).

[99] cf Gerald Spindler and Karin Sein, 'Die endgültige Richtlinie über digitale Inhalte und Dienstleistungen' [2019] Multimedia und Recht 415, 418. Here DCSD, recital 25 is read as excluding cookies information generally, and cookies information that qualifies as personal data specifically.

[100] This outcome was criticised, eg, by Lena Mischau, 'Daten als "Gegenleistung" im neuen Verbrauchervertragsrecht' [2020] Zeitschrift für die gesamte Privatrechtswissenschaft 5 (forthcoming).

[101] For simplicity, we set aside the second exception in DCSD, art 3(1) regarding data processed in order to comply with a legal obligation.

broad definition of 'personal data'[102] and the corresponding interpretation by the Court of Justice of the European Union (CJEU),[103] the exclusion of non-personal data might end up having a marginal impact in practice. It is generally reasonable to assume that non-anonymised location data are more valuable than anonymised data to traders in the B2C sector in terms of allowing pinpointed targeted advertising, refined consumer profile building and individualised pricing models. The first condition nonetheless triggers the general problem of how and where to draw the line between personal and non-personal (including anonymised) data.[104]

The ePrivacy Regulation Proposal suggests that location pings require a device identifier to make them useful in terms of creating heatmaps and ascertaining mobility patterns that are important to the research and development of smart mobility concepts in densely populated cities.[105] Furthermore, depending on the technology and device at play, consumer location data that are collected automatically often come with 'build-in identifiers' such as IP address, device ID and advertiser ID in smartphones. Even when separated from those identifiers, location data are particularly susceptible to re-identification attacks, and within the broader discussion about the sheer feasibility of rendering personal data completely and permanently anonymised, location data present an example in support of arguments that total anonymisation cannot be attained.[106] The upshot is that location data will almost always qualify as personal data under the GDPR (unless sufficiently anonymised before processing under applicable/acceptable technical and legal standards of anonymisation) and thereby fulfil the first condition.

The second condition calls for a careful assessment. Whether the location data that the consumer provides are processed *exclusively for supplying* the digital content/services in accordance with the DCSD depends largely on the facts and circumstances of the individual case. The assessment will be as complex (or as straightforward) as ascertaining the technical, contractual and practical conditions surrounding the exchange. In addition, obligations under the DCSD's supply and

---

[102]GDPR, art 4(1): '"Personal data" means any information relating to an identified or identifiable natural person ("data subject"); an identifiable natural person is one who can be identified, directly or indirectly, in particular by reference to an identifier such as a name, an identification number, location data, an online identifier or to one or more factors specific to the physical, physiological, genetic, mental, economic, cultural or social identity of that natural person.'

[103]Case C-582/14 *Breyer* [2016] EU:C:2016:779. This judgment refers to the definition of 'personal data' under Parliament and Council Directive (EC) 95/46 of 24 October 1995 on the protection of individuals with regard to the processing of personal data and on the free movement of such data [1995] OJ L281/31, art 2(a), which is considered equivalent to the definition of the same concept under the GDPR.

[104]For a recent account, see Michèle Finck and Frank Pallas, 'They Who Must Not Be Identified – Distinguishing Personal from Non-Personal Data under the GDPR' (2019) Max Planck Institute for Innovation and Competition Research Paper No. 19-14 <https://papers.ssrn.com/sol3/papers.cfm?abstract_id=3462948> accessed 21 February 2020.

[105]COM (2017) 10 final: ePrivacy Regulation Proposal, recital 17.

[106]cf Finck and Pallas (104) 30-31. See also, Keßler and McKenzie (n 14).

conformity requirements[107] and perhaps some other sources external to the contract might be relevant.

This restriction under Art. 3(1) is formulated in a very similar way to Art. 6(1)(b) GDPR, which permits the processing of personal data if 'processing is necessary *for the performance of a contract* to which the data subject is party or in order to take steps at the request of the data subject prior to entering into a contract' (emphasis added). At the same time, the GDPR provision is somewhat broader compared to Art. 3(1) DCSD. The latter excludes from the concept of counter-performance the processing of personal data exclusively 'for the *purpose of supplying the digital content or digital service* in accordance with this Directive' (emphasis added). It seems that, at least in some cases, processing for the purpose of supply is a specific type of contract performance necessity. Under this interpretation, it is conceivable that Art. 6(1)(b) GDPR might also capture processing that is not directly related to supplying the contracted subject matter.

The EDPB opined that 'Article 6(1)(b) [GDPR] applies where either of two conditions are met: the processing in question must be objectively necessary for the performance of a contract with a data subject, or the processing must be objectively necessary in order to take pre-contractual steps at the request of a data subject'.[108] In this context, the concept of necessity is applied not strictly under contract law but under data protection (objective) assessment criteria. At the same time, even under such a narrow construction of the legal basis of Art. 6(1)(b) GDPR, it is clear that there is no perfect overlap with Art. 3(1) DCSD. As a result, a valid Art. 6(1)(b) GDPR basis does not exclude *a priori* application of the DCSD, but in practice, processing on this basis will often coincide with situations excluded under Art. 3(1) DCSD. In a legal-economic environment that tolerates the consensual commodification of personal data and simultaneously imposes strict data protection limitations on traders, a successful business model seeking to monetise the data will usually need to rely on processing grounds other than contractual performance necessity, mainly on consent.[109]

Indeed, the importance of users' affirmative consent in situations where location data are being processed by the trader is expected to increase in light of the CJEU jurisprudence on metadata collected by cookies. In the *Planet49* case, the CJEU ruled that a pre-selected checkbox does not fulfil the requirements of consent.[110] Active, informed and specific consent is required for using both personal and

---

[107]DCSD, arts 5-8.

[108]European Data Protection Board, 'Guidelines 2/2019 on the processing of personal data under art 6(1)(b) GDPR in the context of the provision of online services to data subjects' (v. 2.0, 8 October 2019) para 22.

[109]GDPR, art 6(1)(a). Legitimate interests under GDPR, art 6(1)(f) can provide an alternative ground.

[110]Case C-673/17 *Planet49 GmbH v. Bundesverband der Verbraucherzentralen und Verbraucherverbände – Verbraucherzentrale Bundesverband e.V.* [2019] EU:C:2019:246, paras 49-65.

non-personal data covered under the e-Privacy Directive,[111] and the user should have a viable option to refuse the implementation of cookies as 'user consent may no longer be presumed but must be the result of active behaviour on the part of the user'.[112] Similar to data retrieved via cookies (e.g. IP addresses), location data are often collected in the course of a continuous, automated process inherent to using a connected device. The process runs seamlessly in the background without any affirmative action of users to 'hand over' their data and sometimes even without their knowledge.

The prominence of consent is expected to grow under the upcoming ePrivacy Regulation as an important lawful basis of processing 'electronic communications metadata'.[113] Already today, consent is the main lawful basis of processing location data that qualify as sensitive data under Art. 9 GDPR. The claim that users often do not actively provide explicit consent to the collection of their (personal) location data poses a major compliance challenge that relates to the more general problem of how to improve the consent process in digital and online settings.[114]

In the final analysis, whether consumers actively provide the personal (location) data or not is of secondary importance, and in any case, it should not impose a technical limitation on the DCSC's scope. For the opposite conclusion, a convincing normative or economic argument saying that location data provided 'passively' call for a lower degree of consumer protection would have to be made. The question of how to reconcile commercial data as counter-performance models with privacy

---

[111]ibid paras 70-71.

[112]ibid para 56.

[113]Amended Proposal of the ePrivacy Regulation, art 6bff. Shortly before this chapter went to print, the Presidency of the Council of the European Union published a progress report regarding the ePrivacy Regulation Proposal. The Presidency proposed a modification, according to which the processing of electronic communication metadata would be allowed also when it is necessary for the purpose of legitimate interests (i.e., without specific user consent), subject to a number of safeguards. See Council of the European Union, Proposal for a Regulation of the European Parliament and of the Council concerning the respect for private life and the protection of personal data in electronic communications and repealing Directive 2002/58/EC (Regulation on Privacy and Electronic Communications) - Progress Report, 29 May 2020 <https://data.consilium.europa.eu/doc/document/ST-8204-2020-INIT/en/pdf> accessed 26 August 2020.

[114]One way to combat lack of awareness, risk illiteracy and information asymmetry for achieving a better working consent procedure is through visualisation techniques such as privacy icons. See eg Zohar Efroni and others, 'Privacy Icons: A Risk-Based Approach to Visualisation of Data Processing' (2019) 3 European Data Protection Law Review 352. Another way is by applying personal information management systems (PIMS). See EDPS, 'Opinion on Personal Information Management Systems (Opinion 9/2016): Towards more user empowerment in managing and processing personal data' (EDPS 2016) 5 <https://edps.europa.eu/sites/edp/files/publication/16-10-20_pims_opinion_en.pdf> accessed 21 February 2020; Stiftung Datenschutz, 'Policy Paper: New Ways of Providing Consent in Data Protection – Technical, Legal and Economic Challenges' (Stiftung Datenschutz 2017) <https://stiftungdatenschutz.org/fileadmin/Redaktion/Bilder/Abschluss_Studie_30032017/stiftungdatenschutz_PolicyPaper_New_ways_of_providing_consent_in_data_protection_EN_final.pdf> accessed 21 February 2020.

and data protection law and their consent requirements (importantly including Art. 7 (4) GDPR) will remain the paramount challenge.

3.3 *Embedded Digital Content and IoT*

3.3.1 Products Bundled with Digital Elements

After many twists and turns on the issue of goods with embedded digital content, the DCSD adopted a new definition for 'goods with digital elements', meaning 'any tangible movable items that incorporate, or are inter-connected with, digital content or a digital service in such a way that the absence of that digital content or digital service would prevent the goods from performing their functions'.[115] This definition covers what is commonly referred to as IoT devices.[116] IoT devices connect to the internet via IP addresses, and connectivity is by definition essential for them to perform their functions.[117]

The legal scheme explicitly excludes goods with digital elements from the DCSD while making such goods subject to the Sale of Goods Directive (SGD).[118] Since the SGD applies solely to sales contracts,[119] and since its definition of a sales contract does not entertain the concept of data as counter-performance,[120] goods with digital elements for which the consumer provides data instead of a price are covered neither by the DCSD nor by the SGD. It follows that renting, lending and gratis distribution of a consumer IoT device remains outside of the regulative scope of these directives,

---

[115]DCSD, art 2(3).

[116]For an extensive discussion on the concept and meanings of IoT, see Ovidiu Vermesan and others, 'Internet of Things – Strategic Research and Innovation Agenda' in Ovidiu Vermesan and Peter Friess (eds), *Internet of Things* (River Publishing 2014) 11-16.

[117]ibid 12: 'In [the IoT] context the notion of network convergence using IP is fundamental and relies on the use of a common multi-service IP network supporting a wide range of applications and services. The use of IP to communicate with and control small devices and sensors opens the way for the convergence of large, IT-oriented networks with real time and specialised networked applications.'

[118]DCSD, recital 21: 'Directive (EU) 2019/771 [SGD] should apply to contracts for the sale of goods, including goods with digital elements. The notion of goods with digital elements should refer to goods that incorporate or are inter-connected with digital content or a digital service in such a way that the absence of that digital content or digital service would prevent the goods from performing their functions. Digital content or a digital service that is incorporated in or inter-connected with goods in that manner should fall within the scope of Directive (EU) 2019/771 if it is provided with the goods under a sales contract concerning those goods. Whether the supply of the incorporated or inter-connected digital content or digital service forms part of the sales contract with the seller should depend on the content of this contract.'

[119]SGD, art 3.1.

[120]SGD, art 2(1): '"Sales contract" means any contract under which the seller transfers or undertakes to transfer ownership of goods to a consumer, and the consumer pays or undertakes to pay the price thereof.'

unless the transaction for the supply of digital elements can be severed from the transaction concerning the physical good and be treated separately and independently.[121]

This 'distribution of labour' between the DCSD and the SGD means that unless the physical component serves merely as a data carrier of digital content, the SGD applies exclusively to sales contracts of goods that include digital elements. The question of whether the digital element in a given case is essential for the good to perform its functions is to be answered, to a large extent, by the terms of the contract itself and the surrounding circumstances. For IoT devices covered by the SGD, the Directive's protection scheme spreads over the digital components alongside the physical elements. It sets forth specific objective requirements for conformity that are typical to digital content and services, such as the duty to inform the consumer and to supply updates, including security updates that are necessary to keep those goods in conformity.[122] The SGD, however, does not include a detailed provision comparable to Art. 19 DCSD regarding modifications in the digital content or services and the consumer protection safeguards therein.[123]

3.3.2 Application to Location Data

The application of the coverage question to IoT devices is certainly relevant for smart mobility. The consumer devices used for smart mobility usually qualify as goods with digital elements under the DCSD/SGD scheme. Those devices rely on location data and connection to the internet is essential for their proper function and utility. During their operation, they establish connection to remote services that access their location data. As noted, in the absence of transfer of ownership for a price, the consumer protection layer of the DCSC/SGD does not apply. It appears that traders still sell most consumer IoT devices for money.[124] But a shift to business models that more intensively and transparently monetise personal data collected by the device for a considerable discount, a subscription model and/or gratis distribution instead of sales transactions do not seem that farfetched.

Particularly in the consumer IoT and smartphone segments, consumers have a strong incentive to share their location with hardware, software, service and platform providers. Depending on the particular case, sharing location data can dramatically increase personal usability and functionality. The mission of consumer protection

[121]DCSD, recital 21.

[122]SGD, art 7(3).

[123]For more discussion, see Axel Metzger, 'Verträge über digitale Inhalte und digitale Dienstleistungen: Neuer BGB-Vertragstypus oder punktuelle Reform?' (2019) 12 Juristenzeitung 577, 578.

[124]A random list of the 'most popular' IoT devices shows that all the products on the list are currently offered for money—some for a considerable price. See '18 Most Popular IoT Devices in 2020 (Only Noteworthy IoT Products)' (*Software Testing Helps*, 25 December 2019) <www.softwaretestinghelp.com/iot-devices> accessed 21 February 2020.

law at this juncture should be to ensure that consumers, who suffer from information asymmetry vis-à-vis traders, weaker bargaining positions and in some cases total lack of both bargaining power and viable alternatives, are not being exploited. One important element is imposing transparency obligations on traders to enhance consumers' understanding of the context, purposes, implications and risks associated with sharing location.

A comprehensive evaluation of the legal position of EU consumers in the IoT segment should include further regulative instruments, such as the Consumer Rights Directive (2011/83/EU) as recently revised by Directive (EU) 2019/2161 (Consumer Rights Modernisation Directive CRMD).[125] The CRD generally secures broad information rights under Article 5 thereof (including information about the *total price* of the goods or services) as well as specific information requirements for distance or off-premises contracts (Article 6). The revised CRD (to be transposed in national laws by 28 May 2022) borrows many important definitions from the GDPR and the DCSD/SGD scheme.[126] It will apply explicitly 'where the trader supplies or undertakes to supply digital content which is not supplied on a tangible medium or a digital service to the consumer and the consumer provides or undertakes to provide personal data to the trader'.[127]

In principle, CRD rights should apply to contracts regarding IoT goods, namely, both to the physical component of the device and the digital content or service that makes it work. But this is not always the case. For instance, some consumer rights specifically attach requirements concerning pre-contractual information duties[128] or the rights of consumers in the case of withdrawal[129] to digital content. Under the revised CRD, these rights will also apply to digital content/services of goods with digital elements subject to a sales contract, except for cases where the digital content is supplied on a tangible medium and the consumer 'pays' with personal data. This structure suggests that pre-installed digital content on an IoT device does not benefit from the CRD's protections that apply to digital content.

The synopsis sketched above, while only briefly touching upon the genuinely complex matrix of digital consumer protection law in the EU, demonstrates that the implications of the revised CRD for IoT consumers are not easy to pin down. As the consolidated body of consumer protection law emerging under the New Deal for Consumers Initiative of the European Commission and the enactment of the DCSD/SGD becomes more intricate, the exposition, implementation and compliance

[125]Parliament and Council Directive (EU) 2019/2161 of 27 November 2019 amending Council Directive 93/13/EEC and Directives 98/6/EC, 2005/29/EC and 2011/83/EU of the European Parliament and of the Council as regards the better enforcement and modernisation of Union consumer protection rules [2019] OJ L328/7.

[126]CRMD, art 4(1). See referenced and new definitions in the revised CRD to 'goods', 'personal data', 'sales contract', 'service contract', 'digital content' and 'digital service' as well as to 'computability', 'functionality' and 'interoperability'.

[127]CRMD, art 4(2)(b).

[128]CRD, art 5(1)(g)-(h).

[129]CRD, art 9(1), 9(2)(c).

challenges are likely to increase and provide fertile ground for further research and discussion.

4 Conclusion

Location data remain an extremely relevant and dynamic playing field for technology developers, market actors and consumers. As such, they calls for the attention of lawmakers and courts as they come to define the legal boundaries for these dynamics and, to some extent, prescribe the rules of the game. The task of enabling market models with an increasing reliance on data and their consensual exchange in B2C markets and, at the same time, preserving the rights of individuals *as data subjects and consumers* should not be underestimated. Many questions within data protection and privacy law itself as well as questions concerning its interface with other legal domains such as consumer protection and contract law remain unresolved.

Location data, due to their unique significance and role in the digital economy, could play a pivotal role in the process of figuring out this interplay—which is hopefully moving towards a coherent and consistent legal scheme that finds the right balance between personal autonomy, state intervention and market economy. On the one hand, utilising location data is indispensable for numerous technological innovations and key for economic growth. On the other hand, such utilisation poses new risks to individual interests. Whether location data therefore could and should be treated as a unique category of data from a legal perspective is a vexing question that has not yet been extensively discussed, but it certainly deserves some deeper deliberations.

Yes Means No(thing): Bridging Consent in Contract Law and Data Protection in the Context of Smart Mobility

Catalina Goanta

Contents

Abstract This contribution departs from a theoretical question regarding the similarities and differences between informed consent as a concept of contract law on the one hand and as a concept of privacy and data protection on the other hand. As a lot of private urban mobility initiatives (e.g. Uber public transportation) focus on tracking and profiling users for the purpose of data analyses that lie at the core of their business models, informed consent plays a fundamental role in the transactions through which this data is acquired.

This chapter aims to explore the urban mobility context in order to identify and discuss legal issues linked to the tensions between the two legal frameworks shaped by contract law as well as privacy and data protection law. In order to showcase the roots of consent in contract law and follow its clash with an equivalent concept arising from mandatory data protection rules aimed to curtail freedom of contract for protective purposes, it examines the contract as the transactional regime underpinning the legitimacy and legal validity of an agreement between two parties, and looks into models of contract formation and information duties comparatively in contract and data protection scholarship.

Dr. Catalina Goanta is Assistant Professor in Private Law at the Faculty of Law, Maastricht University, Maastricht, the Netherlands, and postdoctoral researcher at Studio Europa (Maastricht Working on Europe) and manages the Maastricht Law and Tech Lab.

C. Goanta (✉)
Faculty of Law, Maastricht University, Maastricht, The Netherlands
e-mail: catalina.goanta@maastrichtuniversity.nl

M. Finck et al. (eds.), *Smart Urban Mobility*, MPI Studies on Intellectual Property and Competition Law 29, https://doi.org/10.1007/978-3-662-61920-9_14

1 Introduction

In twenty-first century society, complex technology is inescapable. The process of embedding technology in the workplace as well as daily life, which began decades ago with the promise of 'more communication at greater speed',[1] constantly challenges the design and application of existing legal and regulatory frameworks. The diffusion of personal computing and internet services has transformed the way in which individuals—as consumers and citizens—exchange information globally.[2] This phenomenon used to be mostly confined to a private sphere: emerging information products and services were designed and used by private parties (e.g. companies such as IBM or consumers at large). Absent strong public structures to regulate technology during the internet's first iteration,[3] regulatory lines were drawn by the companies that provided goods or services through the internet. They relied on a fundamental transactional instrument: the contract. The market practice of drafting and imposing standard contracts on users, which was common among other industries up to that time, prevailed as a model of managing risks and liabilities. Whatever broader concerns may have arisen from these transactions, they were mostly dealt with through standard setting, as '[m]uch of the most general architecture of cyberspace, protocols and standards, has been developed and is controlled by a variety of broadly representative and participatory non-government organisations of internet governance, including the World Wide Web Consortium (W3C)'.[4] At this

[1]John M Eger, 'The Glabal Phenomenon of Teleinformantics: An Introduction' (1981) 14 Cornell International Law Journal 203. See also Timothy L Skelton, 'Internet Copyright Infringement and Service Providers: The Case for a Negotiated Rulemaking Alternative Comments' (1998) 35 San Diego Law Review 219; S Blair Kauffman, 'The Future of Legal Bibliography: The Role of Laserdiscs and Computers in Compiling and Distributing Bibliographies Trends' (1989) 9 Legal Reference Services Quarterly 147.

[2]See for instance Richard T Watson and Leyland F Pitt, 'Personal Computing Ethics: Beliefs and Behaviour' (1993) 13 International Journal of Information Management 287; John A Lehman, 'Personal Computing vs. Personal Computers' (1985) 9 Information & Management 253; Tor Guimaraes and Vasudevan Ramanujam, 'Sources of Personal Computing Problems' (1989) 17 Omega 543.

[3]In this chapter, web 1.0 refers to the early internet, marked by the emergence of the first worldwide internet services, such as the Netscape browser, which displayed static, non-interactive information. See for instance Tim O'Reilly, 'What Is Web 2.0' (*O'Reilly,* 30 September 2015) <www.oreilly.com/pub/a/web2/archive/what-is-web-20.html> accessed 24 March 2020; Diane Murley, 'What Is All the Fuss about Library 2.0 Technology for Everyone...' (2008) 100 Law Library Journal 197; George Bouchagiar, 'Privacy and Web 3.0: Implementing Trust and Learning from Social Networks' (2018) 10(4) Review of European Studies 16; Christopher G Reddick and Donald F Norris, 'Social Media Adoption at the American Grass Roots: Web 2.0 or 1.5?' (2013) 30 Government Information Quarterly 498.

[4]Graham Greenleaf, 'An Endnote on Regulating Cyberspace: Architecture vs. Law Electronic Commerce: Legal Issues for the Information Age' (1998) 21 University of New South Wales Law Journal 593; Nick Doty and Deirdre K Mulligan, 'Internet Multistakeholder Processes and Techno-Policy Standards: Initial Reflections on Privacy at the World Wide Web Consortium The Technology of Piracy' (2013) 11 Journal on Telecommunications & High Technology Law 135;

stage, little to no concern was paid to the impact of this private regulation on public values and interests,[5] apart perhaps from questions regarding the nature of cyberspace[6] and in particular the future of intellectual property rights in the context of piracy.[7]

The advent of the so-called 'sharing economy', which constitutes the second iteration of the internet, namely web 2.0, brought the inherent tensions between the private regulation of internet transactions and public values to the fore.[8] The regulatory vacuums or subsidies enjoyed by platforms earlier on led to the aggregation and consolidation of their power, which has echoed well beyond the private transactions concluded between information intermediaries such as Uber, AirBnb, Google, Facebook or YouTube and their respective users.[9] From this perspective, the discussion to be had about what goes on in cyberspace no longer fits the existing

---

Robert Uerpmann-Wittzack, 'Principles of International Internet Law' (2010) 11 German Law Journal 1245 <www.cambridge.org/core/journals/german-law-journal/article/principles-of-international-internet-law/3E9B0ED4BABDC582FA1A053DDD454987> accessed 27 August 2020.

[5]Matthew Fagin, 'Regulating Speech Across Borders: Technology vs. Values Comment' (2003) 9 (2) Michigan Telecommunications and Technology Law Review 395; Philip J Weiser, 'Law and Information Platforms Symposium - The Regulation of Information Platforms: Overview' (2002) 1 (1) Journal on Telecommunications & High Technology Law 1; Jose MA Emmanuel A Caral, 'Lessons from ICANN: Is Self-Regulation of the Internet Fundamentally Flawed' (2004) 12 International Journal of Law and Information Technology 1; Orly Lobel, 'The Renew Deal: The Fall of Regulation and the Rise of Governance in Contemporary Legal Thought' (2004) 89 Minnesota Law Review 342; Stefan Bechtold, 'Governance in Namespaces Symposium: ICANN Governance' (2002) 36 Loyola of Los Angeles Law Review 1239.

[6]Lyrissa Barnett Lidsky, 'Anonymity in Cyberspace: What Can We Learn from John Doe Publicity, Privacy, and Intellectual Property Meet the First Amendment' (2009) 50 Boston College Law Review 1373; Greenleaf (n 4); Richard A Paul and Lisa H Chung, 'Brave New Cyberworld: The Employer's Legal Guide to the Interactive Internet' (2008) 24 Labor Lawyer 109; Jonathon W Penney, 'Privacy and the New Virtualism' (2007) 10 Yale Journal of Law and Technology 194.

[7]Lidsky (n 6); Joel Reidenberg, 'The Rule of Intellectual Property Law in the Internet Economy Copyright in Context: Institute for Intellectual Property & Informational Law Symposium - Fourth Annual Baker Botts Lecture' (2007) 44 Houston Law Review 1073; Kristin Delaney, 'World Wide Web: Using Internet Governance Structures to Address Intellectual Property and International Development Note' (2006) 32 Brooklyn Journal of International Law 603.

[8]Jenny Kassan and Janelle Orsi, 'The Legal Landscape of the Sharing Economy Symposium: The Local Revolution: How Relationships and Legal Policies Are Helping Create Sustainable Communities Around the Country' (2012) 27 Journal of Environmental Law and Litigation 1; Guy Pessach, 'An International-Comparative Perspective on Peer-to-Peer File-Sharing and Third Party Liability in Copyright Law: Framing the Past, Present, and Next Generations' Questions' (2007) 40 Vanderbilt Journal of Transnational Law 87; Leah Wing, 'Social Impact and Technology: Issues of Access, Inequality and Disputing in the Collaborative Economy' (2014) 1 International Journal of Online Dispute Resolution 150.

[9]Stephen M Feldman, 'Broken Platforms, Broken Communities: Free Speech on Campus' (2018) 27 William & Mary Bill of Rights Journal 949; Shelly Kreiczer-Levy and Ronit Donyets-Kedar, 'Better Left Forgotten: An Argument against Treating Some Social Media and Digital Assets as Inheritance in an Era of Platform Power' (2018) 84 Brooklyn Law Review 703; Clement Salung Petersen, Vibe Garf Ulfbeck and Ole Hansen, 'Platforms as Private Governance Systems - The Example of Airbnb' (2018) 1 Nordic Journal of Commercial Law 38; Weiser (n 5); Cobun Keegan

paradigm, which assumes that the digital realm ought to be shaped according to the rules of the real world. It is the other way around. The shortcomings of private governance have a severe impact on the health and fitness of legal concepts and systems, primarily due to their effect on the values these rules and systems aim to protect.

A prime example of where this tension becomes visible is the context of smart cities.[10] Found at the intersection of the public and private divide, the quest for smart cities reflects on the one hand the interaction between public administration and private actors (such as technology companies) and, on the other hand, a transition from the private sphere in which internet technologies were previously deployed, to the public spheres of cities, including at physical level. Tech companies have been pushing for the development of smart services at the municipal level, including smart mobility, smart healthcare, smart infrastructure and smart building, to name a few examples.[11] To 'smartify' these services, it is necessary to collect and/or channel data into models that are intended to make urban life more fluid, comfortable and safe. While many data protection questions and concerns arise from such information flows and management systems,[12] in the vast majority of situations surrounding smart cities, contracts remain the foundation of the legal architecture used in this process. To have access to Uber's mapping of public transport, users must log into their Uber apps.[13] The Dutch public-private project Green Deal Smart Energy Cities, which is trying to contribute to the agenda of making the Netherlands energy-neutral by 2050, currently rests on existing infrastructures and energy providers and is in turn part of a contractual framework with consumers residing in the country.[14] The same holds true for similar projects on sustainability and energy efficiency deployed

and Calli Schroeder, 'Unpacking Unfairness: The FTC's Evolving Measures of Privacy Harms' (2019) 15 Journal of Law, Economics & Policy 19.

[10]Marloes Dignum, 'E-Governance for Smart Cities Book Review' (2015) 16 Competition and Regulation in Network Industries 309; Lilian Edwards, 'Privacy, Security and Data Protection in Smart Cities: A Critical EU Law Perspective' (2016) 2 European Data Protection Law Review 28; Janine S Hiller and Jordan M Blanke, 'Smart Cities, Big Data, and the Resilience of Privacy' (2016) 68 Hastings Law Journal 309; Nabeel Jurdi, 'Smart Cities and Global Village' (2018) 69 Journal of Law, Policy and Globalization 132; Jan Whittington, 'Remembering the Public in the Race to Become Smart Cities' (2016) 85 University of Missouri-Kansas City Law Review 925; K Sabeel Rahman, 'The New Utilities: Private Power, Social Infrastructure, and the Revival of the Public Utility Concept' (2017) 39 Cardozo Law Review 1621.

[11]Hiller and Blanke (n 10) 317.

[12]Christopher Kuner, 'Reality and Illusion in EU Data Transfer Regulation Post Schrems' (2017) 18 German Law Journal 881 <www.cambridge.org/core/journals/german-law-journal/article/reality-and-illusion-in-eu-data-transfer-regulation-post-schrems/0341A0D14DC345730F9B48A496A968D3> accessed 27 August 2020.

[13]'Uber Transit for Real-Time Public Transit Information in the App' (*Uber*) <www.uber.com/nl/en/ride/transit/> accessed 24 March 2020.

[14]'Green Deal Smart Energy Cities' (*Topsector Energie*) <www.topsectorenergie.nl/tki-urban-energy/kennisdossiers/green-deal-smart-energy-cities> accessed 24 March 2020.

in Spain, Turkey and the United Kingdom.[15] A lot of these initiatives try to respond to valid concerns; the unavoidable reality is that human-made climate change poses a grave danger to the future of our civilization,[16] and technology can be used to curb its effect. However, while the pace of the search for sustainability quickens, solutions may come at the price of overlooking what is necessary to achieve them: curtailing privacy. Perhaps in the context of sustainability, such a trade-off is not out of the question, but a discussion must be had as to whether such a trade-off is actually necessary. In this paper, I argue that the practice of curtailing citizens' control over their transactions need not be encouraged to attain sustainability—and that control is best defined by the giving of consent.

This chapter examines the contract as the transactional regime underpinning the legitimacy and legal validity of an agreement between two parties, and thus discusses consent from the perspective of contract law. What is the role of consent in contract formation? How does it come into being, and how is it recorded? In addition, what standards of quality apply to contractual consent? These questions will be central to Sect. 2. Section 3 will juxtapose reflections on contract law with insights from privacy scholarship in order to define and understand the concept of 'informed consent'. Section 4 discusses the main similarities and differences between the two facets of consent and reflects upon whether they (need to) converge or diverge in the context of smart mobility as a policy pursuing local/regional sustainability. Section 5 concludes the chapter.

This chapter makes several contributions to existing scholarship. First, given their focus on the public interest, privacy and data protection regulation and scholarship have generally developed in isolation from private law. Apart from specific private law fields such as consumer protection, where public interest considerations have led to some literature discussing and arguing for more harmonization between consumer and data protection law,[17] contract law as a whole remains generally detached from most privacy debates. This chapter contributes to furthering the dialogue between the two fields of law[18] by way of a comparison. Second, and more specifically, contract law scholarship has generated copious amounts of evidence regarding information duties in transactions between companies and consumers[19] that shows

[15]'Remourban' (*The Smart Circle*) <www.smart-circle.org/portfolios/remourban/> accessed 24 March 2020. See also Hiller and Blanke (n 10) 317.

[16]'Climate Change: Thousands Invited to Join Citizens Assembly' *BBC News* (2 November 2019) <www.bbc.com/news/science-environment-50264797> accessed 24 March 2020.

[17]Natali Helberger, Frederik Zuiderveen Borgesius and Agustin Reyna, 'The Perfect Match? A Closer Look at the Relationship between EU Consumer Law and Data Protection Law' (2017) 54 CML Rev 1427.

[18]Chris J Hoofnagle, 'Designing for Consent' (2018) 7 Journal of European Consumer and Market Law 162; Helberger, Zuiderveen Borgesius and Reyna (n 17).

[19]Omri Ben-Shahar, 'Fixing Unfair Contracts' (2010) 63 Stanford Law Review 869; Omri Ben-Shahar and Ariel Porat, 'Personalizing Negligence Law' (2016) 91 New York University Law Review 627; Omri Ben-Shahar and Carl E Schneider, 'Coping with the Failure of Mandated Disclosure' (2015) 11 Jerusalem Review of Legal Studies 83; Omri Ben-Shahar and Ariel Porat,

what works and what does not work in this context. Especially in light of the pervasiveness of contracts in everyday life, the more these contracts include privacy policies which serve as consent collection, the more essential it becomes to revisit the discussion regarding the efficiency of mandated disclosures. Finally, the chapter sets out to address the question of consent harvesting in the context of smart mobility, which in itself is linked to sustainability as a local or regional policy.

The contributions made in this chapter mainly take the form of a descriptive legal doctrinal inquiry into contract and privacy, while also relying on empirical findings from law and economics as well as computer science literature to provide further critical reflections on the interaction of these two fields of law at the center of this discussion.

2 Contracts and Consent

This section focuses on contract law, bringing basic contract formation mechanisms to the fore in order to determine what role consent plays therein. Private law defines the body of rules which 'are the ones that touch us most intimately, that mold our contracts, measure our torts, define our private rights, prescribe our private duties, come home to our firesides, enter into our offices, shops and factories and meet us at every turn on our round of daily tasks'.[20] Within it are the transactional dimensions of everyday life for individuals, companies as well as the state, reflecting the basic conditions of a healthy free market. We need property law to determine what is ours, contract law to conclude transactions and to exchange value and tort law to account for behavior outside of these transactions.

So how does contract law deal with consent? A granular answer to this question can only be found in the specific rules that govern contract law in various jurisdictions, as currently there is no harmonized global or European regime of default contract law rules. For this reason, this section relies on general principles of contract law as espoused by countries around the world and more specific examples from

'Personalizing Mandatory Rules in Contract Law Symposium: Personalized Law' (2019) 91 University of Chicago Law Review 255; Omri Ben-Shahar, 'Regulation through Boilerplate: An Apologia' (2014) 112 Michigan Law Review 883; Oren Bar-Gill, 'Seduction by Plastic' (2003) 98 Northwestern University Law Review 1373; Oren Bar-Gill, 'The Behavioral Economics of Consumer Contracts Exchange' (2007) 92 Minnesota Law Review 749; Ariel Porat, 'Private Production of Public Goods: Liability for Unrequested Benefits' (2009) 108 Michigan Law Review 189; David Gilo and Ariel Porat, 'The Hidden Roles of Boilerplate and Standard-Form Contracts: Strategic Imposition of Transaction Costs, Segmentation of Consumers, and Anticompetitive Effects' (2006) 104 Michigan Law Review 983; Rory Van Loo, 'Digital Market Perfection' (2018) 117 Michigan Law Review 815; Shmuel I Becher, 'Unintended Consequences and the Design of Consumer Protection Legislation' (2018) 93 Tulane Law Review 105; Hoofnagle (n 18).

[20] Adolph J Rodenbeck, *Anatomy of the Law: A Logical Presentation of the Parts of the Body of the Law* (Little Brown 1925) 174.

harmonization instruments adopted by the international community to this end as well as further illustrations from national jurisdictions.

As such, the law does not see every promise made by one person to another as a contract. This begs the question: under what conditions do promises become contracts? It is generally acknowledged that a contract is the expression of an agreement between two or more parties wanting to enter into a transaction that produces legal effects.[21] Generally speaking, three essential elements are required when considering the valid conclusion of a contract: there must be an offer, an acceptance and the intention to be legally bound.[22] Each of these aspects is discussed in what follows.

The offer and acceptance model is the most common expression of the *quid pro quo* nature of contracts: one party expresses their will to enter into a transaction by offering something; the other party in turn expresses their own will with respect to the terms of the offer in agreeing to those terms.[23] The Vienna Convention on the Sale of Goods (CISG), addressing contract formation in its Part II, is a good illustration of additional conditions an offer needs to comply with: 'A proposal for concluding a contract addressed to one or more specific persons constitutes an offer if it is sufficiently definite and indicates the intention of the offeror to be bound in case of acceptance'.[24] Similarly, the CISG further exemplifies, in Art. 18, the conditions of a valid acceptance: 'A statement made by or other conduct of the offeree indicating assent to an offer is an acceptance. Silence or inactivity does not in itself amount to acceptance.'[25] In doing so, the CISG expresses a standard which can be found in the vast majority of national legal systems as well: that acceptance can take place in the form of a statement, but also in the form of conduct. California also sees party consent as an essential element for the validity of contracts, as long as it is: (1) free, (2) mutual and (3) communicated by each party to the other.[26] For internet contracting, the latter component has proved problematic because in general, while

---

[21]Hugh Beale and others, *Contract Law: Ius Commune Casebooks for the Common Law of Europe* (Bloomsbury Publishing 2010); Randy E Barnett, 'Some Problems with Contract as Promise' (1991) 77 Cornell Law Review 1022; Randy E Barnett, 'A Consent Theory of Contract' (1986) 86 Columbia Law Review 269; Matthew A Seligman, 'The Error Theory of Contract' (2018) 78 Maryland Law Review 147.

[22]Gregory Klass, 'Intent to Contract' (2009) 95 Virginia Law Review 1437; Gregory Klass, 'Three Pictures of Contract: Duty, Power, and Compound Rule' (2008) 83 New York University Law Review 1726; Barnett, 'Consent Theory of Contract, A' (n 21); Barnett, 'Some Problems with Contract as Promise' (n 21); Anthony J Bellia, 'Contracting with Electronic Agents' (2001) 50 Emory Law Journal 1047.

[23]Günter H Treitel, *The Law of Contract* (10th edn, Sweet & Maxwell 1999) 8.

[24]Art 14.1, United Nations, Vienna Convention on the Law of Treaties, 23 May 1969, United Nations, Treaty Series, vol. 1155, p. 331.

[25]ibid, art 18.1.

[26]Cal. Civ. Code §1565. It is worth mentioning that the Chapter of the Civil Code dealing with consent (§1565-1590) was enacted in 1872. See also George W Kuney and Donna C Looper, *California Law of Contracts* (CEB 2017) §3.2.

consent may be expressed or implied,[27] it is unclear how to determine the nature of consent when it is expressed digitally.

For thousands of years, contracts have been concluded orally or in writing, with the most straightforward example being the use of pen and paper.[28] Although one of the most essential concepts emerging from the principle of freedom of contract is the freedom of form, individuals and businesses around the world tend to conclude contracts in writing for more predictability and to make sure, should a deal fall short of their expectations, that they can always prove their rights and obligations. With the emergence of email services, people could all of a sudden communicate by clicking buttons and sending computer-generated text to one another without writing anything down on a piece of paper. This has fundamentally changed contract law.[29] One of the vital changes it has brought about concerns contract formation, as new models of concluding contracts have emerged. One of these models is clickwrap, namely the concept that if a user clicks on a button or icon to indicate acceptance of general terms, the contract is concluded. A second model is browsewrap, namely the concept that when a user visits or views an internet website, a contract is concluded.[30]

In California, the cradle of internet services since the early 1990s, online contracting has been a rich source of case law. In one of the first cases of its kind, *CompuServe, Inc. v Patterson*,[31] the Sixth Circuit upheld the validity of a choice of

[27] James Chang and Farnaz Alemi, 'Gaming the System: A Critique of Minors' Privilege to Disaffirm Online Contracts' (2012) 2 UC Irvine Law Review 627, 648.

[28] RJ Robertson, 'Electronic Commerce on the Internet and the Statute of Frauds' (1998) 49 South Carolina Law Review 787, 810.

[29] See for instance Peer Zumbansen, 'Contracting in the Internet: German Contract Law and Internet Auctions' (2001) 2(7) German Law Journal <www.cambridge.org/core/journals/german-law-journal/article/contracting-in-the-internet-german-contract-law-and-internet-auctions/A61AA388C6E50BA0656D002148379949> accessed 24 March 2020.

[30] A third model is 'shrinkwrap': if a user opens the packaging of a software product (plastic shrinkwrap) and starts using the software, a contract is concluded. This contract formation model, however, does not necessarily reflect an intention to be legally bound expressed online. Moreover, shrinkwrap agreements grew in importance because of the fact that as of the early days of personal computers, the purchase of software became crucial to the functioning of these machines. This issue thus became part of the greater debate on licensing and IP rights.

[31] *CompuServe, Inc v Patterson* 89 F3d 1257 (6th Cir 1996). See also *MySpace, Inc v TheGlobe.com, Inc* WL 1686966 (CD Cal 2007), dealing with enforceable MySpace clickwrap agreement; *Koresko v RealNetworks, Inc.* 291 F Supp 2d 1157 (ED Cal 2003), dealing with 'I agree' box clicked by user, therefore agreement enforced; *Hoffman v Supplements Togo Mgmt, LLC* 18 A3d 210 (NJ Super 2011) relating to choice of forum clause not enforced because website was structured unfairly; *Caspi v Microsoft Network, LLC* 118, 732 A2d 528 (NJ Super Ct App Div 1999) relating to choice of forum clause enforced, as users had to click 'I agree' or 'I don't agree'; *Forrest v Verizon Communications, Inc* 805 A2d 1011 (DC App 2002): 'A contract is no less a contract simply because it is entered into via a computer'; American Eyewear, Inc v Peeper's Sunglasses 106 F Supp 2d 895 (ND Tex 2000); *Hotmail Corp v Van$ Money Pie, Inc* WL 388389 (ND Cal 1998) on enforcing Hotmail clickwrap agreement with clause prohibiting users from distributing spam; *AV v iParadigms* 544 F Supp 2d 473 (ED Va 2008). See also Steven C Bennett, 'Click-Wrap Arbitration Clauses' (2000) 14 International Review of Law, Computers & Technology 397, 410.

forum clause that required one of the parties to type 'AGREE' at different points in the online document to indicate its intention to be legally bound. This case reflects clickwrap practices.[32] In 1999, when California amended its Civil Code to accommodate the Uniform Electronic Transactions Act, clickwrap agreements became regulated through statute.[33] §1633.14 governs automated decisions and acknowledges in subparagraph 1 that electronic contracts can be concluded even if the users were not aware of or did not review the actions of the electronic agents. A more detailed overview of clickwrap agreements was offered in the Uniform Computer Information Transactions Act (UCITA).[34]

Case law reflects a more turbulent history for browsewrap agreements, as they are generally not considered to be enforceable.[35] This is mostly because courts have found the lack of notice and the non-interactive nature of such agreements to be key

---

[32]See for instance Margaret J Radin, 'Humans, Computers, and Binding Commitment' (2000) 75 Indiana Law Journal 1125, 1162; Mark L Tuft, 'Internet Communications with Prospective Clients When Disclaimers May Not Be Enough' (2006) The Professional Lawyer Symposium 23, 27; Susan Y Chao, 'Contract Law - Electronic Contract Formation - District Court for the Central District of California Holds That a Web-Wrap Site License Does Not Equate to an Enforceable Contract - Ticketmaster Corp v Tickets.com, Inc' (2001) 54 Southern Methodist University Law Review 439, 442.

[33]UCITA §1633.14 mentions:

(a) In an automated transaction, the following rules apply:

(1) A contract may be formed by the interaction of electronic agents of the parties, even if no individual was aware of or reviewed the electronic agents' actions or the resulting terms and agreements.
(2) A contract may be formed by the interaction of an electronic agent and an individual, acting on the individual's own behalf or for another person, including by an interaction in which the individual performs actions that the individual is free to refuse to perform and which the individual knows or has reason to know will cause the electronic agent to complete the transaction or performance.

(b) The terms of the contract are determined by the substantive law applicable to it.

[34]Robert W Hahn and Anne Layne-Farrar, 'An Economic Assessment of UCITA' (2002) 24 Hastings Communications and Entertainment Law Journal 335, 341.

[35]Jeffrey M Jensen, 'Personal Jurisdiction in Federal Courts over International E-Commerce Cases' (2007) 40 Loyola of Los Angeles Law Review 1507, 1551; Francis J Mootz, 'After the Battle of the Forms: Commercial Contracting in the Electronic Age' (2008) 4 I/S: A Journal of Law and Policy for the Information Society 271, 282; see also *Specht v Netscape Communications Corp*, 306 F3d 17 (2d Cir 2002); *Hubbert v Dell Corp* 835 NE2d 113 (Ill App Ct 2005); *Southwest Airlines v Boardfirst, Llc*, 2007 WL 4823761 (ND Tex 2007); *Cvent, Inc v Eventbrite, Inc* 739 F Supp 2d 927 (E D V a 2010); *Nguyen v Barnes & Noble, Inc*, 763 F3d 1171 (9th Cir 2014); *Be In, Inc v Google Inc* 12-CV-03373-LHK (ND Cal 2013); *Hines vOverstock.com, Inc*, 668 FSupp2d 362, 366–67 (ED NY 2009); *Cairo, Inc v Crossmedia Servs, Inc* WL 756610 (ND Cal 2005); *Pollstar v Gigmania, Ltd* 170 F Supp 2d 974 (ED Cal 2000); *Nghiem v Dick's Sporting Goods, Inc* 222 F. Supp. 3d 805 (CD Cal 2016); *Long v Provide Commerce, Inc* 245 CA4th 855 (CA Cal 2016); *Tompkins v 23andMe, Inc* 840 F3d 1016 (9th Cir 2016).

factors in the rejection of their enforcement.[36] However, due to widespread methods of harvesting consent (mostly based on clickwrap), terms of use are generally binding on e.g. platform users,[37] as are additional clauses incorporated in the terms of use by reference.[38]

Regardless of whether it is expressed in person or online, consent is based on the information available to the person expressing it. Should a buyer investigate defects in a second-hand car or compare prices using online tools to make sure a product is really on sale, as an ad may suggest?[39] Should service providers disclose to consumers any potential incompatibilities with existing infrastructures (e.g. in the case of communication services)? The balance of what information parties ought to know and ought to be given when entering a contract depends on the object of the contract as well as the qualities of the parties to the contract. Specifically in European consumer protection, mandatory disclosures have shifted the responsibility from the consumer to the professional party. For instance, Art. 6 of the Consumer Rights Directive lists a host of disclosures that traders must comply with if they transact with European consumers, such as the existence of withdrawal rights, price breakdowns, etc.[40] European law identifies disclosures as the ones exemplified by 'information duties', the role of which is to inform consumers about aspects which may play a role in their decision-making process.[41] How exactly consumers internalize this information is a different matter. Law and economics literature has long been promoting the view that consumers do not really care about information duties because even if they wanted to, the information dumped on them when entering into contracts (e.g. the general terms and conditions) is so overwhelmingly volumi-

---

[36]See for instance *Lima v Gateway, Inc* 886 F Supp 2d 1170 (CD Cal 2012); *Savetsky v Pre-Paid Legal Servs, Inc* WL 604767 (ND Cal 2015).

[37]'Update on Shrinkwrap/Clickwrap/Browsewrap Contracts' (2006) 21 Berkeley Technology Law Journal 552, 554. See also *Register.com, Inc v Verio, Inc*, 356 F. 3d 393 (2d Cir 2004).

[38]*PDC Labs, Inc v Hach Co* WL 2605270 (CD Ill 2009); *Swift v Zynga Game Network, Inc* 805 F Supp 2d 904 (ND Cal 2011).

[39]Jeffrey L Harrison, 'Defects in Consent and Dividing the Benefit of the Bargain: Recent Developments' (2014) 53 University of Louisville Law Review 193; Sebastian Lohsse, 'Information Duties and Defects in Consent' in Reiner Schulze and Perales Viscasillas Pilar, *The Formation of Contract* (Nomos Verlagsgesellschaft mbH & Co KG 2016); Francesco Paolo Patti, '"Fraud" and "Misleading Commercial Practices": Modernising the Law of Defects in Consent' (2016) 12 European Review of Contract Law 307.

[40]Parliament and Council Directive (EU) 2011/83 of 25 October 2011 on consumer rights, amending Council Directive 93/13/EEC and Directive 1999/44/EC of the European Parliament and of the Council and repealing Council Directive 85/577/EEC and Directive 97/7/EC of the European Parliament and of the Council, [2011] OL 304/64.

[41]Lohsse (n 39); Zofia Bednarz, *Breach of Information Duties in the B2C E-Commerce: A Comparative Perspective* (Marcial Pons Ediciones Jurídicas 2019); Great Britain: Law Commission, *Consumer Redress for Misleading and Aggressive Practices: A Joint Consultation Paper* (The Stationery Office 2011).

nous that it is simply impossible for consumers to care about it.[42] This body of literature, although not too popular in the European Union, where the prevalent policy view is that mandated disclosures empower consumers,[43] forms an inherent part of the general development of scholarship on contract and consumer law. It is particularly valuable for the next part of the paper, which deals with the privacy notion of 'informed consent'.

3 Informed Consent as a Privacy Standard

Traditionally subsumed in the expression of fiduciary duties in doctor-patient relationships, informed consent has become a central concept for privacy regulation.[44] The GDPR defines consent in Art. 4(11) as '[. . .] any freely given, specific, informed and unambiguous indication of the data subject's wishes by which he or she, by a statement or by a clear affirmative action, signifies agreement to the processing of personal data relating to him or her'. In addition, consent 'should be given by a clear affirmative act establishing a freely given, specific, informed and unambiguous indication of the data subject's agreement to the processing of personal data relating to him or her, such as by a written statement, including by electronic means, or an oral statement', whereas 'silence, pre-ticked boxes or inactivity should not therefore constitute consent'.[45] Still, the same recital acknowledges that expressions of informed consent could include 'ticking a box when visiting an internet website, choosing technical settings for information society services or another statement or conduct which clearly indicates in this context the data subject's acceptance of the proposed processing of his or her personal data'.[46]

[42]Omri Ben-Shahar and Carl E Schneider, *More Than You Wanted to Know: The Failure of Mandated Disclosure* (Princeton University Press 2014); Omri Ben-Shahar, 'More Failed Nudges: Evidence of Ineffective Behaviorally Informed Disclosures Contracts' (2017) Jotwell: The Journal of Things We Like (Lots) 1.

[43]Dorota Leczykiewicz and Stephen Weatherill, *The Images of the Consumer in EU Law: Legislation, Free Movement and Competition Law* (Bloomsbury Publishing 2016).

[44]Ruth R Faden and Tom L Beauchamp, *A History and Theory of Informed Consent* (Oxford University Press 1986); Fida K Dankar, Marton Gergely and Samar K Dankar, 'Informed Consent in Biomedical Research' (2019) 17 Computational and Structural Biotechnology Journal 463. See also Alexandra Giannopoulou, 'Algorithmic Systems: The Consent Is in the Detail?' (2020) 9 Internet Policy Review <https://policyreview.info/articles/analysis/algorithmic-systems-consent-detail> accessed 24 March 2020; Elettra Bietti, 'Consent as a Free Pass: Platform Power and the Limits of the Informational Turn' (2020) 40 Pace Law Review 310.

[45]Parliament and Council Regulation (EU) 679/2016 of 27 April 2016 on the protection of natural persons with regard to the processing of personal data and on the free movement of such data, and repealing Directive 95/46/EC (General Data Protection Regulation) [2016] OJ L119/1 (GDPR), recital 32.

[46]ibid. See also Christopher F Mondschein, 'Some Iconoclastic Thoughts on the Effectiveness of Simplified Notices and Icons for Informing Individuals as Proposed in Article 12(1) and (7) GDPR'

In the *Planet49* case, Advocate General Szpunar clarified these concepts by establishing 'general principles deriving from the applicable legal instruments on the giving of consent',[47] namely active consent, separate consent and the obligation to fully inform.[48] Active consent is seen by AG Szpunar as stemming from the fact that the user must 'unambiguously' give their consent, as ambiguity can 'only be removed with active, as opposed to passive, behaviour'.[49] The practical impact of this assessment, the AG holds, is that pre-formulated declarations of consent are not unambiguous because it is not clear to what extent the user actually reads them. Separate consent is reflected by a separation between the activity pursued by the consumer on the internet and the act of giving consent. The two actions must be given equal footing, as 'a bundle of expressions of intention, which would include the giving of consent, would be in conformity with the notion of consent'.[50] Lastly, the obligation to fully inform is presented as a 'crystal-clear' acknowledgment made to the user 'whether the activity he pursues on the internet is contingent upon the giving of consent', so that '[a] user must be in a position to assess to what extent he is prepared to give his data in order to pursue his activity on the internet'.[51]

The Court subsequently agreed with this view[52] and determined that pre-ticked boxes do not constitute 'clear affirmative action' reflecting how users would agree to

(2016) 2 European Data Protection Law Review 507; Paul Voigt and Axel von dem Bussche, *The EU General Data Protection Regulation (GDPR): A Practical Guide* (Springer 2017); JC Buitelaar, 'Privacy: Back to the Roots' (2012) 13 German Law Journal 171 <www.cambridge.org/core/journals/german-law-journal/article/privacy-back-to-the-roots/4BF002324861DBEBE0E0C3314709866C> accessed 27 August 2020; Jordan M Blanke, 'Robust Notice and Informed Consent: The Keys to Successful Spyware Legislation' (2005) 7 Columbia Science and Technology Law Review 1; Bart Custers and others, 'Informed Consent in Social Media Use - The Gap between User Expectations and EU Personal Data Protection Law' (2013) 10 SCRIPTed: A Journal of Law, Technology and Society 435; Shara Monteleone, 'Addressing the Failure of Informed Consent in Online Data Protection: Learning the Lessons from Behaviour-Aware Regulation' (2015) 43 Syracuse Journal of International Law and Commerce 69; Eoin Carolan, 'The Continuing Problems with Online Consent under the EU's Emerging Data Protection Principles' (2016) 32 Computer Law & Security Review 462; Yue Liu, 'User Control of Personal Information Concerning Mobile-App: Notice and Consent?' (2014) 30 Computer Law & Security Review 521.

[47]Case C-673/17 *Planet49 GmbH v Bundesverband der Verbraucherzentralen und Verbraucherverbände – Verbraucherzentrale Bundesverband e.V* [2019] EU:C:2019:246, Opinion of Advocate General Szpunar, para 58.

[48]While these principles are mentioned in relation to Parliament and Council Directive 95/46 EC of 24 October 1995 on the protection of individuals with regard to the processing of personal data and on the free movement of such data [1995] OJ L 281/31, AG Szpunar acknowledges that they equally apply to the GDPR as well.

[49]*Planet49* (n 47) para 62.

[50]ibid, para 66.

[51]ibid, para 67.

[52]Case C-673/17 *Planet49 GmbH v Bundesverband der Verbraucherzentralen und Verbraucherverbände – Verbraucherzentrale Bundesverband eV* [2019] EU:C:2019:801.

the processing of their personal data.[53] In addition, the Court expressed that 'it would appear impossible in practice to ascertain objectively whether a website user had actually given his or her consent to the processing of his or her personal data by not deselecting a pre-ticked checkbox nor, in any event, whether that consent had been informed',[54] given that a user might not have read the information in the checkbox or would have failed to see the checkbox if pre-ticked.

Even though it establishes a clear prohibition on pre-ticked boxes for cookie-tracking consent, the *Planet49* judgment leaves out the essential question of what informed consent truly is.[55] The standard expressed in the recitals of the GDPR Preamble seems to leave enough room for the interpretation that consent need not be expressed through a statement alone, but also through behavior. Yet both AG Szpunar and the CJEU agree that such behavior needs to be active and not passive, which casts a lot of doubt on where to draw the line between these two dimensions. Does the main difference between passive and active behavior lie in whether a user needs to perform several other clicks before clicking the 'I agree' button? Hopefully, that is not what the Court actually meant to imply. Still, the argumentation used in the advisory opinion as well as the judgment leads to the conclusion that according to the CJEU, pre-ticked boxes are the main reason why a user would not read the information about how a company tracks them through cookies, which is a grossly flawed behavioral assumption about internet users.

4 The Clash of Consent in the Context of Smart Mobility

Clickwrap and browsewrap agreements highlight the form and scale of questions of contract formation on the internet. First, even contracts for necessaries, such as groceries, are designed to leave a paper trail in daily life in the form of the receipt we get from a supermarket cashier (or as is increasingly the case, self-service scanning and payment machines). For forms of contracts concluded outside of the trader's premises, such as doorstep contracts, paper contracts are quintessential. This explains an initial legal struggle in replacing paper with a digital 'durable medium'.[56] Second, contracting in the real world takes time, whereas digital contracts can be concluded much faster and in higher volumes, which means that information overload is equally fast. Clicking a 'buy' button on a webstore after placing items in a basket and inserting payment details is sufficient for there to be a

[53]ibid, para 61.

[54]ibid, para 55.

[55]Gabriela Zanfir Fortuna, 'Planet49 CJEU Judgment Brings Some "Cookie Consent" Certainty to Planet Online Tracking' (*European Law Blog*, 8 October 2019) <https://europeanlawblog.eu/2019/10/08/planet49-cjeu-judgment-brings-some-cookie-consent-certainty-to-planet-online-tracking/> accessed 24 March 2020.

[56]Catalina Goanta, 'Information Duties in the Internet Era: Case Note on *Content Services Ltd* v. *Bundesarbeitkammer*' (2013) 21 European Review of Private Law 643.

legally binding agreement between a consumer and a company from a contractual perspective. In such a situation, pre-ticked boxes may be seen as an unfair commercial practice, but they have no impact on contract formation to the extent that the consent of the consumer is not vitiated. Yet what may suffice in the eyes of contract law, as we have seen in the previous section, may not suffice in the case of privacy standards, where active behavior is necessary.[57]

To continue this comparison in the context of smart mobility, let us focus on a real-life (anonymized) illustration. Say that a European city wants to improve the well-being, participation, altruism and sustainability awareness of its citizens and asks a private company to develop (among other things) an app that citizens can use to share cars and bikes as a form of pro-social behavior. For every such action, the citizen would be rewarded with points that could be collected to win various prizes, mostly relating to public services (e.g. opera subscription, public transportation subscription, etc.). Given that the app is made and run by a private company (as opposed to the municipality), it will have to govern its relationship with citizens by engaging in contracts with each of the users. No boxes are pre-ticked in signing up for this free service, and the user simply needs to accept the general terms and conditions, which also refer to a privacy policy that explains how the information given by the user will be publicly available on the app, as the app keeps a ranking of the most engaged citizens.

According to contract law, a contract would come into existence once the user clicks the 'I agree' button. It is true that if there were any issues with the general terms—for example, if some of the clauses were deemed unfair—those clauses would not be binding on the consumer. However, such an information service or contract for digital content would still stand. The same goes for information duties. Where information duties are placed under the responsibility of an internet trader, not displaying these duties might lead to administrative fines; nonetheless, *prima facie*, the contract would still stand. In comparison, according to the *Planet49* case, consent must not only be active but also specific, meaning that 'it must relate specifically to the processing of the data in question and cannot be inferred from an indication of the data subject's wishes for other purposes'.[58] If this standard is not respected, the data processor has no legal ground to process consumer data, but this framework does not tackle any effect the lack of this legal ground would have on the contract itself. Furthermore, this raises the question of whether generic terms and conditions would count as 'other purposes' if they are separated from a company's privacy policy. Would both the general terms and the privacy policy in this case be seen as separate documents for which companies need to obtain consent separately? Given the popularity of separating these rules (e.g. privacy policies; general terms; and codes of conduct or community guidelines), as well as their impact on

---

[57]See also Alessandro Mantelero, 'The Future of Consumer Data Protection in the E.U. Re-Thinking the "Notice and Consent" Paradigm in the New Era of Predictive Analytics' (2014) 30 Computer Law & Security Review 643.

[58]*Planet49* (n 47) para 58.

contract formation from the perspective of aligning the expectations of contracting parties, further research is necessary to determine, at the level of specific jurisdictions, whether, and to what extent these rules have a binding nature. Equally, the limitations of freedom of contract which are created through mandatory rules of public order such as those arising from privacy and data protection constitute further evidence regarding the constitutionalization of private law.

An additional complication is that companies change their standard terms (and privacy policies) all the time.[59] If a micromobility company such as Lime updates its general terms and sends a notification to its existing users (with whom the company already has a contract),[60] this can be seen as a subsequent agreement and users could adhere to it by conduct. Using an app for years and continuing to accept its changed general terms by clicking notifications away[61] amounts to a behavioral contracting pattern, and in principle, a user cannot invoke their own lack of active behavior when agreeing to continue with the contractual relationship.[62] Yet applying the privacy standards discussed above may not yield the same result, given that active behavior is now established as central for informed consent. It would be stimulating (if somewhat unfeasible) to consider how this threshold would be theoretically applied to a situation where a Lime user performs the contract (using the e-scooter) right after a privacy update. Would this conduct be enough to be considered informed consent for the subsequent agreement, or would the user first have to click various boxes by themselves for there to be informed consent?

So far, consent remains an abstract concept that is highly contextual. Given the broad definitions in the GDPR as well as the interpretations of the European Court, a quick fix for the coherence issues faced at the intersection of contract and consumer protection is not really in sight. These two fields are not the only ones where competing concepts need to be aligned: in governing digital contracts and collective redress, European consumer law will be increasingly at odds with privacy and data protection regulation in spite of earlier calls for more coherence and coordination within European law.[63]

---

[59]See also Liam Curren and Jane Kaye, 'Revoking Consent: A "Blind Spot" in Data Protection Law?' (2010) 26 Computer Law & Security Review 273.

[60]Mobility companies gather a lot of locational data, and need to explain this process to users. See Aggeliki Tsohou and Eleni Kosta, 'Enabling Valid Informed Consent for Location Tracking through Privacy Awareness of Users: A Process Theory' (2017) 33 Computer Law & Security Review 434.

[61]Given the current complexity of marketing email services (e.g. the use of pixel tracking), it would even be possible for data companies to determine whether users read updates to general terms sent by email.

[62]It is important to note that for a lot of digital content contracts (e.g. with Facebook), there are no incentives for a party to invalidate such a contract. This discussion can, however, play a role in situations where damage may occur (e.g. using a Lime e-scooter and damaging it or damaging additional things), and there needs to be a contractual or extra-contractual assessment of the regime applicable to such damages.

[63]Helberger, Borgesius and Reyna (n 17).

5 Conclusion

This chapter looked into the concept of consent in the context of smart mobility, aiming to explore the urban mobility context in order to identify and discuss legal issues linked to the tensions between contract on the one hand and privacy and data protection law on the other. Given that a lot of private urban mobility initiatives (e.g. Uber public transportation) focus on tracking and profiling users for the purpose of data analyses that lie at the core of their business models, informed consent plays a fundamental role in the transactions through which this data is acquired.

Taking contract law as a starting point, I explored contract formation with an emphasis on the history of digital contracts concluded via browsewrap or clickwrap, paying particular attention to the role of consent in contract formation and giving examples from various national and supranational jurisdictions. These reflections were further compared with insights from privacy scholarship and practice in order to define and understand the concept of 'informed consent' and how this concept converges or diverges with the contractual dimension of consent. The recent ruling of the Court of Justice of the European Union in the *Planet49* case served as an interpretative tool for Art. 4(11) GDPR. The Court's (as well as the AG's) development of a high threshold for the concept of 'informed consent' poses significant coherence questions in the alignment of contract and privacy/data protection.

Perhaps the most important conclusion regarding the intersection of concepts of consent is that the lack of informed consent from a privacy perspective does not affect the validity of a contract from a contract law point of view but can still lead to administrative penalties under the GDPR. This clash of consent*s* can lead to a paradoxical situation where the degree of consent is sufficient for there to be a contract but at the same time—due to a lack of active behavior—insufficient to be considered informed consent. While overall, the GDPR is hailed as a gold standard for data protection, its European concepts by no means fit neatly into the legal systems of Member States, especially when they have spillover effects across different fields of law. We can only hope that additional case law will clarify and crystalize reasonable and cohesive standards surrounding the meaning and value of consent.

Private Ordering of Online Platforms in Smart Urban Mobility: The Case of Uber's Rating System

Rossana Ducato

People have stars, but they aren't the same. For travellers, the stars are guides. For other people, they're nothing but tiny lights. And for still others, for scholars, they're problems. For my businessman, they were gold. But all those stars are silent stars. You, though, you'll have stars like nobody else.
—Antoine de Saint-Exupéry

Contents

This article expands on the research initially conducted for the contribution, Rossana Ducato, Miriam Kullmann and Marco Rocca, 'European Legal Perspectives on Customer Ratings and Discrimination' in Tindara Addabbo and others (eds), *Performance Appraisal in Modern Employment Relations* (Springer 2020). Rossana Ducato is Lecturer in IT Law and Regulation at the University of Aberdeen. She is also affiliated to the CRIDES at UCLouvain. The research for this paper has been conducted with the support of the Erasmus+ Project of the EU Commission, within the framework of the Jean Monnet Network "SHINE. SHaring economy and INequalities across Europe". The European Commission's support for the production of this publication does not constitute an endorsement of the contents, which reflect the views only of the author, and the Commission cannot be held responsible for any use which may be made of the information contained therein.

R. Ducato (✉)
University of Aberdeen, School of Law, Aberdeen, UK
e-mail: rossana.ducato@abdn.ac.uk

M. Finck et al. (eds.), *Smart Urban Mobility*, MPI Studies on Intellectual Property and Competition Law 29, https://doi.org/10.1007/978-3-662-61920-9_15

Abstract Rating and review systems are a self-regulatory mechanism widely used by online platforms, especially in the smart mobility sector. Such systems have already been analysed in empirical studies and legal contributions, in particular in the fields of consumer law and labour law.

This chapter aims to make an original contribution to the current debate from a relatively underinvestigated perspective: how rating and review systems interact with the European data protection framework. As a case study, the chapter will focus on the rating system adopted by Uber, one of the largest shared mobility platforms worldwide.

1 Introduction

Rating and review (R&R) systems are private ordering mechanisms widely used by online platforms. The paradigmatic example is that of multi-sided platforms such as eBay, Amazon, Uber or Airbnb.[1] These platforms, although at different times and in different ways, have introduced R&R systems as a tool to build and maintain trust within their community and to preserve the attractiveness of their services.

The scoring system in particular has played a crucial role for the development of business models in the shared mobility sector, where platform users are able to organise urban and extra-urban rides in real time.[2]

In this context, R&R systems can be seen to perform essentially two functions: (1) informative and (2) self-regulatory.

First of all, R&R systems constitute a reputational mechanism that can help reduce information asymmetry between the parties and promote the overall transparency of the transaction.[3] They represent a source of information which, before the advent of e-commerce, could have been obtained through channels such as advertising, direct experience or recommendations of friends or acquaintances. In

[1]On the notion of multi-sided platforms, see Kevin J Boudreau and Andrei Hagiu, 'Platform Rules: Multi-sided Platforms as Regulators' (2009) 1 Platforms, Markets and Innovation 163; David S Evans, 'Governing Bad Behavior by Users of Multi-sided Platforms' (2012) 27 Berkeley Technology Law Journal 1201.

[2]On the different types and models of business in the shared mobility sector, see Boyd Cohen and Jan Kietzmann, 'Ride on! Mobility Business Models for the Sharing Economy' (2014) 27 Organization & Environment 279.

[3]On the role of R&R systems in the platform economy, see Christoph Busch, 'Crowdsourcing Consumer Confidence: How to Regulate Online Rating and Review Systems in the Collaborative Economy' in Alberto De Franceschi (ed), *European Contract Law and the Digital Single Market: the Implication of the Digital Revolution* (Intersentia 2016); Guido Smorto, 'Reputazione, Fiducia e Mercati' (2016) 1 Europa e Diritto Privato 199; Lene G Braathen Pettersen, 'Rating Mechanisms Among Participants in Sharing Economy Platforms' (2017) 22 First Monday <https://firstmonday.org/ojs/index.php/fm/article/view/7908/6586> accessed 30 December 2019; Sofia Ranchordás, 'Online Reputation and the Regulation of Information Asymmetries in the Platform Economy' (2018) 5 Critical Analysis of Law 127 <https://cal.library.utoronto.ca/index.php/cal/article/view/29508/21993> accessed 30 December 2019.

this sense, R&R systems have codified the 'word of mouth' in the business models, contracts and digital architectures of such platforms.[4]

Reviews and ratings can be defined respectively as feedback (in a textual form) and scores (in a numerical form) given by the platform's users to report their experience with a particular buyer or service provider in a supposedly impartial manner. In addition to that, some platforms also provide aggregate or consolidated ratings, which sum up the single ratings or reviews in an overall assessment. Consolidated ratings can play an important role in supporting the users' decision-making process, addressing some cognitive difficulties and the problem of information overload (the 'wall' of reviews).[5] As Busch stated: 'the use of consolidated ratings thus takes into consideration the problems of bounded attention and bounded rationality and increases the salience (i.e. the cognitive accessibility) of the most important information'.[6]

The second function of R&R systems is self-regulation. On many platforms, users (both service providers and end users) assess each other. This bi-directional evaluation is an incentive for members to behave according to the rules of the community and maintain a high online reputation.[7] A series of private sanctions usually complete the R&R systems: if the user's overall score is below the threshold set by the platform, the personal account can be suspended or deactivated.

On the one hand, the platform aims to maintain a safe and attractive business environment by using this combination of ratings and sanctions. On the other hand, this can have significant consequences for the online and offline activity of its participants: end users may decide not to accept a service from the provider with a low rating or, in the worst case, the user may be excluded from the platform.

R&R systems have already been at the centre of a series of empirical studies[8] and legal analyses, particularly in the areas of consumer[9] and labour

---

[4]Chrysanthos Dellarocas, 'The Digitization of Word-of-Mouth: Promise and Challenges of Online Feedback Mechanisms' (March 2003) MIT Sloan Working Paper No. 4296-03 <https://ssrn.com/abstract=393042> accessed 30 December 2019 or <https://doi.org/10.2139/ssrn.393042> accessed 30 December 2019.

[5]Busch (n 3).

[6]ibid 12.

[7]However, the reciprocity of the evaluation is also one of the reasons why users tend to score high. This distorting effect has been found in platforms such as eBay, where the evaluation is not anonymous and takes place at a delayed point in time. A user who has had a mediocre or negative experience is inclined to leave positive feedback, fearing that the other party might 'retaliate' by leaving a low score. Chrysanthos Dellarocas and Charles A Wood, 'The Sound of Silence in Online Feedback: Estimating Trading Risks in the Presence of Reporting Bias' (2008) 54 Management Science 460; Abbey Stemler, 'Feedback Loop Failure: Implications for the Self-regulation of the Sharing Economy' (2017) 18 Minnesota Journal of Law, Science & Technology 673, 691.

[8]For an overview, see Cristiano Codagnone and Bertin Martens, 'Scoping the Sharing Economy: Origins, Definitions, Impact and Regulatory Issues' (2016) Institute for Prospective Technological Studies Digital Economy Working Paper 22.

[9]See, in particular, Omri Ben-Shahar, 'One-Way Contracts: Consumer Protection without Law' (2010) 6 European Review of Contract Law 221; Christoph Busch and others, 'The Rise of the

law.[10] The paper aims to contribute to the debate from a rather underinvestigated perspective, namely how the data protection framework applies to R&R systems.

As a case study, this chapter will critically analyse the rating system implemented by Uber, one of the major platforms for shared mobility worldwide (Sect. 2). The analysis will focus specifically on 'UberX', i.e. the automated service that—through the eponymous app—matches drivers and passengers within the same city. Considering that scores, reviews, and ratings can qualify as personal data, the contribution identifies and analyses two main points of friction between R&R systems and the General Data Protection Regulation (GDPR):[11] the identification of the appropriate legal basis for processing data (Sect. 3.1) and the limitations to data subjects' rights, in particular their right not to be subject to a solely automated decision-making process (Sect. 3.2). In conclusion, the chapter will formulate guidelines and recommendations to encourage the design of R&R systems that are in line with fundamental data protection principles (Sect. 4).

Research Method

This contribution investigates the Uber R&R system through an empirical analysis of the legal documents available online (Terms and Conditions, Privacy Policy, Deactivation Policy, help pages, etc.). When some information was not available—for instance, the average minimum rating—the specific data were requested directly through the Uber help centre.

All the documents and information refer to 'UberX' (as operating in Belgium). For the purpose of this contribution, the official English version (available for Belgium) of all the documents has been used.

To get more precise information to supplement the textual analysis, I have replicated the passenger's journey on the platform, e.g. by signing up, requesting a ride and assigning a score. A limitation of the present study is that it does not perform the same analysis of the user's journey from the driver's perspective. Therefore, when the user's path is described, it refers to the rider's experience unless otherwise specified.

Platform Economy: a New Challenge for EU Consumer Law?' (2016) 5 Journal of European Consumer and Market Law 3; Marta Cantero Gamito, 'Regulation.com. Self-regulation and Contract Governance in the Platform Economy: a Research Agenda' (2016) 9 European Journal of Legal Studies 53.

[10] Valerio De Stefano, 'The Rise of the Just-in-Time Workforce: On-Demand Work, Crowdwork, and Labor Protection in the Gig-Economy' (2015) 37 Comparative Labor Law and Policy Journal 471; Jeremias Prassl, *Humans as a Service: The Promise and Perils of Work in the Gig Economy* (Oxford University Press 2018); Adrián Todolí-Signes, 'Algorithms, Artificial Intelligence and Automated Decisions Concerning Workers and the Risks of Discrimination: the Necessary Collective Governance of Data Protection' (2019) 25 Transfer: European Review of Labour and Research 465.

[11] Parliament and Council Regulation (EU) 2016/679 of 27 April 2016 on the protection of individuals with regard to the processing of personal data and on the free movement of such data, and repealing Directive 95/46/EC (General Data Protection Regulation) [2016] OJ L119/1 (GDPR).

2 The Uber Rating and Review System

Uber is one of the most popular smart urban mobility platforms in Western countries. Its business model is well known and has already been analysed in several contributions.[12] Established in 2009 in San Francisco, the platform has spread beyond US borders over the last 10 years and expanded its range of services from the transport of passengers to food delivery, bike-sharing and even helicopter rentals.[13]

According to Uber's 'Terms and Conditions',[14] the platform acts as a mere intermediary: its declared role is to facilitate both the matching of supply and demand and the conclusion of a contract between two or more users.

However, such a legal classification has been contested. For instance, in *Asociación Profesional Élite Taxi*, the CJEU affirmed that the intermediation service provided by Uber must be considered as 'inextricably linked to a transport service and therefore covered by the qualification of "services in the transport sector" within the meaning of Art. 58(1) TFEU'.[15] In particular, the Court stressed that the platform

---

[12]For an overview of the legal issues raised by this business model, see Kristofer Erickson and Inge Sorensen, 'Regulating the Sharing Economy' (2016) 5 Internet Policy Review <https://policyreview.info/articles/analysis/regulating-sharing-economy> accessed 30 December 2019; Nayeem Syed, 'Regulating Uberification' (2016) 22 Computer and Telecommunications Law Review 14; Guido Noto La Diega, 'Uber Law and Awareness by Design. An Empirical Study on Online Platforms and Dehumanised Negotiations' (2016) 2 Revue européenne de droit de la consommation/European Journal of Consumer Law 383; Diane M Ring and Shu-Yi Oei, 'The Tax Lives of Uber Drivers: Evidence from Online Forums' (2016) 8 Columbia Journal of Tax Law 56; Alex Rosenblat and Luke Stark, 'Algorithmic Labor and Information Asymmetries: A Case Study of Uber's Drivers' (2016) 10 International Journal of Communication 3758; Ryan Calo and Alex Rosenblat, 'The Taking Economy: Uber, Information, and Power' (2017) 117 Columbia Law Review 1623; Alex Rosenblat and others, 'Discriminating Tastes: Uber's Customer Ratings as Vehicles for Workplace Discrimination' (2017) 9 Policy & Internet 256; Giorgio Resta, 'Digital Platforms and the Law: Contested Issues' (2018) 1 Media Laws 231.

[13]See Cathy Bussewitz, 'Uber Expands Helicopter Service to All Users with iPhones in New York City' (*USA Today*, 15 December 2019) <https://eu.usatoday.com/story/tech/2019/10/03/uber-helicopter-service-expands-all-iphone-users-new-york-city/3855008002/> accessed 30 December 2019.

[14]As indicated at section 2 of Uber's Terms and Conditions (*Uber*) <www.uber.com/legal/it/document/?name=general-terms-of-use&country=belgium&lang=en/> accessed 30 December 2019: 'YOU ACKNOWLEDGE THAT UBER DOES NOT PROVIDE TRANSPORTATION OR LOGISTICS SERVICES OR FUNCTION AS A TRANSPORTATION CARRIER AND THAT ALL SUCH TRANSPORTATION OR LOGISTICS SERVICES ARE PROVIDED BY INDEPENDENT THIRD PARTY CONTRACTORS WHO ARE NOT EMPLOYED BY UBER OR ANY OF ITS AFFILIATES.'

[15]Case C-434/15 *Asociación Profesional Elite Taxi v. Uber Systems SpainSL* [2017] EU:C:2017:981, para 48. For a comment on the judgment, see Philipp Hacker, 'UberPop, UberBlack, and the Regulation of Digital Platforms after the Asociación Profesional Elite Taxi Judgment of the CJEU' (2018) 14 European Review of Contract Law 80; Michèle Finck, 'Distinguishing Internet Platforms from Transport Services: Elite Taxi v. Uber Spain' (2018) 55 CML Rev 1619; Alberto De Franceschi, 'Uber Spain and the "Identity Crisis" of Online Platforms' (2018) 7 Journal of European Consumer and Market Law 1.

could not be regarded as a mere intermediary because it exerts a decisive influence on the conditions under which the drivers provide the service. It is possible to infer such influence from the power of Uber to (1) determine the maximum fare for the ride by means of the Uber app, (2) regulate the payment process and (3) exclude drivers from the platform for reasons related to 'the quality of the vehicles, the drivers and their conduct'.[16]

Although the Court does not specify which instruments are covered under point (3), it is evident that the R&R system is one of the primary means used to assess the driver's performance.[17]

For the present analysis, it is then crucial to understand how Uber's R&R system works in practice.

It can be preliminarily observed that despite the role of R&R in Uber's business model, it is difficult to find clear and complete information about the system before creating a personal account on the platform. In the almost 50 documents available online (Terms and Conditions, Privacy Policy, Community Guidelines, etc.), the R&R system is described in very general terms.[18] The Privacy Policy and some 'help pages' mainly explain the bi-directionality of the mechanism: each passenger can give a score from 1 to 5 to her driver and vice-versa.[19]

Only by registering and using the app it is possible to understand the R&R system in detail. In brief, at the end of the journey, a pop-up window informs the passenger that she can evaluate the driver using the well-known 5-star scale. The user is not obliged to give a score, but if she does, she may leave an explanation (albeit succinctly).

If the passenger decides to give the maximum score (5 stars), the system allows her to send a 'compliment' to the driver. This compliment can be shown in the driver's profile to passengers who are paired with her in the future. Meanwhile, if the passenger assigns a score lower than 5, the system immediately shows a 'headline' close to each 'star'. This is meant to give an idea of the score's meaning: for example, 4 stars, 'Ok, but I had an issue'; 3 stars, 'Disappointing'; 2 stars, 'Bad'; 1 star, 'Terrible'. When the users assign a score <4, the system allows them to select the issue they experienced from a pre-filled list (e.g. 'driving', 'professionalism', 'music', 'conversation'). If the score given by the passenger is ≤ 3 stars, the user is obliged to select at least one of the reasons listed. Otherwise, she cannot submit her score. For grievances independent of the driver's conduct—e.g. 'traffic'—the app records the score without affecting the driver's rating.

---

[16] *Asociación Profesional Elite Taxi* (n 15) para 39.

[17] However, this conclusion is supported by the Case C-434/15 *Asociación Profesional Elite Taxi v. Uber Systems SpainSL* [2017] EU:C:2017:981, Opinion of Advocate General Szpunar. See in particular paras 51-52.

[18] On the contractual 'flora' that characterises the platform, see the critical comment by Guido Noto La Diega and Luce Jacovella, 'UBERTRUST: How Uber Represents Itself to Its Customers Through its Legal and Non-Legal Documents' (2016) 5 Journal of Civil and Legal Sciences 199.

[19] Section IV.C 'Consultation of Evaluations', Uber Privacy Policy (*Uber*) <www.uber.com/global/it/privacy/notice/> accessed 30 December 2019.

Uber then aggregates all the scores concerning a particular user and calculates the arithmetic average, forming the user's rating. This person can then view her own rating through the main menu of the app. With specific modalities and at certain times, passengers can also view the rating of drivers. This last feature underlines an important point. The Uber rating is not shown to the user before she requests the ride. Only after the app has matched a driver and passenger (i.e. when the driver is already heading to the meeting point)[20] is the passenger able to see the identity of the driver, the licence plate number and the rating. Therefore, the rating has no real informative function here because it is not taken into account in the transactional decision-making process of the passenger (unlike in other cases, such as Blablacar or Airbnb). There is, however, a little room for the user to exercise choice: once the rating has been shown and before the driver arrives at the meeting point, the passenger has the chance to cancel the trip. However, this eventuality is residual, firstly because of the limited time window for making such a choice and secondly because the cancellation could cause the user to pay a penalty.

Given this premise, it is possible to conclude that the Uber R&R system is essentially based on ratings, with limited space for reviews. Other users can only view the latter if they are 'compliments'. The explanations (mere 'keywords') that the passenger uses to justify the assignment of a medium-to-low score are not published but transmitted to the platform.

Considering these characteristics and the impossibility of the user choosing her counterparty based on the rating, one can observe that the exclusive function of the Uber rating is what we have defined as 'self-regulation'. The most important—and almost exclusive—consequence related to the rating is that all users' profiles might be deactivated if their score is 'low'.[21] Legally speaking, the deactivation of the account means the unilateral termination of the contract between the user and the platform at Uber's discretion, leaving little doubt about the unfairness of such a provision under the consumer protection framework.

In the light of this consequence, the lack of information about the minimum threshold of the rating required by the platform is even more surprising.

Few details are provided in the document 'Community Uber Guidelines', where it is mentioned that:

> Where applicable, there is a minimum average rating in each city. These may vary between cities because there may be cultural differences in the way people in different cities rate each other. Drivers, riders, couriers, or merchants that don't meet the minimum average rating for

---

[20]The app matches users based on criteria such as proximity. Therefore, the user does not have the option to really choose the counterparty on the basis of her rating.

[21]Section III.B.9, Uber Privacy Policy (*Uber*) <www.uber.com/global/it/privacy/notice/> accessed 30 December 2019. A decision by the California Labor Commission confirms that the minimum average rating to remain on the platform is the same both for drivers and passengers. cf *Uber Techs., Inc. v. Berwick*, No. CGC-15-546378, Cal. App. LEXIS 9488 (Cal. Super. 2015); see also *O'Connor v. Uber Technologies, Inc.*, 82 F. Supp. 3d 1133, 1135 (N.D. Cal. 2015).

> their city may lose access to the Uber app. If you lose access to your account as a result of your rating, we may share information that may help you improve your rating.[22]

Uber states that it does not set the same threshold for all cities, referring to a sort of sociological justification. While the reason for different minimum ratings might be acceptable in the light of specific verifiable parameters, these should at least be communicated to users before the conclusion of a contract and easily accessible on the website/app.

Nevertheless, information about the minimum score and the criteria for determining deactivation is almost absent. At least until December 2018, a deactivation policy was accessible on the Uber platform, but only for four countries (Denmark, Ireland, Puerto Rico and Norway). At the moment, the only deactivation policy still published online is Puerto Rico's, which does not mention the minimum average score that users must maintain.[23]

To give the reader an idea, the minimum average rating is 4.6/5 in San Francisco[24] and 4.5/5 in Brussels.[25]

According to the Community Guidelines, when the user's profile is deactivated, the platform provides suggestions on how to improve the rating. The usefulness of this type of information once the user has lost access to her profile remains doubtful.[26] However, there is a specific condition for drivers: the latter can reactivate their profile if they 'provide proof that [they have] successfully taken a quality improvement course offered by third party experts, available online or in person'.[27]

In addition to the vague and in some cases contradictory information,[28] there are three critical points in the design of Uber ratings that may undermine their reliability.

---

[22] (*Uber*) <www.uber.com/legal/en/document/?name=general-community-guidelines&country=belgium&lang=en> accessed 30 December 2019.

[23] (*Uber*) <www.uber.com/legal/deactivation-policy/pr-en/> accessed 30 December 2019.

[24] As reported in *Uber Techs., Inc. v. Berwick* (n 21).

[25] This information was obtained after sending a direct request to the Uber assistance service on 4 December 2018.

[26] It is interesting to note that the previous version of the Community Guidelines (online at least until 19 November 2019) adopted a 'preventive' approach. They stated that: 'We will alert you over time if your rating is approaching this limit. However, if your average rating still falls below the minimum after multiple notifications, you will lose access to your account as your rating will no longer meet the overall quality standards that riders reasonably expect from drivers when using the Uber app in the relevant city' ((*Uber*) <www.uber.com/legal/community-guidelines/be-en/> accessed 30 December 2019. This link has expired. However, the same provision remains in Porto Rico's deactivation policy: (*Uber*) <www.uber.com/legal/deactivation-policy/pr-en/> accessed 30 December 2019).

[27] (*Uber*) <www.uber.com/legal/en/document/?name=general-community-guidelines&country=belgium&lang=en> accessed 30 December 2019.

[28] By clicking on her rating, the passenger can access a page that provides general information about the rating. Such information is framed in positive terms. Uber reassures passengers who do not have an immaculate rating: 'very few people have a perfect rating, so don't despair if your average isn't 5.0. Things that seem small can matter to your driver—it's easy to accidentally slam a door if you are not thinking about it.' The platform then offers a series of tips to get a high score, such as not

First of all, while the scores given by individuals are the result of a subjective assessment about the overall performance, both individual and aggregate scores are expressed in a number (from 1 to 5 stars),[29] which might create a misleading sense of objectivity.[30] Moreover, since the user does not have to evaluate each aspect of the performance but rather the service as a whole, there is the risk of introducing elements of discretionary decision-making: one can easily imagine that users will assign different weight and importance to various elements of the service. The lack of granularity of the score can therefore generate problems of simplification or, worse, distortion.

A second issue with Uber's rating system concerns the voluntary nature of the evaluation. Neither passengers nor drivers are obliged to score each other's performance at the end of the ride. If this architectural choice favours the usability of the system, it is likely to create some undesirable misrepresentations in the ratings. These are calculated not from the total number of rides made but from the total number of rides evaluated. Therefore, each rating is based on a partial cohort of data, which provides an incomplete picture. Several empirical studies have shown that users are more likely to leave an evaluation in the case of either a highly positive or extremely negative experience.[31] Thus, a voluntary system of rating might not be accurate.

A third issue concerns the reliability of ratings in general and the risk that they become vehicles for unfair practices, prejudices or cognitive bias.[32] Users might complain fraudulently just to get a refund or a discount, give a low score for reasons not related to the performance itself[33] or negatively interpret behaviours that would have been considered neutral if the users had not seen the score first (so-called confirmation bias, i.e. the tendency to find elements that validate our choices or

keeping the driver waiting, being polite, wearing a seat belt, etc. The information page concludes with a paragraph on the importance of ratings: 'ratings foster mutual respect between riders and drivers [...] a high rating is about more than bragging rights among your friends; it's a sign that people enjoyed their time with you. Keep up the good work!' Nothing, however, is mentioned about the other important consequences, should the score not be 'stellar'. The sanction of deactivation is mentioned in a section of the Privacy Policy (Section III.B.9, Privacy Policy Uber (n 21)).

[29]For an overview of the different types of rating systems, see Pettersen (n 3).

[30]The system indeed allows one to give feedback, but these qualitative inputs are limited and, in any case, they do not appear in the final rating.

[31]Chrysanthos Dellarocas and Ritu Narayan, 'A Statistical Measure of a Population's Propensity to Engage in Post-purchase Online Word-of-mouth' (2006) 21 Statistical Science 277.

[32]Rosenblat and others, 'Discriminating Tastes' (n 12).

[33]Unfortunately, the digital environment has replicated some discriminatory practices of the 'analogue age'. See for example Ray Fisman and Michael Luca, 'Fixing Discrimination in Online Marketplaces' (2016) Harvard Business Review <https://hbr.org/2016/12/fixing-discrimination-in-online-marketplaces> accessed 30 December 2019; Benjamin Edelman, Michael Luca and Dan Svirsky, 'Racial Discrimination in the Sharing Economy: Evidence from a Field Experiment' (2017) 9 American Economic Journal: Applied Economics 1.

behaviour).[34] Such problems, which depend on 'human' factors, could be partially counterbalanced in two ways: firstly by imposing an obligation to justify the low score and secondly by giving the possibility to contest the rating.[35]

Regarding the first case, it was already mentioned that Uber does in fact provide a mechanism that obliges the user to leave a justification when giving a negative score. However, this architectural choice—which forces the user to stop, read the information and make a choice—only applies to scores ≤ 3. The user who opts for a 4 is free to send her evaluation immediately without any feedback. Considering that the minimum rating to maintain is around 4.5, it is easy to predict that even 4-star ratings can make a significant difference.

With regard to disputing a rating, on the basis of the information available, it is not clear whether and how the platform provides an option to contest or review ratings.[36]

These three [illegible] points in the design of rating systems seem particularly pernicious if we consider that the decision to exclude a user from the platform could be based on automated means that are not entirely reliable. Such aspects are even more critical when observed from the data protection perspective.

3 Ratings and Reviews: Data Protection Aspects

Ratings and reviews may be qualified as 'personal data' when they relate to an identified or identifiable person.[37] As stated by Art. 29 Data Protection Working Party ('WP29', now the European Data Protection Board, 'EDPB')[38] and confirmed

---

[34]As Stemler (n 7) 694 points out: 'For example, if a passenger has a low rating, an Uber driver may interpret innocuous behaviour, like failing to make small talk, as unfriendly and give the passenger a negative review.'

[35]Bénédicte Drambine, Joseph Jerome and Ben Ambrose, 'User Reputation: Building Trust and Addressing Privacy Issues in the Sharing Economy' (2015) 9ff <https://fpf.org/wp-content/uploads/FPF_SharingEconomySurvey_06_08_15.pdf> accessed 30 December 2019.

[36]ibid 11. On the contrary, in the United States, a specific procedure has been established in cooperation with the *Independent Drivers Guild* to deal with account deactivations due to low ratings ((*IDG*) <https://drivingguild.org/uberdeactivated/> accessed 30 December 2019; (*Uber*, 29 June 2019) <www.uber.com/drive/new-york/resources/appeals/> accessed 30 December 2019). However, the initiative seems to be somewhat limited. First, it is only available to drivers based in New York City (see (*Uber*) <www.uber.com/drive/new-york/resources/improve-your-rating/> accessed 30 December 2019). Moreover, rather than a system to contest the rating, what the platform provides is a system of 'reputation[al] rehabilitation'. Drivers can, in fact, reactivate their account by following an online course on how to improve customer satisfaction.

[37]GDPR, art 4(1) defines personal data as 'any information relating to an identified or identifiable natural person ("data subject"); an identifiable person is one who can be identified, directly or indirectly, by reference in particular to an identifier such as a name, an identification number, location data, an online identifier or to one or more factors characteristic of his physical, physiological, genetic, mental, economic, cultural or social identity'.

[38]Article 29 Data Protection Working Party (WP29), 'Opinion 4/2007 on the concept of personal data' (2007) WP136, 6.

by the CJEU,[39] the concept of personal data includes not only objective information (for example, John is 20 years old) but also subjective information, such as opinions or assessments. Therefore, ratings or reviews expressed in R&R systems may fall within the notion of personal data.

On the one hand, an Uber rating is a summary of subjective opinions given about an identified person (driver or passenger). The consolidated rating would be personal data not only considering its content (John's score is 4.7) but also the purpose of the processing (the assessment of John's performance as a driver or passenger) and the result (the use of the data could lead to the exclusion of John from the platform).[40]

On the other hand, the score assigned by each user has to be considered personal data as well. Hence, the rating can be personal data for a plurality of data subjects: it concerns both the individual who receives the score and the one who gives it.

This interpretation is coherent with the principles expressed in *Nowak*.[41] In that case, concerning access to the results of a professional examination, the CJEU recognised as personal data not only the answers given by the candidate but also the examiner's comments, as their content 'reflects the opinion or the assessment of the examiner of the individual performance of the candidate in the examination, particularly of his or her knowledge and competences in the field concerned'.[42] Furthermore, the comments would relate both to the candidate who receives them and to the examiner who makes them.[43]

[39]Case C-434/16 *Peter Nowak v. Data Protection Commissioner* [2017] EU:C:2017:994, para 42. cf Karolina Podstawa, 'Peter Nowak v Data Protection Commissioner: You Can Access Your Exam Script, Because It Is Personal Data' (2018) 4 European Data Protection Law Review 252; Nadezhda Purtova, 'The Law of Everything. Broad Concept of Personal Data and Future of EU Data Protection Law' (2018) 10 Law, Innovation and Technology 40; Sandra Wachter and Brent Mittelstadt, 'A Right to Reasonable Inferences: Re-thinking Data Protection Law in the Age of Big Data and AI' (2019) Columbia Business Law Review 494.

[40]To determine whether a piece of information refers to an identified or identifiable person, the WP29 suggests taking the three following elements into account: content (the information concerns the person), purpose (the information is or is likely to be used to evaluate the person or to influence his or her behaviour) and outcome (the use of the information may have an impact—even if not necessarily significant—on the rights and interests of the person). These elements are alternative. See, WP29, 'Opinion 4/2007 on the concept of personal data' (2007).

[41]This ruling exceeds the principles of law expressed in the previous Joined Cases C-141/12 and 372/12 *YS c. Minister voor Immigratie, Integratie en Asiel and Minister voor Immigratie, Integratie en Asiel* [2014] EU:C:2014:2081 (hereinafter *YS and others*). In this case, concerning access to a decision about a residence permit, the Court considered that the personal data contained in the so-called 'minute' (the draft decision containing the assessment of the applicant's request) were exclusively the information related to the applicant (name, surname, etc.) and not the information concerning the assessment and application of the law to the situation of the applicant (the so-called 'legal analysis'). For a critical comment, see Evelien Brouwer and Frederik Zuiderveen Borgesius, 'Access to Personal Data and the Right to Good Governance during Asylum Procedures after the CJEU's *YS. and M. and S.* judgment (C-141/12 and C-372/12)' (2015) 17 European Journal of Migration and Law 259; Wachter and Mittelstadt (n 39).

[42]*Nowak* (n 39) para 43.

[43]*Nowak* (n 39) para 45.

The qualification of ratings and reviews as personal data is not a mere exercise in definition. It has a legal consequence that is as simple as it is relevant: the data protection framework will apply. In particular, this means that the processing of such data will have to comply with the fundamental principles of data processing (Arts. 5–6, GDPR), the rules on consent where applicable (Arts. 7–8 GDPR) and, with the clarifications set out below, the provisions for the exercise of data subjects' rights (Arts. 12 et seq.).[44]

Considering the characteristics of the rating system seen in Sect. 2, two significant points of friction with the discipline of the GDPR emerge, namely (1) the opacity surrounding the lawful basis for the processing and (2) the limitations to the exercise of data subjects' rights.

3.1 *Lawful Basis and Processing of Personal Data in the Context of the Rating System*

Article 6 GDPR lists six lawful bases on which the controller may rely in making the processing of personal data legitimate.[45] Such bases are alternative.

In the case study in question, Uber's Privacy Policy mentions a series of bases potentially suitable to ensure the lawfulness of the processing.[46] They are: (1) the consent of the data subject,[47] (2) the necessity for the performance of a contract or a pre-contractual measure,[48] (3) the necessity for the purposes of the legitimate interests pursued by the data controller or third parties[49] and (4) the necessity for the compliance with a legal obligation to which the controller is subject.[50] However,

[44]With specific reference to processing in the employment sector, the GDPR leaves a certain margin of discretionary power to the Member States (GDPR, art 88(1)). In Italy, for example, some specific provisions in this context have been introduced by art 9 of Legislative Decree of 10 August 2018, no. 101 (see Maria Cristina Degoli, 'I Trattamenti in Ambito Lavorativo' in Simone Scagliarini (ed), *Il 'Nuovo' Codice in Materia di Protezione dei Dati Personali. La Normativa Italiana Dopo il d.lgs. n. 101/2018* (Giappichelli 2019); Vincenzo Turco, 'Il Trattamento dei Dati Personali Nell'ambito del Rapporto di Lavoro' in Vincenzo Cuffaro, Roberto D'Orazio and Vincenzo Ricciuto (eds), *I Dati Personali nel Diritto Europeo* (Giappichelli 2019)). However, despite the control exercised by the platform, the qualification of Uber drivers as employees is still contested in many Member States. Consequently, the following analysis will not focus on the special rules applicable in the employment context.

[45]The data controller is defined as 'the natural or legal person, public authority, service or other body which, individually or jointly with others, determines the purposes and means of the processing of personal data' (GDPR, art 4(7)).

[46]See Section III.F 'Reasons for Processing', Uber Privacy Policy (*Uber*) <www.uber.com/global/it/privacy/notice/#choice> accessed 30 December 2019.

[47]GDPR, art 6(1)(a).

[48]GDPR, art 6(1)(b).

[49]GDPR, art 6(1)(f).

[50]GDPR, art 6(1)(c).

it is not possible to reconstruct from the document which lawful basis corresponds to the purpose concerning the processing of rating and scores data.

This is already a problematic point in terms of transparency given that the data controller has the precise obligation to inform data subjects about the relevant conditions of the processing.[51] However, for the aim of this chapter, it is worth investigating what lawful basis might eventually legitimise an instance of processing in which its main purpose is the self-regulation of the platform's environment.

Firstly, to the best of the Author's knowledge, there is no rule in European or domestic law that requires the use of R&R systems in smart mobility platforms. Therefore, Art. 6(1)(c) GDPR is not relevant for our case.

Consent might be a suitable lawful basis for R&R systems in general. However, the particular modality for its obtainment coupled with the platform's business model raises more than one doubt.

According to Art. 4(11) GDPR, consent must be (a) freely given, (b) specific, (c) informed, and (d) unambiguous.[52] In particular, it must consist of a 'clear affirmative act'[53] by the data subject and the controller shall implement exclusively opt-in mechanisms for the obtainment of consent.[54]

A preliminary problem in this context concerns how the consent should be requested. In the platform's registration procedure, there is no specific moment where the controller provides information about the processing (especially about ratings) and asks for consent.

The first time the app is launched on the smartphone, the user is requested to enter her phone number. Once she has typed it in, the user receives a confirmation code to complete the registration (and therefore the contract with the platform). In all these steps, the existence of the T&C or Privacy Policy is not even mentioned.

Registration via the website does not lead to substantially different results. The registration form and the manner the consent is "obtained" raise several concerns. To begin with, the interface is designed in a way that users are led to insert the data necessary for the registration first; then, a big green button invite to "sign up". Only

---

[51]See GDPR, arts 13(1)(c), 14(1)(c). On transparency duties, WP29, 'Guidelines on transparency under Regulation 2016/679' (2018) WP260 rev.01.

[52]Art. 4(11) GDPR. On the requirements for valid consent, see European Data Protection Board (EDPB), 'Guidelines 5/2020 on consent under Regulation 2016/679' (2020) Version 1.1. In the literature, see in particular, Giorgio Resta, 'Revoca del Consenso ed Interesse al Trattamento nella Legge sulla Protezione dei Dati Personali' (2000) Rivista Critica del Diritto Privato 299; Roger Brownsword, 'Il Consenso Informato nella Società dell'Informazione' (2012) XI(3) Salute e Società 161; Fausto Caggia, 'Libertà ed Espressione del Consenso' in Vincenzo Cuffaro, Roberto D'Orazio and Vincenzo Ricciuto (eds), *I Dati Personali nel Diritto Europeo* (Giappichelli 2019); Ingrida Milkaite and Eva Lievens, 'Counting Down to 25 May 2018: Mapping the GDPR Age of Consent Across the EU' (2018) <https://biblio.ugent.be/publication/8561253> accessed 30 December 2019.

[53]GDPR, recital 32.

[54]On the prohibition of opt-out mechanisms for consent, see the recent Case C-673/17 *Bundesverband der Verbraucherzentralen und Verbraucherverbände—Verbraucherzentrale Bundesverband e.V. v Planet49 GmbH* [2019] EU:C:2019:801.

below the button, few lines of text (in a smaller font) recite: "By clicking 'sign up', you agree to Uber's Terms of Use and acknowledge you have read the Privacy Policy". As a matter of fact, the text at the bottom of the registration form does not refer to consent at all.[55] There the user merely confirms that she has read the Privacy Policy.[56]

Furthermore, if drivers are going to qualify as employees of the platform, consent can hardly be an appropriate lawful basis because it is unlikely that it will be freely given.[57] Indeed, the WP29 states that the freedom of consent shall imply that the data subject is in a position to make a real choice and that 'there is no risk of deception, intimidation, coercion or significant negative consequences if he/she does not consent'.[58] As a paradigmatic example of consent that is not freely given, the WP29 refers precisely to the context of employment relationships, where the data subject is in a weaker position vis-à-vis the controller (the employer). In this [illegible] with regard to the processing, especially if consent is a condition of employment.[59]

The third possible option to consider is Art. 6(1)(b) GDPR. However, even taking into account the contractual dimension of the R&R system, it is difficult to argue that the processing is necessary for the performance of the contract between the data subject and the platform or to fulfil any pre-contractual activity requested by the data subject. According to the EDPB, the processing of data cannot be considered necessary if the contractual obligation can be performed without the use of personal data.[60] Considering the contract between the platform and the users, the object is the obligation of the carrier to transfer a person from one place to another (see e.g. Arts. 1678 and 1681 Italian Civil Code).[61] To this end, it is necessary to process, for

[55] Even if the user agrees to the Terms and Conditions of Service, such consent shall not be confused with the consent required under GDPR, art 6(1)(a). See EDPB, 'Guidelines 2/2019 on the processing of personal data within the meaning of Article 6(1)(b) of the General Data Protection Regulation in the context of the provision of online services to data subjects' (2019) point 20.

[56] The only consent that is 'requested' is for marketing purposes, but its modalities raise serious doubts about its validity.

[57] According to GDPR, art 7(4), 'when assessing whether consent is freely given, utmost account shall be taken of whether, *inter alia*, the performance of a contract, including the provision of a service, is conditional on consent to the processing of personal data that is not necessary for the performance of that contract'.

[58] WP29, 'Opinion 15/2011 on the definition of consent' (2011) WP187, 12. See WP29, 'Guidelines on Consent under Regulation 2016/679' (2018) WP259 rev.01.

[59] WP29, 'Opinion 8/2001 on the processing of personal data in the employment context' (2001) WP48. See WP29, 'Opinion 2/2017 on the processing of data at work' (2017) WP249, 6-7.

[60] On the requirements that the data controller may take into account when assessing the necessity of the processing for the purpose of performing the contract: EDPB, 'Guidelines 2/2019'. See in particular point 33.

[61] Uber has been qualified as a service in the transportation sector by the CJEU. Even before the European judgment, Italian courts qualified the contract between the platform and its users as a transport contract according to arts 1678 and 1681, Italian Civil Code (see, for instance, Court of Turin, commercial section, 22 March 2017, no. 1553, in *Foro it.* 2017, 6, I, 2082, with comment by

example, the passenger's destination address. However, the presence of the rating does not appear functional either to the performance of the transportation or to the payment of the fare.[62]

The processing of ratings data might become relevant in the light of the platform's business model: ratings encourage users to behave in a way that keeps their online reputation high while the platform benefits from having a community where users can expect certain standards of conduct from each other. Therefore, the legitimate interest of the controller or third parties can come into play.[63]

However, it is important to stress that Art. 6(1)(f) GDPR is far from being a silver bullet. It cannot be invoked automatically in cases where the controller cannot rely on any other condition listed in Art. 6(1) GDPR. The legitimate interest is perhaps the most complex ground on which the controller can base the processing. It always requires a comparative assessment that weighs the interests of the controller or third parties on the one hand against the impact on data subjects on the other. This assessment must be as granular as possible and shall take into account the appropriate safeguards to reduce the undue impact on the interests, rights or freedoms of the data subject, and, in the light of the principle of accountability, the controller must be able to justify the outcome of such balancing.[64] The assessment should indeed consider the accuracy of the rating mechanism, the possibility of false positives, and the measures to neutralise or minimise the negative consequences for individuals.

Moreover, Arts. 13(1)(d) and 14(2)(b) GDPR explicitly require that where processing is carried out based on the legitimate interest of the controller or third parties, such interest shall be clearly communicated to the data subjects.

However, coming back to the case study, it is not easy to deduce from the Uber Privacy Policy what lawful basis governs the processing of the ratings data and, *a fortiori*, what specific legitimate interest is invoked. Therefore, serious doubts remain as to what legal grounds exist for the processing of ratings in this specific case.

Caputi. See also, Giovanni Basini, 'Innovazione Disruptive e Limiti dell'Azione di Concorrenza Sleale per Violazione di Norme Pubblicistiche, Dopo il Caso Uber-II Parte' (2018) 83 Responsabilità Civile e Previdenza 1316; Giorgio Resta, 'Uber di Fronte alle Corti Europee' (2017) 2 Diritto dell'informazione e dell'informatica 330).

[62]As clarified by the EDPB, just because the ratings data are mentioned in the T&C does not mean that the processing is necessary for the purposes of the contract. See EDPB, 'Guidelines 2/2019', point 28, referring to WP29, 'Opinion 06/2014 on the notion of legitimate interests of the data controller under Article 7 of Directive 95/46/EC' (2014) WP217, 20.

[63]GDPR, art 6(1)(f).

[64]WP29, 'Opinion 06/2014 on the notion of legitimate interests of the data controller under Article 7 of Directive 95/46/EC' (2014) 36.

3.2 Ratings and Limitations to Data Subjects' Rights

Data protection is a fundamental right, established in the CFR and 'constitutionalised' with the entry into force of the Lisbon Treaty.[65] However, it is not an absolute right: it can be restricted in the balancing of conflicting interests, fundamental rights or freedoms.[66]

Data subjects' rights, a manifestation of the broader right to data protection, are no exception: the exercise of the rights in Arts. 15 et seq. GDPR (access, rectification, erasure, limitation of processing, portability, prohibition of solely automated decision-making processes) could, as we will see, be limited in some cases.

In the context of ratings, the right of access (to check what data are processed and how), the right to rectify (to correct inaccurate data), the right to erasure (to delete data in certain circumstances) and the right not to be subject to solely automated decision-making processes that have legal consequences for the data subject (such as exclusion from the platform) play a primary role.

Such rights can be exercised, balanced against the other interests involved according to the concrete circumstances of the processing. In *Nowak*, the CJEU stressed the need to contextualise the exercise of data subjects' rights in relation to the purpose of the processing.[67] For instance, the Court recognised the right of access to personal data but not the right to rectify incorrect answers given by the candidate,[68] nor the right to delete the examiner's comments or corrections.[69] Since the purpose was to verify the knowledge and skills of the candidate at the moment of the examination, the right of rectification and erasure could not extend to the point of depriving the test of its own function. On the contrary, the right of erasure can be exercised once the data are no longer necessary, i.e. when the examination procedure is closed and cannot be challenged,[70] while the right of rectification can be invoked for the correction of material errors, such as the incorrect attribution of one candidate's answers to another.[71]

---

[65] See, Stefano Rodotà, 'Data Protection as a Fundamental Right' in Serge Gutwirth and others (eds), *Reinventing Data Protection?* (Springer 2009); Gloria González Fuster, *The Emergence of Personal Data Protection as a Fundamental Right of the EU* (Springer Science & Business 2014); Orla Lynskey, *The Foundations of EU Data Protection Law* (Oxford University Press 2015); Federico Fabbrini, 'The EU Charter of Fundamental Rights and the Rights to Data Privacy: The EU Court of Justice as a Human Rights Court' (2015) iCourts Working Paper Series, No. 19 <SSRN: https://ssrn.com/abstract=2576214> accessed 30 December 2019.

[66] On the balancing of the right to privacy and data protection with other interests, see Federica Giovanella, *Copyright and Information Privacy: Conflicting Rights in Balance* (Edward Elgar Publishing 2017).

[67] *Nowak* (n 39) para 53.

[68] *Nowak* (n 39) para 52.

[69] *Nowak* (n 39) para 55.

[70] ibid.

[71] *Nowak* (n 39) para 54.

What remains unresolved in the analysis of the CJEU in *Nowak* is whether the right of rectification could cover the content of the examiner's evaluation—more precisely, whether data subjects' rights could be used to ensure the accuracy of the decision-making process. Through a systemic interpretation of the CJEU case law, Wachter and Mittelstadt have observed that in the Court's view the right of rectification cannot be invoked to challenge the accuracy of the logic of the assessment itself or the inferences drawn by it.[72] Two main arguments support this conclusion:[73] on the one hand, the Court in *Nowak* gives some specific examples that relate only to the case of rectification of material errors (i.e. if the comments made by the examiner do not actually record her evaluation of the answers of the candidate);[74] on the other hand, in *Commission v Bavarian Lager*[75] and *YS and others*, the CJEU has affirmed that the scope of data protection law is to guarantee the right to privacy with regard to the processing of data relating to the subject and not to 'ensure the greatest possible transparency of the decision-making process of the public authorities'.[76] Therefore, if the data subject wants to challenge the decision, she should rely on other legal tools and governance mechanisms, such as access requests to administrative documents or existing appeal procedures. However, questions remain as to how to deal with cases that are not covered by *lex specialis*, such as the decision-making process of a private company.[77]

Applying these principles to the case at stake, we must first recall that the intended purpose of the processing of ratings data is to assess the behaviour of users and expel those with a low score. Within this context, it seems there are no grounds to limit the data subject's right to access her rating. However, in order to be an effective tool, the right of access should be designed in a way that the user is able to access her rating in a disaggregated manner (i.e. to see the individual ratings) so that she can be aware not only of the number of stars received but also of the reasons for the complaint. To this end, the rights of other subjects involved should be safeguarded as well (Recital 63 GDPR). Therefore, the platform should put in place technical and organisational measures to ensure compliance with the principle of minimisation, for example by proceeding with the pseudonymisation of the evaluations (creating a mechanism similar to a blind peer-review).[78]

Designed in such a way, the exercise of the right of access would be a useful tool for the user to improve her performance during the contractual relationship. To know

[72]Wachter and Mittelstadt (n 39) 42.

[73]ibid 45.

[74]*Nowak* (n 39) para 54.

[75]Case C-28/08 *European Commission v The Bavarian Lager Co. Ltd* [2010] EU:C:2010:378.

[76]*YS and others* (n 41) para 47.

[77]Wachter and Mittelstadt (n 39) 49. The authors are open to the possibility that the right to rectify assessments might be recognised to data subjects in the future, considering that data protection law has to be interpreted teleologically.

[78]As proposed in Rossana Ducato, Miriam Kullmann and Marco Rocca, 'European Legal Perspectives on Customer Ratings and Discrimination' in Tindara Addabbo and others (eds), *Performance Appraisal in Modern Employment Relations* (Springer 2020).

the reasons behind complaints could be relevant information in terms of orienting the data subject's behaviours and actions. Nevertheless, 'granular' access to the rating might prove to be powerless if the rights of rectification or erasure are not supported.

To this end, as we have seen, the CJEU case law offers a quite narrow interpretation. Considering that the purpose of the rating is essentially to evaluate the user, we can reasonably retain that the right of rectification could allow, for example, the correction of mistakes in the calculation of the average score or in the attribution of the rating to the wrong person. Meanwhile, the right to erasure could be exercised when the rating is no longer necessary (e.g. when the user voluntarily deletes her profile) or, for instance, when discriminatory feedback accompanies the score given by a user. Nevertheless, such hypotheses remain very limited.

More relevant for challenging the consequences of low ratings is the right of the data subject enshrined in Art. 22 GDPR. Such provision recognises the right not to be subject to a decision based solely on automated processing, including profiling which produces legal effects concerning the data subject or affects her in a similarly significant way.[79]

In principle, the decision to deactivate a user's profile can have legal effects on the person, as it entails the termination of the contract between the user and the platform.[80]

Such a procedure can also be considered to be based on profiling, which is defined in the GDPR as 'any form of automated processing of personal data consisting of the use of personal data to evaluate certain personal aspects relating to a natural person, in particular, to analyse or predict aspects concerning that natural person's performance at work, economic situation, health, personal preferences, interests, reliability, behaviour, location or movement'.[81] The rating is the product of the automated

---

[79]In the literature, see Isak Mendoza and Lee A Bygrave, 'The Right not to Be Subject to Automated Decisions Based on Profiling' in Tatiana-Eleni Synodinou and others (eds), *EU Internet Law: Regulation and Enforcement* (Springer 2017); Lee A Bygrave, 'Minding the Machine v2.0: The EU General Data Protection Regulation and Automated Decision Making' in Karen Yeung and Martin Lodge (eds), *Algorithmic Regulation* (Oxford University Press 2019); Elena Gil González and Paul de Hert, *Understanding the Legal Provisions that Allow Processing and Profiling of Personal Data—an Analysis of GDPR Provisions and Principles* (Springer 2019).

[80]The same could be said for platforms using reputational ratings for "pure" informative purposes: if the score of a user is low, this could have an impact on her dignity or on her future chance to enter into contracts. In a case concerning the lawfulness of a reputational system set up by a company, the Italian Data Protection Authority (DPA) stressed the link between data protection and dignity, underlying the necessity to evaluate the impact on the latter caused by the "social projection" of a data subject determined by ratings. In that case, the Italian DPA considered the reputational rating unlawful (Italian DPA, decision no. 488 of 24 November 2016 (Garante per la protezione dei dati personali 2016) <www.garanteprivacy.it/web/guest/home/docweb/-/docweb-display/docweb/5796783> accessed 27 August 2020). The decision was partially reformed by the Tribunal of Rome (decision no. 5715 of 4 April 2018), which established the legitimacy of the reputational rating, being the latter a voluntary system and expression of individuals' private autonomy. The decision has been highly critised in the literature. See, for instance, Giorgio Giannone Codiglione, 'Algoritmi reputazionali e confini dell'autonomia dei privati' (2019) 2 Diritto dell'Informazione e dell'Informatica 520.

[81]GDPR, art 4(1)(4).

aggregation of all the scores given by users who have interacted with the data subject, and such data are used by the controller to analyse or infer the user's behaviour or her performance.

Nevertheless, the right enshrined in Art. 22 GDPR is subject to three exceptions.[82] A solely automated decision-making process with legal consequences for individual users is allowed if the decision is (1) necessary for the performance of the contract between the data subject and the controller, (2) based on the explicit consent of the data subject or (3) authorised by the EU or national law.

For the reasons already given in Sect. 3.1, none of these three conditions might apply in the context at stake. If this is the case, a rating system based on a solely automated decision-making process that leads to the exclusion of a user should not be adopted in principle. Nevertheless, if an automated-decision making system is legit under Art. 22—e.g. there is a truly informed explicit consent—the platform should deploy a system for allowing the exercise of the rights recognised at Art. 22 (3) GDPR (right to obtain human intervention on the part of the controller, to express data subject's point of view and to contest the decision).

However, it is not entirely clear whether the process directed at the deactivation of profiles is solely automated in the case of Uber. In its Privacy Policy, the platform uses vague and generic terms to allude to the fact that a low score 'could' be a cause for exclusion. There is no certainty about the sanction and the precise consequences of the envisaged processing. This formulation raises more than one concern as to its compliance with the principle of transparency and purpose limitation. Anyhow, according to this wording, it should be understood that the decision made by the platform involves at some point the presence of the 'human in the loop'.[83]

Even assuming that the decision is not fully automated within the meaning of Art. 22 GDPR, the platform performs a decision-making process which remains subject to the fundamental data protection principles in any case.

In this regard, the design of Uber's rating system, as seen in Sect. 2, raises several doubts, particularly with reference to the principle of accuracy.[84] Such principle requires, first and foremost, that the data processed shall be accurate. However, the EDPB adopts a broad interpretation, suggesting that the controller should take into account not only the accuracy of personal data as such but also the accuracy of the profiling or the (not exclusively) automated decision-making process at all stages

[82]GDPR, art 22(2).

[83]However, such human involvement must be meaningful. The WP29 has been clear in affirming that the controller cannot circumvent art 22 by introducing a merely fictitious form of human control: 'for example, if someone routinely applies automatically generated profiles to individuals without any actual influence on the result, this would still be a decision based solely on automated processing' (WP29, 'Guidelines for automated decision making and profiling' (2018) WP251 rev.01, 23). In other words, art 22 will still apply if the controller does not provide for a supervisory mechanism that allows for effective oversight and intervention in the decision-making process.

[84]GDPR, article 5(1)(d).

(from the collection of the data to the application of the profile to the individual).[85] Interestingly, the EDPB stresses that 'even if raw data is recorded accurately, the dataset may not be fully representative or the analytics may contain hidden bias'.[86]

Such an opinion is particularly noteworthy because it seems to go one step further than *Nowak* and prefigure some form of assessment for the accuracy of not only the content but also the logic of the decision-making. This conclusion can be confirmed if we intepret systematically Art. 5(1)(b) and Recital 71, where the GDPR stresses that controllers should 'implement technical and organisational measures appropriate to ensure, in particular, that factors which result in inaccuracies in personal data are corrected and the risk of errors is minimised'. Among the 'factors' affecting the accuracy of the output data there might be input data, for instance, but also what Hallinan and Borgesius call the 'interpretative framework' used for generating the assessment.[87] Therefore, to return to our case, even if the result of the rating is formally correct because the system meticulously collects all the scores given by individuals, it is not necessarily accurate. Firstly, the evaluation is optional. The rating is, in fact, the arithmetic average of the total of voluntarily given scores, not the total of all rides. Secondly, in the absence of appropriate safeguards (e.g. audit mechanisms), the individual scores can be a token of more or less conscious forms of discrimination. The user could complain fraudulently just to gain an advantage; in some cases, she could give a medium-low score without being required to give a reason; or the rating itself could influence her.[88]

When the dataset or the analytics are not entirely reliable, decisions based thereupon can be flawed to the detriment of individuals. Lacking appropriate guarantees to ensure the accuracy of the data, including with regard to the various stages of the decision-making, the processing risks coming into conflict with the principle of accuracy from a substantive point of view.

---

[85]WP29, 'Guidelines for automated decision making and profiling' (2018) 13. See also the recent contribution by Dara Hallinan and Frederik Zuiderveen Borgesius, 'Opinions Can Be Incorrect (in Our Opinion)! On Data Protection Law's Accuracy Principle' (2020) 10 International Data Privacy Law 1, where the authors argue that the principle of accuracy does and should apply to opinions (either they are human-generated, algorithm-generated or human-algorithm-mix generated opinions). In particular, Hallinan and Borgesius retain that the principle of accuracy is applicable not only to the facts at the basis of an opinion but also to the interpretative framework used in generating that opinion.

[86]WP29, 'Guidelines for automated decision making and profiling' (2018) 13.

[87]Hallinan and Borgesius (n 85).

[88]For a discussion of each example, see above Sect. 2.

4 Recommendations for the Star System

The considerations made regarding the case study lead us to question what function and purpose R&R systems should have for ensuring the fair development of shared mobility platforms. This section will outline some suggestions and guidelines for pushing the design of R&R systems in this direction.

A preliminary question that has to be addressed is whether a rating mechanism (and the corresponding data processing) is necessary and, if yes, at what conditions. The adoption of a reputational system is not prohibited *a priori* by the law, and the GDPR offers a preliminary toolkit for untangling the most pressing concerns. For instance, the GDPR requires that data must be processed in accordance with the fundamental principles enshrined in Art. 5. The lawfulness of the processing requires, first and foremost, that any activity involving personal data be conducted on a legitimate legal basis. The identification of such a basis is intertwined with the purpose of the processing and its concrete modalities of execution. Therefore, if the purpose is informative rather than self-regulatory, the assessment can differ.

A rating system can be established on a voluntary basis. Among the conditions that make the processing lawful, the main one is the data subject's consent, provided that its four fundamental conditions are ensured: consent must be free, informed, specific and unambiguous. However, even by designing the appropriate choice architecture to obtain users' genuine consent for a given purpose, consent may not be an adequate lawful basis in some cases, for example, because of the particular relationship between the parties. This situation could occur where there is an imbalance of power between the controller and the data subject, such as in an employment context or where 'the performance of a contract, including the provision of a service, is dependent on the consent despite such consent not being necessary for such performance'.[89]

An alternative legal basis might be represented by the necessity to perform a contract or any pre-contractual measure requested by the data subject. However, the necessity must interpreted narrowly. In the opinion of the EDPB, the processing must be 'objectively necessary for a purpose that is integral to the delivery of that contractual service to the data subject' and the controller shall demonstrate how 'the main subject-matter of the specific contract with the data subject cannot, as a matter of fact, be performed if the specific processing of the personal data in question does not occur'.[90] If the object of smart mobility contracts is considered to be 'transportation', the processing performed via the rating is unlikely to be necessary for the performance of the contractual obligations.

Given the importance of ratings for the business model of shared mobility platforms (and the chance that consent can be legitimately withdrawn), the controller could opt for the legitimate interest basis. However, such a legitimate interest (of the

---

[89]GDPR, art 7(4) and recital 43. On this point, see also WP29, 'Guidelines on Consent under Regulation 2016/679' (2018) 8-9.

[90]EDPB, 'Guidelines 2/2019', point 30.

platform itself or other users) must be balanced against the fundamental rights or freedoms of the data subject in a comparative assessment that takes into account the appropriate safeguards, including those related to proportionality and transparency, to reduce any disproportionate impact on users.

More generally, before adopting any R&R system, adequate mechanisms should be considered to ensure the *spectrum* of data subjects' rights. In particular, appropriate measures shall be put in place to (1) inform data subjects about the functioning of the decision-making process, (2) allow the granular access to scores and reviews in the balancing with other individuals' rights (3) prevent potential distorting or discriminatory effects of the rating ex ante (by design) and ex post (e.g. via auditing mechanisms), and (4) ensure the principle of accuracy in the design of the R&R system and at all stages of its deployment. This latter point would certainly include the possibility to correct scores given by mistake (material errors). However, if we follow the broad interpretation of the GDPR, the principle of accuracy should apply not only to data as such but also to the interpretation model incorporated in the R&R system, whether the automated decision-making process falls under Art. 22 GDPR or not. This means firstly that the principle of accuracy should be ensured by default. This could also imply for the data controller not to use a R&R system if it is not possible to guarantee a sufficient level of precision in light of the decision to be taken. Secondly, the respect of the principle of accuracy should pave the way to the exercise of the rights that are its direct manifestation: the right to rectification and erasure. Furthermore, when the process is fully automated (and there is one of the conditions listed at Art. 22(2) GDPR), the rating can be also challenged through the rights enshrined at Art. 22(3) GDPR.[91]

Finally, few concrete measures of data minimisation, inspired by the case study, can be mentioned. For instance, when the purpose of the rating is essentially disciplinary, there is no apparent necessity of showing a user's rating to the other platform's users. The communication of this information to another subject is superfluous given the limited decision-making space of the latter in relation to the choice of the counterparty. Moreover, the communication of the rating could create a vicious circle if we take into account the effects of confirmation bias. The availability of the rating might unduly influence the individual score given by another user, which then flows again into the overall rating.

On the contrary, when the rating has a substantially informative function, its communication might be useful for the individual transactional decision. However, in this case, the principle of minimisation would require, for example, ensuring that

[91] Interestingly, a recent law from the Region of Lazio (Italy) introduced a specific provision to protect 'digital workers'. Art. 7 of Regional Law (Lazio) no. 4 of 12 April 2019 establishes that the Region shall encourage any activity aimed at ensuring: (1) the transparency of the evaluation incorporated in the reputational rating, and (2) an impartial review mechanism in case the digital worker contests the result of the rating. Such provisions are in line with the Italian data protection framework and can be indirectly derived from it. However, the initiative is interesting because it envisages some form of public engagement in the governance of a specific aspect of the gig-economy.

the rating is only shown to registered users when requesting or offering a ride, not to any internet surfer. Furthermore, appropriate measures to prevent potential misleading effects should be taken in this context.[92]

5 Conclusions

The ability to assess one's peers and make this assessment available to other users has been one of the reasons for digital platforms' success. Ratings can potentially help create a trusted environment, allowing users to rely on each other's performance reasonably. After all, how many people would accept a ride from a stranger if it were not an Uber driver? Or how many would trust an individual's driving skills if they could not check her Blablacar reviews first?

One of the main functions of R&R systems is to provide information about the user's reputation. However, such systems are also meant to regulate the behaviour of users and maintain the platform as an attractive network. As we have seen, the self-regulatory function of rating systems such as the one adopted by Uber raises a few concerns from a data protection standpoint. The analysis of this model has provided a paradigmatic case study not only to verify how R&R systems have been developed in practice but also to isolate those aspects that deserve special attention when controllers implement reputational systems.

To this end, it has been observed that a decision-making process based solely on the automated aggregation of scores and resulting in the exclusion of users from the platform is highly problematic under the current data protection framework. Therefore, in developing an R&R system, the controller should ensure the presence of effective human oversight, where the person in charge considers further elements in addition to the results of the rating and ensures the fairness of the assessment.

In any case, whether the automated decision making process falls under Art. 22 GDPR or not, the fundamental question as to the reliability of reputational systems remains. Despite the potential benefits and the promise of greater transparency, R&R mechanisms are still far from being a perfect tool for assessing the quality of a performance. In the absence of adequate safeguards, such as algorithmic audits and the appropriate design of the scoring system, ratings may serve as a vehicle for prejudice and discrimination, affecting the rights or interests of the subjects receiving the evaluation. It is therefore essential to ensure that the principle of substantive accuracy is respected in the design of rating systems and that the processing of personal data, including the associated decision-making, is accurate at all stages.

---

[92]For example, the controller could demonstrate its minimisation of disproportionate consequences for data subjects by complying with technical standards, where they exist (e.g. ISO 20488:2018, Online consumer reviews—Principles and requirements for their collection, moderation and publication). Such standard has been modelled on the French standard NF Z74-501 (accessed 30 December 2019).

Challenges to Locational Privacy: The Transformation of Urban Mobility

Jonathan Andrew

Contents

Abstract Pervasive, always-on wireless networks increasingly surround citizens. These systems bridge physical spaces and the virtual world to deliver greater efficiencies in urban mobility. Efforts to develop transportation and mobility infrastructure are subjecting populations to the influence of technologies that monitor individuals and group movements within our communities—and to determine interactions, associations and transactions at an increasingly finer degree of granularity. A concern is whether existing assessments of established technologies and their human rights impacts are apt to be applied to these novel technological innovations relating to mobility data: does the degree of originality these new advancements represent indeed require that we adopt a fundamentally different approach to their appraisal? Locational privacy constitutes a specific facet of privacy and has recently acquired prominence in discussions regarding urban mobility stemming from developments in ICT. As citizens, our own individual movements are aiding the development of more granular, sophisticated registers of activities linked to our mobility through the collection and processing of personal data. Crucially, there has been little examination to date, especially within Europe, as to why locational privacy is especially relevant to the safeguard of the right to privacy in urban settings.

Jonathan Andrew, is Associate Research Fellow, Geneva Academy of International Humanitarian Law and Human Rights, Geneva, Switzerland.

J. Andrew (✉)
Geneva Academy of International Humanitarian Law and Human Rights, Geneva, Switzerland
e-mail: jonathan.andrew@geneva-academy.ch

M. Finck et al. (eds.), *Smart Urban Mobility*, MPI Studies on Intellectual Property and Competition Law 29, https://doi.org/10.1007/978-3-662-61920-9_16

1 Introduction

The technologies evolving with the development of nascent urban mobility solutions foresee the collection and processing of personal data in a multitude of different spaces, in real time and in many different forms, including potentially a diverse range of location-related data.[1] In urban environments, efforts to develop more intelligent transportation and mobility infrastructure are increasingly subjecting our daily lives to the influence of technologies that possess the capabilities to monitor individuals and groups within our communities, and to determine interactions and transactions at an increasingly finer degree of detail.[2] Forecasts that smart city infrastructure may portend an era of omnipresent surveillance reflect the possibility of a wholesale explosion in the growth of both the spatial scope and temporal coverage of the capability to monitor citizens' movements.[3]

The utility of the Internet of Things (IoT) devices being developed for deployment in urban infrastructure is largely dependent upon the increasing precision, augmentation and diversification of localisation services. Localisation services depend upon location data and capitalise on the premise that information relating to the individual is more relevant, and hence more valuable, where it is linked to their location.[4] As such, location awareness is integral to the effectiveness of networked devices and services.[5]

The collection of location data relating to human mobility raises pertinent questions as to whether data that notionally has been anonymised may in fact be subject to processing that allows for identification of specific individuals, thus constituting personal data.[6] In addition, we also need consider how cutting edge research on

---

[1]Institute for Prospective Technological Studies (IPTS), 'Security and Privacy for the Citizen in the Post-September 11 Digital Age: A Prospective Overview Report to the European Parliament Committee on Citizens Freedoms and Rights, Justice and Home Affairs' (IPTS 2003) <ftp://ftp.jrc.es/pub/EURdoc/20823-ExeSumm.pdf> accessed 12 September 2019.

[2]David Lyon, *Surveillance studies: An overview* (Cambridge 2007) 12. See also: Robert Kitchin, 'The Real-Time City? Big Data and Smart Urbanism' (2014) 79 GeoJournal 1, 11.

[3]Marc Langheinrich, 'Privacy Invasions in Ubiquitous Computing' (Workshop on Socially-informed Design of Privacy-enhancing Solutions in Ubiquitous Computing 2002) <http://citeseerx.ist.psu.edu/viewdoc/download?doi=10.1.1.6.6743&rep=rep1&type=pdf> accessed 28 August 2019.

[4]Joint Research Centre of the Commission and the Institute for Prospective Technological Studies (IPTS), 'Future bottlenecks in the information society' (IPTS 2001) 104 <https://op.europa.eu/en/publication-detail/-/publication/9e10023b-b5da-45cb-b9bb-f05a0676322d> accessed 20 August 2019.

[5]Indeed, the significance of the issue of location data and the subsequent triggers applied by the provisions of the EU legal instruments which confer the obligations incumbent upon data controllers and data processors to protect individuals' privacy and right to data protection was highlighted very early on in the development of mobile communications networks. See further: Commission, 'A comprehensive approach on personal data protection in the European Union' COM (2010) 609 final.

[6]Kristina Irion and Giacomo Luchetta, 'Online Personal Data Processing and EU Data Protection Reform: Report of the CEPS Digital Forum' (Center for European Policy Studies (CEPS) April

embedded sensors' collection of location data and other personal data in relation to an individual's activity is further driving the evolution of biometrics that infer intimate aspects of a person's physiology related to mobility.[7] Purported patterns pertaining to the attributes of location data are increasingly forming the basis for forward-sighted predictions of citizens' behaviour.[8] Thus, more widespread sensing of people's movement, coupled with advancements in analytical capabilities rendered by enhanced data mining of large datasets, presage significant challenges for society.[9] On the other hand, we might ask ourselves whether, however, these

---

2013) 72 <www.ceps.eu/wp-content/uploads/2013/04/TFR%20Data%20Protection_0.pdf> accessed 28 August 2019; Douwe Korff, 'Data Protection Laws in the EU: The Difficulties in Meeting the Challenges Posed by Global Social and Technical Developments' (2010) Kantor and Centre for Public Reform Working Paper 2 <https://papers.ssrn.com/sol3/papers.cfm?abstract_id=1638949> accessed 12 September 2019.

[7]Muhammad Shoaib and others, 'Towards Physical Activity Recognition Using Smartphone Sensors' (2013) IEEE 10th International Conference on Ubiquitous Intelligence & Computing 80 <https://ieeexplore.ieee.org/abstract/document/6726194> accessed 21 August 2019.

[8]Jason Millar, 'Core Privacy: A Problem for Predictive Data Mining' in Ian Kerr, Valeria Steeves and Carole Lucock (eds), *Lessons from the Identity Trail: Anonymity, Privacy and Identity in a Networked Society* (New York, Oxford University Press 2009) 106. Similarly, Phillips underscores the primacy of behavioural monitoring as an objective of ubiquitous location tracking, identifying the abnormal from a background of normalcy: David Phillips, 'Ubiquitous Computing, Spatiality, and the Construction of Identity: Directions for Policy Response' in Ian Kerr, Valeria Steeves and Carole Lucock, *Lessons from the Identity Trail: Anonymity, Privacy and Identity in a Networked Society* (New York, Oxford University Press 2009) 310. In a similar vein, Gonzalez and others argue in their research that, in contrast with the random trajectories predicted of humans, our movements follow simple reproducible patterns and, as such, knowledge of the intrinsic similarity of our travel patterns could prove transformative the monitoring and predictive modeling of human mobility: Marta C Gonzalez, César A Hidalgo and Albert L Barabási, 'Understanding individual human mobility patterns' (2008) 453 Nature 779. Freiwald also asserts that cellular networks afford sufficient resolution in allowing for detailed inferences to be drawn relating to individual patterns of movement, noting that the short-term irregularity and imprecision of specific data points is adequately compensated for by the larger datasets of location data furnished over time: Susan Freiwald, 'Cell Phone Location Data and the Fourth Amendment: A Question of Law, Not Fact' (2011) 70 Maryland Law Review 731, 732. For further examples see also: Julie Cohen, 'Privacy, Visibility, Transparency, and Exposure' (2008) 75 University of Chicago Law Review 186. Refer also to Boyd and Crawford's account of the issues of apophenia (erroneous pattern recognition), which advocates particular caution in relation to the processing of large datasets of personal data: Danah Boyd and Kate Crawford, 'Six Provocations for Big Data: a Decade in Internet Time' (2011) Symposium on the Dynamics of the Internet and Society 4, 5 <https://papers.ssrn.com/sol3/papers.cfm?abstract_id=1926431> accessed 16 March 2020. See also: David Bollier, *The Promise and Peril of Big Data* (The Aspen Institute 2010) 13.

[9]Cohen's work on the relationship between networked information technologies and their propensity to shape and configure those using such systems is particularly insightful: Julie Cohen, *Configuring the Networked Self: Law, Code, and the Play of Everyday Practice* (Yale University Press 2012). Also see: Paul Ohm, 'Changing the Rules: General Principles for Data Use and Analysis' in Julia Lane and others (eds), *Privacy, Big Data and the Public Good: Frameworks for Engagement* (Cambridge University Press 2014). See further: Predrag Klasnja and others 'Exploring Privacy Concerns About Personal Sensing' in Hideyuki Tokuda and others (eds), *Pervasive Computing* (Springer 2009) 176-183. Refer also to: Shoshana Zuboff, 'Big Other:

concerns are not entirely novel or unfamiliar: successive generations of ICT applications in the past have created a certain disquiet, and yet we've learned as a society to adapt.

2 The Dichotomy of Public and Private Spaces

Public authorities, local and national governments and regional entities such as the European Union have progressively engaged in allocating greater resources to study the possible uses of new technologies within smart cities, enhanced by the collection and processing in particular of location data from communications networks.[10] Strategy studies have also highlighted how future policy interventions and management of decisions relating to the operation of vital transportation infrastructure will in part be shaped by contextualisation and analyses derived from the mapping of individuals' mobility patterns across metropolitan spaces.[11]

Also relevant to the discussion of the development of urban mobility and infrastructure development is the intrinsic character of physical spaces. To date, in privacy law, physical spaces have been characterised by way of an elementary dichotomy, where space is characterised as either 'public' or 'private'.[12] In contrast, in behavioural psychology recent research has highlighted the complexity of delineating spaces. Seclusion plays an important function in affording scope to shape privacy, which reflects its intrinsic value in influencing development of our identities and our sense of selfhood.[13] However, other studies have highlighted the

Surveillance Capitalism and the Prospects of an Information Civilization' (2015) 30 Journal of Information Technology 75.

[10]See for instance: Karima Kourtit, Peter Nijkamp and Daniel Arribas-Bel, 'Smart Cities in Perspective: A Comparative European Study by Means of Self-Organizing Maps' (2012) 25 Innovation: The European Journal of Social Science Research, 229; Anthony Townsend, *Smart Cities: Big Data, Civic Hackers, and the Quest for a New Utopia* (W W Norton & Co 2013); Michael Batty and others, 'Smart Cities of the Future' (2012) 214(1) The European Physical Journal Special Topics 481.

[11]Ionna D Constantiou and Jannis Kallinikos, 'New Games, New Rules: Big Data and the Changing Context of Strategy' (2015) 30 Journal of Information Technology 44.

[12]For instance, Seidman asserts that the private sphere constitutes the diametric opposite to the public nature of government, within which citizens can freely develop their own individual, personalised relationships. See further: Louis Seidman, 'Public Principle and Private Choice' (1987) 96 Yale Law Journal 1026. Tene, in contrast, has contended that the private and public dichotomy has been irreversibly transformed, claiming citizens accept location being tracked and broadcast. See: Omer Tene, 'Privacy: The New Generations' (2010) 1 International Data Privacy Law 15. Refer also to Gary Marx's discussion of conceptual borders and the capability of comprehensive monitoring to invade public and private spheres: Gary Marx, 'Murky Conceptual Waters: the Public and the Private' (2001) 3 Ethics and Information Technology 157.

[13]See for example: Daniel Solove, 'Reconstructing Electronic Surveillance Law' (2004) 72 George Washington Law Review 1264, 1708 in which Solove asserts that: 'Freedom is not just the absence of restraints; it is a mental state, a felt reality in both structure and sentiment.' See also: Erving

relationship of context to personal privacy, framing our everyday existence as a continual navigation of dichotomies, such that the individual traverses a plurality of distinct realms.

Litigation in Europe concerning the right to privacy is filled with elucidations as to *how* society must allow for individuals to move unimpeded, exercise their choice to freely interact and benefit from their mobility, but they rarely elucidate in comprehensive terms precisely *why* this liberty is necessary for a democratic society.[14] Thus, a broader concern is how existing assessments of established technologies and their human rights impact are apt to be applied to novel technological innovations relating to mobility data: does the degree of originality these new advancements represent indeed require we adopt a fundamentally different approach to their appraisal?

Locational privacy constitutes a specific facet of privacy and, whilst the concept of locational privacy is not in itself new, its recently acquired prominence in discussions regarding urban mobility stems from developments in ICT: increasingly our mobility is mediated and facilitated through these innovations.[15] As citizens, our own individual movements are aiding the development of more granular, sophisticated registers of activities linked to our mobility through the collection and processing of personal data.[16] Crucially, there has been little examination to date,

---

Goffman, *The Presentation of Self in Everyday Life* (Doubleday 1959) 75; Jason Millar, 'Core Privacy: A Problem for Predictive Data Mining' in Ian Kerr, Valerie Steeves and Carole Lucock (eds), *Lessons From The Identity Trail: Anonymity, Privacy and Identity in a Networked Society* (Oxford University Press 2009).

[14]See for example the deliberations of the ECtHR in the following cases: *Uzun v Germany* App no 35623/05 (ECtHR, 2 September 2010); *Liberty and others v United Kingdom* App no 58243/00 (ECtHR, 1 July 2008); *Peck v United Kingdom* App no 44647/98 (ECtHR, 28 January 2003).

[15]See for example Jerome E Dobson and Peter F Fisher, 'Geoslavery' (2003) Institute of Electrical and Electronics Engineers (IEEE) Tech and Society Magazine 48. Moreover, Shokri and others affirm the importance of understanding the broader impact of location data collection and processing, whereby 'a trace is not only a set of positions on a map. The contextual information attached to a trace tells much about the individuals' habits, interests, activities, and relationships: ... the negative side-effects of insufficient location privacy are becoming more and more threatening': Reza Shokri, 'Quantifying Location Privacy' (Security and Privacy IEEE Symposium, Berkeley CA, 2011) 247.

[16]Bridwell's research has highlighted how the growth of ubiquitous location sensing prompts serious concerns for individual location privacy. See: Scott A Bridwell, 'The Dimensions of Locational Privacy', in Harvey J Miller, *Societies and Cities in the Age of Instant Access* (Springer 2007) 209-225. Refer also to Mike Crang and Stephen Graham, 'Sentient Cities: Ambient Intelligence and the Politics of Urban Space' (2007) 10 Information, Communication and Society 789-791. Also noteworthy is Schulhofer's discussion of spheres of privacy: Stephen J Schulhofer, 'An International Right to Privacy? Be Careful What You Wish For' (2016) 14 International Journal of Constitutional Law 238.

especially within Europe, as to why locational privacy is especially relevant to the safeguarding of the right to privacy in urban settings.[17]

2.1 *Locational Privacy and Its Association with Mobility*

In essence, research has largely focused on exploring the notion that the monitoring of movements may impede the formation of respective individual identities; indeed, this premise has been the subject of relatively extensive examination.[18] Locational privacy has also been justified on the basis that it enables citizens to avail themselves of opportunities to circulate and communicate with others in different spaces, and especially within public spaces: a phenomenon that also contributes toward safeguarding the vital social processes that are dependent upon these interactions.[19] The linkage made between human relationships, privacy, intimacy and the development that supports decisional autonomy has lately represented an important area of study for the analysis of the specific performative function of location.[20]

Studies on surveillance have, however, underscored the extent to which observation of citizens can promote anxiety and undermine personal interactions with others; this in turn may then impact associational behaviours, which are then subject to misinterpretation.[21] In this context, the work of Hildebrandt is relevant for its focus on the manner by which interferences render changes to the individual's

[17]North American scholarship has in contrast been centered upon the impact of novel forms of surveillance of the monitoring of citizens' movements. See further: Daniel Solove, 'Reconstructing Electronic Surveillance Law' (2004) 72 George Washington Law Review 1708. The work of Uteck too has reviewed in detail the possible impact of location monitoring, and has expressed the consternation that such surveillance could inflect a genuine sea change in the extent to which monitoring of our movements could permeate a society. This pervasiveness surveillance could provoke unwelcome influences that engender subtle changes in our behavior, in turn proving disruptive to social interaction: Anne Uteck, 'Ubiquitous Computing and Spatial Privacy' in Ian Kerr, Valerie Steeves, and Carole Lucock (eds), *Lessons from the Identity Trail: Anonymity, Privacy and Identity in a Networked Society* (Oxford University Press 2009) 89.

[18]Wider-ranging concerns expressed by Novotny and Spiekermann have highlighted how developments in personal data processing may present risks to the fundamental rights of citizens: 'Personal information is also the core of two facets that constitute humanity: identity and dignity . . . as more personal information is collected, used, packaged, and leveraged, more conflict arises around how people can retain control of their identities and protect their dignity': Alexander Novotny and Sarah Spiekermann, 'Personal Information Markets and Privacy: A New Model to Solve the Controversy' (2012) <http://ssrn.com/abstract=2148885> accessed 28 August 2019.

[19]This duality recalls the incisive observation of Brandeis argued in *Whitney*, whereby liberty must be valued 'both as an end and as a means'. *Whitney v California*, 274 US 357 (1927).

[20]We enact our identity by way of the selective preferences we exercise in the situational and spatial relationships within our respective environments. This elucidation of location privacy reflects our ability to move freely, which contributes toward the formation of identity, and assimilates both a spatial and informational dimension. See: Phillips (n 8) 306-308.

[21]Solove (n 17).

mental state (for example, in respect of the sense of seclusion).[22] The effects therefore require much more detailed examination if we are to better determine these interdependencies, and to better understand the intrinsic value of locational privacy. Heretofore, the role of locality in relation to autonomy, social formation, and organisation between peers and other aspects of associative behaviour has been limited: the study of both individual self-determination and the formation of interpersonal relations has largely been aspatial.[23]

We must therefore adopt a forward-looking perspective to discern how the evolution of urban mobility with the integration of information technologies with the collection and processing of location data will influence understanding of the normative basis for the existing legal framework established at the European level. As such, this review is important with particular regard to understanding the impact the institutional entrenchment of the technologies and methods of mobility tracking and monitoring may inhere once they have become integrated within public institutions, such as law enforcement agencies and civic authorities.[24] Crucially, as regards European citizens' level of comprehension as to how data protection and privacy rights have come into being, surveys have consistently shown that their understanding of the legal framework at both the national and regional levels is extremely limited.[25]

It should be noted that the lack of appraisal given to locational privacy does not diminish its importance. Rather, we may reconcile the comparative inattention given this topic of research in part to the need to consider that, historically, practical constraints limited the availability of the means to determine an individual's location at any particular time. In the past, methods of collecting and processing location data were invariably relatively resource intensive as the technological means of effectively monitoring an individual's mobility patterns were far more limited; primarily it was this burden that had historically limited more widespread general application of the monitoring of people's movements.

However, technological advancements now allow for the pervasive and unrelenting collection and processing of personal location data attributable to an individual's

---

[22]Hildebrandt and others have contended that human rights enable the creation of a 'sphere of individual autonomy or self-determination and in doing so, they protect individuals against excessive steering of their lives and doings; they contribute to the creation of the private sphere.' See further: Future of Identity in the Information Society (FIDIS), 'D7.4: Implications of Profiling Practices on Democracy and Rule of Law' (FIDIS 2005) 13 <www.fidis.net/resources/fidis-deliverables/profiling> accessed 24 August 2019. Taylor has asserted that autonomy relates to an individual's integrity and identity, and the ability to exercise agency in defining one's own behaviour and persona; Charles Taylor, 'Responsibility for Self' in Amélie Rorty (ed), *The Identities of Persons* (University of California Press 1976) 281-301.

[23]Rob Kitchin and Martin Dodge, *Code/Space: Software and Everyday Life* (MIT Press 2011) 13.

[24]See Further: Michael Levi and David Wall, 'Technologies, Security, and Privacy in the Post-9/11 European Information Society' (2004) 31 Journal of Law and Society 194.

[25]See, for instance: Dara Hallinan, Michael Friedewald and Paul McCarthy, 'Citizens' Perceptions of Data Protection and Privacy' (2012) 28 Computer Law and Security Review 263, 267.

movements.[26] Thus, while locational privacy is an established notion, it has thus far remained underdeveloped conceptually and, as a result, has been under appreciated in respect of its inherent value in furnishing citizens' capacity to enjoy wider fundamental freedoms. Today, continuous, pervasive and unrelenting monitoring of citizens' movements for the purpose of enhancing urban mobility in the smart city environment is increasingly realisable. Anticipation of concerns relating to the possible interferences into the fundamental rights of citizens must also be considered in the light of the topicality of surveillance as a broader issue.

2.2 *Surveillance and the Delineation of Domains*

Scholarship on technologies has in recent times underscored the propensity of surveillance to subject a greater number of persons and spaces to monitoring.[27] Research has also highlighted the growing importance of our examining the relevance of location and mobility to citizens' perception of how privacy relates to formulations of autonomy and personal identity.[28] Critically, an understanding of human mobility is more central to our wider comprehension of what makes us unique as individuals; and yet, to date, mobility as a subject has remained relatively intangible, elusive and under-theorised an object of study.[29]

An initial concern is how best to apply safeguards where existing formulations that delineate the scope and the nature of privacy protections prove challenging to apply in the context of urban mobility; emerging technology developments in this

---

[26]See: Peter Swire and Kenesa Ahmad, '"Going Dark" Versus a "Golden Age for Surveillance"' (*Center for Democracy & Technology*, 28 November 2011) <https://cdt.org/insights/'going-dark'-versus-a-'golden-age-for-surveillance'/> accessed 20 August 2019.

[27]Masa Galič, Tjerk Timan and Bert J Koops, 'Bentham, Deleuze and Beyond: An Overview of Surveillance Theories from the Panopticon to Participation' (2017) 30 Philosophy and Technology 9. See also: Jean Camp and Kay Connelly, 'Beyond Consent: Privacy in Ubiquitous Computing (Ubicomp)' in Alessandro Acquisti and others (eds), *Digital privacy: Theory, Technologies, and Practices* (Auerbach Publications 2008) 327-343; Michal Kosinski, David Stillwell and Thore Graepel, 'Private Traits and Attributes are Predictable from Digital Records of Human Behavior' (2013) 110 Proceedings of the National Academy of Sciences of the United States of America (PNAS) 5802.

[28]Rouvory and Pullet, for example, affirm that informational self-determination implies that an individual must be in a position to exercise control over the data that are available about him/her and, in particular, the implications of the use of those data: Antoinette Rouvory and Yves Poullet, 'The Right to Informational Self-Determination and the Value of Self-Development: Reassessing the Importance of Privacy for Democracy' in Serge Gutwirth and others (eds), *Reinventing Data Protection* (Springer 2009) 51.

[29]Cresswell asserts in this regard that mobility must be more deeply scrutinised for '... study it we must for mobility is central to what it is to be human. It is a fundamental geographical facet of existence and, as such, provides a rich terrain from which narratives—and, indeed, ideologies—can be, and have been, constructed': Tim Cresswell, *On the Move: Mobility in the Modern Western World* (Taylor & Francis 2006) 1.

sphere may elude straightforward classification. In turn, advances in information technology question how we draw distinctions between the self, our location and our immediate environment; the tenability of conceptual and contextual assumptions that relate to the temporal and spatial parameters of privacy are in consequence also placed under examination.[30] In the context of 'private life', the European Court of Human Rights (ECtHR) has recalled that the notion is a broad one, which is not susceptible to exhaustive definition.[31] Furthermore, of relevance too within this context is the ECtHR having asserted that: 'Moreover, public information can fall within the scope of private life where it is systematically collected and stored in files held by the authorities.'[32] Monitoring activity, whether overt or covert, must meet the Strasbourg court's tests pursuant to the reasonableness of interferences allowed for under Art. 8(2), whereby it noted surveillance was 'tolerable under the Convention only in so far as strictly necessary for safeguarding the democratic institutions.'[33]

With the increasing integration of IoT devices into networks within urban settings, it can be difficult to determine how personal data is distinguished from non-personal data. Applying the existing legal framework for personal data protection to IoT presents challenges where one necessarily distinguishes between personal and non-personal data. Information that identifies or is reasonably likely to identify an individual (either directly or indirectly) should be differentiated from information that does not. Indeed, differentiation between types of location data, and whether such data constitutes 'personal data' is rendered more complex where one determines the primary concept of *agency* in respect of how data is collected.[34] In the context of surveillance, long-established criteria for establishing distinctions between the monitoring of persons (both in terms of individuals and groups) versus physical objects are now subject to review where even the term 'device' in itself is

---

[30]Many different ways of defining privacy in relation to the physical environment and the individual sphere have been attempted. Seeking to distinguish the different realms that engage privacy, Rosenberg determines that it may be distinguished in respect of three distinct spheres, whereby geographic privacy constitutes the protection of the immediate sphere surrounding the person; privacy of the person refers to the respect and the protection of the individual's mind and body, whilst informational privacy concerns the control of what personal data can be gathered, stored, processed or selectively disseminated, and how this should be achieved: Richard Rosenberg, *The Social Impact of Computing* (Academic Press 1992).

[31]*Niemietz v Germany* (1992) Series A no 251-B, s 29.

[32]*Rotaru v Romania* App no 28341/95 (ECtHR, 4 May 2000) s 43.

[33]*Klass and Others v Germany* (1978) Series A no 28, s 42.

[34]Meints notes in this respect that not only is the accuracy of data questionable in many cases, but also that 'the accuracy of linkage to a specific individual in the case of personal profiling. This can be a severe problem if a personal profile is created on basis of data which is only thought to belong to the specific person, but in fact belongs to others.' Thus a profile that is assigned to a specific person may constitute a hybrid or, indeed, even be entirely constructed from another individual's data: FIDIS (n 22).

open to question.[35] Whether data is 'personal data', and how one establishes whether any associated location data collected or processed falls within the remit of existing data protection legislation is potentially subject to a significant paradigmatic shift.

As has already been discussed, the integration of pervasive sensing capabilities within urban environments will likely generate in the future an even larger volume of data that, when processed using continuing evolving complex data mining techniques, or collated with data provided by other networked sensors, will potentially be utilised to furnish new and novel inferences relating to the citizen. These secondary uses may constitute a repurposing[36] of personal data that was originally collected. Furthermore, the phenomenon of 'sensor fusion' with smart city networks dictate that the data collected by two disconnected devices can, when combined, be utilised to develop information and provide greater insight than would be possible with the data furnished by either device in isolation.[37]

The combination of data sources may reveal unexpected inferences; for example, where location data is analysed in conjunction with measurements of an individual's heart rate and respiration, potentially yielding detailed information relating a person's physical state relative to their locality and environment.[38] As such, a sensor in a consumer device collecting location data (for example, a personal health monitor or vehicle 'black box' event recording device) can collect data that may be processed for many purposes beyond that particular sensor's intended original use or context.[39]

---

[35]Michael Gleeson, Stéphanie Faber and Caroline Egan, 'ICO Raises Awareness of the Privacy Implications of the Internet of Things' (*Lexology*, 2014) <www.lexology.com/library/detail.aspx?g=99ea0f7c-5c18-4f2f-b98f-9f650f33fc40> accessed 20 August 2019.

[36]Note: 'Data reuse' refers to the 'taking of a data asset and using it more than once for the same purpose', whereas 'data repurposing' refers to the 'taking of a data asset previously used for one (or more) specific purpose(s) and using that data set for a completely different purpose'. See: David Loshin, 'Data Governance and Quality: Data Reuse vs. Data Repurposing' in David Loshin, *The Practitioner's Guide to Data Quality Improvement* (Elsevier 2011) 349.

[37]David L Hall and James Llinas, 'An Introduction to Multi-sensor Data Fusion' (1997) 85 Institute of Electrical and Electronics Engineers (IEEE) 6; Richard Beckwith, 'Designing for Ubiquity: The Perception of Privacy' (2003) 2 IEEE Pervasive Computing 40, 43; Kaivan Karimi, 'The Role of Sensor Fusion and Remote Emotive Computing (Rec) in the Internet Of Things' (Freescale 2013) 6-7 <http://perma.cc/FP82-HK55> accessed 12 September 2019.

[38]Scott Peppet, 'Regulating the Internet of Things: First Steps Toward Managing Discrimination, Privacy, Security, and Consent' (2014) 93 Texas Law Rev 85.

[39]It has been noted that IoT sensor data are so rich, accurate, and fine-grained that data from any given sensor context may be valuable in a wide variety of different information contexts. In this context, Peppet asserts: 'The technical problem created by the Internet of Things is that sensor data tend to combine in unexpected ways, giving rise to powerful inferences from seemingly innocuous data sources … in a world of connected sensors, everything may reveal everything', ibid 119.

2.3 Repurposing Data and the Challenges of Ubiquitous Sensing Capabilities

Indeed, the challenges presented by the repurposing of data are amplified by the increased collection of data implicit to both the IoT and urban mobility infrastructure environments, as the use of data for purposes in addition to those originally specified is more serious a consideration where sensing and monitoring capabilities proliferate. Furthermore, repurposing of data may be contemplated prior even to the initial collection of data. The concern has been raised that public authorities, in particular law enforcement authorities, may seek access to data collected by other parties for specified purposes: a 2013 briefing paper to the EU Commission on IoT underscored how such activity might potentially violate individuals rights to privacy and the protection of their personal data, and in addition impact more widely the public's social acceptance of such technologies. Another critical concern is that greater monitoring of aspects of a citizen's behaviour through urban infrastructure will afford scope to profile and determine in-depth associations relating to the individual that extend to include their personal interests, relationships and activities: all such aspects may increasingly be determined through advanced processing techniques of data.

The increasing availability of location data from monitoring mobility clearly affords scope for greater theorisation of the role performed by space in the constitution of rights-based concerns such as privacy. Indeed, the inherent complexity of conceptualising the questions that arise from the consideration of locality in relation to the individual is rendered all the more vexing where spaces themselves within networked urban environments may be seen as subtly evolving layers of context and practices that actively influence and shape social relations.[40]

The widespread deployment of sensing devices permits data collection allowing for further processing that enables profiling of citizens on a scale previously unimagined: this reflects the comprehensiveness of the granularity of the information the data provides. Whilst initially appearing relatively benign in terms of its capacity to differentiate, movement-related location data, in conjunction with individuals' other types of personal data, may originate an intrusive form of individual profiling in which new and invidious types of discrimination may challenge existing safeguards to citizens' fundamental rights.

However, from the outset one needs recognise too that constructive discrimination can occur in a value-neutral sense, based on detailed appraisal of distinctions made on the bias of an almost infinite number of differences that exist in individuals' characteristics, preferences and activities.[41] Notwithstanding this concession,

[40] Refer to, for example, Kitchen and Dodge's discussion of the role played by public and private spaces in relation to their intersection with software and the creation of new spatialities of everyday life and new modes of governance and creativity: Kitchin and Dodge (n 23) 12-14.

[41] The Oxford Dictionary takes discrimination in this sense to mean 'the recognition and understanding of the difference between one thing and another.' In contrast, discrimination may also

differentiations based on the analysis of personal data will prove problematic where there exists no coherent means by which automated processing can algorithmically distinguish between lawful and non-lawful discrimination. Furthermore, it is important to recognise that discrimination may be either direct or indirect. In data analysis direct discrimination can occur when decisions are made in connection to sensitive attributes (whether the prejudice or bias is acknowledged or not), whilst indirect discrimination occurs when decisions are made based on non-sensitive attributes that are strongly correlated with biased sensitive ones.[42]

The processing of personal data in connection with the identification of an individual's location could result in unlawful discrimination on the basis of grounds such as gender, race, colour and religion.[43] In connection with the particular contribution location data may perform in respect of generating enhanced profiles, analysts have underscored the considerable risks associated with monitoring and surveillance of mobility.[44] Where it has been suggested by specialists that these technological advancements may risk being further developed in an uncontrolled manner, absent the safeguards necessary to protect fundamental rights, we need consider whether the existing legal framework is indeed apt to ensure the requisite

---

constitute prejudicial treatment which involves denying opportunities to members of one group in favour of other groups: See: Oxford Dictionaries online (*OxfordLanguages*) <http://www.oxforddictionaries.com> accessed 20 August 2019. In this context, Tene and Polonetsky have highlighted how the meaning of the term 'discrimination' has become highly charged; the data mining of personal data collected by IoT sensors could be legitimate, where we may overlook the fact that entirely reasonable distinctions that differentiate and discriminate between persons may be justifiable, noting: 'In our daily life, we draw distinctions (i.e., discriminate) all the time. A person sitting next to us on a plane is tall or short, agitated or relaxed, attractive or unattractive, young or old—there is an endless list of such adjectives; and our attitudes and actions towards that person will vary accordingly.' See further: Omer Tene and Jules Polonetsky, 'Judged by the Tin Man: Individual Rights in the Age of Big Data' (2013) 11 Journal of Telecommunications and High Technology Law 351.

[42]Indeed, in this regard efforts to determine whether and how statistical analysis may allow patterns of discrimination to be discovered in datasets is only at an early stage of research. See for example: P Priya and J C Miraclin Joyce Pamila, 'Identification of Direct and Indirect Discrimination in Data Mining' in Azami Zaharim and others, *Recent Advances in Electrical and Computer Engineering: Proceedings of the 2014 International Conference on Circuits, Systems, Signal Processing, Communications and Computers (CSSCC '14)* (Venice, Italy, 15-17 March 2014, Wseas LLC 2014); Salvatore Ruggieri, Dino Pedreschi and Franco Turini, 'Data Mining for Discrimination Discovery' (2010) 4(2) ACM Transactions on Knowledge Discovery from Data 1.

[43]Peppet (n 38) 117.

[44]The reflections provided by the WP29 on IoT are especially apposite in that agencies such as the European Data Protection Supervisor (EDPS) asserted at the early stages of development of IoT that the expert group's interpretation and guidance on the application of existing laws and principles would constitute a requisite for sustaining a coherent approach. See further: European Data Protection Supervisor (EDPS), 'Internet of Things: Ubiquitous Monitoring in Space and Time' (European Privacy and Data Protection Commissioners' Conference, Prague, 29-30 April 2010) 7 <https://secure.edps.europa.eu/EDPSWEB/webdav/shared/Documents/EDPS/Publications/Speeches/2010/10-04-29_Speech_Internet_Things_EN.pdf> accessed 28 August 2019.

level of protection to individuals.[45] In many cases for the individual it proves unrealistic for their being able to comprehend how location is tracked, whether in respect of their own movement relative to a fixed device or, as is more usual, where the device itself moves directly in conjunction with the individual as her/his position changes.[46]

Moreover, as the ability to electronically monitor individuals' locations *en masse* is a relatively new phenomenon, our understanding remains relatively limited as to the extent citizens perceive it may inhibit the realisation of their fundamental rights. This impediment in turn also reinforces the premise that citizens themselves might not fully comprehend the scope of the tracking of their location, and thus are constrained in their ability to reason and make decisions, which constitutes the primary basis for informed consent.

The challenges inherent to applying existing safeguards to fundamental rights to the development of smart cities were acknowledged from the very outset.[47] Currently, the evolution of these systems is such that they at present consist of a loose connection of disparate networks—though in time this situation will evolve such that greater organisation will allow far more powerful analytics and data-mining capabilities: in effect, a 'network of networks'.[48] A fundamental difficulty this ubiquity generates is that with data processing so pervasive, based on this proliferation of sensing capabilities into the most trivial of appliances and every day practices, it becomes ever more difficult to discern both where and how each individual's personal activities are subject to data processing. As such the need to comprehend the challenges this presents to the protection of citizens' fundamental rights to

[45]For example, the WP29 has warned that the fundamental rights of citizens of the EU are at stake; it contends that the development of IoT raises 'new and significant personal data protection and privacy challenges' that 'could go as far as developing a form of surveillance of individuals that might be considered as unlawful under EU law.' The WP29 further cautions that 'IOT raises important security concerns, where security breaches could entail significant privacy risks for the individuals whose data are processed in such contexts.' Article 29 Data Protection Working Party (WP29), 'Opinion 8/2014 on the on Recent Developments on the Internet of Things' (2014) WP223.

[46]As regards the former, technological developments now allow for parties to install fixed systems that can actively monitor an individual's movements prior to initiating any form of process pertaining to the accession of consent. See for instance: Raffaele Bruno and Franca Delmastro, 'Design and Analysis of a Bluetooth-based Indoor Localisation System' in Marco Conti and others (eds), *Personal Wireless Communications* (Springer 2003).

[47]In this context the EDPS, for example, affirmed that the combination of technological developments with 'new global realities' rendered applying the existing legal principles pertaining to data protection particularly challenging, principally on the basis that the Directive, it believed, had not accounted for such eventualities. Indeed, in this respect, rather curiously it asserted that such challenges might only partially 'be solved by interpretation and flexibility': EDPS (n 44).

[48]See: Dave Evans, 'The Internet of Things: How the Next Evolution of the Internet Is Changing Everything' (CISCO Internet Business Solutions Group 2011) 4 <www.cisco.com/web/about/ac79/docs/innov/IoT_IBSG_0411FINAL.pdf> accessed 28 August 2019.

privacy and personal data protection remains critical.[49] At the heart of the concept of intelligent urban mobility networks is the notion that 'embedded intelligence' in individual items detects and processes data relating to changes in their physical state.[50] It is this ambient, pervasive perceptivity that distinguishes the technology in its capacity to perform surveillance of individuals on an unprecedented level, particularly as concerns its ability to monitor responses to environmental factors.[51]

Guarantees of ever improving acuity in detection and monitoring, coupled with assurances as to the increasing reliability of progressively more detailed deductions made on the basis of the analysis of location data, should be treated with caution. It should be recalled that the roll-out of services are still very much in the early stages of maturation, and that the viability of their advantages for society remains open to debate. It is crucial therefore that we take sufficient care to examine how the existing scope of protective safeguards is best applied based on an objective elucidation of the functionality inherent to the technologies.

However, at the same time we must also avoid unwittingly jumping to conclusions based upon 'worst-case' type scenarios in which the most probable use of technologies in given scenarios, based upon emerging trends, is disregarded in favour of plotting speculative projections that promise more hazardous, but relatively improbable, developments of smart urban mobility infrastructure. Information pertaining to physical location, mobility and micro-scale movements relating to an individual can provide the observer with considerable insight into the habits and exploits of the individual. Research has shown that a very short time spent monitoring the mobility of citizens can render an extremely detailed and nuanced representation of a person's private life.[52]

---

[49]Indeed, the former EU Commissioner for the Digital Agenda Neelie Kroes has asserted that the Internet of Things 'is surrounded by a value system: as it comes so close to the heart of everyday life, social relations and daily services, it needs a broad societal consensus to fulfill its potential', thus reaffirming the concern that the collection and processing of personal data relating to highly intimate aspects of citizens' lives could portend enormous impacts on the rights to privacy and data protection. See: Neelie Kroes, 'Bringing European Values to the Internet of Things' (2nd Annual Internet of Things Conference, Brussels, 1st June 2010) 2 <https://ec.europa.eu/commission/presscorner/detail/en/SPEECH_10_279> accessed 28 August 2019.

[50]FTC, 'FTC Seeks Input on Privacy and Security Implications of the Internet of Things' (*Federal Trade Commission*, 2013) 13 <http://www.ftc.gov/policy/public-comments/initiative-484> accessed 12 September 2019.

[51]The EDPS highlighted at an early juncture in the evolution of smart cities and IoT the inherent challenges to privacy and data protection presented by an environment in which every single action of objects and individuals can be monitored from a spatial and temporal perspective, reflecting what the agency foresaw as a 'lack of "natural" limits which were preserving the privacy of the data subject so far.' As such, the issue arises as to how effective limits may in fact be set in order that the availability of this powerful monitoring capability may be regulated effectively. See: EDPS (n 44).

[52]Thomas Louail and others, 'From Mobile Phone Data to the Spatial Structure of Cities' (2014) 4 Scientific Reports 5276 <https://doi.org/10.1038/srep05276> accessed 20 August 2019; Marta C Gonzalez, César A Hidalgo and Albert L Barabási, 'Understanding Individual Human Mobility Patterns' (2018) 453 Nature 779; Thomas Louail and others, 'Uncovering the Spatial Structure of Mobility Networks' (2015) 6 Nature Communications 1.

Significant resources have already been invested to further develop the application of information and communications technologies based upon location and temporal awareness capabilities to mobility and transportation networks. In contrast, however, the discourse amongst lawyers, ethicists and policymakers has lagged. In particular, dialogue concerning the appropriacy and efficacy of the legal framework to appreciate and effectively regulate innovations in the tracking of human mobility has to date been relatively limited. As a result, today our understanding of the interconnectedness of location with mobility and our apprehension of the value of the spaces we inhabit and move within relative to our conceptualisation of fundamental rights remains decidedly underdeveloped. Furthermore, at issue is how location-aware information technology will influence the interrelationship of the different fundamental rights affected, such as privacy, the right to the protection of personal data, freedom of movement and freedom of assembly and association.

With technologies becoming increasingly context-aware towards the intrinsic value of sensing and monitoring capabilities of the immediate environment, the need to ascertain whether the established premises that underpin current conceptual approaches to location data collection and processing remain tenable is thus ever more acute. The study of the utilisation of location data is of additional value for the insight it may provide in relation to broader, extant issues pertinent to data protection and privacy rights currently. The binary distinction whereby the right to privacy is conceived as a negative right, whilst related concepts such as identity and personality formation are viewed as positive constructs, is an increasingly difficult notion to preserve at a time when technological advancements are reshaping our interactions in every sphere of our lives.

3 Conclusions

Potentially, the same technological advances rendering these more networked, interconnected communities can also afford greater scope for our understanding of the complexity these developments yield. However, this same complexity also portends the growth of expansive sociotechnical systems that may prove increasingly challenging to comprehend and, in turn, manage and control effectively in consideration of the wider democratic interests of society. Whilst governments, public authorities and other agencies may eagerly anticipate the considerable opportunities to understand with increasing spatial and temporal resolution the utilisation of public facilities and structures by citizens, at the same time important questions surface as to suitability of the existing regulatory and legal frameworks to oversee the augmentation in surveillance inhered in this nascent exploitation of enhanced monitoring capability.

Comprehension of the challenges faced in the advent of new mobility monitoring technologies is further complicated by the necessity of resolving the effect of more extensive movement tracking in meaningful, measurable terms: the risk of interferences in our fundamental rights can only be determined where intrusions are qualified succinctly, and their impact rendered in unambiguous, quantifiable terms. Conventionally, the framing of such interferences has been based upon more traditional notions of visibility, which may more easily be understood by the layperson. In contrast, new methods of tracking individuals' locations underscore the salience of novel, non-visual methods of surveillance which may later be used to discern data subjects' behaviours and preferences based on their distinct and unique pattern of movement. Furthermore, besides being largely hidden, covert and, increasingly, unremitting, the acquisition of people's mobility data is inherently indiscriminate in terms of the scope of the everyday activities monitored.

Moreover, customary distinctions drawn between physical and abstract virtual spaces are increasingly problematic in privacy terms. Questions will inevitably arise as to how we seek to delineate events that are either categorised as 'online' or 'offline' within urban environments that incorporate sensing and monitoring capabilities, and how such determinations relate in a spatial context, representing a 'collapsing distinction' between online and offline contexts that blurs not only our relationships, but also our identities.[53] European citizens will find themselves increasingly surrounded by pervasive, always-on wireless networks; these systems will continue to bridge physical spaces and the virtual world. The challenges society faces in this respect are intrinsically multi-disciplinary, and require solutions—and hence further research—that cross the boundaries of traditional disciplines.

[53]In this regard, US Supreme Court Justice Anthony Kennedy duly noted: 'Minds are not changed in streets and parks as they once were. To an increasing degree, the more significant interchanges of ideas and shaping of public consciousness occur in mass and electronic media.' Thus, increasingly relevant to our framing expressive association between individuals are the distinctions made between traditionally defined geographic, spatial environments and nascent conceptions of the metaphysical. See: *Denver Area Educational Telecommunications Consortium, Inc. v FCC*, 518 US 727 (1996) 802-803 (Opinion of Justice Anthony Kennedy, concurring in part and dissenting in part).

The manufacturer's authorised representative in the EU is Springer Nature Customer Service Centre GmbH, Europaplatz 3, 69115 Heidelberg, Germany. If you have any concerns regarding our products, please contact ProductSafety@springernature.com

Printed and bound by CPI Group (UK) Ltd, Croydon, CR0 4YY
30/09/2026
02225492-0018